CONGRESSIONAL ELECTIONS

Campaigning at Home and in Washington

CONGRESSIONAL ELECTIONS

Campaigning at Home and in Washington

Second Edition

Paul S. Herrnson
UNIVERSITY OF MARYLAND

CQ
PRESS

A Division of Congressional Quarterly Inc.
Washington, D.C.

Copyright © 1998 Congressional Quarterly Inc.
1414 22nd Street, N.W.,
Washington, D.C. 20037

Printed in the United States of America

Cover design: Paula Anderson

Library of Congress Cataloging-in-Publication Data

Herrnson, Paul S., 1958–
    Congressional elections : campaigning at home and in Washington /
Paul S. Herrnson. — 2nd ed.
        p.   cm.
    Includes bibliographical references and index.
    ISBN 1-56802-379-0
    1. United States. Congress—Elections. 2. Electioneering—United
States. 3. Campaign funds—United States. 4. Political action
committees—United States.   I. Title.
JK1976.H47   1997
324.973'0928—dc21   97-41261
                                                              CIP

In Memory of
Harry Perlman

Contents

Preface

When CQ Press invited me to write a second edition of this book I was delighted. For one thing, the invitation suggested that the first edition had been well received, which is music to the ears of any author. More important, the invitation gave me the opportunity to analyze recent changes that have taken place in congressional elections. These include the massive growth in "soft money" contributions and expenditures, the escalation of party agenda-setting efforts, the legalization of party independent expenditures, the introduction of party and interest group issue advocacy campaigns, the emergence of tax-exempt interest group organizations as partisan political campaigners, and the expanded roles of members of Congress as contributors to and fund-raisers for other candidates.

This edition, like the first, is about congressional elections and their implications for Congress and, more generally, for American government. Most congressional elections are contests between candidates who have vastly unequal chances of victory. Incumbents generally win because of their own efforts and because many challengers find themselves in a catch-22 situation. Without name recognition, challengers and candidates for open seats have trouble raising funds, and without funds, they cannot enhance their name recognition or attract enough support to run a competitive race. This conundrum hints at a fundamental truth of congressional elections: candidates wage two campaigns, one for votes and one for money and other resources. The former takes place in the candidate's district or state. The latter is conducted primarily in the Washington, D.C., area, where many political consultants, political action committees (PACs), and the parties' national, senatorial, and congressional campaign committees are located. The two campaigns are waged almost concurrently, but candidates and their organizations must conceptualize the campaigns as separate and plot a different strategy for each.

Although this book focuses on congressional election campaigns, considerable attention is given to voters, candidates, governance, and campaign reform. I have gathered information from candidates, campaign aides, party strategists, PAC managers, journalists, and other political insiders to describe their goals, strategies, decision-making processes, and roles in congressional campaigns. I have also assessed the influence that the efforts of these individuals and groups have on election outcomes.

The conclusion I draw is that the norms and expectations associated with congressional campaigns affect who runs, the kinds of organizations the candidates assemble, how much money they raise, the kinds of party and interest group support they attract, the strategies and communications techniques they use, and whether they win or lose. The need to campaign for votes and resources, in turn, affects how members of Congress carry out their legislative responsibilities, and the kinds of reforms they are willing to consider. These observations may seem intuitive, but they are rarely discussed in studies of voting behavior and are usually overlooked in research that focuses on the role of money in politics. Given their importance, it is unfortunate that congressional campaigns have received so little attention in the scholarly literature.

The candidates, parties, and PACs that have participated in congressional elections at the close of the millennium are all systematically analyzed. The analysis is based on interviews with and completed questionnaires from more than 450 House and Senate candidates and other political insiders, as well as on campaign finance data furnished by the Federal Election Commission and information collected from campaign organizations, party committees, PACs, and other interest groups. Case studies of individual campaigns supply concrete illustrations for the generalizations produced by the systematic data analysis. Insights are drawn from my own past participation in congressional campaigns. The evidence supports the thesis that the campaigns that candidates wage at home for votes and in Washington for money and campaign assistance have a significant effect on the outcomes of congressional elections. It shows that the activities of party committees, interest groups, campaign volunteers, and journalists are also important.

Scholars using this book as a classroom text might be interested in reviewing the questionnaires I used to collect information from congressional campaigns. They turned out to be valuable research tools for students in my congressional elections seminars, who have used them to guide their field research on campaigns. I have made the questionnaires, my class assignments, and other course materials available on the publisher's Web page: http://books.cq.com (navigate to the "Free Resources" area).

The publication of this book required the cooperation of many individuals and institutions. I am indebted to the hundreds of individuals who consented to be interviewed, completed mail questionnaires, or shared election targeting lists and other campaign materials with me. Their participation in this project was essential to its success.

The Graduate Research Board and the Academy of Leadership of the University of Maryland provided financial support for the project. The Department of Government and Politics provided a stimulating environment in which to work. Peter Burns, Mary Fitzgerald, and Peter Francia provided valuable assistance during various stages of the research. Robert Biersack and Michael Dickerson of the Federal Election Commission furnished information and assistance at several junctures. Chris Bailey, Jim Gimpel, Stephen Salmore, Frank Sorauf, and Ric Uslaner made valuable suggestions for the first edition of the book. William Bianco, Thomas Kazee, and Sandy Maisel made helpful recommendations for revising it. Biersack, Gimpel, Uslaner, and Clyde Wilcox commented on various parts of the second edition. The suggestions of several anonymous readers were also useful. Brenda Carter and Gwenda Larsen at CQ Press and Joanne S. Ainsworth of Ainsworth Editorial Services played a vital role in helping to prepare the manuscript. I am delighted to have the opportunity to express my deepest appreciation to all of them.

Finally, a few words are in order about the person to whom this book is dedicated. My uncle, Harry Perlman, did not live to see the completion of this book, but his contributions to it were critical. The construction jobs he gave me were the most important form of financial aid I received while pursuing my college education. His ideas about politics and philosophy helped me to appreciate the virtues of democratically held elections and to recognize the inferiority of other means of transferring political power. His unwavering belief that people can be taught to value what is good about their political system and to recognize its shortcomings was a source of inspiration that helped me complete this book.

CONGRESSIONAL ELECTIONS

Campaigning at Home
and in Washington

Introduction

Elections are the centerpiece of democracy. They are the means Americans use to choose their political leaders, and they give those who have been elected the authority to rule. Elections also furnish the American people with a vehicle for expressing their views about the directions they think this rule ought to take. In theory, elections are the principal mechanism for ensuring "government of the people, by the people, [and] for the people."

An examination of the many different aspects of the electoral process can provide insight into the operations of our political system. Separate balloting for congressional, state, and local candidates results in legislators who represent parochial interests, sometimes to the detriment of the formation of national policy. Private financing of congressional campaigns, which is consistent with Americans' belief in capitalism, favors incumbents and increases the political access of wealthy and well-organized segments of society. Participatory primaries, which require congressional aspirants to assemble an organization in order to campaign for the nomination, lead candidates to rely on political consultants rather than on party committees for assistance in winning their primaries and general elections. These factors encourage congressional candidates and members of Congress to act more independently of party leaders than do their counterparts in other democracies.

Congressional elections are affected by perceptions of the performance of government. Americans' satisfaction with the state of the economy and with the nation's foreign policy, as well as with their own standard of living, provides a backdrop for elections and a means for assessing whether presidents, individual representatives, and Congress as an institution have performed their jobs adequately. Issues related to the internal operations of Congress—such as the perquisites enjoyed by members—can affect congressional elections. Conversely, congressional elections can greatly affect the internal operations of Congress, the performance of government, and the direction of domestic and foreign policy. Major political reforms and policy reversals generally follow elections in which there has been substantial congressional turnover.

One of the major themes developed in this book is that campaigns matter a great deal to the outcome of congressional elections. National conditions are significant, but their impact on elections is secondary to the decisions and actions of candidates, campaign organizations, party committees, organized interests, and other individuals and groups. This comes as no surprise to those who toil in campaigns, but it is in direct contrast to what many scholars would argue.

In order to win a congressional election or even to be remotely competitive, candidates must compete in two campaigns: one for votes and one for resources. The campaign for votes is the campaign that generally comes to mind when people think about congressional elections. It requires a candidate to assemble an organization and to use that organization to target key groups of voters, select a message they will find compelling, deliver that message, and get supporters to the polls on election day.

The other campaign, which is based largely in Washington, D.C., requires candidates to convince the party officials, political action committee (PAC) managers, political consultants, and political journalists who are the leaders of the nation's political community that their races will be competitive and worthy of support. Gaining the backing of these various individuals is a critical step in attracting the money and campaign services that are available in the nation's capital and in other major urban centers. These resources enable the candidate to run a credible campaign back home. Without them, most congressional candidates would lose their bids for election.

In this book I present a systematic assessment of congressional election campaigns that draws on information from a wide variety of sources. Background information on the more than 13,000 major-party contestants who ran for the House between 1978 and 1996 furnished me with insights into the types of individuals who try to win a seat in Congress and the conditions under which they run. Personal interviews and survey data provided by more than 450 candidates and campaign aides who were involved in the 1992, 1994, and 1996 House and Senate elections permitted analysis of the organization, strategies, tactics, issues, and communications techniques used in congressional campaigns. They also provided insights into the roles that political parties, PACs, and other groups play in those contests.

Case studies of forty House campaigns conducted in the elections of 1992 through 1996 illustrate with concrete examples the generalizations drawn from the larger sample. These include many typical elections, such as Republican representative Constance A. Morella's victory over Democratic challenger Donald Mooers in Maryland's 8th congressional district, as well as a few unusual contests, such as the hotly contested race in Texas's 25th congressional district. The latter race took several strange turns after the Supreme Court ruled that three nearby districts had been racially gerrymandered, and required that the boundaries of Texas's 25th district and twelve others be redrawn and their primary results nullified.

Many close contests, such as the rematch between Republican representative Fred Heineman and Democrat David E. Price, whom Heineman had defeated two years earlier in North Carolina's 4th congressional district, are also discussed. Some races are included because of the role of scandal or district partisanship. A seven-term incumbent, Nicholas Mavroules, D-Mass., lost his Democratic-leaning 6th congressional district seat to the Republican challenger, Peter G. Torkildsen, in 1992 after being indicted on charges of bribery and influence peddling, but Torkildsen lost it four years later to the Democratic challenger, John F. Tierney. Other House campaigns are covered because they include members of the Republican freshman class of 1994, who came to Washington wearing "Majority Maker" buttons on their lapels. Many of their 1996 reelection campaigns were extremely competitive and the focus of intense party and interest group activity.

Most of the discussion focuses on House candidates and campaigns because they are easier to generalize about than Senate contests. Differences in the sizes, populations, and political traditions of the fifty states and the fact that only about one-third of all Senate seats are filled in a given election year make campaigns for the upper chamber more difficult to discuss in general terms. Larger, more diverse Senate constituencies also make Senate elections less predictable than House contests. Nevertheless, insights can be gained into campaigns for the upper chamber by contrasting them with those waged for the House.

Interviews with party officials, conducted over the course of the 1992 through 1996 elections, give insights into the strategies used by the Democratic and Republican national, congressional, and senatorial campaign committees. Similar information provided by the managers of a representative group of PACs is used to learn about PAC contribution strategies. Campaign contribution and spending data furnished by the Federal Election Commission (FEC) are used to examine the role of money in politics. Newspapers, press releases, advertising materials distributed by individual campaigns, and World Wide Web sites furnish examples of the communications that campaigns disseminate. Collectively, these sources of information, along with scholarly accounts published in the political science literature and insights drawn from my own participation in congressional and campaign politics, have permitted a comprehensive portrayal of contemporary congressional election campaigns.

In the first five chapters an examination is made of the strategic context in which congressional election campaigns are waged and the major actors that participate in those contests. In Chapter 1 I discuss the institutions, laws, party rules, and customs that are the framework for congressional elections. The framework has a significant impact on who decides to run for Congress; the kinds of resources that candidates, parties, and interest groups bring to bear on the campaign; the strategies they use; and who ultimately wins a seat in Congress. I also focus on the setting for the congressional elections held during the 1990s, with special emphasis on 1996.

Chapter 2 contains a discussion of candidates and nominations. I examine the influence of incumbency, national conditions, and the personal and career situations of potential candidates on the decision to run for Congress. I also assess the separate contributions that the decision to run, the nomination process, and the general election make toward producing a Congress that is overwhelmingly white, male, middle-aged, and drawn from the legal, business, and public service professions.

The organizations that congressional candidates assemble to wage their election campaigns are the subject of the third chapter. Salaried staff and political consultants form the core of most competitive candidates' campaign teams. These professionals play a critical role in formulating strategy, gauging public opinion, fund-raising, designing communications, and mobilizing voters.

The campaign for money and other election resources is the focus of Chapters 4 through 6. Chapter 4 includes an analysis of the goals, decision-making processes, and election activities of party committees. I discuss many recent innovations, including party independent expenditures and issue advocacy. In Chapter 5 I concentrate on the goals, strategies, and election efforts of PACs and other interest group organizations. Among the innovations it covers are business- and union-sponsored issue advocacy campaigns and the political activity of groups that enjoy tax-exempt status. The topic of Chapter 6 is fund-raising from individuals in the candidates' own states, in Washington, and in the nation's other major political and economic centers. It is clear from these chapters that Washington-based elites have a disproportionate effect on the conduct of congressional elections.

In Chapters 7 through 9 I concentrate on the campaign for votes. A discussion of voters, campaign targeting, issues, and other elements of strategy make up Chapter 7. Campaign communications, including television, radio, direct mail, and field work are the focus of Chapter 8. The subject of winners and losers is taken up in Chapter 9. In it I analyze what does and does not work in congressional campaigns.

In Chapter 10 I address the effect of candidate-centered elections on the activities of individual legislators and on Congress as an institution. The final chapter takes up the highly charged topic of campaign reform. I recommend specific reforms and discuss the obstacles that must be overcome before meaningful campaign reform is enacted.

CHAPTER 1

The Strategic Context

Congressional elections, and elections in the United States in general, are centered more on the candidates than are elections in other modern industrialized democracies. In this chapter I discuss the candidate-centered U.S. election system and explain how the Constitution, election laws, and the political parties form the system's institutional framework. I explain how the nation's political culture and recent developments in technology have helped this system flourish. The influence that the political setting in a given election year has on electoral competition and turnover in Congress is also covered. The setting includes some predictable factors such as the decennial redrawing of House districts, some highly likely occurrences such as the wide-scale reelection of incumbents, and transient, less predictable phenomena, such as congressional scandals. All these aspects of the setting influence the expectations and behavior of potential congressional candidates, the individuals who actually run for Congress, political contributors, and voters.

THE CANDIDATE-CENTERED CAMPAIGN

Candidates, not political parties, are the major focus of congressional campaigns, and candidates, not parties, bear the ultimate responsibility for election outcomes. These characteristics of congressional elections are striking when viewed from a comparative perspective. In most democracies, political parties are the principal contestants in elections, and campaigns focus on national issues, ideology, and party programs and accomplishments. In the United States, parties do not actually run congressional campaigns nor do they become the major focus of elections. Instead, candidates run their own campaigns, and parties may contribute money or election services to them. A comparison of the terminology commonly used to describe elections in the United States and that used in Great Britain more than hints at the differences. In the United States, candidates are said to *run* for Congress, and they do so with or without party help. In Britain, on the other hand, candidates are said to *stand* for election to Parliament, and their party runs most of the campaign. The difference in terminology only slightly oversimplifies reality.

Candidates are the most important actors in American congressional elections. Most of them are self-selected rather than recruited by party organizations. All of them must win the right to run under their party's label through a participatory primary, caucus, or convention, or by scaring off all opposition. Only after they have secured their party's nomination are major-party candidates assured a place on the general election ballot. Independent and minor-party candidates can get on the ballot in other ways, usually by paying a registration fee or collecting several thousand signatures from district residents.

The nomination process in most other countries, in contrast, begins with a small group of party activists pursuing the nomination through a "closed" process that allows only formal, dues-paying party members to participate.[1] Whereas the American system amplifies the input of primary voters and in a few states caucus participants, these other systems respond more to the input of local party activists and place more emphasis on peer review.

The need to win a party nomination forces congressional candidates to assemble their own campaign organizations, formulate their own election strategies, and conduct their own campaigns. The images and issues that they convey to voters in trying to win the nomination carry over to the general election. The efforts of individual candidates and their campaign organizations have a larger impact on election outcomes than the activities of party organizations and other groups.

The candidate-centered nature of congressional elections has a fundamental impact on virtually every aspect of campaigning, including who decides to run, the kinds of election strategies the candidates employ, and the resources that are available to them. It affects the decisions and activities of party organizations, PACs, other interest groups, and journalists. It also has a major influence on how citizens make their voting decisions and on the activities that successful candidates carry out once they are elected to Congress. Finally, the candidate-centered nature of the congressional election system affects the election reforms that those in power are willing to consider.

THE INSTITUTIONAL FRAMEWORK

In designing a government to prevent the majority from depriving the minority of its rights, the framers of the Constitution created a system of checks and balances to prevent any one official or element of society from amassing too much power. Three key features of the framers' blueprint have profoundly influenced congressional elections: the separation of powers, bicameralism, and federalism. These aspects of the Constitution require that candidates for the House of Representatives, Senate, and presidency be chosen by different methods and constituencies. House members were and continue to be elected directly by the people. Senators were originally chosen by their state legislatures but have been selected in statewide elections since the passage of the Seventeenth Amendment in 1913. Presidents have always been selected through the electoral college. The means for filling state and local offices were omitted from the Constitution, but candidates for these positions were and continue to be elected independently of members of Congress.

Holding elections for individual offices separates the political fortunes of members of Congress from one another and from other officials. A candidate for the House can win during an election year in which his or her party suffers a landslide defeat in the race for the presidency, experiences severe losses in the House or Senate, or finds itself surrendering its hold over neighboring congressional districts, the state legislature, the governor's mansion, and various local offices. The system encourages House, Senate, state, and local candidates to communicate issues and themes that they perceive to be popular in their districts even when these messages differ from those advocated by their party's leader. The system does little to encourage teamwork in campaigning or governance. In 1990 many Republican congressional candidates took a "no new taxes" pledge, a pledge that was diametrically opposed to the tax increase signed into law by their party's standard-bearer, President George Bush. In 1993 many congressional Democrats opposed the North American Free Trade Agreement (NAFTA), which was championed by Democratic president Bill Clinton. These acts would be labeled party disloyalty and considered unacceptable under a parliamentary system of government with its party-focused elections, but they are entirely consistent with the expectations of the framers of the U.S. Constitution. As James Madison wrote in *Federalist* no. 46,

> A local spirit will infallibly prevail . . . in the members of Congress. . . .
> Measures will too often be decided according to their probable effect, not on
> the national prosperity and happiness, but on the prejudices, interests, and
> pursuits of the governments and people of the individual States.

When congressional candidates differ from their party's presidential nominee or national platform on major issues, they seek political cover not only from the Constitution but also from state party platforms, local election manifestos, or fellow party members who have taken similar positions.

Of course, congressional candidates usually adopt only those issue positions that are held by other party candidates for the House, Senate, or presidency. In 1932 most Democrats embraced Franklin D. Roosevelt's call for an activist government to battle the Great Depression. In 1994 most Republican candidates for the House, as well as some candidates for the Senate and some state legislatures, embraced the issues outlined in their party's Contract with America.[2] In 1996 many Democratic candidates for the House and Senate supported the positions articulated in the party's Families First Agenda and the Democratic platform.

Federal and state laws further contribute to the candidate-centered nature of congressional elections. Originally, federal law regulated few aspects of congressional elections, designating only the number of representatives a state was entitled to elect. States held congressional elections at different times, used different methods of election, and set different qualifications for voters. Some states used multimember at-large districts, a practice that awarded each party a share of congressional seats proportional to its share of the statewide popular vote; others elected their House members in odd years, which minimized the ability of presidential candidates to pull House candidates of their own party into office on their coattails. The financing of congressional campaigns also went virtually unregulated for most of the nation's history.

Over the years, Congress and the states passed legislation governing the election of House members that further reinforced the candidate-centered nature of congressional elections at the expense of parties. The creation of geographically defined, single-member, winner-take-all congressional districts was particularly important in this regard. These districts, which were mandated by the Apportionment Act of 1842, encouraged individual candidates to build locally based coalitions. Such districts gave no rewards to candidates who came in second, even if their party performed well throughout the state or in neighboring districts.[3] Thus, candidates of the same party had little incentive to work together or run a party-focused campaign. Under the multimember district or general ticket systems that existed in some states prior to the act and continue to be used in most European nations, members of parties that finish lower than first place may receive seats in the legislature. Candidates have strong incentives to run cooperative, party-focused campaigns under these systems because their electoral fortunes are bound together.

The timing of congressional elections also helps to produce a candidate-centered system. Because the dates are fixed, with House elections scheduled biennially and roughly one-third of the Senate up for election every two years, many elections are held when there is no burning issue on the national agenda. Without a salient national issue to capture the voters' attention, House and Senate candidates base their campaigns on local issues or on their personal qualifications for holding office. Incumbents stress their experience, the services they provide to constituents, or seniority, whereas challengers attack their opponents for casting congressional roll-call votes that are out of sync with the views of local voters, for pandering to special interests, or for "being part of the problem in Washington." Open-seat races focus mainly on local issues, the candidates' political experience, or character issues.

In contrast, systems that do not have fixed election dates, including most of those in western Europe, tend to hold elections that are more national in focus and centered on political parties. The rules regulating national elections in those systems require that elections be held within a set time frame, but the exact date is left open. Elections may be called by the party in power at a time of relative prosperity, when it is confident that it can maintain or increase its parliamentary majority. Elections also may be called when a burning national issue divides the nation and the party in power is forced to call a snap election because its members in parliament are unable to agree on a policy for dealing with the crisis. In contrast to congressional elections, which are often referenda on the performance of individual officeholders and their abilities to meet local concerns, these elections focus on national conditions and the performance of the party in power.

Because the boundaries of congressional districts rarely match those for statewide or local offices and because terms for the House, the Senate, and many state and local offices differ from one another, a party's candidates often lack incentives to work together. House candidates consider the performance of their party's candidates statewide or in neighboring districts to be a secondary concern, just as the election of House candidates is usually not of primary importance to candidates for state or local office. Differences in election boundaries and timing also encourage a sense of parochialism in party officials that is similar to that in their candidates. Cooperation among party organizations can be achieved only by persuading local, state, and national party leaders that it is in their mutual best interest.

Although the seeds for candidate-centered congressional election campaigns were sown by the Constitution and election laws, it was not until the middle of the twentieth century that the candidate-centered system firmly took root. Prior to the emergence of this system, during a period often called the "golden age of political parties," party organizations played a major role in most election campaigns, including many campaigns for Congress. Local party organizations, often referred to as old-fashioned political machines, had control over the nomination process, possessed a near monopoly over the resources needed to organize the electorate, and provided the symbolic cues that informed the electoral decisions of most voters.[4] The key to their success was the ability to command the support of large numbers of individuals who were able to persuade friends and neighbors to support their party's candidates. It was not until the demise of the old-fashioned machine and the emergence of new campaign technology that the modern candidate-centered system finally blossomed.

Reforms intended to weaken political machines played a major role in the development of the candidate-centered system. One such reform was the adoption of the Australian ballot by roughly three-quarters of the states between 1888 and 1896.[5] This government-printed ballot listed every candidate for each office and allowed individuals to cast their votes in secret, away from the prying eyes of party officials. The Australian ballot replaced a system of voting in which each party supplied supporters with its own easily identifiable ballot that included only the names of its own candidates. The Australian ballot, by ensuring secrecy and simplifying split-ticket voting, made it easy for citizens to focus on candidates rather than parties when voting. This type of ballot remains in use today.

State-regulated primary nominating contests, which were widely adopted during the Progressive movement of the early 1900s, deprived party leaders of the power to handpick congressional nominees and gave that power to voters who participated in their party's nominating election.[6] The merit-based civil service system, another progressive reform, deprived the parties of patronage. No longer able to distribute government jobs or contracts, the parties had difficulty maintaining large corps of campaign workers.[7] Issues, friendships, the excitement of politics, and other noneconomic incentives could motivate small numbers of people to become active in party politics, but they could not motivate enough people to support a party-focused system of congressional elections.

Congressional candidates also lacked the patronage or government contracts needed to attract large numbers of volunteer workers or to persuade other candidates to help them with their campaigns. By the mid–twentieth century the "isolation" of congressional candidates from one another and from their own party organizations was so complete that a major report on the state of political parties characterized congressional candidates as the "orphans of the political system." The report, which was published by the American Political Science Association's Committee on Political Parties, went on to point out that congressional candidates "had no truly adequate party mechanism available for the conduct of their campaigns, . . . enjoy[ed] remarkably little national or local support, [and] have mostly been left to cope with the political hazards of their occupation on their own."[8]

Voter registration and get-out-the-vote drives were about the only area of electioneering in which there was, and remains, some cooperation among groups of candidates and party committees. But even here the integration of different party committees and candidate organizations—and especially those involved in congressional elections—was and continues to be short of that exhibited in other democracies.

The Federal Election Campaign Act of 1974 and the amendments, regulatory rulings, and court decisions that have shaped federal campaign finance law (collectively known as the FECA) further reinforced the pattern of candidate-centered congressional elections.[9] The original 1974 law placed strict limits on the amount of money parties could contribute to or spend directly on behalf of their congressional candidates. It further limited the parties' involvement in congressional elections by placing ceilings on individual contributions and an outright ban on corporate, union, or trade association contributions to the accounts the parties use to campaign directly for federal candidates. Moreover, the FECA provided no subsidies for generic, party-focused campaign activity.[10]

The law's provisions for political parties stand in marked contrast to the treatment given to parties in other democracies. Most of these countries provide subsidies to parties for campaign and interelection activities.[11] The United States is the only democracy in which parties are not given free television and radio time.[12] The support that other democracies give to parties is consistent with the central role they play in elections, government, and society, just as the lack of assistance afforded to American parties is consistent with the candidate-centered system that has developed here.

Lacking independent sources of revenue, local party organizations are unable to play a dominant role in the modern cash-based system of congressional campaign politics.[13] The national and state party committees that survived the reform movements and changes in federal election laws lack sufficient funds or staff to dominate campaign politics. Perhaps even more important, party leaders have little desire to do so. They believe a party should bolster its candidates' campaigns, not replace them with a campaign of its own.[14]

Nevertheless, the evolution of campaign finance law has enabled parties to play a greater role in recent congressional elections. The 1979 amendment to the FECA exempted from federal contribution and spending limits voter registration drives, get-out-the vote efforts, and other grass-roots activities sponsored by state and local party committees. It also allowed these organizations to distribute slate cards and other materials that list federal candidates without reporting these activities to the FEC. The amendment created a legal loophole that permits campaign spending that is technically outside of the federal campaign finance system but is used to influence the outcome of federal elections. The funds that flow through this loophole, commonly referred to as "soft" money (as opposed to the "federal" or "hard" money that is spent inside the system), include contributions that come from sources and in amounts banned under the federal system. Some soft money contributions are collected from corporations, unions, and wealthy individuals in amounts in excess of $1 million.[15]

Most soft money is raised and spent by political parties, but other groups, some of which are closely affiliated with party committees, also collect and distribute soft money in order to influence federal elections. Party soft money expenditures surpassed $160 million during the 1996 contests.[16] The soft money activity of interest groups cannot be accounted for because it does not have to be reported to the FEC. Soft money has become one of the most controversial components of the election system, and its elimination has become a major goal of political reformers.

Another change in the campaign finance system that has increased the role of interest groups in elections concerns the use of funds collected by tax-exempt organizations for political use.[17] These groups, classified as 501(c)(3) and 501(c)(4) organizations in the federal tax code, do not pay taxes because they purportedly exist for charitable, educational, or other civic purposes rather than earning profits. In recent years, however, some tax-exempt groups have carried out activities designed to influence congressional and other elections. Among these groups are GOPAC, the Abraham Lincoln Opportunity Foundation, and the Progress and Freedom Foundation, which were part of House Speaker Newt Gingrich's, R-Ga., political operation; Americans for Tax Reform, a group that has close ties with the Republicans; and Vote Now '96, a voter registration group that focuses on demographic groups that are traditionally loyal to Democrats.[18]

A series of court decisions, including one that was handed down in the midst of the 1996 election season, increased the activities that parties, PACs, and other interest groups can use to influence federal elections.[19] These rulings allow these organizations to spend unlimited sums of hard or soft money on issue advocacy advertisements that resemble ads that in the past could only be financed with hard money. Most issue advocacy ads are nearly identical to hard money ads in that they praise or criticize federal candidates by name or feature their likenesses. The only major visible difference is that issue advocacy ads cannot *expressly* call for a candidate's election or defeat.[20] The courts also asserted the parties' right to make unlimited independent expenditures on campaign communications that *directly* advocate the election or defeat of a federal candidate as long as these expenditures are made with hard money and without the candidate's knowledge or consent. Party and interest group independent expenditures, issue advocacy campaigns, and voter mobilization efforts have significantly increased these organizations' influence in congressional elections. It is unlikely that these efforts will do away with the candidate-centered nature of congressional elections, but they have significantly altered it.

POLITICAL CULTURE

Historically, American political culture has supported a system of candidate-centered congressional elections in many ways, but its major influence stems from its lack of foundation for a party-focused alternative. Americans have traditionally held a jaundiced view of political parties. *Federalist* no. 10 and President George Washington's farewell address are evidence that the framers and the first president thought a multitude of overlapping, wide-ranging interests preferable to class-based divisions represented by ideological parties. The founders designed the political system to encourage pragmatism and compromise in politics and thus to mitigate the harmful effects of factions. Although neither the pluralist system championed by the framers of the Constitution nor the nonpartisan system advocated by Washington has been fully realized, both visions of democracy have found expression in candidate-centered campaigns.

Congressional elections test candidates' abilities to build coalitions of voters and elites from diverse individuals. The multiplicity of overlapping interests, lack of a feudal legacy, and relatively fluid social and economic structure in the United States discourage the formation of class-based parties like those that have developed in most other democracies.[21] The consensus among Americans for liberty, equality, and property rights and their near-universal support for the political system further undermine the development of parties aimed at promoting major political, social, or economic change.[22]

Americans' traditional ambivalence about political parties has found expression during reform periods. The Populist movement of the 1890s, the Progressive movement that came shortly after it, and the rise of the New Left in the 1960s all resulted in political change that weakened the parties. Turn-of-the-century reformers championed the Australian ballot, the direct primary, and civil service laws for the explicit purpose of taking power away from party bosses.[23] Similarly, the reform movement that took hold of the Democratic Party during the 1960s and 1970s opened party conventions, meetings, and leadership positions to the increased participation of previously underrepresented groups. The reforms, many of which were adopted by Republican as well as Democratic state party organizations, made both parties more permeable and responsive to pressures from grass-roots activists. They tremendously weakened what little influence party leaders had over the awarding of nominations, giving candidates, their supporters, and issue activists more influence over party affairs.[24]

Post–World War II social and cultural transformations undermined the parties even further. Declining immigration and increased geographic mobility eroded the lower-class ethnic neighborhoods that were an important source of party loyalists. Increased educational levels encouraged citizens to rely more on their own judgment and less on party cues in political matters. The development of the mass media gave voters less-biased sources of information than the partisan press. The rise of interest groups, PACs, and other forms of functional and ideological representation created new arenas for political participation and new sources of political cues.[25] The aging of the parties, generational replacement, and the emergence of new issues that cut across existing fault lines led to the decline of party affiliation among voters and to more issue-oriented voting.[26] These developments encouraged voters to rely less on local party officials and opinion leaders for political information.[27] Cultural transformations created a void in electoral politics that individual candidates and their organizations came to fill.

Current attitudes toward the parties reflect the nation's historical experience. Survey research shows that most citizens believe that parties "do more to confuse the issues than to provide a clear choice on the issues," and "create conflict where none exists." Half of the population believes that parties make the political system less efficient and that "it would be better if, in all elections, we put no party labels on the ballot."[28]

Negative attitudes toward the parties are often learned at an early age. Many schoolchildren are routinely instructed to "vote for the best candidate, not the party." This lesson appears to stay with some of them into adulthood. A month before the 1986 congressional elections, less than 10 percent of all registered voters maintained that the candidate's political party would be the biggest factor in their vote decision. Candidates and issues ranked higher.[29]

Although American history and culture extol the virtues of political independence and candidate-oriented voting, the electoral behavior of citizens does provide an element of partisanship in congressional elections. Roughly two-thirds of all voters are willing to state that they identify with the Democratic or Republican Party. About 60 percent of all self-identified independents hold attitudes and exhibit political behaviors similar to those of partisans.[30] In 1986, the same year in which so few registered voters stated that they planned to cast their votes chiefly on a partisan basis, nearly three-quarters of all voters cast their ballots along party lines.[31] Such high levels of party-line voting are common in contemporary American politics, and partisanship is among the best predictors of voting in congressional elections, ranking second only to incumbency. The fact that roughly 85 percent of the voting population perceives, retains, and responds to political information in a partisan manner means that elections are not entirely candidate-centered.[32] Yet the degree of partisanship that exists in the contemporary United States is not strong enough to encourage a return to party-line voting or to foster the development of a party-focused election system.

CAMPAIGN TECHNOLOGY

Political campaigns are designed to communicate ideas and images that will motivate voters to cast their ballots for particular candidates. Some voters are well-informed, have strong opinions about candidates, issues, and parties, and will vote without ever coming into contact with a political campaign. Others will never bother to vote, regardless of the efforts of the politicians. Many voters need to be introduced to the candidates and made aware of the issues in order to become excited enough to vote in a congressional election. The communication of information is central to democratic elections, and those who are able to control the flow of information have tremendous power. Candidates, campaign organizations, parties, and other groups employ a variety of technologies to affect the flow of campaign information and win votes.

Person-to-person contact is one of the oldest and most effective approaches to winning votes. Nothing was or is more effective than having a candidate, or a candidate's supporters, directly ask voters for their support. During the golden age of parties, local party volunteers assessed the needs of voters in their neighborhoods and delivered the message that, if elected, their party's candidates would help voters achieve their goals.[33] Once these organizations lost their control over the flow of political information they became less important, and candidate-assembled campaign organizations became more relevant players in elections.

The dawning of the television age and the development of modern campaign technology helped solidify the system of candidate-centered congressional elections.[34] Television and radio studios, printing presses, public opinion polls, high-speed computers, and sophisticated targeting techniques are well suited to candidate-centered campaign organizations because they, and the services of the political consultants who know how to use them, can easily be purchased. Congressional candidates can assemble organizations that meet their specific needs without having to turn to party organizations for assistance, although many candidates request their parties' help.

New technology has encouraged a major change in the focus of most congressional election campaigns. It has enabled campaigns to communicate more information about candidates' personalities, issue positions, and qualifications for office. As a result, less campaign activity is now devoted to party-based appeals. Radio and television were especially important in bringing about this change because they are well suited to conveying images and less useful in providing information about abstract concepts, such as partisan ideologies.[35] The overall effect of the electronic mass media is to direct attention away from parties and toward candidates.

The increased focus on candidate imagery that is associated with the "new style" of campaigning encourages congressional candidates to hire professional technicians to help them convey their political personas to voters.[36] Press secretaries, pollsters, issue researchers, fund-raising specialists, and media experts are commonplace in most congressional campaigns. Local party activists became less important in congressional elections as the importance of political consultants grew and the contributions of semiskilled and unskilled volunteers diminished. The introduction of direct-mail fund-raising and the emergence of PACs further increased the candidate-centered character of election campaigns because they provided candidates with the means for raising the contributions needed to purchase the services of campaign consultants.

Changes in technology transformed most congressional campaigns from labor-intensive grass-roots undertakings, at which local party committees excelled, to money-driven, merchandised activities requiring the services of skilled experts. Most local party committees were unable to adapt to the new style of campaign politics.[37] Initially, party committees in Washington, D.C., and in many states were also unprepared to play a significant role in congressional elections. However, the parties' national, congressional, and senatorial campaign committees and several state party organizations proved more adept at making the transition to the new-style politics. They began to play a meaningful role in congressional election campaigns during the late 1970s and early 1980s.[38]

THE POLITICAL SETTING

Candidates, campaign managers, party officials, PAC managers, and others who are active in congressional elections consider more than the institutional framework, available technology, and culturally and historically conditioned expectations of voters when planning and executing electoral strategies. They also assess the political setting, including the circumstances in their district, their state, or the nation as a whole. At the local level, important considerations include the party affiliation, tenure, and intentions of the incumbent or other potential candidates, and the partisan history of the seat. Relevant national-level factors include whether it is a presidential or midterm election year, the state of the economy, presidential popularity, international affairs, and the public's attitude toward the government. In 1992 the populist anti-Washington senti-ments that crystallized in the independent presidential candidacy of Ross Perot were significant. Similarly, hostile sentiments directed at congressional Demo-crats and President Clinton led to the Republican takeover of Congress in 1994. Disapproval of the two federal government shutdowns and some elements of the "Republican revolution" helped make many 1996 congressional elections competitive.

Of course, one's perspective on the limits and possibilities of the political setting depends largely on one's vantage point. Although they talk about the competition and are, indeed, wary of it, congressional incumbents, particularly House members, operate in a political setting that works largely to their ben-efit. As explained in later chapters, incumbents enjoy significant levels of name recognition and voter support, are able to assemble superior campaign organi-zations, and can draw on their experience in office to speak knowledgeably about issues and claim credit for the federally financed programs and improve-ments in their state or district. Incumbents also tend to get favorable treatment from the press. Moreover, most can rely on loyal followers from previous cam-paigns for continued backing: supporters at home tend to vote repeatedly for incumbents, and supporters in Washington and the nation's other wealthy cit-ies routinely provide incumbents with campaign money.

Things look different from the typical challenger's vantage point. Most chal-lengers, particularly those who possess some political experience, recognize that most of the cards are stacked against an individual who sets out to take on an incumbent. Little in the setting in which most congressional campaigns take place favors the challenger. Most challengers lack the public visibility, money, and campaign experience to wage a strong campaign. Moreover, because those who work in and help finance campaigns recognize the strong odds against challengers, they usually see little benefit in helping them. As a result, high incumbent success rates have become a self-fulfilling prophecy. Between 1950 and 1990, House incumbents enjoyed reelection rates of better than 90 per-cent; the 1990 and 1992 elections returned to Congress 96 percent and 88 percent, respectively, of those who sought to keep their jobs. Even with the tidal wave that swept away thirty-four Democrats in the House in the 1994 elec-tions, just over 90 percent of all House incumbents who wished to remain in office did so.[39] With some important exceptions, most experienced politicians wait until an incumbent retires before running for office. Thus, many House seats fail to attract meaningful competition.

Elections for open seats are highly competitive. They attract extremely qualified candidates who put together strong campaign organizations, raise huge amounts of money, and mount lively campaigns. Even House candidates of one party campaigning for seats that have been held by the other party for decades are often viable and attract substantial resources, media attention, and votes.

Senate elections have been more competitive than contests for the lower chamber. Senate reelection rates ranged from 55 percent to almost 97 percent between 1946 and 1996. Between 1986 and 1996 less than 3 percent of all Senate incumbents had no major-party opponent, and 54 percent of those involved in contested races won by 60 percent or more of the two-party vote. Thirteen percent of all senators seeking reelection during this span were defeated.[40]

There are many explanations for the relative lack of competition in House elections. Some districts are so dominated by one party that few individuals of the other party are willing to commit their time, energy, or money to running for office. In many cases, the tradition of one-party dominance is so strong that virtually all the talented, politically ambitious individuals living in the area join the dominant party. When an incumbent in these districts faces a strong challenge it usually takes place in the primary, and the winner is all but guaranteed success in the general election.[41]

Uncompetitive House districts are sometimes the product of the redistricting process. In states where one party controls both the governorship and the state legislature, partisan gerrymandering is often used to maximize the number of House seats the dominant party can win. In states where each party controls at least some portion of the state government, compromises are frequently made to design districts that protect congressional incumbents. Party officials and political consultants armed with computers, election returns, and demographic statistics can "pack" and "crack" voting blocs in order to promote either of these goals.[42] The result is that large numbers of congressional districts are designed to be uncompetitive.

The desire of incumbents to retain their seats has changed Congress in ways that help discourage electoral competition. Most of those who are elected to Congress quickly understand that they will probably never hold a higher office because there are too few of such offices to go around. Like most people, they do everything in their power to hold on to their jobs. Congress has adapted to the career aspirations of its members by providing them with resources that can be used to increase their odds of reelection. Free mailings, WATS lines, district offices, and subsidized travel help members gain visibility among their constituents. Federal "pork-barrel" projects also help incumbents win the support of voters.[43] Congressional staffs help members write speeches, respond to constituent mail, resolve problems that constituents have with executive branch agencies, and follow the comings and goings in their bosses' districts.[44] These perquisites of office give incumbents tremendous advantages over challengers. They also work to discourage those experienced politicians who could put forth a competitive challenge from taking on an entrenched incumbent.

The dynamics of campaign finance have similar effects. Incumbents have tremendous fund-raising advantages over challengers, especially among PACs and wealthy individual donors. Many incumbents build up large war chests to discourage potential challengers from running against them. With the exception of millionaires and celebrities, those challengers who decide to contest a race against a member of the House or Senate typically find they are unable to raise the funds needed to mount a viable campaign.

Given that the cards tend to be so heavily stacked in favor of congressional incumbents, most electoral competition takes place in open seats. Open-seat contests draw a larger than usual number of primary contestants. They also attract significantly more money and election assistance from party committees, PACs, and individuals than do challenger campaigns.[45] Special elections, which are called when a seat becomes vacant because of an incumbent's resignation, are open-seat contests that tend to be particularly competitive and unpredictable. They bring out even larger numbers of primary contenders than normal open-seat elections, especially when the seat that has become vacant was formerly held by a longtime incumbent.

The concentration of competition in open-seat elections and the decennial reapportionment and redistricting of House seats have combined to produce a ten-year, five-election cycle of political competition. Redistricting leads to the creation of many new House seats and the redrawing of the boundaries of numerous others. It encourages an increase in congressional retirements, leads more nonincumbents than usual to run for the House, and thereby increases competition in many House elections.[46]

Another cyclical element of the national political climate that can influence congressional elections is the presence or absence of a presidential election. Presidential elections have higher levels of voter turnout than midterm elections, and they have the potential for coattail effects. A presidential candidate's popularity can become infectious and lead to some increase in support for the party's congressional contestants. A party that enjoys much success in electing congressional candidates during a presidential election year is, of course, likely to lose some of these seats in the midterm election that follows.[47] An unpopular president can further drag down a party's congressional contestants.[48] Presidential election politics had a strong impact on the election of 1932, in which the Democrats gained ninety seats in the House and thirteen seats in the Senate. The Democratic congressional landslide was a sign of widespread support for the Democratic presidential candidate, Franklin D. Roosevelt, as well as a repudiation of the incumbent president, Herbert Hoover, and his policies for dealing with the Great Depression.[49] Although coattail effects have declined since the 1930s, Ronald Reagan's 1980 presidential campaign is credited with helping the Republicans gain thirty-three seats in the House and twelve seats in the Senate.[50] Bill Clinton's presidential elections were conspicuous for their lack of coattails. Democrats lost ten House seats and broke even in the Senate in 1992; they gained only ten seats in the House and lost two seats in the Senate in 1996. Coattail effects are rarely visible when a presidential candidate wins by margins as small as Clinton's 43 percent of the popular vote in 1992 and 49 percent in 1996.

Congressional candidates who belong to the same party as an unpopular president also run the risk during midterm elections of being blamed for the failures of their party's chief executive.[51] The Republicans' forty-nine-seat House and four-seat Senate losses in 1974 grew out of a sense of disgust about the Nixon administration's role in the Watergate break-in and President Ford's decision to pardon Nixon.[52] The Democrats' loss of fifty-two seats in the House and eight seats in the Senate in 1994 was caused largely by voter animosity toward Clinton, dissatisfaction with his party's failure to enact health care reform or a middle-class tax cut, and the Republicans' successful portrayal of the White House and the Democratic-controlled Congress as corrupt and out of step with the views of most voters.[53]

The economy, foreign affairs, and other national issues have some effect on congressional elections. The president's party often loses congressional seats in midterm elections when economic trends are unfavorable, although the relationship between economic performance and congressional turnover has been weakening in recent years.[54] Foreign affairs may have contributed to the Democrats' congressional losses in 1972 during the Vietnam War.[55] Americans, however, tend to be less concerned with "guns" than with "butter," and so international events generally have less of an effect on elections than domestic conditions.

Other national issues that can affect congressional elections are civil rights, social issues, and the attitudes of voters toward political institutions. The civil rights revolution, the women's movement, urban decay, the emergence of the hippie counterculture, and the protests they spawned influenced voting behavior during the 1960s and 1970s.[56] Political scandal, and the widespread distrust of government that usually follows, can lead to the defeat of politicians accused of committing ethical transgressions, but as the 1974 and 1994 elections demonstrate, individual members of Congress who are not directly implicated in scandal can also suffer because of it.

National issues are likely to have the greatest effect on congressional elections when candidates take unambiguous stands on them.[57] Presidential politics are likely to have the greatest influence on congressional elections when voters closely identify congressional candidates with a party's presidential nominee or an incumbent president. House and Senate candidates generally respond strategically to national politics in order to improve their electoral fortunes. When their party selects a popular presidential candidate or has a popular incumbent in the White House, congressional candidates ally themselves with that individual in order to take advantage of the party cue. When their party selects an unpopular nominee or is saddled with an unpopular president, congressional candidates seek to protect themselves from the effects of partisanship by distancing themselves from the comings and goings of the executive branch. The party-focused campaigns that Democratic congressional candidates ran during the New Deal era and in 1996 and that Republicans mounted during the height of Ronald Reagan's presidency exemplify the former strategy. The independent, nonpartisan campaigns that many congressional Republicans carried out in 1990, 1992, and 1996 and Democrats carried out in 1994 are representative of the latter.

RECENT CONGRESSIONAL ELECTIONS

The political settings that shaped the opportunities presented to politicians, parties, interest groups, and ultimately voters in the 1980s and early to middle 1990s had some important similarities. All but the 1994 midterm elections took place during a period of divided control, which made it difficult to credit or blame only one party for the government's performance or the nation's affairs. Most of the elections also took place under the shadow of a weak economy and were haunted by the specter of huge budget deficits.

Civil rights and racial and gender discrimination were issues in many campaigns during the 1990s as a result of the highly publicized studies of the unequal salaries and advancement prospects for women and African Americans, the beating of the African American motorist Rodney King by four white police officers in Los Angeles, and the riots that ensued in that city when the officers were found not guilty. The Senate Judiciary Committee's treatment of Anita Hill and her allegations of sexual harassment against Supreme Court nominee Clarence Thomas during his confirmation hearings called further attention to racial and gender issues. Gay rights found its place on the agenda as the nation debated the military's long-standing policy against homosexuals serving in the military. The allegations of sexual harassment that led Robert Packwood, R-Ore., to resign from the Senate called further attention to the concerns of traditionally unempowered groups.

A final arena in which civil rights issues were fought was redistricting. In 1986 the Supreme Court ruled that any gerrymandering of a congressional district that purposely diluted minority strength was illegal under the 1982 Voting Rights Act.[58] Most states interpreted the ruling cautiously, redrawing many of the districts after the 1990 census with the explicit purpose of giving one or more minority group members better-than-even chances of being elected to the House. Several groups opposed the majority-minority seats, claiming they were unconstitutional. Their successful lawsuits led to the redrawing of many congressional districts in Florida, Georgia, Louisiana, North Carolina, and Texas after the 1992 elections. They also nullified the results of several primary contests and forced three run-off elections to be held in Texas in December 1996. Even the 1998 House elections promise to be influenced by the redistricting that followed the 1990 census. Both Virginia's 3rd congressional district, which was drawn to promote the election of an African American, and New York's 12th congressional district, which was designed to elect a Hispanic, were overturned in federal court after the 1996 elections.[59] The irony of these decisions, and pending lawsuits, is that the redistricting process will start all over again in 2000, undoubtedly inspiring new legal challenges.

Dissatisfaction with the political establishment in Washington also occupied a prominent position on the political agenda at the close of the twentieth century. Gridlock and the federal government's inability to solve problems associated with drug abuse, crime, the environment, rising health care costs, the unsatisfactory performance of the nation's schools, the deficit, and a myriad of other seemingly intractable issues resulted in voter frustration with national politicians. Much of this hostility was directed toward Congress, and many incumbents responded with a strategy that had served them well in the past—running for reelection by campaigning against Congress itself.[60]

Political scandal and the anti-Washington mood gave open-seat and challenger candidates for Congress many powerful issues to use in campaigns during the 1990s. The Keating Five scandal, which implicated five senators in improperly lobbying federal bank regulators on behalf of Charles Keating, who was a major campaign supporter, ignited anti-Congress sentiments in 1990. Congressional pay raises and the scandal-tainted resignations of House Speaker Jim Wright, D-Texas, and House Democratic Whip Tony Coelho, D-Calif., added fuel to the fire during that same year. In 1992 the flames of anti-Congress sentiment were further fanned by the House banking scandal, which revealed that 325 current or former House members had made 8,331 overdrafts at the House bank; by the House Post Office scandal, which implicated some high-ranking House members and staff in exchanging stamps for money; and by the savings and loan crisis, which left American taxpayers footing a bill for failed banking institutions that is estimated to reach $180 billion.[61] Not surprisingly, support for the national legislature reached an all-time low prior to the 1994 elections, with polls estimating that roughly three-fourths of all Americans disapproved of Congress's performance.[62]

Political scandal, congressional perquisites, the federal deficit, and government gridlock are easily identifiable issues that can be used effectively against congressional incumbents and others who are identified with the Washington establishment. In 1994 conditions were ripe for the Republicans to pick up a significant number of congressional seats. Public hostility toward Washington, Democratic control of both the executive and legislative branches of the national government, and the Democrats' historical association with the growth of federal programs and the bureaucracy put that party in a precarious position. Moreover, Clinton's early missteps on health care reform, gays in the military, and tax cuts, and allegations of ethical misconduct by the president and his administration, served to energize Republican candidates and their supporters while demoralizing Democrats and their allies. Under Gingrich's leadership, the Republicans capitalized on these circumstances by running a nationalized anti-Washington campaign that drew on the Contract with America.[63]

Following their takeover of Congress in 1994, House Republicans passed most elements of their contract.[64] The public supported congressional reform, crime control, welfare reform, a balanced budget amendment, and other contract provisions that would promote a smaller, less expensive government. However, it objected to GOP plans to grant $240 billion in tax cuts to the wealthiest elements in society while reducing future Medicare funding by $270 billion, and cutting appropriations for Medicaid, education, and environmental protection. The federal government shutdowns, which were largely blamed on Gingrich, increased public misgivings about the Republican Congress. Just as the missteps of Democrats laid the foundation for a nationalized political campaign in 1994, those of Republicans laid the foundation for one in 1996. Democrats sought to capitalize on the Republicans' difficulties by campaigning against what they labeled "the extremist Republican Congress" and offering their Families First Agenda, which included several modest policy proposals that were designed to appeal to middle-income and blue-collar families.

The political setting for the congressional elections of 1992 through 1996 produced greater competition than had the races of the previous decade, par-

TABLE 1-1

Number of Unchallenged and Defeated House Incumbents

	1982	1984	1986	1988	1990	1992	1994	1996
Incumbent unchallenged by major-party opposition in general election	49	63	71	81	76	25	54	20
Incumbent defeated								
In primary	10	3	3	1	1	19	4	2
In general election	29	16	6	6	15	24	34	20

Sources: Compiled from various editions of *Congressional Quarterly Weekly Report.* The primary and general election results are from Norman J. Ornstein, Thomas E. Mann, and Michael J. Malbin, *Vital Statistics on Congress, 1995–1996* (Washington, D.C.: Congressional Quarterly, 1996), 60.

Note: The 1982 and 1992 figures include incumbent-versus-incumbent races.

ticularly in House contests (see Table 1-1). Nineteen House incumbents lost their primaries in 1992—a post–World War II record—and another thirty-four lost in the general election two years later—the most since the post-Watergate housecleaning of 1974. Relatively few incumbents enjoyed the luxury of running unopposed by a major-party candidate in the 1992 through 1996 elections.

The increased competitiveness of recent House elections is even more apparent once the candidates are divided into categories based on the "marginality" of the districts in which they ran. During the post-redistricting elections of 1982, 38 percent of all major-party House candidates ran in marginal districts. Included in this group are the 15 percent of the candidates classified as "incumbents in jeopardy," on the basis of their having lost the general election or won by a margin of 20 percent or less of the two-party vote; the 15 percent of the candidates who opposed them—labeled "hopeful challengers"; and the 8 percent of the candidates—classified as open-seat "prospects"—who ran in contests that were decided by 20 percent or less of the two-party vote (see Table 1-2).[65]

The 1992 post-redistricting House elections were slightly more competitive than those in 1982 because a greater number of retirements led to an increase in the number of marginal open-seat races. However, the 1994 and 1996 elections witnessed even more competitive contests. Forty-three percent of the candidates who ran in 1994 were involved in marginal contests, as compared with only 31 percent who ran in 1984; 38 percent of 1996 House candidates were also involved in close contests, as compared with 25 percent ten years earlier. The growth in competitive races was not merely the result of an increase in

TABLE 1-2

Competition in House Elections

	1982	1984	1986	1988	1990	1992	1994	1996
Incumbents								
In jeopardy	15%	13%	9%	8%	15%	14%	17%	15%
Shoo-ins	27	34	35	39	32	25	27	29
Challengers								
Hopefuls	15	13	9	8	15	14	17	15
Likely losers	27	34	35	39	32	25	27	29
Open-seat candidates								
Prospects	8	5	7	5	5	13	9	8
Long shots	7	1	4	3	1	9	5	4
(N)	(750)	(736)	(720)	(712)	(696)	(794)	(766)	(812)

Source: Compiled from Federal Election Commission data.

Notes: Figures are for general election candidates in major-party contested races, excluding incumbent-versus-incumbent races, runoff elections, and contests won by independents. Incumbents in jeopardy are defined as those who lost or who won by 20 percent or less of the two-party vote. Shoo-ins are incumbents who won by more than 20 percent of the two-party vote. Hopeful challengers are those who won or who lost by 20 percent or less of the two-party vote. Likely loser challengers are those who lost by more than 20 percent of the two-party vote. Open-seat long shots are those whose election was decided by more than 20 percent of the two-party vote. Some columns do not add to 100 percent because of rounding.

open-seat contests following House retirements. There was also an increase in the number and competitiveness of contested incumbent-challenger races, especially in the South and in districts where first-term House members sought to defend their seats.[66] The value of incumbency, although still significant, diminished in the 1990s.

The Senate elections held in the first half of the 1990s were not much different from those held in the previous decade in regard to the challenges presented to incumbents (see Table 1-3). Only two members of the upper chamber were defeated in a primary between 1990 and 1996. In 1992 the Cook County recorder of deeds, Carol Moseley-Braun, defeated Sen. Alan Dixon in the Illinois Democratic primary. In the 1996 Republican Senate primary in Kansas, Rep. Sam Brownback defeated Sen. Sheila Frahm, who had been appointed to take Robert Dole's Senate seat after Dole left the Senate to run for president. Moreover, when the classification scheme used for House candidates is applied to the Senate it becomes clear that the incumbent-challenger contests of the early and middle 1990s were somewhat more competitive than those that preceded them (see Table 1-4).

TABLE 1-3

Number of Unchallenged and Defeated Senate Incumbents

	1982	1984	1986	1988	1990	1992	1994	1996
Incumbent unchallenged by major-party opposition in general election	0	1	0	0	5	1	0	0
Incumbent defeated								
In primary	0	0	0	0	0	1	0	1
In general election	2	3	7	4	1	4	2	1

Sources: Compiled from various issues of *Congressional Quarterly Weekly Report.* The primary and general election results are from Norman J. Ornstein, Thomas E. Mann, and Michael J. Malbin, *Vital Statistics on Congress, 1995–1996* (Washington, D.C.: Congressional Quarterly, 1996), 61.

What did change were the numbers and competitiveness of open seats. During the 1980s, 18 percent or fewer Senate candidates were involved in open-seat contests. In 1992, this number jumped to 24, and in 1996 it reached 41 percent—a record that is likely to stand for some time. Moreover, only 6 percent of the 1996 open-seat contestants ran in races that were decided by more than 20 percent of the vote.

The competitiveness of recent congressional elections and the large number of open seats in both chambers ensured the appearance of many new faces in Congress. Over 50 percent of the members of the 105th Congress took their seats after the 1992 elections. As a group, those sworn into the 102d through the 105th Congresses were more diverse than previous classes. The House opened its first session of the 105th Congress with thirty-three more women, fifteen more African Americans, and eight more Hispanics than the 101st. Change generally comes slower to the upper chamber. Nevertheless, the number of female senators increased by seven, and the elections of Moseley-Braun and Ben Nighthorse Campbell, R-Colo., in 1992 meant that African Americans and Native Americans would enjoy demographic representation in the upper chamber.[67]

Despite this diversity, the vast majority of newcomers had at least one thing in common with one another and with their more senior colleagues: they came to Congress with significant political experience under their belts. Almost 90 percent of the new House members elected to the 105th Congress had previously held another public office, served as a party official, worked as a political aide or consultant, or run for Congress at least once before getting elected. Of the eight freshmen who had not held an elective or unelective political post, two—Reps. John Sununu, R-N.H., and Harold Ford Jr., D-Tenn.—were the

TABLE 1-4

Competition in Senate Elections

	1982	1984	1986	1988	1990	1992	1994	1996
Incumbents								
In jeopardy	26%	17%	20%	17%	20%	22%	23%	21%
Shoo-ins	20	27	20	24	25	16	14	9
Challengers								
Hopefuls	26	17	20	17	20	22	23	21
Likely losers	20	27	20	24	25	16	14	9
Open-seat candidates								
Prospects	10	10	12	12	3	21	14	35
Long shots	0	3	6	6	7	3	11	6
(N)	(66)	(64)	(68)	(66)	(60)	(68)	(707)	(68)

Source: Compiled from Federal Election Commission data.

Notes: Figures are for general election candidates in major-party contested races. Incumbents in jeopardy are defined as those who lost or who won by 20 percent or less of the two-party vote. Shoo-ins are incumbents who won by more than 20 percent or less of the two-party vote. Hopeful challengers are those who won or who lost by 20 percent or less of the two-party vote. Likely loser challengers are those who lost by more than 20 percent of the two-party vote. Open-seat prospects are those whose election was decided by 20 percent or less of the two-party vote. Open-seat long shots are those whose election was decided by more than 20 percent or less of the two-party vote. Some columns do not add to 100 percent because of rounding.

sons of famous politicians, and another, Rep. Jo Ann Emerson, R-Mo., was elected to take her deceased husband's seat. All the senators elected for the first time in 1996 had previously held elective office, except for Sens. Susan Collins, R-Me., and Chuck Hagel, R-Neb., both of whom had previously worked as congressional aides.

CHAPTER 2

Candidates and Nominations

Can I win? Is this the right time for me to run? Who is my competition likely to be? These are the kinds of questions that have always gone through the minds of prospective candidates. During the golden age of political parties, party bosses helped individuals make up their minds whether or not to run for Congress. In many places the bosses' control over the party apparatus was so complete that, when in agreement, they could guarantee the nomination to the person they wanted to run. Moreover, receiving the nomination was usually tantamount to winning the election because strong political machines were usually located in one-party areas.[1]

After the golden age, party leaders had less control over the nomination process and less ability to ensure that the individuals they recruited would, in fact, win the nomination. Contemporary parties are no longer the primary recruiters of congressional candidates. Parties continue to play a role in encouraging some individuals to run for office and in discouraging others. But they serve more as vehicles that self-recruited candidates use to advance their careers than as organizations that can make or break those careers. Party recruitment has been largely replaced by a process referred to as candidate emergence.[2]

In this chapter I examine who decides to run for Congress, how potential candidates reach their decisions, and the influence that different individuals and groups have on these decisions. I also examine the impact of political experience on a candidate's prospects of winning the nomination and the influence of nominations and general elections on the representativeness of the national legislature.

STRATEGIC AMBITION

The Constitution, state laws, and the political parties pose few formal barriers to running for Congress, enabling virtually anyone to become a candidate. Members of the House are required to be at least twenty-five years of age, to have been U.S. citizens for at least seven years, and to reside in the state they represent. The requirements for the Senate are only slightly more stringent. In addition to residing in the state they represent, senators must be at least thirty years old and have been U.S. citizens for at least nine years. Some states bar prison inmates or individuals who have been declared insane from running for office, and most states require candidates to pay a small filing fee or to collect anywhere from a few hundred to several thousand signatures prior to having their names placed on the ballot. As is typical for election to public offices in many democracies, a dearth of formal requirements allows almost anyone to run for Congress. And well over 1,500 people declare themselves candidates in most election years.

Although the formal requirements are minimal, other factors, related to the candidate-centered nature of the electoral system, favor individuals with certain personal characteristics. Strategic ambition, which is the combination of a desire to get elected, a realistic understanding of what it takes to win, and an ability to assess the opportunities presented by a given political context, is one such characteristic that distinguishes most successful candidates for Congress from the general public. Most successful candidates must also be self-starters, since the electoral system lacks a tightly controlled party-recruitment process or a well-defined career path to the national legislature. And, because the electoral system is candidate-centered, the desire, skills, and resources that candidates bring to the electoral arena are the most important criteria separating serious candidates from those who have little chance of getting elected. Ambitious candidates, sometimes referred to as *strategic, rational,* or *quality* candidates, are political entrepreneurs who make rational calculations about when to run. Rather than plunge right in, they assess the political context in which they would have to wage their campaigns, consider the effects that a bid for office could have on their professional careers and families, and carefully weigh their prospects for success.[3]

Strategic politicians examine many institutional, structural, and subjective factors when considering a bid for Congress.[4] The institutional factors include filing deadlines, campaign finance laws, prohibitions for or against preprimary endorsements, and other election statutes and party rules. The structural factors include the social, economic, and partisan composition of the district, its geographic compactness, the media markets that serve it, the degree of overlap between the district and lower-level electoral constituencies, and the possibilities that exist for election to some alternative office. One structural factor that greatly affects the strategic calculations of nonincumbents and is prone to fluctuate more often than others is whether an incumbent plans to run for reelection.

Potential candidates also assess the political climate in deciding whether to run. Strategic politicians focus mainly on local circumstances, particularly whether a seat will be vacant or the results of the previous election suggest that an incumbent is vulnerable.[5] National forces, such as a public mood that favors Democrats or Republicans or challengers or incumbents, are usually of secondary importance. The convergence of local and national forces can have a strong impact on the decisions of potential candidates. The widespread hostility the public directed at Congress and its members played a major role in shaping the pool of candidates that competed in the 1992, 1994, and 1996 primaries and general elections.[6] These forces motivated many House incumbents to retire.[7] They also encouraged many would-be House members to believe that a seat in Congress was not beyond their reach. Favorable circumstances and these candidates' positive self-assessments encouraged them to think they could win the support of local, state, and national political elites, raise the money, build the name recognition, and generate the momentum needed to propel them into office.[8]

Incumbents

For House incumbents the decision to run for reelection is usually an easy one. Congress offers its members many reasons to want to stay, including the ability to affect issues they care about, a challenging environment in which to work, political power, and public recognition. It is also an ideal platform for pursuing a governorship, cabinet post, or even a seat in the oval office. Name recognition and the advantages inherent in incumbency—such as paid staff and the franking privilege (which have an estimated worth of more than $1.5 million over a two-year House term)—are two factors that discourage strong opposition from arising.[9] Furthermore, House members recognize that the "home styles" they use to present themselves to constituents create bonds of trust that have important electoral implications.[10]

Incumbents undertake a number of additional preelection activities to build support and ward off opposition. Many raise large war chests early in the election cycle in order to intimidate potential opponents.[11] Many also keep a skeletal campaign organization intact between elections and send their supporters campaign newsletters and other political communications. Some even shower their constituents with greeting cards, flowers, and other gifts.[12] Their congressional activities, preelection efforts, and the fact that they have been elected to Congress at least once before make most incumbents fairly secure in the knowledge that they will be reelected.

Under certain situations, however, incumbents recognize that it may be more difficult than usual for them to hold on to their seats. Redistricting, for example, can change the partisan composition of a House member's district or it can force two incumbents to compete for one seat.[13] A highly publicized ethical transgression usually weakens an incumbent's reelection prospects. A poor economy, an unpopular president or presidential candidate, or a wave of antigovernment hostility also has the potential to bring down legislators who represent marginal districts. These factors can influence incumbents' expectations about the quality of the opposition they are likely to face, the kinds of reelection campaigns they will need to wage, the toll those campaigns could take on themselves and their families, and their desire to stay in Congress.

When the demands of campaigning outweigh the benefits of getting reelected, strategic incumbents retire. Elections that immediately follow redistricting are often preceded by a jump in the number of incumbents who retire, as was the case in 1952, 1972, 1982, and 1992 (see Figure 2-1). Elections held during periods of voter frustration, congressional scandal, or incivility within Congress itself are also preceded by high numbers of retirements.[14] A combination of redistricting, anti-incumbent sentiments, and a decline in comity in the House, led 15 percent of all House members to retire in 1992—a post–World War II record. The numerous hard-fought elections that took place in 1994 inspired many congressional retirements in 1996.

Elections that occur following upheaval within Congress itself are also marked by large numbers of congressional retirements. The political reforms passed during the mid-1970s, which redistributed power from conservative senior House members to more liberal junior ones, encouraged many senior members to retire from the House.[15] The Republican takeover of the House in 1994 also encouraged large numbers of Democrats, and some Republicans, to retire. For the Democrats, retirement was preferable to waging a reelection campaign that, if successful, would result in their continuing to suffer the powerlessness associated with being in the minority. For the Republicans, it was preferable to enduring the indignity of being defeated for a committee chairmanship or some other leadership post. Rep. Norman Mineta, D-Calif., former chair of the Public Works and Transportation Committee, retired nine months into the 104th Congress, reportedly for the former reason. Rep. Carlos Moorhead, R-Calif., who was the senior Republican member of two committees going into the 104th Congress and ended up chairing neither of them, was influenced by the latter.[16]

The individuals who are most likely to retire from Congress are senior mem-

FIGURE 2-1
Number of Retirements by House Incumbents, 1950–1996

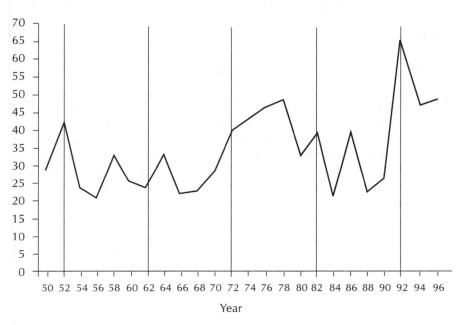

Year

Sources: Compiled from various issues of *Congressional Quarterly Weekly Report* and Norman J. Ornstein, Thomas E. Mann, and Michael J. Malbin, *Vital Statistics on Congress, 1995–1996* (Washington, D.C.: Congressional Quarterly, 1996), 62.

bers who decide they would rather enjoy the fruits of old age than face a tough opponent, members who find their districts largely obliterated, members who belong to the minority party, and those who are implicated in some kind of scandal.[17] The period just before the 1996 elections was marked by several retirements that were motivated by these reasons. Rep. Anthony C. Beilenson, D-Calif., a sixty-four-year-old Democrat who was reelected by just over 3,500 votes in 1994, was among those who chose to retire rather than wage a difficult reelection campaign against a strong opponent. Rep. Cleo Fields, D-La., who was elected in 1992, decided to leave Congress after a three-judge federal panel disassembled his district, which had held an African American majority. Reps. Enid Greene, R-Utah, and Wes Cooley, R-Ore., who had just been elected in 1994, were among those whose retirements were related to scandal. Greene and her estranged husband Joe Waldholtz were accused of campaign finance violations and personal financial improprieties. Cooley was charged with and later convicted of lying about his military record, and he and his wife were accused of hiding the date of their marriage so that she could continue to collect a widow's benefit stemming from her first marriage to a veteran.[18] Others who are likely to retire include those shorn from positions of power, such as Mineta and Moorhead.

Nonincumbents

The conditions that affect the calculations of strategic incumbents also influence the decision making of nonincumbents who plan their political careers strategically.[19] Redistricting has a tremendous impact on these individuals. More state and local officeholders run for the House in election cycles that follow redistricting than in other years (see Figure 2-2).[20] Many of these candidates anticipate the opportunities that arise from the creation of new seats, the re-

FIGURE 2-2

Number of House Primary Candidates by Political Experience, 1978–1996

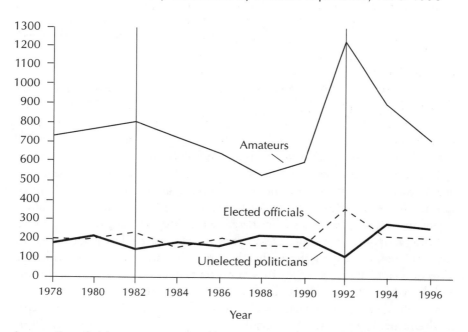

Sources: Compiled from various issues of *Congressional Quarterly Weekly Report* and other sources cited in note 20.

Note: Includes nonincumbent candidates for major-party nominations only.

drawing of old ones, or the retirements that often accompany elections after redistricting. The effects of redistricting and the anti-incumbent mood that gripped the nation encouraged roughly 350 candidates who had officeholding experience to run in 1992. Voter hostility toward the nation's capital and the possibility for change encouraged 210 elected officials and former officeholders to run in 1994 and another 209 to run in 1996.

Candidates who have significant campaign and political experience but who have never held elective office also respond to the opportunities that emerge in specific election years. These "unelected politicians" include legislative and executive branch aides, political appointees, state and local party officials, political consultants, and individuals who have previously lost a bid for Congress. Most of these politicians think strategically. Prior to deciding to run, they monitor voter sentiment, assess the willingness of political activists and contributors to support their campaigns, and keep close tabs on who is likely to oppose them for the nomination or in the general election.

Unelected politicians differ from elected officials and former officeholders in their perceptions of what constitutes a good time to run. For example, individuals with elective experience were more likely than unelected politicians to view the post-redistricting elections of 1992 favorably. The major reason for this difference is that the candidacies of the elected officials weighed heavily in the strategic calculations of the unelected politicians. Unelected politicians appreciate that most elected officials possess more name recognition and fundraising advantages than they do. Unelected politicians typically balk at the opportunity to contest a primary against an elected official, even when other circumstances appear favorable. However, if a candidate with elective experience does not come forward, individuals with other significant forms of political experience will usually run.

Political amateurs are an extremely diverse group, and it is difficult to generalize about their political decision making. Only a small subgroup of amateurs, referred to as *ambitious amateurs,* behave strategically, responding to the same opportunities and incentives that influence the decisions of more experienced politicians. Most amateurs do not spend much time assessing these factors. *Policy amateurs,* comprising another subgroup, are driven by issues, whereas *experience-seeking* or *hopeless amateurs* run out of a sense of civic duty or for the thrill of running itself.[21]

Record numbers of amateurs ran in the 1982 and 1992 elections. A few were ambitious challengers, who, after weighing the costs of campaigning and the probability of winning, declared their candidacies. Many policy and experience-seeking amateurs were also compelled to run in the early and middle 1990s. These elections provided political landscapes that were ideal for running advocacy-oriented or anti-incumbency campaigns. Calls for change and relentless government-bashing in the media provided reform-minded candidates from both parties with ready-made platforms. The Contract with America and supporting issue papers, campaign manifestos, and Republican recruitment efforts helped inspire more GOP than Democratic candidates to run in 1994—the first time in decades. The legislation proposed and enacted by the Republican-led 105th Congress inspired many policy-oriented Democratic and GOP candidates to run in 1996. The possibilities for turnover in the three elections attracted all types of amateurs.

What appears to be a year of opportunity for strategic politicians of one party is often viewed as a bad year by their counterparts in the other. Democrats with experience in lower office considered 1978 and 1982 to be good years to run for the House; Republicans with comparable levels of experience did not (see Figure 2-3). In 1978 many Democrats believed that the lingering

FIGURE 2-3

House Primary Candidacies of Politicians by Party and Experience, 1978–1996

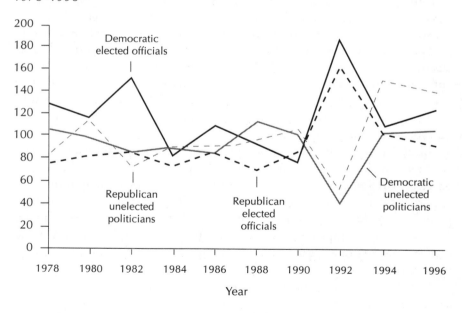

Sources: Compiled from various issues of *Congressional Quarterly Weekly Report* and other sources cited in note 20.

Note: Includes candidates for major-party nominations only.

effects of the Watergate scandal and the retirements of forty-nine House members improved their electoral prospects. In 1982 many Democrats expected to benefit from the sluggish economy and declining popularity of President Reagan.[22]

Republicans, in contrast, judged 1980 to be a good year. Double-digit inflation and the failures of Jimmy Carter's presidency encouraged many experienced Republicans to run for Congress while discouraging qualified Democratic candidates.[23] The 1990 elections also attracted many highly qualified Republican candidates while discouraging the candidacies of similarly qualified Democrats. Many of these GOP members apparently thought that the Keating Five scandal (which implicated four Democrats and only one Republican), the congressional pay raise, the forced retirements of House Speaker Jim Wright and House Majority Whip Tony Coelho, and the diffuse hostility that voters were directing at Congress could be used to whip up sentiment against Democratic incumbents.

The 1992 election was somewhat unusual in that strategic politicians of both parties judged it to hold tremendous possibilities. The effects of redistricting, a weak economy, congressional scandal, and voter antipathy encouraged record numbers of Democratic and Republican officeholders to run for Congress. The 1994 election witnessed a significant decline in candidates with elective experience from both parties, but especially Democrats. Democratic and Republican unelected politicians, however, saw greater opportunities that year, perhaps because of the decline in the number of politicians with elective experience who chose not to run.

The Republican takeover of Congress had a significant effect on both parties' recruitment for the 1996 elections. The number of Republican candidates with elective or significant nonelective experience decreased slightly after 1994. Many individuals in the GOP's candidate pool undoubtedly believed that their party had captured virtually every vulnerable Democrat-held seat in the tidal wave of 1994. Many Democratic elected officials also opted not to run in 1996. Demoralized by their party's low standing in the polls, the president's unpopularity, and the House Republicans' initial legislative success, they anticipated that 1996 would offer another hostile electoral setting for their party. Not wanting to risk a political defeat, many declined the opportunity to run against GOP freshmen, including some who probably would have been vulnerable to a strong challenge. Democratic unelected politicians filled the void in some of these districts; political amateurs did likewise in others.

Because it is so difficult to defeat an incumbent, usually most of the best-qualified office seekers wait until a seat opens, either through the retirement or the death of the incumbent, before throwing their hats into the ring.[24] Once a

TABLE 2-1

The Effect of Seat Status on Nonincombent Candidates for House
Nominations in 1996

	Democrats			Republicans		
	Elected officials	Unelected politicians	Political amateurs	Elected officials	Unelected politicians	Political amateurs
Open seat	43%	30%	25%	56%	28%	32%
Democratic incumbent seeking reelection	8	10	12	38	57	56
Republican incumbent seeking reelection	48	61	62	6	15	12
(N)	(122)	(104)	(335)	(87)	(143)	(348)

Sources: Compiled from various issues of *Congressional Quarterly Weekly Report* and other sources cited in note 20.

Note: Some columns do not add to 100 percent because of rounding.

seat becomes vacant, it acts like a magnet, drawing the attention and candidacies of many individuals. Usually several strategic politicians will express interest in an open seat. Forty-three percent of the Democratic elected officials who ran for the House in 1996 and 56 percent of their Republican counterparts ran in the 11 percent of the races in which there was no incumbent at the beginning of the election season (see Table 2-1).[25]

Incumbency discourages strategic competition, especially within one party. Only 8 percent of the Democratic elected officials who ran for the House in 1996 were willing to challenge one of their party's incumbents for the nomination. Their Republican counterparts were similarly gun shy about attempting to commit political fratricide: only 6 percent were willing to challenge a GOP House member in the primary.

The candidacies of elected officials contrast with those of unelected politicians and amateur candidates. Unelected politicians and political amateurs are more willing to engage in internecine warfare with one of their party's House incumbents or to run in a primary for a seat that is controlled by an incumbent from the opposing party. These candidates have fewer political costs to weigh than do elected officials when considering whether to enter a congressional primary. Prospective candidates who do not hold an elective office do not have to give up a current office in order to run for Congress, as do most officeholders whose positions are coterminous with congressional elections.[26] They also do not have to be concerned about the effect a defeat could have on an established political career.

Others Involved in the Decision to Run

The drive to hold elective office may be rooted in an individual's personality and tempered by the larger political environment, but potential candidates rarely reach a decision about running for Congress without touching base with a variety of people.[27] Nearly all candidates single out their family and friends as being highly influential in their decision to enter or forgo the race.[28] More than one young, talented, experienced, and well-connected local politician who wanted a seat in Congress has remarked only half in jest that family members would probably shoot them if they decided to run. Family concerns, financial considerations, and career aspirations have kept many ambitious and highly regarded local politicians from running for Congress.

Political parties, labor unions, other organized groups, and political consultants can also affect a prospective candidate's decision, but they have far less impact than the people who are directly involved in an individual's daily life. Potential candidates usually discuss their plans with these groups only after mulling for a long time the idea of running. Sometimes, would-be candidates approach local party leaders, fellow party members in the House or the Senate, or officials from their party's state, national, congressional, or senatorial campaign committee to learn about the kinds of assistance that would be available should they decide to run. On other occasions the party initiates the contact, seeking to nurture the interest of good prospects.

Barred from simply handing out the nomination, party leaders can influence a prospective candidate's decision to run in a variety of ways. State and local party leaders can help size up the potential competition and try to discourage others from contesting the nomination.[29] In some states party leaders can help a candidate secure a preprimary endorsement, but this does not guarantee nomination.

Members of Congress and the staffs of the Democratic and Republican congressional and senatorial campaign committees often encourage prospective candidates to run. Armed with favorable polling figures and the promise of party assistance in the general election, they search out local talent. Promising individuals are invited to meet with members of Congress and party leaders in Washington and to attend campaign seminars. They are also given lists of PACs and political consultants who possess some of the resources and skills needed to conduct a congressional campaign.[30] That is where national party involvement usually ends. When more than one candidate signs up to run for a nomination, the national parties usually remain neutral unless a primary challenger seriously threatens an incumbent.

Party recruitment is especially important and difficult when local or national forces favor the opposing party. Just as a strong economy or popular president can encourage members of the president's party to run, it can discourage members of the opposition party from declaring their candidacies, most notably when an incumbent of the opposing party is seeking to remain in the seat. Sometimes the promise of party support can encourage a wavering politician to run under what at the outset appear to be less than optimal conditions.

Recruiting candidates to run for traditionally uncompetitive seats is not a major priority, but party committees work to prevent those seats from going uncontested. According to staffers from both parties' congressional and senatorial campaign committees, getting candidates to run for these seats is an important part of building for the future. These candidacies can strengthen state and local party committees by giving them a campaign on which to focus and deepening the farm team from which candidates emerge. They also help prepare a party for opportunities that might arise when an incumbent retires, House districts are redrawn, or a scandal or some other event changes the partisan dynamics in the district. GOPAC, a political committee that was headed by Rep. Newt Gingrich prior to his becoming Speaker of the House, played a major role in recruiting Republicans to run for office, including many who helped the GOP win its House majority in 1994.

Labor unions, PACs, and other organized groups typically play more limited roles in candidate recruitment than parties. A few labor PACs and some trade association committees, such as the Committee on Political Education (COPE) of the American Federation of Labor–Congress of Industrial Organizations (AFL-CIO) and the American Medical Association's AMPAC take polls to encourage experienced politicians to run.[31] Others, such as the National Federation of Independent Business PAC, sponsor campaign training seminars to encourage individuals who support the group's position to run for the House. Some PACs, such as the pro-women Women's Campaign Fund, EMILY's List, and WISH List, search out members of specific demographic groups and offer them financial and organizational support.[32] Labor unions focus most of their candidate-recruitment efforts, and campaign activities in general, on Democrats. Ideological PACs are among the most aggressive in searching out candidates, and many offer primary assistance to those who share their views. Few corporate PACs become involved in recruiting candidates because they fear offending incumbents.

Finally, political consultants can become involved in a potential candidate's decision making. In addition to taking polls and participating in candidate-training seminars, consultants can use their knowledge of a state or district to assist a would-be candidate in assessing political conditions and sizing up the potential competition. Politicians who have had long-term relationships with consultants usually seek their advice prior to running for Congress.

<h3 style="text-align:center">PASSING THE PRIMARY TEST</h3>

There are two ways to win a major-party nomination for Congress: in an un-contested nominating race or by defeating an opponent. It is not unusual for incumbents to receive their party's nomination without a challenge. Even in the 1992 elections, which were marked by a record number of nonincumbent candidacies, 52 percent of all representatives and 42 percent of all senators who sought reelection were awarded their party's nomination without having to defeat an opponent.

Incumbent Victories in Uncontested Primaries

Victories by default occur mainly when an incumbent is perceived to be invul-nerable. The same advantages of incumbency and preelection activities that make incumbents confident of reelection make them seem invincible to those contemplating a primary challenge. Good constituent relations, policy repre-sentation, and other job-related activities are sources of incumbent strength. A hefty campaign account is another.

The loyalties of political activists and organized groups also discourage party members from challenging their representatives for the nomination. While in office, members of Congress work to advance the interests of those who sup-ported their previous election, and in return they routinely receive the support of these individuals and groups. With this support comes the promise of en-dorsements, campaign contributions, volunteer campaign workers, and votes. Would-be primary challengers often recognize that the groups whose support they would need to win the nomination are often among the incumbent's staunchest supporters.

Senior incumbents also benefit from the clout—real and perceived—that comes with moving up the ranks of the congressional leadership. Rep. Vic Fazio, D-Calif., who completed his ninth term in Congress in 1996, is typical of most senior incumbents, who are routinely awarded their party's nomination with-out more than a token fight. Fazio could have been vulnerable to a primary challenge in 1996 because as chair of the House Democratic Caucus he could have been tied to the anti-Washington sentiments that gripped the nation. Nevertheless, only one Democrat, Rodger McAfee, a political researcher, chose to oppose Fazio in the primary. This was McAfee's second challenge to Fazio. He lost the first one in 1994 by 50 percent of the vote. Fazio was unchallenged for the nomination in the previous election.

One of the reasons that no experienced politician was willing to challenge Fazio is that he had performed his job as a representative well: he returned to California often, he maintained three district offices to provide constituent services, and he voted in accordance with his constituents' views on most issues. As a member of the Appropriations Committee, he had brought many federal grants and projects to his constituents and state.[33]

Fazio was and continues to be an excellent fund-raiser. By the close of the 1995 calendar year, three months before the date of the primary election, he had already raised more than $372,500. His campaign spending in the 1994 election—nearly $2 million—and the fund-raising records he set as chairman of the Democratic Congressional Campaign Committee (DCCC) easily intimidated most primary challengers.

Fazio has also enjoyed the support of many national and local interest groups. In 1996, as in previous years, he received the support of the California chapter of the National Abortion and Reproductive Rights Action League, the United Auto Workers, and the AFL-CIO. He also won awards from the groups' local affiliates and other organizations. The backing that Fazio received from these groups deprived would-be primary challengers of much of the organizational and financial support that they would need to win. Finally, most of the Democratic politicians who would normally be included on a list of Fazio's rivals or potential successors could be counted among his political allies.[34]

Junior incumbents rarely have the same kind of clout in Washington or as broad a base of support as senior legislators, but because they tend to devote a great deal of time to expanding their bases of support they too typically discourage inside challenges.[35] Junior members also may receive special attention from national, state, and local party organizations. Both the DCCC and the National Republican Congressional Committee (NRCC) hold seminars immediately after the election to instruct junior members on how to use franked mail, town meetings, and the local press to build voter support. Prior to the start of the campaign season these party committees advise junior members on how to defend their congressional roll-call votes, raise money, and discourage opposition.[36]

State party leaders also give junior members of Congress advice and assistance. In 1992 Rep. James Moran, D-Va., received what is perhaps the most important form of help state party leaders can bestow upon a candidate: a supportive district. Democrats in Virginia's capital redrew the state's congressional map with an eye toward improving Moran's reelection prospects. They added heavily Democratic areas to the district, let it be known that they considered this Moran's seat, and even invited one of his potential rivals to run in another congressional district.[37]

Local party activists, who form the pool of potential candidates from which inside opposition usually emerges, are generally more inclined to help junior legislators than challenge them because these activists often worked to elect that individual in the first place. Their loyalties tend to be especially strong when the seat is competitive or was held by the opposition party for a long period of time. As several Democrats in Moran's district explained, teamwork was essential in winning the seat and the same team that helped elect Moran would discourage other Democrats from running against him.[38]

Considerations of teamwork rarely protect House members who are vulnerable because of scandal. These incumbents face stronger challenges from within their own party than do others. Experienced politicians are often willing to take on an incumbent who is toiling under the cloud of scandal.

Contested Primaries with an Incumbent

When incumbents do face challenges for their party's nomination, they almost always win. Of the ninety House members who were challenged for their party's nomination in 1996, only two were defeated: Greg Laughlin, R-Texas, who had switched parties early in the 104th Congress, was defeated by former GOP congressman Ron Paul, and Barbara-Rose Collins, D-Mich., who was accused of using campaign funds for personal use, was defeated by state representative Carolyn Cheeks Kilpatrick. Typically, only those members of Congress who have allegedly committed an ethical transgression, lost touch with their district, or suffer from failing health run a significant risk of falling to a primary challenger.

What kinds of challengers succeed in knocking off an incumbent for the nomination? The answer is candidates who have had significant political experience. Only 16 percent of the Democrats and 8 percent of the Republicans who sought to defeat an incumbent in a primary in 1996 had been elected officials (see Table 2-2). Yet, they were the only candidates to wrest a party nomination away from an incumbent that year. Elected officials typically succeed where others fail because they are able to take advantage of previous contacts to gain the support of the political and financial elites who contribute to or volunteer in political campaigns. They can readily make the case that they know what it takes to get elected. Some of these candidates consciously use a lower-level office as a steppingstone to Congress.[39]

TABLE 2-2

Political Experience and Major-Party Nominations for the House in 1996

	Primary challenges to incumbent		Primary contests to challenge an incumbent		Primary contests for an open seat	
	Demo-crats	Repub-licans	Demo-crats	Repub-licans	Demo-crats	Repub-licans
Level of experience						
Elected officials	16%	8%	18%	11%	32%	24%
Unelected politicians	16	31	19	26	18	20
Political amateurs	68	61	63	63	50	56
(N)	(62)	(67)	(331)	(311)	(168)	(200)
Primary winners						
Elected officials	100%	100%	22%	12%	46%	42%
Unelected politicians	0	0	16	26	15	27
Political amateurs	0	0	62	61	39	31
(N)	(1)	(1)	(201)	(170)	(54)	(51)
Primary success rates						
Elected officials	10%	20%	76%	64%	47%	45%
Unelected politicians	0	0	51	55	26	35
Political amateurs	0	0	59	53	25	14

Sources: Compiled from various issues of *Congressional Quarterly Weekly Report* and other sources cited in note 20.

Notes: Figures are for nonincumbents only and exclude a few elections in which the nominating contest was not conclusive. Some columns do not add to 100 percent because of rounding.

Kilpatrick's victory over Collins in Michigan's 15th congressional district in the Democratic primary in 1996 is typical of a nomination contest in which a challenger knocks off an incumbent. Collins, who had been in Congress for three terms and was the ranking member on the Postal Service Subcommittee of the House Government Reform and Oversight Committee, was counting on an easy reelection in 1996. Her Detroit-based black majority district had given her 80 percent of the vote or better in her previous three elections, and no strong GOP challengers had shown interest in running for the seat. In the spring of 1996, however, her hold over her seat began to weaken as she became the subject of several scandals. On May 31, the FEC reported to the House ethics committee that it had reason to believe that Collins had violated contribution limits during her 1990 primary campaign by accepting two loans totaling $75,000 that were guaranteed by others. Later that summer the U.S. Justice Department revealed that it was investigating Collins for allegedly spending money allocated for her congressional office to pay for personal expenses. The House ethics committee also acknowledged that it was investigating whether Collins had misused money intended for scholarships for students in her district. These accusations made her vulnerable to a strong challenge, which was provided by Kilpatrick, who had been in the state legislature since 1979. Others who sought to take advantage of Collins's vulnerability were George Hart and Henry Stallings II, both state senators; Douglass Diggs, a funeral home manager; and attorneys Leon Jenkins and Godfrey Dillard.[40]

Collins drew heavy criticism from her opponents and the media. She was berated for missing one-fourth of all House votes in 1995, including a bill to protect black churches by imposing greater federal penalties for arson. She was also criticized for holding a rally with and accepting the endorsement of Louis Farrakhan, the controversial leader of the Nation of Islam. Reports that Collins held a fund-raising event at a Detroit strip club that included performances by male and female dancers further harmed her reelection effort.[41]

Collins and Kilpatrick dominated the contest. Collins sought to portray herself as a victim of racist and sexist attacks, stating, "I have come under some of the most vicious and racist and vile attacks ever seen upon an African American woman. . . . Just like they crucified Jesus Christ, murdered Malcolm X, assassinated Martin Luther King. . . . That's how they come after me."[42] Collins's inflammatory rhetoric appeared to harm her cause more than help it. She lost to Kilpatrick by 51 percent to 31 percent of the vote in Michigan's August 6 primary.

Open Primaries

Opposing-incumbent primaries are those primaries in which an incumbent of the opposing party has decided to seek reelection. A second type of open nomination, called an open-seat primary, occurs in districts in which there is no incumbent seeking reelection. Both types of primaries attract more candidates than contests in which a nonincumbent must defeat an incumbent in order to win the nomination, but opposing-incumbent primaries are usually the less hotly contested of the two.

Political experience is usually a determining factor in opposing-incumbent primaries. Elected officials do especially well in Democratic primaries. In 1996 they comprised 18 percent of the candidates, 22 percent of the winners, and enjoyed a nomination rate of 76 percent. Elected officials accounted for a smaller portion of the Republican candidates and winners in opposing-incumbent primaries, and they enjoyed a success rate of 64 percent. Fewer unelected politicians ran in Democratic than Republican opposing-incumbent primaries in 1996. The Republicans made up a larger percentage of the primary winners and enjoyed a greater success rate in winning the nomination than their Democratic counterparts. Political amateurs overwhelmed the other candidates both in numbers and in the percentages that won their primaries, but as one would expect, their overall success rates in the primaries were relatively low.

The Republican primaries held in Virginia's 8th congressional district during the early and mid-1990s are typical of most opposing-incumbent nominating contests in that the local heavyweights sat them out in order to pursue safer options. In 1992, U.S. District Attorney Henry Hudson and former House member Stan Parris, arguably two of the best potential Republican candidates, opted not to seek the nomination to challenge the Democratic incumbent, James P. Moran. Hudson instead chose to become head of the U.S. Marshal's Office, and Parris accepted an appointment to the St. Lawrence Seaway Commission. This enabled Kyle McSlarrow, a GOP conservative activist to defeat Bill Cleveland, a Capitol Hill police officer, and Joe Vasipoli, a member of the city council in Alexandria, Virginia, for the nomination.[43] The next two Republican contests in the 8th district produced even thinner fields of candidates. In 1994 McSlarrow went unchallenged. In 1996 John Otey, a defense contractor, won the nomination without opposition.

Open-seat primaries are the most competitive of all nominating contests. They typically attract many highly qualified candidates, often pitting one elected official against another. Relatively large numbers of candidates with officeholding experience ran for open seats in 1996, and they enjoyed high success rates in being nominated. Significant numbers of political amateurs also ran, but they enjoyed less success than did elected officials and unelected politicians.

The Democratic and Republican primaries in Illinois's 20th congressional district, like most open-seat primaries, were hard-fought contests that featured many qualified candidates. The contests' dynamics were influenced by the chain of events that led Rep. (now Sen.) Richard Durbin, D-Ill., to vacate the seat he had held for fourteen years. Sen. Paul Simon, D-Ill., let it be known well before the beginning of the campaign season that he would be retiring from politics, prompting Durbin to declare his intentions to run for the Senate early in the election cycle. This left Durbin's Democratic-leaning moderate-to-conservative district in southwestern Illinois up for grabs.

The Republican primary was the more heavily contested of the two, drawing a total of seven candidates. Three of these had considerable political experience: John Shimkus, who served as treasurer of Madison County from 1989 through 1996 and had waged a hard-fought campaign for the seat in 1992, holding

Durbin to his smallest reelection margin; Carl Oblinger, the Sangamon County Clerk and former mayor of Chatham; and Patrick Baikauskas, a legislative liaison for the Illinois Department of Mental Health, congressional aide, and gay rights advocate. The other candidates were James Zerkle, an attorney; Richard Angel, a private investigator and retired California police officer; Dave Green, a twenty-four-year-old house painter; and Bill Owens, a construction engineer and member of the John Birch Society.[44]

The Republican primary contest was spirited. Four of the candidates spent in excess of $40,000 each, and the two front-runners, Shimkus and Oblinger spent about $140,000 and $250,000, respectively. When the polls closed on March 19, Shimkus emerged victorious with 51 percent of the vote, Oblinger came in second with 19 percent, and the remaining ballots were divided among the five other candidates.

Unlike the GOP contest, the Democratic primary was not hotly contested. Jay Hoffman, a state representative who had shown himself to be a strong labor supporter and conservative on social issues, succeeded in discouraging the other experienced politicians in the area from joining the race. His sole opponent was Samuel Cahnman, an attorney who ran unsuccessfully for the state senate in 1986. Hoffman dominated the campaign. He outspent Cahnman by three-to-one, received Durbin's endorsement, and went on to win the nomination with 84 percent of the vote.[45]

NOMINATIONS, ELECTIONS, AND REPRESENTATION

The electoral process—which transforms private citizen to candidate to major-party nominee to House member—greatly influences the makeup of the national legislature. Those parts of the process leading up to the general election, especially the decision to run, play an important role in producing a Congress that is not demographically representative of the U.S. population. The willingness of women and minorities to run for Congress during the last few decades and of voters to support them have helped make the national legislature somewhat more representative in regard to gender and race. Still, in many respects Congress does not mirror American society.

Occupation

Occupation has a tremendous effect on the pool of House candidates and on the candidates' prospects for success. Individuals who claim law, politics, or public service (many of whom have legal training) as their profession are a

TABLE 2-3

Occupational Representativeness of 1996 House Candidates and Members of the 105th Congress

Occupation	General population	Nomination candidates	General election candidates	House members
Agricultural or blue-collar workers	26%	7%	5%	4%
Business or banking	12	21	20	22
Clergy or social work	—	1	1	—
Education	2	10	11	14
Entertainer, actor, writer, or artist	1	2	2	1
Law	—	22	28	35
Medicine	1	4	4	3
Military or veteran	1	1	—	—
Politics or public service	—	20	18	14
Other white-collar professionals	17	13	11	6
Outside work force	35	—	—	—
Unemployed	4	—	—	—
Unidentified, nonpolitical occupation	—	—	—	—
(N)	(248,718,000)	(1,543)	(863)	(435)

Sources: General population figures are from U.S. Department of Commerce, Bureau of the Census, *Statistical Abstract of the United States* (Washington, D.C.: U.S. Government Printing Office, 1992), xii, 18, 392–394; candidate occupation data are from various issues of *Congressional Quarterly Weekly Report* and other sources cited in note 20.

Notes: Figures include all 1996 major-party House candidates and all members of the 105th Congress, including Rep. Bernard Sanders, I-Vt. Dashes = less than 0.5 percent. The figures for the general population are from 1990. Some columns do not add to 100 percent because of rounding.

minuscule portion of the general population but comprise 42 percent of all nomination candidates, 46 percent of all successful primary candidates, and 49 percent of all House members (see Table 2-3). The analytical, verbal, and organizational skills required to succeed in the legal profession or in public service help these individuals undertake a successful bid for Congress.[46] The high salaries that members of these professions earn give them the wherewithal to take a leave of absence from work so they can campaign full time. These highly paid professionals can also afford to make the initial investment that is needed to get a campaign off the ground. Moreover, their professions place many attorneys and public servants in a position to rub elbows with political activists and con-tributors whose support can be crucial to winning a House primary or general election.

Business professionals and bankers are not as overrepresented among nomi-nation candidates, major-party nominees, or House members as are public ser-vants and lawyers, but persons in business tend to be successful in congressional elections. Many possess money, skills, and contacts that are useful in politics. Educators (particularly college professors), entertainers, and other white-collar professionals also enjoy a modicum of success in congressional elections. Of these, educators comprise the most successful group of candidates. They rarely possess the wealth of lawyers and business professionals, but educators frequently have the verbal, analytical, and organizational skills that are needed to get elected.

Just as some professions are overrepresented in Congress, others are underrepresented. Disproportionately few persons employed in agriculture or blue-collar professions either run for Congress or are elected. Even fewer stu-dents, homemakers, and others who are considered outside the work force at-tempt to win a congressional seat.

Closely related to the issue of occupation is wealth. Personal wealth is a sig-nificant advantage in an election system that places a premium on a candidate's ability to raise and spend money. Thirteen percent of the House is made up of millionaires, far outstripping the less than one-half of 1 percent of the general population who enjoy similar wealth.[47]

Gender

Far fewer women than men run for Congress (see Figure 2-4). Less than 14 percent of all contestants for major-party nominations in 1996 were female. Women are underrepresented among congressional candidates for many rea-sons. Active campaigning demands greater time and flexibility than most people—but in particular, women—can afford. Women continue to assume primary parenting responsibilities in most families, a role that is difficult to combine with long hours of campaigning. It is only since the 1980s that sig-nificant numbers of women have entered the legal and business professions, which often serve as training grounds for elected officials and political activists. Women also continue to be underrepresented in state legislatures and other elective offices, which commonly serve as steppingstones to Congress.[48]

Once women decide to run, gender does not affect their election prospects.[49] Women are just about as likely as men to advance from primary candidate to nominee to House member.[50] As more women come to occupy lower-level offices or to hold positions in the professions from which congressional candi-

FIGURE 2-4

Gender Representativeness of 1996 House Candidates and Members
of the 105th Congress

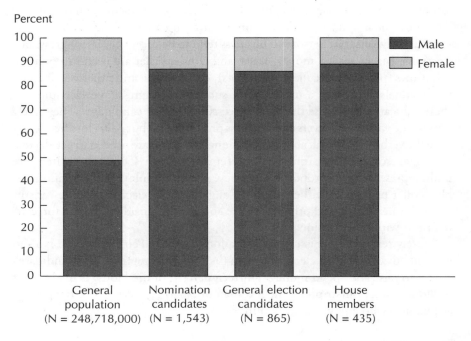

Percent

Sources: General population figures are from U.S. Department of Commerce, Bureau of the Census, *Statistical Abstract of the United States* (Washington, D.C.: U.S. Government Printing Office, 1992), xii, 18, 392–394; candidate gender data are from various issues of *Congressional Quarterly Weekly Report* and other sources cited in note 20.

Notes: Figures include all 1996 major-party House candidates and all members of the 105th Congress, including Rep. Bernard Sanders, I-Vt. The figures for the general population are from 1990.

dates usually emerge, the proportion of women candidates and members of Congress can be expected to increase.

Age

Congressional candidates are also somewhat older than the general population, and this is only partly due to the age requirements imposed by the Constitution. The average candidate for nomination is more than twice as likely to be forty to fifty-four years of age as twenty-five to thirty-nine (see Figure 2-5). Moreover, successful nomination candidates tend to be older than those whom

FIGURE 2-5

Age Representativeness of 1996 House Candidates and Members
of the 105th Congress

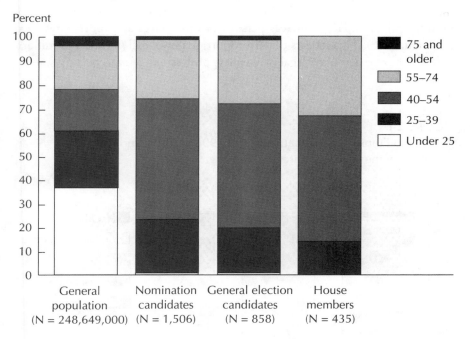

Percent

	75 and older
	55–74
	40–54
	25–39
	Under 25

General
population
(N = 248,649,000)

Nomination
candidates
(N = 1,506)

General election
candidates
(N = 858)

House
members
(N = 435)

Sources: General population figures are from U.S. Department of Commerce, Bureau of the Census, *Statistical Abstract of the United States* (Washington, D.C.: U.S. Government Printing Office, 1992), xii, 18, 392–394; candidate age data are from various issues of *Congressional Quarterly Weekly Report* and other sources cited in note 20.

Notes: Figures include 1996 major-party House candidates and all members of the 105th Congress, including Rep. Bernard Sanders, I-Vt. The figures for the general population are from 1990. The N's differ from those in Figures 2-4 and 2-6 because of missing data.

they defeat. The selection bias in favor of those who are forty to seventy-four continues into the general election; as a result, Congress is made up largely of persons who are middle-aged or older.

The underrepresentation of young people is due to an electoral process that allows older individuals to benefit from their greater life experiences. People who have reached middle age typically have greater financial resources, more political experience, and a wider network of political and professional associates to help them with their campaigns. Moreover, a formidable group of people who are forty to seventy-four years old—current representatives—also benefit from considerable incumbency advantages.

Race and Ethnicity

Race and ethnicity, like gender, have a greater effect on candidate emergence than on electoral success.[51] Whites are heavily overrepresented in the pool of nomination candidates, whereas persons of other races are underrepresented (see Figure 2-6). This reflects the disproportionately small numbers of minorities who have entered the legal or business professions or who occupy state or local offices.

FIGURE 2-6
Racial and Ethnic Representativeness of 1996 House Candidates and Members of the 105th Congress

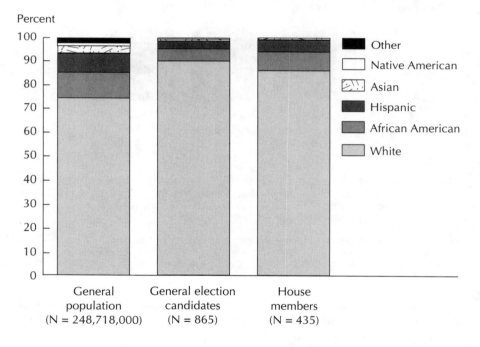

Sources: General population figures are from U.S. Department of Commerce, Bureau of the Census, *Statistical Abstract of the United States* (Washington, D.C.: U.S. Government Printing Office, 1992), xii, 18, 392–394; candidate race data are from various issues of *Congressional Quarterly Weekly Report* and other sources cited in note 20.

Notes: Figures include all 1996 major-party House candidates and all members of the 105th Congress, including Rep. Bernard Sanders, I-Vt. The figures for the general population are from 1990.

Once minority politicians declare their candidacies, they have fairly good odds of winning. The recent successes of minority House candidates are largely due to redistricting processes that were intended to promote minority representation.[52] A few House members, such as Ron Dellums, a fourteen-term African American Democrat from California's 9th congressional district, and Jay Kim, a three-term Korean American GOP member from California's 41st congressional district, were elected from seats that were not specifically carved to promote minority representation in Congress. Still, most minority candidates are elected in districts that have large numbers of voters belonging to their racial or ethnic group, and once they win these seats they tend to hold them. All but one of the incumbents who had occupied majority-minority seats were reelected in 1996, after the courts mandated that their districts had to be redrawn.[53] The success of these members can be attributed to their ability to build multiracial coalitions and the advantages that incumbency conferred on them.

Party Differences

Public servants and members of the legal profession comprise a large portion of each party's candidate pool, but more Republican candidates come from the business world, and many Democratic candidates are educators (see Table 2-4).

TABLE 2-4
1996 Major-Party Nomination and General Election Candidates and House Members of the 105th Congress

	Nomination candidates		General election candidates		House members	
	Demo-crats	Repub-licans	Demo-crats	Repub-licans	Demo-crats	Repub-licans
Occupation						
Agricultural or blue collar workers	6%	8%	4%	6%	3%	5%
Business or banking	15	26	15	26	14	29
Clergy or social work	1	1	1	1	1	—
Education	12	8	13	10	16	12
Entertainer, actor, writer, or artist	2	2	2	2	2	1
Law	25	18	32	24	39	32
Medicine	4	4	4	4	2	4

(Table continues)

TABLE 2-4
(continued)

	Nomination candidates		General election candidates		House members	
	Demo-crats	Repub-licans	Demo-crats	Repub-licans	Demo-crats	Repub-licans
Military or veteran	—	1	—	1	—	—
Politics or public service	23	17	22	14	20	9
Other white-collar professionals	11	15	8	13	4	8
Outside work force	—	—	1	—	—	—
Unidentified, not politics	—	—	—	—	—	—
(N)	(743)	(800)	(430)	(435)	(206)	(228)
Gender						
Male	83%	90%	81%	90%	86%	93%
Female	17	10	19	10	14	7
(N)	(743)	(800)	(430)	(435)	(206)	(228)
Age						
Under 25	—	—	—	—	—	—
25–39	20	26	15	24	10	14
40–54	52	50	55	50	54	54
55–74	27	24	28	25	34	32
75 and older	2	—	1	—	2	—
(N)	(726)	(780)	(428)	(430)	(206)	(228)
Race and Ethnicity						
White	n.a.	n.a.	86%	94%	75%	97%
African American	n.a.	n.a.	8	3	16	1
Hispanic	n.a.	n.a.	5	3	7	3
Other	n.a.	n.a.	1	2	1	—
(N)	(n.a.)	(n.a.)	(430)	(435)	(206)	(228)

Sources: Compiled from various issues of *Congressional Quarterly Weekly Report* and other sources cited in note 20.

Notes: Figures are for all major-party nomination candidates, all major-party general election candidates, and all major-party members of the 105th Congress (which excludes Rep. Bernard Sanders, I-Vt.). Dashes = less than 0.5 percent; n.a. = not available. Some data are missing for the age representation of nomination and general election candidates. Some columns do not add to 100 percent because of rounding.

These differences reflect patterns of support that exist for the parties among voters. The GOP's overrepresentation of business professionals continues through each stage of the election, as does the Democrats' overrepresentation of educators.

Candidates from the business, legal, and public service professions account for the largest occupational differences between the parties. Attorneys from both parties do well in House elections, but lawyers and career public servants are more heavily overrepresented in the Democratic than the Republican Party. Business executives, in contrast, have a bigger presence in the ranks of Republican legislators. Even though Republicans have historically been viewed as the defenders of the rich, members of both parties are found among Congress's wealthiest members.[54]

More women run for Democratic than Republican nominations for Congress. This gender gap reflects the greater number of women who identify with the Democratic Party and that party's greater acceptance of female candidates. Democratic and Republican women enjoy similar success rates in congressional primaries, but Democratic women are more successful in getting elected to the House than are their GOP counterparts.

Democratic primary candidates tend to be somewhat older than their Republican counterparts, reflecting the different orientations of the individuals in the parties' candidate pools. Democratic primary candidates are more likely to come from the ranks of politicians and to consider a congressional election as a somewhat risky opportunity to take a step up the career ladder. Members of the Republican candidate pool are more apt to have careers in the private sector. Many run for Congress before they have taken major strides in their profession, recognizing that if they wait too long they may have advanced too far professionally to want to sacrifice their career in order to run.[55] The initial age difference between Democratic and Republican candidates lays the foundation for an uneven trend toward a middle-aged Congress that continues through the primary and the general election.

The parties also draw candidates from different racial and ethnic groups. Republican primary contestants are overwhelmingly white, as are the GOP's nominees and House members. The Democratic Party attracts candidates from a wider array of groups. These patterns reflect the parties' electoral coalitions.

THE SENATE

The Senate historically has been less demographically representative than the House, but it, too, has been moving toward more accurately mirroring the U.S.

population in some important ways. After the 1990 elections, the Senate had only two women. It also had two Asian American members (both from Hawaii), but no Native Americans or African Americans. Over 60 percent of its members were at least fifty-five years of age. Senate members came from a variety of occupations, but roughly 47 percent were lawyers. Another 25 percent were drawn from the business and banking communities, and 8 percent were journalists. An additional 8 percent were educators, and 6 percent were from the agricultural sector.[56] The remainder held a variety of positions, with 4 percent claiming politics or public service as their profession. In short, descriptions of the Senate as a bastion for white, middle-aged, professional men are very close to the mark.

Part of the reason that the Senate has been slower to change than the House is that Senate terms are six years, and only one-third of the upper chamber is up for election at a time. Other reasons have to do with the heightened demands of Senate campaigns. As statewide races, Senate primary and general election campaigns require larger amounts of money, more extensive organizations, and more complex strategies than do House campaigns. Successful Senate candidates generally possess more skill, political connections, and campaign experience than do their House counterparts. The fact that so many members of the Senate had extensive political experience prior to their election suggests that the dearth of women and minorities in lower-level offices may help to explain why the upper chamber is changing more slowly than the lower. In order to gain seats in the Senate, members of traditionally underrepresented groups have had first to place citizens in the offices that serve as steppingstones to that body. As more women, African Americans, and members of other underrepresented groups are elected or appointed to local, state, and federal offices, their numbers in the Senate will probably increase.

Nevertheless, a single election can have a great effect on the Senate's makeup. After the polls closed in 1992, five more women had secured seats in the upper chamber, including the Senate's first African American woman, Carol Moseley-Braun (D-Ill.). In addition, the Senate prepared to swear in its first Native American, Ben Nighthorse Campbell. Neither the 1994 nor the 1996 election had as big an impact on the demographic makeup of the Senate as that of 1992, but the 1996 election did result in a net increase of one female senator.

Even though traditionally underrepresented groups have increased their numbers in the Senate, this does not mean that the upper chamber has become a place of employment for individuals with a diverse array of backgrounds. Fifty-one senators in the 105th Congress were drawn from the legal profession. Another twenty-three were drawn from the business and banking communities, six were educators, and seven had backgrounds in public service. An additional four were journalists and three were from the agricultural sector. The remainder held positions ranging from veterinarian to social worker. Over 60 percent were fifty-five years of age or older.[57]

Most senators had significant political experience prior to getting elected. Forty-one of the senators in the 105th Congress had previously served in the U.S. House of Representatives, twelve had been governors of their states, twelve had previously held some other statewide office, nine had been state legislators, and twelve had served in a local office. Another ten had served as party officials, political aides, or presidential appointees or had previously run for the Senate. Only four senators—Robert Bennett, R-Utah, Bill Frist, R-Tenn., Orrin Hatch, R-Utah, and Frank Lautenberg, D-N.J.—were elected to the Senate without having previously held elective office or some other significant political position.

Although senators are more likely than representatives to have to defend their nominations, Senate primaries tend to be less competitive than those for the House. Between 1982 and 1996 Alan Dixon and Sheila Frahm were the only two senators who sought to be renominated and were defeated. The relative ease with which members of the Senate secure renomination can be attributed to a number of factors besides the tremendous demands that Senate primary contests make on challengers. For one thing, senators and Senate candidates are highly strategic. Like their counterparts in the House, members of the Senate use their office to help their state receive its share of federal projects, to garner positive coverage in the press, and to build support among voters. Senators, like representatives, also build huge campaign treasuries to discourage potential opponents. Finally, as the retirements in 1992 of Sen. Alan Cranston, D-Calif., Sen. Dennis DeConcini, D-Ariz., and Sen. Don Riegle, D-Mich.—who were implicated in the Keating Five scandal—and the thirteen voluntary retirements that occurred in 1996 attest, most members of the Senate are shrewd enough to recognize when it is time to retire. The effect that scandal, aging, infirmity, and declining support have on Senate turnover tends to be felt more through strategic retirements than primary defeats.

Still, the most qualified opponent that a senator is likely to face in a primary is a current House member or some other elected official.[58] Because these individuals are also highly strategic, only a few are willing to risk their current positions by picking a primary fight. Most prefer to wait until a seat becomes open.

When an incumbent does announce his or her retirement, or a member of the opposite party appears vulnerable, political parties and interest groups help to shape the field of Senate candidates by encouraging potential candidates to declare their candidacies. These organizations promise the same types of support, under the same kinds of circumstances, to potential Senate candidates as they offer to House candidates. Party organizations rarely become involved in contested Senate primaries even though they may promise a candidate from hundreds of thousands to millions of dollars in campaign support upon winning the nomination. The parties' senatorial campaign committees are singled out by candidates as the most influential organizations in the candidate-recruitment process. Nevertheless, the decision to run for the Senate, like the decision to run for the House, is a personal one. Family and friends, issues, and a desire to improve government or become a national leader are more influential in the decisions of candidates to run for the Senate than are political organizations.[59]

CHAPTER 3

The Anatomy of a Campaign

Most House and Senate candidates relied on state and local party committees to wage their campaigns during the parties' golden age. An individual candidate's "organization" was often little more than a loyal following within the party. By the mid-1950s, few congressional candidates could count on party organizations to obtain their nominations and wage their campaigns. Senate campaigns became significantly more professional during the 1950s and 1960s; House campaigns followed suit during the 1970s.[1] The decline of the political machine and the legal and systemic changes that fostered it led to the development of the modern campaign organization.[2] Highly specialized, professional organizations dominate contemporary campaigns for Congress. In this chapter I describe these organizations, focusing on the personnel who work in them and how they spend their money.

CAMPAIGN ORGANIZATIONS

Candidates need to achieve several interrelated objectives to compete successfully in an election, including raising money, formulating a strategy, and communicating with and mobilizing voters. Specialized skills and training are required to meet many of these objectives. Senate campaigns, which are larger and must typically reach out to more voters, employ more paid staff and consultants than do their House counterparts.

The biggest factor in House campaigns is incumbency. Assembling a campaign organization is an easy task for incumbents. Most merely reassemble the personnel who worked on their previous campaign. A substantial number of incumbents keep elements of their organizations intact between election cycles.

Some of these organizations consist only of a part-time political aide or fund-raiser. Others are quite substantial, possessing the characteristics of a permanent business. They own a building and have a large professional staff, a fund-raising apparatus, an investment portfolio, a campaign car, an entertainment budget, and a team of lawyers, accountants, and consultants on retainer. The average House incumbent spent roughly $207,600 on organizational maintenance during the two years leading up to the 1996 election.[3] Speaker Newt Gingrich put together the "Cadillac" of campaigns, spending more than $1,947,800 on overhead during 1995 and 1996, including $411,000 on staff, $67,400 on rent, and $147,400 on computers, furniture, other office equipment, and supplies.[4]

Few House challengers or open-seat candidates possess even a temporary organization capable of contesting a congressional election until just before their declaration of candidacy. Nonincumbents who have held an elective post usually possess advantages over those who have not in assembling a campaign organization. Some have steering committees, "Friends of 'Candidate X'" clubs, or working relationships with political consultants from previous campaigns. Candidates who have never held an elective office but have been active in politics usually have advantages over political amateurs in building an organization. Previous political involvement gives party committee chairs, political aides, and individuals who have previously run for office some knowledge of how to wage a campaign and ties to others who can help them. The organizational advantages that incumbents possess over challengers are usually greater than those advantages that experienced nonincumbents have over political amateurs.[5]

Virtually every House member's campaign organization is managed by a paid staffer or some combination of paid staffer, outside consultant, and volunteer (see Table 3-1). Very often the campaign manager is the administrative assistant or chief of staff in the House member's congressional office. Administrative assistants and other congressional staffers routinely take leaves of absence from their jobs to work for their boss's reelection. Incumbents who are in jeopardy are more likely than shoo-ins to hire a paid staffer to handle day-to-day management and a general consultant to assist with campaign strategy. Most hopeful challengers have professionally managed campaigns, but just over half of all challengers involved in uncompetitive races are managed by a paid staffer or general consultant. Many of these campaigns rely on volunteer managers instead.

Open-seat campaigns fall between campaigns waged by incumbents and challengers. A large number of open-seat prospects rely on a combination of paid staffer and general consultant to manage their campaigns. Many open-seat candidates who are considered long shots also had professional managers, but a

TABLE 3-1

Staffing Activities in House Elections

	Incumbents			Challengers		Open-seat candidates	
	All	In jeopardy	Shoo-ins	Hope-fuls	Likely losers	Pros-pects	Long shots
Campaign management							
Paid staff	65%	85%	78%	68%	41%	70%	49%
Consultant	19	23	15	23	10	31	20
Political party	1	—	—	2	1	—	4
Interest groups	2	4	—	4	2	2	—
Volunteer	24	6	14	20	43	18	40
Not used	4	—	4	—	11	4	—
Press relations							
Paid staff	61%	84%	68%	64%	36%	54%	47%
Consultant	14	21	11	7	11	27	12
Political party	1	—	—	2	—	2	8
Interest groups	1	—	1	—	1	2	—
Volunteer	24	11	16	19	45	29	40
Not used	4	2	4	2	6	4	—
Issue and opposition research							
Paid staff	42%	63%	48%	36%	25%	52%	38%
Consultant	22	37	22	19	8	34	16
Political party	15	4	4	26	25	16	12
Interest groups	7	2	10	9	8	8	4
Volunteer	31	20	14	39	42	40	40
Not used	7	6	13	—	11	2	4
Fund-raising							
Paid staff	53%	77%	67%	58%	22%	65%	57%
Consultant	24	40	30	28	7	28	20
Political party	4	6	—	4	2	6	8
Interest groups	5	9	1	6	5	10	—
Volunteer	41	21	28	44	59	36	56
Not used	4	—	1	6	7	6	4
Accounting/FEC reporting							
Paid staff	64%	84%	80%	65%	43%	63%	60%
Consultant	13	19	19	9	4	16	12
Political party	1	—	—	4	—	2	8
Interest groups	1	2	1	—	1	—	—
Volunteer	42	11	22	57	63	53	56
Not used	2	—	1	2	6	2	—

(Table continues)

TABLE 3-1
(continued)

	Incumbents			Challengers		Open-seat candidates	
	All	In jeopardy	Shoo-ins	Hope-fuls	Likely losers	Pros-pects	Long shots
Polling							
Paid staff	8%	9%	8%	6%	7%	6%	7%
Consultant	60	94	70	70	24	84	33
Political party	7	6	4	7	10	2	25
Interest groups	4	4	3	6	4	4	4
Volunteer	8	—	3	13	17	2	17
Not used	14	2	13	—	39	10	8
Media advertising							
Paid staff	24%	29%	24%	26%	19%	24%	20%
Consultant	61	81	72	62	29	82	49
Political party	2	2	—	—	2	—	8
Interest groups	1	—	—	2	2	—	—
Volunteer	15	2	3	17	36	6	20
Not used	5	2	4	2	12	4	4
Get-out-the-vote drives							
Paid staff	39%	60%	93%	37%	17%	42%	24%
Consultant	5	8	6	2	—	10	4
Political party	29	50	29	19	29	24	28
Interest groups	20	28	21	23	16	24	24
Volunteer	50	39	43	66	51	72	56
Not used	6	2	7	7	10	2	4
Legal advice							
Paid staff	11%	14%	14%	10%	6%	12%	9%
Consultant	13	20	20	13	4	10	17
Political party	10	15	7	15	12	6	12
Interest groups	3	2	3	6	2	4	0
Volunteer	39	22	29	43	46	59	50
Not used	24	26	29	22	26	16	12
Average number of activities performed by paid staff or consultants	5.5	7.4	6.5	5.6	3.1	6.2	5.0
(N)	(331)	(48)	(72)	(54)	(83)	(49)	(25)

Source: The 1992 Congressional Campaign Study.

Notes: Figures are for general election candidates in major-party contested races, excluding a small number of atypical races. Dashes = less than 0.5 percent. Figures for interest groups include labor unions. Some columns do not add to 100 percent because some activities were performed by more than one person or group or because of rounding.

substantial portion of them relied on volunteers for campaign management. Few campaigns are managed by personnel provided by a political party or interest group, regardless of their competitiveness.

Professional staff carry out press relations in most campaigns. Nearly 85 percent of all incumbents in close races hire a paid staffer, frequently a congressional press secretary who is on a leave of absence, to handle their relations with the media. A significant number of incumbents, particularly those involved in competitive contests, hire campaign consultants to issue press releases and handle calls from journalists. Challengers and open-seat candidates are less likely than incumbents to depend on paid staff to handle their press relations. More than 80 percent of all open-seat prospects and 70 percent of all hopeful challengers, however, rely on paid staff or professional consultants for this purpose.

Issue and opposition research is often carried out by a combination of professional staff, outside consultants, and volunteers. Nonincumbents in one-sided races, who generally have less money than incumbents and candidates running for competitive open seats, depend more heavily on volunteers to conduct research. Many nonincumbents also depend on party organizations, particularly the Democratic and Republican congressional campaign committees, for research. Since at least the mid-1980s the National Republican Congressional Committee, which is the wealthier and more heavily staffed of the two campaign committees, has furnished more candidates with opposition and issue research than has its Democratic counterpart.[6]

Fewer incumbents than nonincumbents depend on their party's congressional campaign committee for research materials because their congressional staffs routinely provide much of the information they need. One of the perquisites of office is having a staff that can write memos on the major issues facing the nation and the district. These are normally drafted to help House members represent their constituents, but the political payoffs from them are significant. In fact, both congressional campaign committees offer training seminars for House members to inform them of how legally to utilize their congressional staff for political purposes.

Fund-raising is a campaign activity that requires skill and connections with individuals and groups who are able and willing to make political contributions. Most campaigns use a mix of a paid campaign staffer, a private consultant, and volunteers to raise money. Incumbent campaigns are especially likely to use paid staff. Some incumbents hire experts in direct mail and big donor fund-raising specialists to collect contributions continuously between elections. They also hire staff with accounting skills to file their Federal Election Commission reports. Fewer nonincumbent campaigns have a salaried employee or professional consultant in charge of raising funds or accounting. Challenger and open-seat campaigns in one-sided contests rely heavily on volunteers. One of the ironies of congressional elections is that challengers, who have the greatest need to raise and spend money, often cannot afford to pay an experienced fund-raiser.

Polling and advertising are two specialized aspects of campaigning that are handled primarily by political consultants who are hired on a contractual basis. Most candidates running for marginal seats hire an outside consultant to conduct polls or receive a professionally taken poll from a party committee, labor union, or some other interest group. Most safe incumbents also obtain surveys from professional pollsters. Very few incumbents forgo the opportunity to have a poll done.

Open-seat and challenger campaigns for competitive seats rely almost as much on professionally conducted polls as do incumbent campaigns. The major difference between them is that fewer incumbent campaigns rely on a party committee or a PAC to furnish them with a poll. Challengers and open-seat candidates in lopsided races, who could also benefit from accurate public opinion information, are substantially less likely to purchase the services of a professional pollster. Many of these candidates opt not to conduct a survey in order to reserve their money for some other campaign activity.

Incumbents are the most likely to have professionally produced campaign communications. Virtually every incumbent hires a media consultant or uses some combination of media consultant and campaign aide to produce television commercials, radio advertisements, and direct mail. Open-seat candidates in closely contested races are just as likely as incumbents who find themselves in similar circumstances to hire professional media consultants. Competitive challengers are less likely to hire a professional media consultant, and challengers and open-seat candidates in one-sided contests, who face the biggest hurdles in conveying a message and developing name recognition among voters, are by far the least likely to employ the services of a media consultant.

Parties, PACs, and other groups figure prominently in the field activities of virtually all campaigns. Incumbents depend as much, if not more, on these groups as do challenger and open-seat candidates. Where these campaigns differ is that the majority of incumbents also assign paid staffers to carry out voter registration and get-out-the-vote drives, whereas the majority of nonincumbents depend on volunteers for voter mobilization efforts. Democratic House candidates receive significantly more help with mobilizing voters from unions, reflecting their party's historical ties with the labor movement.

Most House campaigns depend on volunteers for legal counseling. More incumbents than nonincumbents keep an election-law expert on the payroll or on a retainer, but incumbents also draw heavily on the services of volunteers. The fact that only 24 percent of all House campaigns were waged without the assistance of an attorney reflects the complexity of modern elections and the legal codes that govern them.

The overall professionalism of contemporary House campaigns is reflected in the fact that the average campaign uses paid staff or political consultants to carry out five or six of the preceding nine activities (see the bottom of Table 3-1). The typical incumbent campaign uses skilled professionals to carry out roughly seven of these activities, and open-seat prospects and hopeful challengers use skilled professionals for six. Candidates in uncompetitive races are significantly less reliant on professional help. Nonincumbents who are officeholders and unelected politicians assemble more professional campaign organizations than do political amateurs.[7]

The organization that Rep. Connie Morella assembled to conduct her 1996 reelection campaign in Maryland's 8th congressional district is typical of those assembled by most shoo-in incumbents (who win by more than 20 percent of the vote). Since 1986, Morella, a Republican and former schoolteacher and community college professor, has represented a wealthy, ethnically diverse district that has a high proportion of federal workers and retirees. Despite the fact that registered Democrats outnumber registered Republicans by nearly two to one, the 8th district has been one of the safest seats since Morella was elected. Following her initial victory, the representative has never won by less than 60 percent of the vote.

Morella began the 1996 election with the same core campaign team she had used during the last few elections. William Miller Jr., the chief of staff in her congressional office, managed the campaign, after taking a leave from his congressional duties in September. Linda DiVall of American Viewpoints in Alexandria, Virginia, did the campaign's polling. The campaign hired no other outside consultants. It carried out its campaign activities independently from the NRCC and the Republican state and county party committees in order to reinforce Morella's reputation for independence. Instead, it relied on its nine full-time staffers, three part-timers, and hundreds of volunteers to perform campaign activities, ranging from designing the candidate's television, radio, and direct-mail ads to handing out literature at metro stops and in neighborhoods. Issue research that had been carried out in the representative's office formed the foundation for the campaign's briefing materials. Had Morella perceived the race to have been more competitive, she would have hired more outside consultants to carry out some of these activities.[8]

The campaign team that Don Mooers put together to run against Morella was underfunded and understaffed, as is typical of most campaigns waged by challengers who lose by more than 20 percent of the vote. Mooers, who had been in the Peace Corps and worked for the State Department prior to leaving his job in December 1996 in order to run, was not a professional politician.[9] His only political experience was as a member of Montgomery County's Democratic Central Committee. His campaign was managed by Stephen Neill, a veteran of several Maryland campaigns. The rest of the Mooers team was comprised of volunteers, including hundreds of people who helped with literature drops, stuffed envelopes, worked phone banks, canvassed neighborhoods, and campaigned door-to-door with the candidate. Because they were not up for reelection, numerous local Democratic politicians also volunteered to help Mooers campaign.[10]

Mooers was not on the DCCC's target list. His campaign received the standard package of campaign services the committee delivers to challengers that it perceives to be fighting steep uphill battles. This included a report of voting patterns broken down by precinct, other targeting analyses, generic issue research, and generic television footage that the candidate used as the foundation for his TV ads. The Montgomery County Democratic Committee provided some phone banks and volunteers, as did the Maryland Democratic State Central Committee.[11]

The 1996 campaign of Rep. Fred Heineman, R-N.C., is typical of those run by House incumbents in jeopardy (those who lost or won by less than 20 percent of the vote). Heineman, a House freshman, represented a diverse district that includes Raleigh (the state capital), Chapel Hill, several smaller cities, and several suburban and rural areas. The 4th congressional district was one of the most competitive House seats during the 1980s.[12] David Price, whom Heineman defeated in 1994, wrested it from the one-term incumbent William Cobey by a twelve-point margin in 1986, defended it against experienced and well-funded opponents in both 1988 and 1990, and then faced only token opposition in 1992, prior to being defeated by Heineman in 1994.

Before the 1996 campaign season began, Heineman, who had never held political office before defeating Price, anticipated that he would face a strong challenger. Heineman had been a police officer in New York City prior to becoming Raleigh's chief of police and then retiring.[13] Heineman had defeated Price by a mere 1,115 votes in a Democratic-leaning district in 1994—a year when strong Republican tides reverberated throughout the nation, especially in the South. Heineman and his advisers recognized that the district would be targeted by the Democrats and had heard rumors that Price was strongly considering a rematch.[14]

Heineman assembled a highly professional team to mount his reelection effort. He hired veteran campaigner Courtney Malveaux as his campaign manager and James McLaughlin, of Fabrizio and McLaughlin Associates, of Alexandria, Virginia, as his general consultant and pollster. Nancy Bocskor, a prominent

GOP PAC fund-raiser located in Arlington, Virginia, organized his big dollar fund-raising events. Colin Chapman of Welch Norman Communications of West Virginia produced his direct mail. Earl Ashe of Jefferson Marketing, a well-known Republican media firm in the district, produced the campaign's television and radio ads. During the last month of the campaign, Mike Scanlon, Heineman's press secretary, took a leave of absence from his congressional duties to assist with managing the campaign and to handle media relations. Sean O'Brien, of Raleigh, handled most of the campaign's local fund-raising events, and several part-timers rounded out the paid staffers. Roughly one hundred volunteers staffed phone banks, canvassed the district, and participated in literature drops.[15] The NRCC provided the campaign with $60,000 worth of consulting services, and the Republican state party helped with telephone banks. Some field work was coordinated with local party organizations, but the campaign carried out most of its own field efforts because it had more volunteers than most GOP committees in the district.

The campaign organization that David Price assembled to reclaim the 4th district seat was typical for a well-funded challenger in a hotly contested race. Price had been a Duke University political science professor, North Carolina Democratic State Committee chair, and congressional aide, before serving four terms in Congress. Price's 1996 campaign employed numerous high-powered political consultants from the Washington area. Joe Goode, who had worked for Greenberg Research, a leading Democratic polling firm, was the campaign's manager. Rich Schlackman, of the Campaign Performance Group, produced the campaign's direct mail. Linda Davis of Creative Campaign Consultants, raised money from PACs and solicited large contributions from individuals. Cooper-Secrest of Alexandria, Virginia, did Price's polling. Saul Shorr, of Shorr and Associates of Philadelphia, produced the campaign's television and radio commercials.[16]

The campaign's press secretary, director of field operations, scheduler, and the head of its small donor program were all from the 4th district. Its researcher was an out-of-towner who had relocated to the area just before the campaign. Some of these individuals had experience working on Capitol Hill as congressional aides. These five full-time workers were assisted by approximately one hundred volunteers who helped the campaign in a variety of tasks, including stuffing envelopes, staffing phone banks, and accompanying the candidate as he knocked on doors in their neighborhoods.[17]

The DCCC furnished Price with extensive opposition research and information on Heineman's roll-call votes. The DCCC commissioned the National Committee for an Effective Congress (NCEC), a leading liberal PAC, to provide the Price campaign with the precinct-level demographic and vote analysis that guided most of its targeting. In addition, the DCCC gave the Price team advice on how to respond to Heineman's media attacks and provided the campaign with generic talking points that Price included in some of his speeches.[18]

The North Carolina Democratic State Committee assisted Price with field activities, which were run cooperatively with the Clinton-Gore campaign and with DNC "coordinated campaign" efforts in Raleigh. The coordinated campaign conducted literature drops and registration and get-out-the-vote drives on behalf of the party's presidential, congressional, state, and local candidates. The coordinated campaign was particularly helpful in mobilizing voters in the African American community.[19]

The campaigns waged by the Democrat Jay Hoffman and the Republican John Shimkus in Illinois's 20th congressional district resemble those waged by most open-seat prospects in races decided by margins of 20 percent or less. Each candidate hired three veteran campaign aides to manage their campaigns, coordinate their field activities, handle press relations, raise money in the district, and carry out other relatively nontechnical campaign activities. The candidates were able to draw on an exceptionally large pool of political activists for volunteers because the district includes Springfield, the state capital. They also turned to some nationally renowned consultants for specialized campaign activities. Hoffman hired three Washington-based firms: the Feldman Group handled polling; Fenn, King, Murphy, and Putnam provided media advertising and general consulting services; and Fraioli and Company did the campaign's PAC and big donor fund-raising. Shimkus hired Midwest Public Affairs of Chicago for PAC fund-raising and Russo, Marsh, and Raper of Washington for campaign communications, including television, radio, and direct mail. Wirthlin Worldwide of McLean, Virginia, took the polls. Both candidates received strategic assistance and advice from their party's congressional campaign committee.[20]

CAMPAIGN BUDGETS

The professionalism of contemporary congressional campaigns is reflected in how they budget their money. House candidates spend roughly 76 percent of their campaign funds communicating with voters and 18 percent on overhead (see Figure 3-1).[21] Polling and other research account for the final 6 percent. The amounts budgeted for electronic media reveal the importance that modern communication techniques play in most House campaigns. The typical campaign spends approximately 11 percent of its budget on radio and 18 percent on television. Next comes direct mail, which accounts for roughly 18 percent. Newspaper ads account for almost 4 percent. The remaining 25 percent is spent

FIGURE 3-1
The Budget of a Typical House Campaign

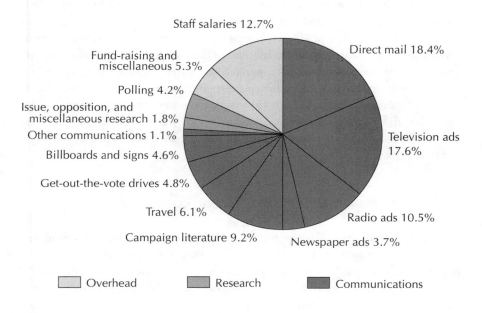

Staff salaries 12.7%

Fund-raising and
miscellaneous 5.3%

Polling 4.2%

Issue, opposition, and
miscellaneous research 1.8%

Other communications 1.1%

Billboards and signs 4.6%

Get-out-the-vote drives 4.8%

Travel 6.1%

Campaign literature 9.2%

Direct mail 18.4%

Television ads
17.6%

Radio ads 10.5%

Newspaper ads 3.7%

☐ Overhead   ▨ Research   ▧ Communications

Source: The 1992 Congressional Campaign Study.

Notes: Figure is for general election candidates in major-party contested races. N = 319.

largely on travel, registration and get-out-the-vote drives, billboards, yard signs, campaign literature, and other field activities.

One of the most interesting things about congressional elections is how few differences there are among campaigns waged by different kinds of candidates. The largest differences are that challengers allocate about 10 percent more funds than incumbents for campaign communications and compensate by scrimping on overhead and polling. Challengers also spend less on television advertising and more on campaign literature than do incumbents. Candidates in contests decided by 20 percent or less of the two-party vote allocate a larger portion of their funds to television than candidates in one-sided races.

Of course, candidates tailor their campaign budgets to suit the nature of their districts. Neither the Heineman nor the Price campaigns spent much on radio, choosing instead to commit the largest portion of their expenditures to television advertising to take advantage of the relatively inexpensive media market that encompasses the entire district.[22] Morella and Mooers, whose district has many rush-hour commuters, advertised extensively on local radio stations.[23]

The overall similarity in campaign budgets is remarkable given the different sums that incumbent, open-seat, and challenger campaigns spend. The widespread availability of campaign technology, the tremendous growth of the political consulting industry, and the increase in the numbers of campaign seminars sponsored by campaign institutes, parties, and interest groups have fostered a set of shared expectations about how a campaign should spend its funds. These expectations are reinforced when campaign personnel negotiate their salaries and draw up budgets, when political consulting firms set their rates, and when party officials and PAC managers scrutinize campaign budgets prior to giving a contribution.

SENATE CAMPAIGNS

Senate campaigns are more expensive, run by more professional organizations, and attract more party assistance than do House campaigns. Senate candidates rely primarily on paid staffs and nationally known political consultants to develop their strategies and carry out their campaigns. Most Senate incumbents keep a substantial organization intact between elections. The typical senator spent almost $1.1 million in overhead to maintain a campaign organization over the six-year period prior to the 1994 election.[24] Overhead costs increased significantly over the course of the 1996 election cycle, when Sen. John Kerry, D-Mass., spent almost $3 million on organizational maintenance, including $1,615,000 on staff salaries, $220,000 on rent, and $359,000 on computer equipment and office supplies.[25]

Senate campaigns often have combinations of individuals sharing responsibilities for various aspects of the campaign. Virtually every campaign assigns a paid aide to work with a mass media advertising firm to develop the candidate's communications. Opposition research is typically conducted by a campaign aide in conjunction with a private consultant or party official. Campaign staff, consultants, volunteers, party committees, and interest group representatives make substantial contributions to Senate candidates' fund-raising efforts. Most Senate campaigns also hire one or more field managers to participate in coordinated voter mobilization efforts that draw on the resources of national, state, and local party committees. Democratic Senate candidates also coordinate their field work with labor unions, and most Senate candidates of both parties rely on volunteers to help with their voter registration and get-out-the-vote efforts.

The major difference in spending between Senate and House contests is in the allocation of media expenditures. The average Senate campaign spends almost 30 percent of its money on television advertising, whereas the typical House campaign spends only a quarter of its money on television. Senate campaigns also allocate far smaller portions of their budgets to radio advertising, campaign literature, newspaper ads, billboards, and yard signs than do House contestants. The differences in communications expenditures reflect both the greater practicality and the necessity of using television advertising in statewide races.

CHAPTER 4

The Parties Campaign

Political parties in the United States have one overriding goal: to elect their candidates to public office. Policy goals are secondary to winning control of the government. Nevertheless, the parties' electoral influence has waxed and waned as the result of legal, demographic, and technological changes in American society and reforms instituted by the parties themselves. During the golden age of political parties, local party organizations dominated elections in many parts of the country. They picked the candidates, gauged public opinion, raised money, disseminated campaign communications, and mobilized voters, most of whom had strong partisan allegiances. "The parties were, in short, the medium through which the campaign was waged."[1]

By the 1950s, most state and local party organizations had been ushered to the periphery of the candidate-centered system. Party organizations at the national level had not yet developed into repositories of money and campaign services for congressional candidates. Most contenders for the House and Senate were largely self-recruited and relied on campaign organizations that they themselves had assembled to wage their bids for office. Professional consultants helped fill the void left by deteriorating party organizations, providing advice about fund-raising, media, polling, and campaign management to clients who were willing to pay for it.[2]

During the late 1970s and early 1980s, first Republican and then Democratic national party organizations in Washington, D.C., began to adapt to the candidate-centered system.[3] This system emphasizes campaign activities requiring technical expertise and in-depth research. Many candidates, especially nonincumbents running for the House, lack the money or professional knowhow needed to run a modern congressional campaign. Candidates' needs created the opportunity for party organizations to assume a more important role in congressional elections.[4] The national parties responded to these needs, not by doing away with the candidate-centered election system but by assuming a more important role in it.[5] In this chapter I discuss the role that party organizations play in congressional elections, including their influence on the agendas around which campaigns are fought, the kinds of assistance they give to House and Senate candidates, the strategies that inform their giving, how they select candidates for support, and the effects of their assistance on candidates' campaigns.

NATIONAL AGENDA SETTING

Contemporary House elections are usually fought on local issues, and Senate elections typically focus on statewide concerns. When national issues find their way into these contests, congressional candidates usually emphasize their local implications. Since the early 1980s, Democratic and Republican congressional leaders produced lengthy issues handbooks and "talking points" for congressional candidates that focus on national issues and include instructions on how to use party rhetoric and statistics compiled in Washington to address local concerns.[6] Many candidates found these materials useful, but the materials were not intended to produce nationalized campaigns and did not do so.

Nevertheless, congressional elections are not always dominated by local issues. In 1932 the Great Depression dominated the national political agenda and the outcomes of many House and Senate races. In 1974 the Democrats nationalized the elections on Watergate, the Nixon administration's ethic lapses, and reform issues. During the 1994 elections, House Republicans set a national agenda that had two foci. The first focus was on the ethical and policy failures of the Clinton administration and House Democrats. Republican leaders published pamphlets criticizing the president's policy performance and leadership and the "special interest" culture they asserted had developed in the House under forty years of Democratic control.[7] These publications provided the anti-Washington rhetoric used by many GOP candidates and inspired the high-tech television commercials that made Democratic congressional candidates appear to metamorphose, or "morph," into President Clinton. The publications also provided much of the substance for discussions broadcast over conservative radio shows and on *GOP-TV,* the Republicans' cable television show.

The House Republicans' second focus was on the Contract with America, the ten-point program that was developed under the direction of then-minority whip Newt Gingrich. The contract included a call for a balanced budget amendment, welfare reform, term limits, and seven other planks based on popular ideas. More than 370 Republican House members and candidates affixed their signatures to the contract at a formal ceremony that took place on the Capitol steps, and many campaigned on contract issues.[8] Even though only one-third of the public had heard of the contract prior to the election, the document and supporting research provided GOP candidates with valuable talking points. The Republicans' nationalized campaign helped them win control of both houses of Congress for the first time in forty years.

The elections of 1996 were also nationalized, but to a lesser extent than in 1994. The Democrats had a bigger role in setting the political agenda than the Republicans. Led by President Clinton, the Democrats sought to paint congressional Republicans as "extremists" who wanted to cut appropriations for Medicare, Medicaid, and education to pay for tax breaks for the rich; who would turn corporate polluters loose on the environment; and who shut down the federal government in order to force their will on the American people. The Democrats portrayed themselves as the champions of working Americans. The early public relations campaign undertaken by the Democratic National Committee (DNC) and the Families First Agenda developed by congressional Democrats focused on moderate policy proposals in areas such as health care, education, and the environment.

The Republicans had hoped to set a campaign agenda in 1996 that focused on the bills they had passed as part of the Contract with America. However, they were put on the defensive by public reaction to the government shutdowns and the Democrats' early media campaign. This led many GOP candidates to try to "denationalize" their elections by emphasizing their independence from Speaker Gingrich.

Several other factors worked to prevent the 1996 election from becoming fully nationalized. A situation of divided government—a Democratic president and a Republican-controlled Congress—made it difficult for either party to claim full credit or to place full blame on the other party for the government's performance. The modesty of the proposals outlined in the congressional Democrats' Families First Agenda and divisions within both parties' ranks prevented partisan lines from crystallizing as clearly as they had in 1932, 1974, and 1994. More important, the GOP's acceptance of a compromise budget that was heavily influenced by the Clinton administration and the president's signing the Republican welfare bill helped to blur partisan distinctions. The 1994 and 1996 elections demonstrate the potential for parties to nationalize congressional elections and the limits to their ability to do so.

THE NATIONAL, CONGRESSIONAL, AND SENATORIAL
CAMPAIGN COMMITTEES

Party organizations in the nation's capital have developed into major sources of campaign money, services, and advice for congressional candidates. The Democratic National Committee and the Republican National Committee (RNC) focus most of their efforts on presidential elections but also pay attention to gubernatorial, statehouse, and a small number of mayoral elections. They also work to set the national campaign agenda and strengthen state and local organizations. The national committees' involvement in House and Senate elections tends to be relatively limited. It includes conducting candidate training seminars; furnishing candidates with party platforms, campaign manifestos, and "talking points"; and coordinating with congressional, senatorial, state, and local party campaign committees to mobilize partisan voters. Congressional candidates in search of money, election services, or assistance in running their campaigns rarely turn to their national committee for help.[9]

The parties' congressional and senatorial campaign committees, sometimes referred to as the "Hill committees," have developed into major support centers for House and Senate candidates.[10] The congressional campaign committees focus their efforts on House races, and the two senatorial campaign committees focus on Senate contests. All four Hill committees set fund-raising records in 1996, as did the parties' national and state local organizations. The DCCC amassed a budget of just under $39.0 million, and its Republican rival raised nearly $92.8 million. The two senatorial committees—the Democratic Senatorial Campaign Committee (DSCC) and the National Republican Senatorial Committee (NRSC)—raised approximately $45.0 million and $92.8 million, respectively.[11]

The chairs, vice chairs, and members of the Hill committees are all members of Congress who are selected by their colleagues in the House or Senate. In addition, the Hill committees employ many highly skilled political professionals. During the 1996 elections the DCCC and DSCC employed 64 and 38 full-time staff, and their Republican counterparts had 64 and 150 full-time employees.[12] For the most part, the members of each committee function like a board of directors, setting priorities and giving staff the support they need to raise money, recruit candidates, and participate in campaigns. The staffs oversee the committees' daily operations, are influential in formulating party strategies, and play a major role in the implementation of those strategies. The campaign committee staffs are divided along functional lines; different divisions are responsible for administration, fund-raising, research, communications, and campaign activities.[13]

As major centers of political expertise and campaign support, the Hill committees are expensive to operate. Between 1995 and 1996 approximately 50 percent of the DCCC's funds and 45 percent of the DSCC's money were used to pay for voter lists, computers, media studios, staff salaries, fund-raising, loan repayments, and other overhead. The NRCC and NRSC spent even more on these activities, committing approximately 55 percent and 48 percent of their funds to them.

STRATEGY, DECISION MAKING, AND TARGETING

The Hill committees have a common overriding goal of maximizing the number of seats their parties hold in Congress.[14] They become heavily involved in some elections, giving selected candidates large contributions and making substantial expenditures on their behalf. They also give these candidates strategic, research, technical, and transactional assistance. The last form of help enables candidates to raise the money and other resources needed to conduct a congressional campaign. Finally, the Hill committees participate with the national committees and state and local party organizations in generic, party-focused election activities that are designed to help candidates for Congress and other offices get elected.

The campaign committees try to focus most of their efforts on competitive House and Senate contests. Protecting incumbents in jeopardy is a major priority. Pressures from nervous incumbents can skew the distribution of committee resources from competitive challenger and open-seat candidates toward members of Congress who hold safe seats. The funds available to a committee can also affect the way it distributes its resources. Other institutional forces that affect committee decision making are the aspirations of its chair and other members. The two individuals who had the most significant roles in modernizing the NRCC and DCCC, former representatives Guy Vander Jagt and Tony Coelho, used their chairmanships as vehicles for advancement in the ranks of the House leadership.[15] Their respective successors, Reps. Bill Paxon, R-N.Y., and Vic Fazio, D-Calif., followed in their footsteps, with Paxon becoming chairman of the House Leadership Group and Fazio being elected chair of the House Democratic Caucus following their campaign committee chairmanships.

National political and economic conditions are additional factors that influence which candidates get campaign resources. When the president is popular and the economy is strong, the campaign committees of the president's party usually invest more resources in challenger and open-seat races. Conversely, the out-party committees use more of their resources to support incumbents. When national conditions do not favor the president's party, the patterns are reversed: the in-party committees take a defensive posture that favors incumbents, and the out-party committees go on the offensive, using more of their resources to help nonincumbents.[16] The unpredictable nature of national political conditions and economic trends and of events that take place in states and congressional districts means that committee decision making and targeting are necessarily imperfect. As a result, some safe incumbents and uncompetitive nonincumbents inevitably receive committee assistance, whereas some competitive nonincumbents get little or no help.

The conditions surrounding the elections held in the early and mid-1990s made strategic decision making and targeting difficult, especially for the two House campaign committees.[17] Redistricting, a process that is always fraught with ambiguities, was complicated by racial redistricting issues that delayed many 1992 House elections while districts were being redrawn. It also introduced complications into several 1994 and 1996 contests for the same reason. Court battles over majority-minority House seats in Illinois, New York, and Virginia that persisted beyond the 1996 elections continued to threaten to require that the boundaries of these seats and neighboring districts be moved.[18]

Redrawn or newly created seats are only one of several factors that complicate the committees' tasks. The president's popularity often shifts up and down, making it difficult for the committees to decide whether to pursue an offensive or a defensive strategy. Congressional scandals and the hostility that voters now routinely direct toward Congress result in some incumbents unexpectedly finding themselves in jeopardy. This gives some challengers a correspondingly unexpected boost. The late retirements of some House members and the primary defeats of others further complicate the committees' efforts.

Because of the uncertainty surrounding the recent elections, the NRCC and DCCC have drawn up huge "watch" lists of "opportunity," or competitive, races and have had difficulty paring those lists. During the 1992 elections, each watch list initially included approximately 300 elections. The lists were shortened over the course of the campaign season, but going into the last week of the election each committee listed more than 150 races as top priorities—more than three times the number they had included at that point in the 1990 election. During the 1994 and 1996 elections the committees initially targeted about 160 seats apiece before they pared their lists down to about 75 races, which included approximately 50 percent more contests than were targeted in most elections held in the 1980s.[19]

Individual candidates are selected for placement on the committees' watch lists on the basis of several criteria. The competitiveness of the district and incumbency are the first two considerations. Candidates running in districts that were decided by close margins in the last election or who are competing for open seats are likely to be placed on a committee's watch list. In 1996 about eighty seats, most of them held by Republicans who were first elected in 1994, were considered top targets by the DCCC and the NRCC.

The strength of the candidate is another consideration in the case of nonincumbents. Those who have had political experience or have celebrity status are likely to be targeted for assistance. Challengers and open-seat contestants who assemble professional campaign organizations are also likely to receive support. Having a professional organization assures the committee that the resources it contributes will be used properly; this is especially true if campaign committee officials are familiar with the consultants who have been hired.[20]

A variety of idiosyncratic factors can also come into play when the committees select the candidates who will be given the most support initially. An incumbent who is accused of committing an ethical transgression, perceived to be out of touch with people in the district, in poor health, or in trouble for some other reason is a likely candidate for extra committee help. These difficulties often provoke a response by the other party's campaign committee, resulting in the incumbent's opponent also benefiting from extra party money and campaign services.

Although party leaders work aggressively to recruit women and minorities to run for Congress, neither party uses gender or race as a criterion for determining who gets campaign assistance. Ideology is also not used to select candidates for support. Women, minorities, liberals, and conservatives are targeted only to the degree their races are expected to be competitive.[21] As Deborah Flavin, a former NRCC official, explained,

> At the NRCC, our only ideology is that you have a "big R" by your name.
> There is no litmus test on any issue. We ask candidates how they feel on "issue X" and "issue Y." Then, we help them articulate what they feel. We are here to help Republicans win.[22]

The committees' lists of competitive elections are revised throughout the election cycle. Regional coordinators who monitor congressional races within designated parts of the country, advise their colleagues in Washington about the latest developments in individual elections. As a result, some candidates drop in priority and are cut off from party help and others gain more committee attention and support.[23] Because of the tremendous uncertainty surrounding recent House elections, both the Democratic and Republican congressional campaign committees have begun to distribute their resources incrementally. Rather than drop a large quantity of money or extensive election services in a candidate's lap early in the campaign season, the committees distribute them piecemeal in response to the candidate's ability to meet a series of discrete fund-raising and organizational goals. Incumbents usually meet these quickly, but the goals pose more formidable hurdles for challengers and open-seat candidates. Nonincumbents who meet their goals in a timely fashion are usually within reach of victory at the end of the election season and receive substantial party support. Of course, a party committee's ability to give them these contributions is limited by available funds.

CAMPAIGN CONTRIBUTIONS AND COORDINATED EXPENDITURES

Party contributions to candidates in congressional elections are restricted by the Federal Election Campaign Act. National, congressional, and state party campaign committees can each give $5,000 to a House candidate at each stage of the election process: primary, runoff, and general election.[24] The parties' national and senatorial campaign committees can give a combined total of $17,500 in an election cycle to a candidate for the Senate. State committees can contribute an additional $5,000 to Senate candidates.

Parties can also spend larger sums of money on behalf of individual candidates. These outlays, referred to as "coordinated expenditures" because they can be made in direct coordination with a candidate's campaign, typically are for campaign services that a Hill committee or some other party organization gives to an individual candidate or purchases from a political consultant on the candidate's behalf. Coordinated expenditures often take the form of polls, television commercials, radio ads, fund-raising events, direct-mail solicitations, or issue research. They differ from campaign contributions in that both the party and the candidate share control over them, giving the party the ability to influence some aspects of how the campaign is run. Originally set in 1974 at $10,000 for all national party organizations, the limits for coordinated expenditures on behalf of House candidates are adjusted for inflation and reached $30,910 in 1996.[25] The limits for national party coordinated expenditures in Senate elections vary by state population and are also indexed to inflation. In 1996 they ranged from $61,820 per committee in the smallest states to $823,690 in Texas. If an election had been held in the nation's most populous state—California—in 1996, the expenditure limit would have been set at $1,409,249.

State party committees are authorized to spend the same amounts in coordinated expenditures in House and Senate races as the parties' national organizations, but some state party committees do not have the funds to do so. In races in which a state party lacks resources and a national party organization—usually the parties' congressional or senatorial campaign committee—deems it important for the party to spend as much money as possible, the state and national party organizations form "agency agreements" that transfer the state party's quota for coordinated expenditures to the national party.[26] In situations in which a state party has enough money to make the maximum legal contribution and coordinated expenditure in a targeted congressional race but has other priorities, such as a gubernatorial election or state legislative elections, national party organizations may induce the state party to spend their hard money in the congressional election by offering them a "money swap." In these agreements, national party organizations make campaign contributions to state or local candidates or soft money transfers to state party organizations in sums that are equal to or slightly greater than the amounts they would like the state parties to spend in congressional races.[27] Agency agreements and money swaps enable Washington-based party organizations to coordinate a national spending strategy in congressional elections.

Coordinated expenditures are the vehicle of choice for most party activity in congressional elections (see Table 4-1). Their higher limits, the possibility for creating agency agreements, and the control they afford party committees in candidates' campaigns make coordinated expenditures an attractive avenue for party involvement. Coordinated spending also enables the parties to take advantage of economies of scale when purchasing and distributing campaign services. Because the parties purchase the services of political consultants in large quantities, they pay below-market rates, which enables them to provide candidates with services whose true market value exceeds the FECA's coordinated expenditure limits.[28]

The four Hill committees determine the parties' congressional campaign spending strategies, and they deliver most of the parties' campaign services. During the 1996 elections the NRCC spent more than $8.5 million in the campaigns of Republican House candidates, about $1.8 million more than the DCCC. The RNC and NRSC spent an additional $1.2 million on House campaigns, largely in response to NRCC requests.[29] Republican national committees distributed almost $3 million more in contributions and coordinated expenditures than their Democratic counterparts. The Republicans also outspent the Democrats in Senate races. Nevertheless, the gap between the two parties has closed considerably over the previous eight election cycles.[30]

Democratic and Republican state and local party committees spent $1.6 million and $1.1 million, respectively, in the 1996 House elections. This accounts for only 14 percent of all party spending made directly in House campaigns. Washington-based party organizations generally outspend state and local organizations in Senate elections. Although House and Senate campaigns are waged locally, national party organizations play a bigger financial role in them than do state and local organizations.

TABLE 4-1

Party Spending in the 1996 Congressional Elections

	House		Senate	
	Contributions	Coordinated expenditures	Contributions	Coordinated expenditures
Democratic				
DNC	$24,311	$2,458	$3,115	$27,520
DCCC	1,020,936	5,689,644	14,817	0
DSCC	10,000	353	530,000	8,396,776
State and local	469,630	1,091,447	142,328	635,556
Total Democratic	$1,524,877	$6,783,902	$690,260	$9,059,852
Republican				
RNC	$486,132	$648,679	$272	$10,412,507
NRCC	1,199,387	7,329,880	60,399	0
NRSC	55,000	0	641,500	308,319
State and local	887,349	261,599	314,528	293,235
Total Republican	$2,627,868	$8,240,158	$1,016,699	$11,014,061

Source: Federal Election Commission, "FEC Reports Major Increase in Party Activity for 1995–96," press release, March 19, 1997.

Note: Figures include party spending in all congressional elections, including primaries, runoffs, and uncontested races.

Party organizations distribute most of their money to candidates in close elections (see Table 4-2).[31] The Democrats' allocation patterns for House candidates in 1996 are indicative of an aggressive, offensive strategy. Their party committees directed 77 percent of their contributions and coordinated expenditures to challengers and open-seat candidates. The remaining money was committed to incumbents. The minority party frequently takes a more aggressive posture than does the majority party in congressional elections.

Democratic money was fairly well targeted. The party committees delivered 40 percent of their funds to hopeful challengers, 20 percent to open-seat prospects, and 17 percent to Democratic incumbents in jeopardy. The party's ability to distribute 77 percent of its funds to candidates in elections that were decided by twenty or fewer percentage points (or in situations in which a challenger defeated an incumbent by a larger margin) is a vast improvement over previous years, such as 1992, when it distributed only 53 percent of its funds to candidates in close races.[32] The improved targeting is due to there being fewer

TABLE 4-2

The Allocation of Party Money in the 1996 Congressional Elections

	House		Senate	
	Democrats	Republicans	Democrats	Republicans
Incumbents				
In jeopardy	17%	37%	16%	34%
	(44)	(75)	(5)	(9)
Shoo-ins	6	2	—	3
	(112)	(125)	(2)	(4)
Challengers				
Hopefuls	40%	26%	27%	19%
	(75)	(44)	(9)	(5)
Likely losers	13	6	1	1
	(125)	(112)	(4)	(2)
Open-seat candidates				
Prospects	20%	23%	52%	41%
	(32)	(32)	(12)	(12)
Long shots	4	6	4	2
	(18)	(18)	(2)	(2)
Total ($, thousands)	$7,860	$9,987	$9,246	$11,513
	(406)	(406)	(34)	(34)

Source: Compiled from Federal Election Commission data.

Notes: Incumbents in jeopardy are defined as those who lost or who won by 20 percent or less of the two-party vote. Shoo-ins are incumbents who won by more than 20 percent of the two-party vote. Hopeful challengers are those who won or who lost by 20 percent or less of the two-party vote. Likely loser challengers are those who lost by more than 20 percent of the two-party vote. Open-seat prospects are those whose election was decided by 20 percent or less of the two-party vote. Open-seat long shots in one-party districts are those whose election was decided by more than 20 percent of the two-party vote. Figures include contributions and coordinated expenditures by all party committees to general election candidates in major-party contested races, excluding a small number of atypical races that were decided in runoffs or won by independents. They do not include soft money expenditures. Some columns do not add to 100 percent because of rounding. The numbers of candidates are in parentheses. Dash = less than 0.5 percent.

Democratic incumbents clamoring for party resources and to DCCC decision makers' learning to resist pressures from nervous but safe incumbents.

Republicans usually spend money more effectively than their Democratic counterparts.[33] GOP committees pursued a moderately defensive strategy in 1996, delivering 37 percent of their funds to incumbents in jeopardy. Republican freshmen in jeopardy were singled out for special help. Although they comprised under 12 percent of all Republican candidates in major-party contested races, they received 30 percent of the party's funds.[34] Republican party organizations distributed only 14 percent of their funds to candidates in uncompetitive contests, whose chances of victory were unlikely to change because of additional party funds.

Several factors account for the disparities in party targeting. First, the Republican party organizations have traditionally taken a more businesslike and less politicized approach to allocating campaign funds. The Democratic Party's greater diversity, DCCC committee members' greater involvement in committee decision making, and the leadership aspirations of DCCC chairs and members made it difficult for the committee to pursue its stated goal of maximizing House seats. Second, the NRCC has been one step ahead of the DCCC in gathering campaign information: the Republican committee was the first to have staff observing campaigns in the field and the only House campaign committee to have permanent field staff in 1996.[35] This gave it an advantage over the DCCC in targeting. Third, many safe Democratic incumbents used the DCCC's media center, inflating the figures for party money spent in connection with shoo-in races.[36]

It is relatively easy for the parties to target their money in Senate elections. DSCC and NRSC officials have to assess their candidates' prospects in only thirty-three or thirty-four races per election, and those races take place within borders that do not shift every ten years because of redistricting. Polling data are also available for all of them. As a result, virtually all the parties' funds are spent in close elections. In 1996 the Democrats spent all but 5 percent of their money in competitive contests, favoring open-seat prospects and hopeful challengers, followed by incumbents in jeopardy. The Republicans distributed all but 6 percent of their funds to candidates in close elections, favoring open-seat prospects and challengers over incumbents in jeopardy. Both parties perceived open-seat elections to be where some hard-fought battles would take place, with the Democrats being more aggressive than the Republicans.

In addition to distributing campaign contributions and coordinated expenditures directly to candidates, the Hill committees have recently begun to encourage the flow of "party-connected" contributions from incumbents' "leadership" (or "member") PACs and reelection accounts to needy candidates, such as nonincumbents and some new members. Although leadership PACs are technically political action committees rather than party organizations and member-to-candidate contributions are not the same as party contributions, those who make these contributions share some of the party committees' objectives.[37]

During the 1996 elections current and former members of Congress, mostly incumbents seeking reelection, contributed more than $8.6 million from their

TABLE 4-3

Party-Connected Contributions in the 1996 Congressional Elections

	House		Senate	
	Democrats	Republicans	Democrats	Republicans
Candidate contributions	$1,566,047	$2,068,861	$102,988	$135,568
Other members and retirees	290,125	203,141	153,104	106,960
Leadership PACs	993,424	3,499,107	132,500	1,587,328
Total	$2,849,596	$5,771,109	$388,592	$1,829,856

Source: Compiled from Federal Election Commission data.

Note: Figures are for contributions from candidates, members of Congress not up for reelection in 1996, retired members, and leadership PACs to candidates in all congressional elections, including primaries, runoffs, and uncontested races.

campaign accounts or leadership PACs to 576 primary and general election House candidates (see Table 4-3). They gave an additional $2.2 million to 57 candidates for the Senate. The biggest contributors were congressional leaders and policy entrepreneurs. Reps. Robert Matsui, D-Calif., and Robert Livingston, R-La., led their respective parties in individual contributions, each giving more than $90,000 from their own war chests. Speaker Gingrich, and Democratic Leader Richard Gephardt, D-Mo., led their congressional parties in leadership PAC dollars, contributing $771,500 and $461,095, respectively. Campaign America, a PAC associated with the former Senate majority leader Robert Dole and former vice president Dan Quayle gave $819,681—the largest sum associated with congressional retirees. Party-connected contributions exceeded contributions distributed by formal party organizations by almost $5 million in 1996.

Party-connected money was distributed strategically, the vast majority of it going to candidates in competitive contests (see Table 4-4). The major difference between party-connected contributions and money contributed by party organizations is that the distribution of party-connected funds favors incumbents somewhat more. This reflects the fact that individuals who contribute party-connected funds, like party committees, are concerned with maximizing the number of seats under their party's control, but they also want to do favors for congressional colleagues that they can collect on later.[38] Party-connected contributions demonstrate that parties have become important vehicles for redistributing wealth among congressional candidates.

TABLE 4-4

The Distribution of Party-Connected Money in the 1996 Congressional Elections

	House		Senate	
	Democrats	Republicans	Democrats	Republicans
Incumbents				
In jeopardy	28%	53%	20%	28%
	(44)	(75)	(5)	(9)
Shoo-ins	9	7	3	8
	(112)	(125)	(2)	(4)
Challengers				
Hopefuls	39%	15%	32%	18%
	(75)	(44)	(9)	(5)
Likely losers	4	3	1	1
	(125)	(112)	(4)	(2)
Open seats				
Prospects	16%	18%	40%	39%
	(32)	(32)	(12)	(12)
Long shots	3	4	4	7
	(18)	(18)	(2)	(2)
Total (thousands)	$2,489	$5,159	$361	$1,769
	(406)	(406)	(34)	(34)

Source: Compiled from Federal Election Commission data.

Notes: Figures are for contributions from candidates, members of Congress not up for reelection in 1996, retired members, and leadership PACs to general election candidates in major-party contested races, excluding a small number of atypical races that were decided in runoffs or won by independents. The numbers of candidates are in parentheses.

CAMPAIGN SERVICES

The parties' congressional and senatorial campaign committees provide selected candidates with assistance in specialized campaign activities, such as management, gauging public opinion, issue and opposition research, and communications.[39] They also provide transactional assistance, acting as brokers between candidates and the PACs, individual contributors, political consultants, and powerful incumbents who possess some of the money, political contacts, and campaign expertise that candidates need. The DCCC and the NRCC typically become closely involved in the campaigns of candidates on their watch lists and have little involvement in others. The DSCC and the NRSC work with virtually all their Senate candidates.

Campaign Management

Candidates and their campaign organizations can get help from their Hill committees with hiring and training campaign staff, making strategic and tactical decisions, and other management-related activities. The committees maintain directories of campaign managers, fund-raising specialists, media experts, pollsters, voting list vendors, and other political consultants that candidates and managers can use to hire staff and purchase campaign services. Committee officials sometimes recommend particular consultants, especially to House challengers and open-seat candidates, some of whom are involved in their first major campaign.[40]

The six Washington party organizations also train candidates and managers in the latest campaign techniques. The DCCC and the NRCC hold training seminars at their headquarters for incumbents that cover such topics as staying in touch with constituents, getting the most political mileage out of franked mail, defending unpopular votes, and PAC fund-raising. The two congressional campaign committees also work with the national committees to host seminars for challengers and open-seat candidates around the country. These focus on more basic subjects, such as the "stump" speech, filing campaign finance reports with the FEC, and building coalitions. Even long-term members of the House and Senate find the seminars beneficial as reminders of what they ought to be doing.

Over the course of the 1996 election cycle, the RNC established campaign management "colleges" and held seminars in forty-one states that served 6,000 Republican candidates and activists.[41] The NRCC organized three four-day candidate schools. It also established a "campaign college" that enrolled 110 congressional aides and Washington political activists, who attended seminars a couple of nights a week over a seven-week period.[42] The NRSC held two campaign seminars, one of which focused exclusively on fund-raising and other new campaign techniques, that attracted representatives from twenty-two campaigns.

The Democrats, led by the DNC, held three campaign training sessions in Washington and four in different states that trained approximately 3,000 campaign operatives in general management, research, communications, fund-raising, and field activities.[43] The DCCC held an additional three seminars for challengers and open-seat candidates.[44] The DSCC trained nonincumbents and their campaign aides in fund-raising, political research, and other activities.[45]

The Hill committees' field representatives and political staffs in Washington also serve as important sources of strategic advice. Because they follow House and Senate elections nationwide and can draw on experiences from previous election cycles, the committees are among the few organizations that have the knowledge and institutional memory to advise candidates and their managers on how to deal with some of the dilemmas they encounter. The political staffs of the congressional campaign committees are usually most heavily involved in the planning and tactical decision making of open-seat and challenger candidates. However, they also provide a great deal of advice to House freshmen, members running in heavily redrawn districts, and those in close races.

Gauging Public Opinion

Many candidates receive significant assistance in gauging public opinion from national party committees. The DNC and RNC disseminate the findings of nationwide polls in newsletters and memoranda that they distribute to members of Congress, party activists, and congressional candidates. The parties' congressional and senatorial campaign committees commission hundreds of district and statewide polls and targeting studies in a given election cycle. The committees use recruitment surveys to show potential candidates the possibilities of waging competitive races, benchmark polls to inform declared candidates of their levels of support and of public opinion on the major issues, and tracking polls to assist a small group of candidates who are running neck-and-neck with their opponents at the end of the campaign season. Some of these surveys are paid for entirely by a Hill committee and reported to the FEC as an in-kind contribution or coordinated expenditure. Most are jointly financed by a committee and the candidates the polls serve.

Parties have significant advantages over individual candidates when it comes to purchasing polls. Parties are able to get polls at discount rates because they contract for so many of them. Parties can also use their extensive connections with polling firms to arrange to "piggyback" questions on polls that are taken for other clients. Benchmark polls, which can be useful weeks after they were taken, give party committees special opportunities to provide candidates with highly useful information at low cost. A party can purchase a poll for roughly $10,000 and give it to a candidate as an in-kind contribution or coordinated expenditure that is valued at a mere fraction of that amount if they turn it over using a depreciation option allowed by the FEC.[46]

All six Washington party organizations commission national polls to research issues that they expect to occupy a prominent position on the national agenda. In 1996 the Republican national party committees distributed just over $47,400 in polling services to thirteen House candidates, whereas the Democrats distributed more than $1,419,700 in polls to 108 House contenders. Four Republican Senate candidates received about $124,400 from GOP committees, whereas 18 Democratic candidates received almost $697,200 from their party.[47] According to DSCC political director Gail Stoltz, these expenditures are worthwhile: "It's a good investment to spend $10,000 before deciding whether to spend over a million dollars in a state."[48]

Selected candidates also receive precinct-level targeting studies from the Hill committees. The DSCC and DCCC use geodemographic data provided by the NCEC to help their candidates develop targeting strategies. These data are matched with previous election results and current polling figures and used to guide the candidates' direct-mail programs, media purchases, voter mobilization drives, and other campaign efforts.[49] Republican candidates receive similar targeting assistance from the NRCC's and NRSC's political divisions.

Issue and Opposition Research

During the 1980s party organizations in Washington became major centers for political research. The DNC and RNC extended their research activities in several directions, most of which were and continue to be focused on the party rather than directed toward the candidates. The national committees routinely send materials on salient national issues to candidates for Congress, governorships, and state legislatures, to "allied" consultants and interest groups, and to activists at all levels. Party research typically includes statistics, tables, and charts that are drawn from major newspapers, the Associated Press wire service, the Lexis/Nexis computerized political database, and government publications. It weaves factual information with partisan themes and powerful anecdotes to underscore major campaign issues. Some individuals receive this information through the U.S. mail, but most get it by way of the thousands of "blast-faxes" that the committees transmit daily during the campaign season.[50] Many journalists and political commentators are also sent issue research—albeit with a partisan spin—by the national committees.

The congressional and senatorial campaign committees also disseminate massive amounts of issue-related materials by mail, fax, and the Internet to candidates, party activists, and partisan political consultants. During the last few congresses, both parties' House and Senate leaderships distributed "talking points," memoranda, pamphlets, and issues handbooks designed to help candidates develop issue positions, write speeches, and prepare for debates. More important than this generic research are the more detailed materials that the

Hill committees distribute to individual candidates. Each committee routinely distributes information on the substance and political implications of congressional roll-call votes. Many nonincumbents, who are unable to turn to congressional aides, the Library of Congress, or Washington-based interest groups for information on important issues, use this information to develop policy positions. Challengers also use it to plan attacks on incumbents.

The two House campaign committees assemble highly detailed issue research packages for candidates involved in some competitive races. These packages present hard facts about issues that are important to local voters and talking points that help candidates discuss these issues in a thematic and interesting manner. During the 1996 elections, the DCCC provided individualized research packages to fifty campaigns, mostly those being waged by challengers and open-seat candidates. The packages presented detailed information on how Republican House members' votes on Medicare, Medicaid, the budget, and other major issues would affect different groups of constituents. Included in them were district-specific estimates of the number of senior citizens and poor people who would be deprived of adequate health care, the number of university hospitals that would lose federal funding and be forced to close, and the number of students whose college loans would be cut under Republican budget proposals.[51]

The NRCC provided similar kinds of detailed research to fifty challengers, fifty open-seat contestants, and nine incumbents, most of whom were freshmen, in 1996. This research highlighted how the constitutional amendment to balance the budget, welfare reform, the crime bill, and other popular Republican legislation would help people living in individual congressional districts.[52] The committee also conducted "vulnerability studies" to help several Republican freshmen and a few other House members respond to attacks it anticipated would be made by their opponents.

Campaign Communications

The Hill committees assist selected candidates with campaign communications. The DCCC and the NRCC own state-of-the-art television and radio production facilities and furnish candidates with technical and editorial assistance in producing television and radio ads. The committees have satellite capabilities that enable candidates to beam television communications back to their districts to interact "live" with voters. This technology is extremely popular with incumbents from western states, who are not able to get back to their districts as frequently as those living on the East Coast or in the Midwest. Each media center produces several "generic" or "doughnut" ads that they customize to incorporate the names and voices of individual candidates. All these resources are made available to candidates at below-market rates.

Twenty-one candidates, mostly incumbents, used the NRCC's media center to produce television commercials and twenty-three used it to produce radio spots in 1996.[53] The committee provided eighteen other House candidates with more comprehensive media packages in which it developed advertising themes and scripts and arranged for advertisements to be aired on local television or radio stations. In previous elections the NRCC had furnished many more candidates with full-service advertising assistance. Following the GOP takeover of the House, however, committee leaders decided they could better serve more candidates by devoting their energies to creating issue advocacy ads (discussed below). Recognizing that the majority of their candidates were incumbents, the NRCC leaders decided that most Republicans in close House races were in a position to hire their own media consultants.[54]

The DCCC also makes its production and editing facilities available to House candidates, but it does not provide them with comprehensive media packages. The majority of Democratic House candidates hire media consultants to provide the content for their ads. Some of those who cannot afford to hire high-powered media consultants, mostly House challengers in uncompetitive races, use one or more of the twelve generic ads produced by the committee's Harriman Communications Center as the foundation for their TV commercials. The DCCC gave virtually every Democratic House candidate $20,000 in credits that could be redeemed at the communications center, and its staff estimated that roughly 70 percent of the candidates, mostly incumbents, redeemed them.[55]

The DSCC and NRSC play a less direct role in developing Senate candidates' campaign communications. Rather than produce television, radio, or direct-mail advertisements, committee staff comment on ads created by private consultants. Sometimes the committees finance these ads through in-kind contributions and coordinated expenditures. Both committees have Internet sites that display candidate information. The NRSC also provides radio actuality services, which enable candidates to record a campaign message or a pseudo-interview that local stations can access by dialing a toll-free number and then broadcast to their listeners. Although their direct involvement is limited, the senatorial campaign committees do play influential roles in campaign communications. As will be discussed later, committee independent expenditures and issue advocacy can affect Senate elections significantly. Senatorial and congressional campaign committee issue research and communication activities have clearly contributed to the nationalization of American politics.

Fund-Raising

In addition to providing contributions, coordinated expenditures, and campaign services directly to candidates, and steering party-connected contributions to them, the Hill committees help selected candidates raise money from individuals and PACs. To this end, the committees give the candidates strategic advice and fund-raising assistance. They also furnish PACs and other Washington insiders with information that they can use when formulating their contribution strategies and selecting individual candidates for support.

All six national party organizations give candidates tips on how to organize fund-raising committees and events. The Republican Hill committees and the DSCC even furnish some candidates with contributor lists, with the proviso that the candidates surrender their own lists to the committee after the election. Sometimes the parties host high-dollar events in Washington or make arrangements for party leaders to attend events held around the country either in person or via satellite television uplink. The Speaker of the House and other congressional leaders can draw lobbyists, PAC managers, and other big contributors to even the most obscure candidate's fund-raising event. Of course, nothing can draw a crowd of big contributors like an appearance by the president.

The committees also steer large contributions from wealthy individuals, PACs, or members of Congress to needy candidates. It is illegal for the parties to "earmark" checks they receive from individuals or PACs for specific candidates, but committee members and staff can suggest to contributors that they give to one of the candidates on the committee's watch list. Sometimes they reinforce this message by sending out fund-raising letters on behalf of a candidate, sponsoring events that list congressional leaders as the event's hosts, or organizing joint fund-raising events after which the committee and the candidates split the proceeds evenly.[56]

The Hill committees also give candidates the knowledge and tools needed to raise PAC money. The committees help candidates design "PAC kits" they can use to introduce themselves to members of the PAC community.[57] They also distribute lists of PACs that include the name of a contact person at each PAC and indicate how much cash the PAC has on hand, so candidates will neither waste their time soliciting committees that have no money nor take no for an answer when a PAC manager claims poverty but still has funds. Candidates are coached on how to fill out the questionnaires that some PACs use to guide their contributions and how to build coalitions of local PAC contributors so they can raise money from national PACs. All four Hill committees make meeting rooms and telephones available to facilitate PAC fund-raising, which cannot be legally conducted on Capitol grounds.

The committees also help candidates raise money from PACs by manipulating the informational environment in which PACs make their contribution decisions. The committees' PAC directors work to channel the flow of PAC money toward their party's most competitive congressional contenders and away from their opponents. This is an especially difficult task to perform for House challengers and open-seat candidates because they are largely unknown to the PAC community. Some junior House members need to have attention called to their races. The PAC directors often call on party leaders, committee and subcommittee chairs, or ranking members to attend a candidate's fund-raising event or to telephone a PAC manager on the candidate's behalf.

The Hill committees use several methods to circulate information about House and Senate elections to PACs and other potential contributors. The committees publicize their targeting lists and contribution activities to draw the attention of PACs and wealthy individual contributors. The committees also host receptions, often referred to as "meet and greets," at their headquarters and national conventions to give candidates, especially nonincumbents, an opportunity to ask PAC managers for contributions. Campaign updates are mailed or faxed to about one thousand of the largest PACs on a weekly basis during the peak of the election season to inform them of targeted candidates' electoral prospects, financial needs, poll results, endorsements, campaign highlights, and revelations about problems experienced by their opponents. Streams of communications are also sent to the editors of the *Cook Political Report,* the *Rothenberg Political Report,* and other political newsletters that handicap congressional races. A favorable write-up in one of these can help a nonincumbent raise more PAC money.

The Hill committees also hold briefings to discuss their opportunity races and to inform PAC managers about their candidates' progress. These are important forums for networking among campaign finance elites. They give PAC managers the opportunity to ask Hill committee staffers questions about specific campaigns and provide them with the chance to discuss contribution strategies among themselves.

The campaign committees' PAC directors and party leaders spend a tremendous amount of time making telephone calls on behalf of their most competitive and financially needy candidates. Some of these calls are made to PAC managers who are recognized leaders of PAC networks. The DCCC and DSCC, for example, work closely with the NCEC and the AFL-CIO's COPE; their GOP counterparts work closely with the Business-Industry Political Action Committee (BIPAC). The committees encourage these "lead" PACs to endorse the party's top contestants and to communicate their support to other PACs in their networks.

One of the more controversial ways that the Hill committees raise money for needy candidates is by "leveraging" it. Campaign committee staff organize functions and clubs that promise PAC managers, lobbyists, and others access to congressional leaders in return for large contributions. Following the Republican takeover of Congress, Majority Whip Tom DeLay, R-Texas, greeted lobbyists with a list that categorized the four hundred largest PACs as "Friendly" or "Unfriendly," depending on the proportion of their contributions that went to Republicans in the 1994 elections, to hammer home the message that groups that wanted access to Republican leaders would be expected to give most of their PAC money to GOP candidates and party committees in the future.[58]

The Hill committees also use "buddy systems" to match financially needy but promising nonincumbents and freshmen with committee chairs and other powerful incumbents for fund-raising purposes. The incumbents offer their partners advice on campaign-related topics and use their influence to persuade PAC managers and individuals who have made large contributions to their campaigns to contribute to their "buddy."[59] The buddy system's impact on fund-raising is hard to estimate, but Speaker Newt Gingrich is said to have persuaded more than 150 House members from safe seats to raise $50,000 each, either for colleagues who were in jeopardy or competitive nonincumbents during the 1996 elections.[60]

The Hill committees are important intermediaries in the fund-raising process because they help needy challengers, open-seat candidates, and incumbents raise money from other PACs, other candidates, and individuals who make large contributions. The committees have created symbiotic relationships with some PACs, resulting in parties' becoming important brokers between candidates and contributors.[61] The relationships are based largely on honest and reliable exchanges of information about the prospects of individual candidates. Hill committee officials and PAC managers recognize that accurate information is the key to this relationship and to the ability of both groups to help candidates.

Party communications to PACs are somewhat controversial because they can harm some individual candidate's fund-raising prospects. Candidates who receive their Hill committee's endorsement derive significant fund-raising advantages from such communications, but nonincumbents who do not are usually unable to collect significant funds from PACs. Some PAC managers justify refusing a contribution request because a nonincumbent was not included on a Hill committee's watch list. Hill committee fund-raising efforts can create both winners and losers in congressional elections.

Grass-Roots Activities

Not all of the campaign assistance that House and Senate candidates get from parties comes from Washington, and not all of it is given by the parties' congressional and senatorial campaign committees. Some state and local party committees give candidates assistance in a few of the aspects of campaigning discussed above, but these committees tend to be less influential than the Hill committees in areas requiring technical expertise, in-depth research, or connections with Washington PACs and political consultants.[62] State and local party committees do, however, provide congressional candidates with substantial help in grass-roots campaigning. Most state committees help fund and organize registration and get-out-the-vote drives, set up telephone banks, and send campaign literature to voters.[63] Many local parties conduct these same activities as well as canvass door-to-door, distribute posters and lawn signs, put up billboards, and engage in other types of campaign field work.[64]

Some of this activity is organized and paid for by the state and local party organizations themselves; however, a significant portion of it is funded by party committees in Washington under the guise of the coordinated campaign—a cooperative party-building and voter mobilization program that is funded mainly by national party organizations. Most of the money that national party organizations spend in coordinated campaigns is targeted to states and localities that are critical to their presidential, senatorial, or congressional candidates' success.[65] These expenditures enable party organizations in the nation's capital to influence locally executed, grass-roots activities that benefit the entire party ticket.

The Democratic national, congressional, and senatorial campaign committees spent roughly $40 million on coordinated campaigns in 1996. This includes hard and soft money used in state and local party-building programs for direct-mail expenses, to purchase voter lists, and to set up telephone banks. According to Don Fowler, DNC's national chairman, that committee alone spent approximately $20 million to contact roughly 14.3 million people through direct mail and 11 million through telemarketing calls.[66]

The DNC also spent considerable sums to mobilize racial and ethnic minorities. It spent about $5 million on generic advertisements that used ethnic radio, television, and newspaper outlets to deliver a pro-Democratic message to African Americans, Hispanics, and Asian Americans, sometimes in languages other than English.[67] It gave a few hundred thousand dollars to the National Coalition for Black Voter Participation, the Rainbow Coalition, and the A. Philip Randolph Institute to help them get minority voters to the polls.[68]

The Republicans spent a record $48.3 million on their "Victory '96" program. The RNC transferred $15.3 million to GOP state party organizations for grass-roots activities. Republican state committees spent an additional $33 million. These resources enabled the party to deliver 84.8 million pieces of targeted political mail and make 14.5 million voter identification or get-out-the-vote calls. The RNC also gave an unprecedented $4.6 million in soft money to Americans for Tax Reform (ATR), an antitax group with ties to the RNC chairman Haley Barbour, and $1.4 million to a few right-to-life groups and other conservative tax-exempt, nonprofit organizations that are allied with the GOP.[69] Republican Hill committees have also distributed funds to many right-to-life groups.

Funneling money through interest groups provides parties with structural, institutional, and strategic benefits. First, these organizations have more credibility than the party committees on certain issues. For example, ATR had greater credibility on tax cuts with antitax voters than did the RNC. Second, groups have their own mailing lists, educational activities, communications networks, and outreach programs. Third, giving campaign funds to these groups helps to keep them from abandoning a party's coalition and backing other candidates. Finally, by giving money to outside groups the parties are able to spend additional sums to help their candidates without violating federal election laws that regulate the amount of soft money a national party can spend in individual states.[70] Party leaders have established tax-exempt groups since the 1980s, mostly to help prepare for presidential nominating contests.[71] Court rulings that allow parties and other groups to carry out election-related issue advocacy campaigns have created new incentives for individuals to form these groups and for party committees to support them.

INDEPENDENT EXPENDITURES AND ISSUE ADVOCACY

Issue advocacy campaigns consist of advertisements that parties (and some interest groups) use to encourage citizens to support or oppose public policies or to praise or criticize specific federal candidates. Television and radio are the media most often employed for these ads, but sometimes direct mail is used. Although they can have direct implications for congressional elections, issue advocacy ads *cannot expressly* advocate the election or defeat of a candidate. Unlike candidate ads, issue advocacy ads that appear on television or radio do not qualify for lowest unit rate charges. They differ from party coordinated expenditures in that they can be made using soft money.[72]

Whether issue advocacy ads can be coordinated with a candidate's campaign is a matter that is under challenge in the courts, but some coordination did occur in 1996. Much of the party money used to finance issue advocacy campaigns originates at the national level and is transferred to state party committees. All six national party organizations, as well as many state party committees, sponsored issue advocacy ads during the 1996 elections.

Party independent expenditures, in contrast, are like independent expenditures made by PACs in that they *can expressly* call for the election or defeat of a federal candidate so long as the expenditure is made with hard money and without the candidate's knowledge or consent. Like issue advocacy campaigns, they do not qualify for lowest unit rate charges. Nearly all the party independent expenditures in the 1996 elections were intended to influence Senate races. The Republicans made nearly $10 million in independent expenditures: $4.7 million was spent to advocate the election of fourteen Republican Senate candidates, and another $5.2 million was spent to advocate the defeat of thirteen Democratic Senate candidates.[73] The Democrats spent nearly $1.3 million against six Republican Senate candidates and another $50,000 advocating the election of three Democratic candidates. Virtually all the independent expenditures were spent in races decided by twenty points or less.[74]

Independent spending, especially Republican spending, played a major role in several elections. GOP independent expenditures broke the million dollar mark in three states. Republican independent expenditures exceeded 20 percent of the Republican candidates' spending in eight states and 44 percent in five states. In Wyoming, the Republicans made $960,792 in independent expenditures in behalf of their party's nominee, state senator Michael Enzi, which was almost exactly the amount that Enzi spent in the race. Without the Republican independent expenditures the Democratic nominee, former secretary of state Kathy Karpan, would have had a 13 percent spending advantage over Enzi. With the money, Enzi and the GOP enjoyed a 61 percent advantage over Karpan and the Democrats. Enzi's twelve-point victory was not solely due to the Republican's independent expenditures, but Republican spending played an important role in achieving it.

The Democratic Party's independent expenditures were important but less impressive than those of the Republican Party. Democratic Party independent spending exceeded 25 percent of Democratic candidates' expenditures in only one race, 18 percent in a second contest, and 12 percent in a third. The rest of the Democrats' independent expenditures amounted to less than 10 percent of the funds spent by the candidates themselves.

The DNC, DCCC, RNC, and NRCC made no independent expenditures in the 1996 elections. Spokespersons for these committees explained that their existing staffs were too involved in individual campaigns to have authorized expenditures that could have legally qualified as independent. The committees would have had to create new independent expenditure divisions, comprised of newly hired staff and consultants, in order to make the expenditures—an undertaking that would have had significant overhead costs. Issue advocacy ads provided them with a better alternative in that they did not impose heavy overhead costs and could be partially financed with soft money.[75]

In 1996, party committees used independent expenditures and issue advocacy campaigns to increase their influence in congressional elections. The DNC was the first party committee to broadcast issue advocacy ads to help a candidate. It began televising ads in mid-October 1995 in order to counteract President Clinton's low standing in the polls. Don Fowler and presidential adviser Dick Morris advocated using TV to get out the message that the president was doing a good job and to paint the Republican-controlled Congress as a group of radical extremists who wanted to help large corporations and wealthy individuals at the expense of working people. TV ads focusing on GOP proposals to downsize the growth of Medicare and Medicaid, cut spending on education, allow corporations to pollute the environment, and cut taxes for the wealthy were aired in states critical to the president's reelection prospects, and their impact on congressional elections was unmistakable. The $42.4 million that the DNC spent on issue advocacy ads over the course of the election helped set the national political agenda and the tone for many House and Senate campaigns.[76]

The DCCC and the DSCC ran issue advocacy campaigns that complemented those spearheaded by the DNC. The DCCC transferred $8.5 million to Democratic state committees to help finance television ads that were aired in the districts of sixty marginal House members, most of whom were Republican freshmen.[77] In addition to criticizing House Republicans, many of the ads touted the congressional Democrats' Families First Agenda.

The DSCC transferred an additional $10 million for issue advocacy ads to fourteen states that hosted the nation's closest Senate races. The committee also made independent expenditures in the form of television ads in Georgia, Kansas, Maine, New Hampshire, and Oregon, states hosting five of the closest Senate races. Prior to making these ads, the committee had to reassign some of its staff. According to Stoltz, the only staff or consultants who were allowed to become involved in the independent expenditure activities in the five races were those who had had no previous involvement in the campaigns.[78]

The Republicans waited until late March, when Sen. Robert Dole had clinched the nomination, to launch their issue advocacy campaign. The party's initial ads were financed by the RNC and designed to boost Dole's image at a time when he had virtually run out of federal matching primary funds. The RNC spent $20 million between March and its August national convention, when the Dole campaign received its general election funds.[79] Although these ads were primarily intended to influence the presidential contest, their impact reverberated in campaigns at all levels.

The NRCC televised six issue advocacy ads in the districts of Republican candidates involved in competitive elections.[80] The first three ads were designed to remind voters of GOP accomplishments and to clarify for the public its positions on welfare reform, congressional reform, and Medicare. They cost $7 million and were aired in thirty House districts from the third week in July through Labor Day. The second three ads sought to counter the anti-Republican media campaign waged by organized labor and the Democrats, to remind voters of some of the policy failures of the Clinton administration, and to discourage them from electing a Democratic Congress.[81] These ads, which were cosponsored by the RNC, cost roughly $20 million and were broadcast in fifty-eight districts from October 5 through election day.[82]

The NRSC took a different route from that of its House counterpart or Democratic rival, setting up a special division composed of twelve full-time staffers to handle its issue advocacy and independent expenditure advertising. The new division was located in office space outside of the committee's headquarters and its members were instructed not to discuss its activities with other NRSC staff, except for the purpose of filing FEC reports. The group hired consultants who neither worked for the committee nor for the candidates whose races were targeted for issue advocacy or independent expenditure advertisements. The committee's main pollster and general consultant was Arthur Finkelstein, but the independent expenditure group hired Keren Mahoney, Inc., for general consulting and to take over half a dozen polls in twenty-seven states.[83]

The NRSC spent only about $2 million to televise issue advocacy ads in five states during the 1996 elections. The ads focused on welfare reform, the Republican plan to balance the budget, and Republican spending priorities. Between April and October 3, which marked the end of the Senate session, the NRSC aired prime-time ads in Iowa, Minnesota, and Montana that were tailored to highlight vulnerabilities in Democratic candidates' records. In Minnesota, for example, the committee ran a series of TV and radio ads calling Sen. Paul Wellstone, D-Minn., "embarrassingly liberal" and accusing him of being "stuck in the sixties, decades out of touch." The NRSC also spent small sums in Michigan and West Virginia for the purpose of throwing Democratic senators Carl Levin and Jay Rockefeller, both of whom held safe seats, off stride.[84]

The 1996 election shows that parties can use independent expenditure and issue advocacy ads to influence the national political agenda and the agendas in individual House and Senate contests. One high-powered Republican operative who was responsible for his Hill committee's issue advocacy and independent expenditure ads compared his role to that of a chef who prepares a meal. The expenditures allowed the committee "to set the place settings and let others select from what was already on their plate."[85] Once the party had set the agenda with issues and themes that worked to the advantage of their candidate, the operative explained, "the candidate could select what he preferred from among them and force them down the opponent's throat."[86] Party spending is especially important in states that have late primaries because candidates often emerge from them with little cash with which to try to set the agenda and only seven or eight weeks to woo general election voters.

Party issue advocacy and independent expenditure ads are also important late in the election. The ads can supplement a candidate's advertisements and catch an opponent off guard and without the funds needed to respond. The ads also have the benefit of limiting the media time that might otherwise be purchased by an opponent. Another advantage of airing attack ads against an opposing party's candidates, including safe incumbents such as Levin and Rockefeller, is that the ads can encourage the candidates to spend more time at home and less time traveling the country raising money for challengers and needy colleagues. Finally, the effect of issue advocacy and independent expenditure ads is usually magnified many times over because they routinely receive free media coverage.

THE IMPACT OF PARTY CAMPAIGNING

How valuable do House and Senate candidates find the campaign services they receive from party organizations? When asked to rate the importance of campaign assistance from local, state, and national party organizations, PACs, unions, and other groups in aspects of campaigning requiring professional expertise or in-depth research, candidates and campaign aides involved in recent House elections ranked their party's Hill committee first. With respect to campaign management, about one-third of all House candidates and campaign aides consider their party's congressional campaign committee to be at least moderately helpful.[87] Roughly 40 percent gave similar assessments for Hill committee assistance in gauging public opinion. Over half of all House contestants report that committee issue research plays at least a moderately important role in their campaigns, with 20 percent describing it as very important and another 11 percent asserting that it is extremely important. More than 40 percent of the House contestants, mostly challengers, also rely heavily on their congressional campaign committee for opposition research. About 30 percent of all House campaigns receive significant DCCC or NRCC help in developing their communications. Slightly more candidates and campaign aides find that Hill committees are moderately important to their fund-raising efforts; however, campaigners report receiving greater fund-raising assistance from PACs and other interest groups. The DCCC and NRCC are also rated lower than are state and local party organizations and interest groups in grass-roots activities. The lower rating reflects their lack of direct involvement in these aspects of campaigning.

The evaluations by House candidates and campaign aides indicate that most congressional campaign committee help is given to candidates in close races, which reflects the parties' goal of winning as many seats in Congress as possible. The evaluations also show that Hill committee assistance is generally more important to hopeful challengers and open-seat prospects than to incumbents in jeopardy, reflecting the fact that incumbents' electoral difficulties are rarely the result of an inability to raise money, assemble a campaign organization, or communicate with voters.

Nevertheless, the Hill committees go to great lengths to protect their endangered incumbents. The NRCC, for example, played an important role in helping endangered first-term Republicans defend their seats in 1996. It provided the typical freshman in jeopardy with $61,500, which was just a few hundred dollars less than the legal maximum in campaign contributions and coordinated expenditures and more than twice what it gave to other incumbents in competitive races. The committee also held special seminars to teach the freshmen how to exploit their incumbency for campaign purposes, created a three-person division for incumbent protection to give them strategic advice, steered millions of PAC dollars in their direction, and made them the focus of most of their issue advocacy advertisements. The DCCC also endeavored to help its vulnerable freshmen, providing them with an average of $33,100 in campaign contributions and coordinated expenditures—roughly $4,100 more than it gave to other incumbents in jeopardy. Most Democratic freshmen also received a great deal of fund-raising assistance and campaign advice and benefited from party-sponsored issue advocacy ads. A political consultant would have charged a candidate tens of thousands of dollars for these services, but the congressional campaign committees' staffs provided this help free to candidates in close races.

One freshman Democrat, Rep. Ken Bentsen of Texas, received a tremendous amount of help. On June 13, 1996, less than three months before election day and three months after Texas held its primary, the Supreme Court ruled against three majority-minority districts in Texas, throwing many House elections into turmoil.[88] A three-judge panel completed drawing new lines for the three seats and several surrounding congressional districts, including Bentsen's, on August 6. Several candidates, however, petitioned the Supreme Court to allow the 1996 elections to be held under the original districting because party nominees had already been selected and their campaigns were under way. On September 4, the Court ruled that the new districts would stand.[89] Bentsen found himself locked in a divisive eleven-person general election contest in a heavily redrawn district. The race included another Democrat, eight Republicans, and a Socialist Workers Party candidate. Bentsen won the election with 34 percent of the vote, but his failure to win by a majority meant that the election would have to be decided in a runoff against the second-place finisher, Republican Dolly Madison-McKenna, who had garnered 17 percent of the vote. Democratic incumbents rallied to help Bentsen, whose seat was always considered marginal. Democratic party committees gave Bentsen $23,500 in cash and made $56,035 in coordinated expenditures on his behalf. Democratic leadership PACs gave Bentsen $22,500. Democratic candidates, almost all incumbents, gave him $101,750 from their reelection accounts, and a few retired members contributed $4,500. As a group, the party committees, candidates, and leadership PACs provided the Bentsen campaign with 12 percent of its financial resources. Moreover, the DNC, DCCC, and DSCC transferred almost $4.1 million to pay for issue advocacy ads and grass-roots efforts designed to help Bentsen and other Texans on the Democratic ticket.

The Republicans also became heavily involved in the race, although Madison-McKenna was not as big a priority as many GOP House freshmen. Republican party committees gave Madison-McKenna $54,000 in contributions and coordinated expenditures, Republican leadership PACs contributed $22,500, and Republican candidates gave another $39,600, accounting for 17 percent of her campaign resources. The RNC, NRCC, and NRSC also transferred more than $2.6 million to help her and other Texas GOP candidates.

Most Senate candidates and campaign aides give evaluations of Hill committee assistance that are as favorable as those given by House candidates. The senatorial campaign committees are rated above any other group in every area of campaigning, except providing information about voters, voter mobilization, and volunteer recruitment. State and local party organizations and interest groups were ranked higher on these.[90]

More important to Senate candidates in competitive races is that their party's senatorial campaign committee is a bigger source of campaign resources than any other single group. In 1996 the parties gave three candidates more than $1 million each in cash and campaign services, and another ten candidates more than $500,000 each, excluding independent expenditures. The Enzi-Karpan race demonstrates how important party activity can be in a Senate election. In addition to the nearly $961,000 the Republican Party made in independent expenditures, party committees contributed $140,500 to Enzi, and GOP members of Congress, congressional retirees, and leadership PACs gave him another

$50,200. These funds account for more than 62 percent of the hard money that was spent directly to help Enzi's cause. Hard money connected to the Democratic Party, by contrast, accounted for only 11 percent of the funds dedicated to advancing Karpan's candidacy.

The Supreme Court rulings that opened the door to party independent expenditures and issue advocacy campaigns have increased the role of party organizations in congressional elections. They have also increased the length of federal campaigns and the amounts of money spent on them. In the absence of a major revision of the current law that survives a Supreme Court challenge, for which reformers have been waiting for well over a decade, party influence in campaign agenda setting, communications, and voter mobilization is likely to grow. Republican party organizations are wealthier than their Democratic counterparts, and GOP party committees, particularly at the national level, have traditionally played a larger role in House and Senate elections. The Democrats have increased their involvement in congressional campaigns, but Republican party committees continue to maintain a significant edge in House and an overwhelming lead in Senate elections. At least in the immediate future, the loosening of federal restrictions on party spending is likely to be more to the advantage of the Republicans than the Democrats.

CHAPTER 5

The Interests Campaign

Organized interests, pejoratively referred to as "special" interests, have always been involved in American elections. During the earliest days of the Republic, leaders of agricultural and commercial groups influenced who was on the ballot, the coverage they received in the press, and the voting patterns that determined election outcomes. As the electorate grew and parties and candidates began to spend more money to reach voters, steel magnates, railroad barons, and other captains of industry increased their roles in political campaigns. Labor unions counterorganized with manpower and dollars.[1] Religious and ethnic groups also influenced elections, but their financial and organizational efforts paled next to those of business and labor.

Interest groups continue to flourish at the close of the twentieth century, and several developments have significantly affected their roles in congressional elections. The growth in the number of organizations that located or hired representatives in Washington led to the formation of a community of lobbyists that was, and continues to be, attuned to the rhythms of legislative and election politics. The enactment of the FECA led to the development of the modern political action committee—the form of organizational entity that most interest groups use to carry out the majority of their federal campaign activities. Court decisions handed down in recent years allow interest groups to use new ways, including issue advocacy campaigns, to spend money in congressional elections.

This chapter covers the growth and development of the PAC community in Washington and the role that PACs play in congressional elections. In it I analyze the motives that underlie PAC strategies and activities, the methods that PACs use to select candidates for support, and the distribution of PAC contributions and independent expenditures. I also examine other forms of interest group activity, including issue advocacy campaigns.

THE RISE OF PACS

Although interest groups have been active in campaigns throughout American history, it was not until 1943 that the first political action committee, the Committee on Political Education, was founded by the Congress of Industrial Organizations.[2] A PAC can be best understood as the electoral arm of an organized interest. Interest groups form PACs to give campaign assistance to federal, or in some cases state or local, candidates with the hope of influencing election outcomes, the formation of public policy, or both. Most PACs have a sponsoring, or parent, organization, such as a corporation, labor union, trade association, or other group. However, for ideological and other "nonconnected" PACs, the PAC is the organization itself.

The FECA set the scene for the PAC explosion of the mid-1970s. One of the goals of the act was to dilute the influence of moneyed interests on federal elections. The act limited individuals to a maximum contribution of $1,000 per candidate at each stage of the election—primary, general election, and runoff (if a runoff is required)—for a total of $3,000. It also imposed an aggregate annual limit of $25,000 on an individual's contributions to all federal candidates, federal party committees, and PACs. It barred corporations, labor unions, trade associations, cooperatives, and other organized groups from giving contributions directly to candidates for federal office.

By limiting the total contributions that a candidate could collect from any one source, the FECA encouraged candidates to solicit smaller donations from a broader array of interests and individuals. The act also encouraged many interest groups to establish PACs. Although the FECA never mentioned the term *political action committee,* it allowed for "a multicandidate committee" that raises money from at least fifty donors and spends it on at least five candidates for federal office, to contribute a maximum of $5,000 per candidate at each stage of the election.[3] The law encouraged people to give money to PACs by setting a low ceiling on individual contributions to candidates. The law's lower ceiling on direct individual contributions to candidates makes PAC contributions a popular vehicle among wealthy individuals who wish to influence congressional elections.

In November 1975, in an advisory opinion written for Sun Oil Company, the FEC counseled the company that it could pay the overhead and solicitation costs of its PAC, thereby freeing the PAC to spend all the funds it collected from donors on federal elections.[4] The *SunPAC* decision clarified a gray area in the law and, in the process, made PACs a much more attractive vehicle for collecting and disbursing funds. The advisory ruling contributed to an explosion in the number of PACs that lasted from the mid-1970s to the mid-1980s.

The Supreme Court's ruling in *Buckley v. Valeo* allowed PACs to make unlimited independent expenditures (expenditures made without the knowledge or consent of a candidate or his or her campaign organization) in congressional and presidential elections.[5] Both the FEC advisory opinion and the Supreme Court decision created new opportunities for organized groups to participate in politics. The advisory opinion was especially important, encouraging a wide range of political leaders, business entrepreneurs, and others to form new PACs.

Between 1974 and the 1996 elections, the PAC community grew from just over 600 to 4,528 committees (see Figure 5-1).[6] Most of the growth occurred in the business sector, with corporate PACs growing in number from 89 in 1974 to 1,836 in 1996. Labor unions, many of which already had PACs in 1974, created the fewest new PACs, increasing the number from 201 to 358. The centralization of the labor movement into a relatively small number of unions greatly limited the growth of labor PACs. In addition, three new species of political action committee—the nonconnected PAC (mostly ideological and issue-oriented groups), and PACs whose sponsors are either cooperatives or corporations without stock, such as the Southern Minnesota Sugar Cooperative and the Aircraft Owners and Pilots Association—emerged on the scene in 1977. The nonconnected PACs are the most important of these. They grew to number 1,259 by 1996; the combined total for the two other types of PACs reached only 179 that year.

The growth in the number of PACs was accompanied by a tremendous increase in their activity. PAC contributions to congressional candidates grew from $12.5 million in 1974 to just under $215.4 million in 1996, including about $201.4 million to House and Senate candidates who competed in the 1996 elections.[7] Corporate and other business-related PACs accounted for most of that growth (see Figure 5-2). In 1996, corporate PACs accounted for almost 36 percent of all PAC contributions to congressional candidates, followed by trade PACs, which accounted for 28 percent. Union PACs gave 22 percent of all contributions received by congressional candidates, and nonconnected PACs gave 11 percent. PACs sponsored by cooperatives and corporations without stock contributed the final 4 percent.

A very small group of PACs is responsible for most PAC activity. A mere 180 PACs, just under 4 percent of the entire PAC community, contributed roughly $124.7 million between 1995 and 1996, representing approximately 57 percent of all PAC money given in that election (see Table 5-1). Each of these committees, which are clearly the "big guns" of the PAC community, gave more than $250,000 to federal candidates. These include PACs sponsored by such corporations, trade associations, and unions as United Parcel Service, the National Association of Realtors, and the National Education Association, as well

FIGURE 5-1

The Growth in the Number of Registered PACs, 1974–1996

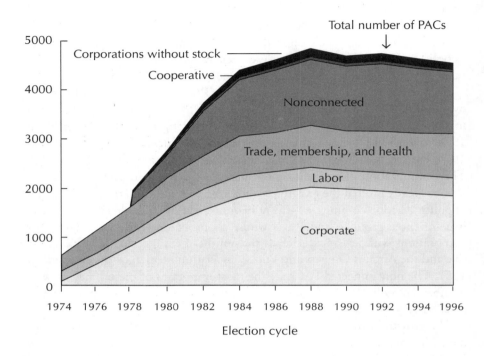

Sources: Joseph E. Cantor, *Political Action Committees: Their Evolution, Growth, and Implications for the Political System* (Washington, D.C.: Congressional Research Service of the Library of Congress, 1984), 88; various Federal Election Commission press releases.

as nonconnected PACs such as Voters for Choice/Friends of Family Planning, and the Adam Smith Political Action Committee.

Another 6 percent of all PACs are "major players," each having contributed between $100,001 and $250,000 to congressional candidates during the 1996 elections. These committees, which include the American Express PAC, the American Insurance Association PAC, the Association of Flight Attendants' "Flight PAC," the National Right to Life PAC, and Washington PAC (WASHPAC, a pro-Israel group), accounted for just over 19 percent of all PAC contributions. The big guns and major players are particularly influential because their wealth allows them to contribute to virtually every candidate whose election is of importance to them.

FIGURE 5-2

The Growth of PAC Contributions in Congressional Elections, 1974–1996

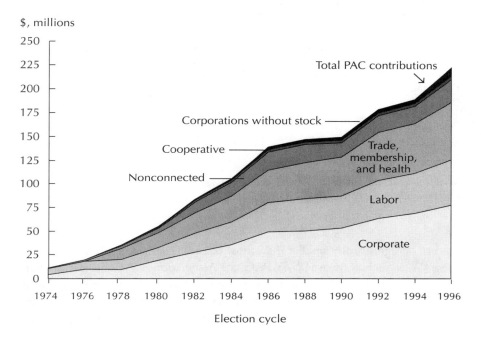

$, millions

Total PAC contributions

Corporations without stock

Cooperative

Nonconnected

Trade, membership, and health

Labor

Corporate

Election cycle

Sources: Joseph E. Cantor, *Political Action Committees: Their Evolution, Growth, and Implications for the Political System* (Washington, D.C.: Congressional Research Service of the Library of Congress, 1984), 88; various Federal Election Commission press releases.

The "players" are those PACs that have the resources to give a significant contribution to many but not all of the candidates they wish to support. They comprise 8 percent of all PACs, and include the Coors Employees' PAC, the Distilled Spirits Council PAC, the International Longshoremen's and Warehousemen's Union PAC, and the Conservative Victory Committee (CVC). Each of the players contributed between $50,001 and $100,000 during the 1996 elections, accounting for roughly 11 percent of all PAC contributions.

The contributions of the next group of PACs, which might be labeled the "junior varsity," are clearly constrained by their size. These PACs each contributed between $5,001 and $50,000. They comprise 29 percent of the PAC community and gave almost 12 percent of all PAC contributions. Their donations

TABLE 5-1

The Concentration of PAC Contributions in the 1996 Congressional
Elections

	PACs' total contributions					
	Over $250,000	$100,001–$250,000	$50,001–$100,000	$5,001–$50,000	$1–$5,000	$0
Percentage of all PACs	4	6	8	29	20	34
(N)	(180)	(261)	(353)	(1,307)	(910)	(1,517)
Percentage of all PAC contributions	57	19	11	12	1	0
($, millions)	(124.7)	(40.9)	(24.9)	(26.5)	(1.8)	(0)

Source: Compiled from Federal Election Commission, "PAC Activity Increases in 1995–96 Election Cycle,"
press release, April 22, 1997.

tend to be significantly smaller than those of the larger PACs. The managers of
these PACs, such as the AMWAY PAC, the Association of American Publishers
PAC (AAP), the Federal Manager's Association PAC, and Republicans for Choice
PAC, commonly have to answer requests for contributions by stating that they
support the candidate and would like to give a contribution but do not have
the money.

The next group, the "small fry," each gave between $1 and $5,000, accounting for just under 1 percent of all PAC contributions during the 1996 elections.
They include the Bacardi Corporation PAC, the PGA Tour PAC, and the Connecticut Portuguese PAC. These committees, which comprise about 20 percent
of the PAC community, play a marginal role in the funding of congressional
elections.

Finally, 1,517 PACs gave no money in the 1996 elections. Of these, 700 are,
for all practical purposes, defunct.[8] Although they registered with the FEC,
they spent no money to collect contributions, pay off debts, or cover the costs
of committee administration during the 1996 election cycle.

STRATEGY, DECISION MAKING, AND TARGETING

PAC goals and strategies are more diverse than those of the two major parties.
Some PACs follow "ideological" strategies designed to increase the number of
legislators who share their broad political perspective or positions on specific,

often emotionally charged issues such as abortion. These PACs are similar to political parties in that they consider congressional elections as opportunities to alter the composition of Congress and view the electoral process as their primary vehicle for changing or reinforcing the direction of public policy.[9]

Ideological PACs give most of their contributions to candidates in close elections, where the PACs have the biggest chance of affecting an election outcome. However, some of these committees also make contributions and independent expenditures in connection with uncompetitive contests in order to attract attention to either themselves or politicians who share their views. Gaining visibility for themselves and their ideas is important because it helps these PACs raise money.

PACs following ideological strategies rarely give money to members of Congress for the sake of gaining access to the legislative process. The issues these PACs support are often linked to values so fundamental that legislators would not be expected to change their views in response to a contribution or visit by a lobbyist. Prior to giving a contribution, many of these PACs, and some others, require candidates to complete questionnaires that elicit their views on certain issues.

Other types of PACs pursue "access" strategies designed to provide the group with the ability to gain at least an audience with members of Congress.[10] These PACs view elections pragmatically. For them, an election is a prime opportunity to shore up relations with members of Congress who work on legislation that is of importance to their parent organization. Elections give these PACs the opportunity to create goodwill with powerful legislators or at least minimize the enmity of legislators who disagree with them. Elections thus lay the groundwork for later lobbying efforts.

A PAC that follows an access strategy is likely to contribute most of its money to incumbents. Members of the House and Senate who chair committees or subcommittees, occupy party leadership positions, or are policy entrepreneurs with influence over legislation are likely to be given large contributions regardless of the competitiveness of their contests.[11] In fact, many access-oriented PACs give contributions to legislators who do not even have opponents. Giving to incumbents enables these PACs to accomplish their goal of ensuring access while also meeting organizational imperatives such as backing a large number of winners and contributing to candidates who represent districts that contain many of the PAC's supporters.

Access-oriented PACs also give significant sums to candidates for open seats. Most of these candidates have good chances of winning but need large amounts of money to run competitive campaigns. Giving an open-seat prospect a large contribution is useful to an access-oriented PAC because it can create goodwill, laying the groundwork for productive relations with a future member of Congress.

Access-oriented PACs tend to ignore challengers because most of them are likely to lose. Giving a challenger a contribution is often considered a waste of money and could lead to serious repercussions from an incumbent. Moreover, backing challengers has a high probability of reducing a PAC's win-loss record and could lead to criticism of the PAC's manager. The managers of access-oriented PACs that decided not to support challenger or open-seat candidates know that should these candidates win, they could make amends later by helping them retire their campaign debts.

PACs that use access strategies rarely make independent expenditures to help or attack candidates because of the publicity these expenditures can generate. Independent expenditures could harm a corporate PAC, for example, if they anger congressional incumbents, upset some of the PAC's donors, or call undue attention to the group. Such publicity could lead to charges that a group is trying to buy influence and could hinder the achievement of its goals.

The largest group of PACs practice "mixed" strategies. They give contributions to some candidates because those candidates share the PAC's views, and they give to others because they wish to improve their access to legislators who work on policies the group deems important. Contributions motivated by the former reason are usually distributed to candidates in competitive contests. Contributions informed by the latter motive are given to incumbents who are in a position to influence legislation that is important to the PAC.

In some cases the two motives clash; for example, when a highly qualified challenger who represents the PAC's views runs a competitive race against an incumbent in a position of power. In these situations PACs usually support the incumbent, but sometimes they contribute to both candidates. PACs that follow mixed strategies and PACs that follow pure access strategies are less likely than ideological PACs to make independent expenditures.

PAC Strategy and the Political Environment

PACs, like most other groups and individuals involved in politics, are strategic actors that respond to their environment in ways that enable them to pursue their goals.[12] During the 1970s most PACs used ideological strategies that followed partisan lines. They backed candidates who supported the positions adhered to by their organizational sponsors. Business-oriented PACs, including corporate and trade committees, largely supported Republican candidates. Labor organizations, which were and continue to be the most consistently partisan of all PACs, regularly gave 90 percent of their contributions to Democrats. In time, many business-oriented committees shifted from ideological to access or mixed strategies. These PACs, with the encouragement of former DCCC chair Tony Coelho, redirected their support from Republican House challengers to incumbents, many of whom were Democrats.[13]

Perhaps the clearest strategic response by PACs takes place after partisan control of one or both chambers of Congress changes hands. When control of the Senate switched from the Democrats to the Republicans in 1981 and back to the Democrats in 1987, many access-seeking PACs switched their contributions to Senate candidates, mainly incumbents, who belonged to the new majority party.[14] Similarly, following the 1994 GOP takeover of both the House and the Senate, these PACs gave most of their funds to Republicans, once again reversing their previous contribution patterns.[15]

Because of their desire to influence the composition of Congress, ideologically oriented PACs are the most likely to capitalize on the conditions peculiar to a specific election. A PAC that uses an access-seeking strategy, such as a corporate or trade committee, is less affected by a particular electoral setting, unless changing conditions are almost certain to influence its parent group's ability to meet with key legislators and their staffs. The strategic changes in PAC behavior that occurred in the early 1980s were the result of committees learning how to get the most legislative influence for their dollars and the increasing aggressiveness of incumbent fund-raising.[16] Those that occurred following the 1994 elections were a response to the change in partisan control of Congress.

Making strategic adjustments in anticipation of political change is more difficult. The manager of an access-oriented PAC who believes that a member of Congress is likely to go from having little to major influence in a policy area, for instance, may have difficulty persuading the PAC's board of directors to raise the member's contribution from a token sum to a substantial donation. The manager's prospects of convincing the board that the PAC should totally revamp its strategy because partisan control of Congress might change are slim. For example, many corporate and trade PACs, whose support of a pro-business agenda suggests they would want to support Republicans who have real prospects for victory, did not support Republican challengers during the 1994 elections. Some of the managers of these PACs may have been attuned to the fact that a confluence of anti-Washington sentiments, strong Republican challengers, and vulnerable Democratic incumbents enhanced the challengers' prospects, but their PAC's decision-making process made it impossible for them to change its contribution patterns in anticipation of the Republicans' stunning success.

PAC Decision Making

The decision-making processes that PACs use to select individual candidates are affected by a PAC's overall strategy, wealth, organizational structure, and location.[17] Ideological PACs spend more time searching for promising challengers to support than do PACs that use access-seeking or mixed strategies. Ideological committees are also more likely than other PACs to support nonincumbents in congressional primaries. Wealthy PACs tend to spend more time searching for promising nonincumbents simply because they can afford to fund more candidates.[18] Federated PACs whose organizational affiliates are spread across the country typically have to respond to the wishes of these constituents when making contributions.[19] Nonconnected PACs and PACs that are sponsored by a single corporation or cooperative, in contrast, are less constrained by the need to please a diverse and far-flung constituency. Committees located in the nation's capital have more information available to them about the relative competitiveness of individual races because they can plug into more communications networks than can PACs located in the hinterlands.[20]

The decision-making processes of PACs vary according to the PACs' organizational capacities. The Realtors PAC, a large institutionalized committee with headquarters in Washington, was formed in 1969.[21] This federated PAC, which is sponsored by the National Association of Realtors (NAR), receives its money from PACs sponsored by the NAR's 1,800 local affiliates and state associations located in all fifty states plus the District of Columbia, Guam, Puerto Rico, and the Virgin Islands. Realtors give donations to these affiliated PACs, which each pass 35 percent of their revenues to the national PAC. In 1996 the NAR's national PAC distributed $2.1 million in contributions, making it the eighth largest big gun in that election.

The Realtors PAC employs a mixed strategy to advance the goals of the real estate industry. As do most other institutionalized PACs, it has explicit criteria for selecting candidates for support and uses a complex decision-making procedure. Incumbency and candidates' policy proclivities, electoral competitiveness, and local support are important determinants of who gets a contribution. Party affiliation, ideology, and personal friendship are secondary concerns. Committee assignments, a member's voting record on real estate issues, and the ability to affect real estate interests are additional criteria used to evaluate incumbents, who are typically given preference over challengers.

The PAC's contribution decisions are made by a twenty-five-member board of trustees that is appointed by the NAR's president. The decisions are guided by input from local realtors who interview candidates, evaluate congressional voting records and other policy-related information, assess the competitiveness of the election, consult with NAR political field staff, and then make a contribution recommendation to the Realtors PAC affiliate in their state. The state association reviews the material and then makes its recommendation to the PAC's board in Washington. PAC staff members in the nation's capital prepare an analysis of every candidate who has been recommended for support by a state association, and the board then reviews the contests race by race. The board meets three or four times in nonelection years and up to eight times during an election year to make its contribution decisions.

Decisions on independent expenditures are made by a separate group that is also appointed by the NAR's president. Strong supporters of real estate issues who are involved in competitive races are targeted for independent expenditures. The PAC commissions polls to evaluate the competitiveness of the elections and to determine the kinds of expenditures that could be helpful in each situation. Most take the form of direct mail or mass media communications that address issues related to the price of home ownership and the like.

The decision-making process of the Realtors PAC is similar to that of other institutionalized committees, such as AT&T's PAC, the American Medical Association's PAC (AMPAC), and Clean Water Action-Vote Environment (CWAVE) PAC.[22] It relies on a combination of factual information, local opinion, and national perspective to determine which candidates to support. The requirement that a board formally approve all recommendations is also typical, as is the ability to conduct research on individual elections in-house. The PAC's lack of participation as either a source or a user of the information available in Washington communications networks is unusual for a PAC located in the nation's capital, but its size, federated structure, and tremendous resources enable it to make decisions with information it has collected independently of other committees.

At the opposite end of the spectrum from the Realtors PAC are the noninstitutionalized PACs. The CVC is a nonconnected ideological committee that was founded in 1987 by L. Brent Bozell to help elect conservative candidates.[23] During the 1996 elections, the CVC contributed $73,000 to candidates for Congress—all but $1,000 of it to Republicans. The PAC pursued a highly aggressive electoral strategy, making 60 percent of its contributions to nonincumbents and another 30 percent to House freshmen. All the recipients of the CVC's largesse, some of whom lost in primaries, were involved in competitive races. WASHPAC, another nonconnected committee, was founded in 1980 by Morris J. Amitay, formerly the executive director of the American Israel Public Affairs Committee (AIPAC), to promote a secure Israel and strong American-Israeli relations.[24] It spent $144,250 in congressional elections in 1996, contributing the vast majority of its money to incumbents. The AAP PAC is a small trade committee founded in 1973 to represent the interests of the publishing community. Its manager, Dianne Rennert, distributed just over $6,500 in 1996, all of which went to incumbents.[25]

These three PACs—and thousands of other noninstitutionalized committees—are essentially one-person operations with one-person decision-making processes. Noninstitutionalized PACs rely primarily on personal contacts with candidates and other Washington insiders for the political information that guides their contribution decisions. The CVC's Bozell, for example, requires candidates who solicit CVC support to demonstrate their conservatism by pledging to support a balanced budget amendment, the line-item veto, and tax relief. He contacts the staffs of the Free Congress PAC, the National Right to Work PAC, and other conservative committees to learn about the competitiveness of different races.

Amitay, who started WASHPAC as a hobby, peruses candidates' speeches and press releases and incumbents' voting records and letters to constituents to gauge their support for Israel. He exchanges information about the competitiveness of different elections when meeting with other pro-Israel political activists. For Rennert, collecting the information needed to distribute the AAP PAC's money is a simple task because the committee routinely contributes all its funds to incumbents who are in a position to influence legislation that affects the publishing community. She keeps abreast of developments in congressional contests through the many fund-raising events she attends or organizes. All three PAC managers are open to the suggestions of individuals who give donations to their committees, but they generally do not make contributions to candidates solely on the basis of donor suggestions.

Noninstitutionalized PACs and multitudes of other one-person organizations use informal decision-making processes. Their lack of formal rules and procedures allows their managers great flexibility in choosing candidates for support. Their limited staff resources force the PAC managers to turn to others for election-related information. These PACs are in a better position than more institutionalized committees to adjust their initial strategies in response to changing electoral conditions. Of course, in the case of very small committees, such as the Connecticut Portuguese PAC, this is true only as long as their money holds out.

Between the institutionalized PACs and the small, one-person organizations are semi-institutionalized committees that possess some of the characteristics of the PACs in the other two groups. These PACs, which include FHP Health Care (FHP) PAC, usually have staffs of two to four people. The staffs are big enough to allow for a functional division of labor and to require the adoption of some concrete decision rules, but they are not big enough to rely solely on their own research when making contribution decisions. For instance, FHP PAC, a corporate committee that has consistently pursued an access strategy, has a two-person staff and a very active board of directors.[26] It contributed $85,919 during the 1996 elections.

PACs with semi-institutionalized organizations typically rely on their staffs to learn where candidates stand on the issues and to collect information from Washington-based PACs and party communities about the competitiveness of various races. FHP PAC, which is located in California, gets its political intelligence from its donors, the company's Washington office, the National Association of Business PACs, the DNC, the RNC, and the four Hill committees. Like most other semi-institutionalized committees, it has a board of directors that approves the PAC's overall strategy but gives its manager discretion in making individual contribution decisions. Managers of these PACs do not have as much flexibility as the managers of one-person committees, but they have more freedom than the managers of institutionalized PACs.

Lead PACs comprise a final group of committees. These PACs, which include the NCEC, COPE, and BIPAC, are as complex organizationally as the institutionalized PACs.[27] They are every bit as thorough in their research and decision making as are the institutionalized committees and are motivated by ideological or policy goals. They differ from other committees in that they carry out research and select candidates for support with an eye toward influencing the decisions of other PACs. Much of the research conducted by lead PACs is oriented toward assessing the electability of individual candidates. Like the Hill committees, these PACs spend much time, money, and energy disseminating information about specific campaigns to other PACs. They occupy central positions in the networks of PACs, lobbyists, and individual contributors in the Washington fund-raising community.

CONTRIBUTIONS

PACs contributed a total of $200.7 million to major-party candidates in the 1996 congressional elections. Corporate PACs accounted for the most PAC contributions, followed by trade groups, labor committees, and nonconnected PACs. Corporations without stock and cooperatives contributed the least, giving less than $6.8 million (see Table 5-2).

Incumbents have laid claim to the lion's share of PAC money since the PAC boom of the 1970s. Since the mid-1980s, business-related PACs have been among the most incumbent-oriented committees, adhering more closely to an access-oriented strategy than labor or ideological PACs. In 1996, corporate

TABLE 5-2

PAC Contributions in the 1996 Congressional Elections (in thousands)

| | House | | Senate | | |
	Democrats	Republicans	Democrats	Republicans	Total
Corporate	$15,427	$35,830	$3,656	$14,638	$69,551
Trade, mem-bership, and health	16,254	27,758	3,504	8,523	56,039
Cooperative	989	1,216	215	329	2,749
Corporations without stock	1,231	1,774	344	663	4,012
Labor	36,848	2,564	6,519	388	46,319
Nonconnected	6,577	8,560	2,368	4,491	21,996
All PACs	$77,326	$77,702	$16,606	$29,032	$200,666

Source: Compiled from Federal Election Commission data.

Note: Figures are for PAC contributions to all major-party candidates, including candidates in primaries, runoffs, and uncontested races.

PACs made 88 percent of their House contributions to incumbents involved in major-party contested races (see Table 5-3), distributing 52 percent of them to shoo-ins. These committees donated little to House challengers, and made a mere 9 percent of their House contributions to open-seat candidates. Corporate PACs made only 45 percent of their House contributions to candidates in competitive races, reflecting their goal of maintaining good relations with current members and their lack of concern with changing the composition of Congress.

Corporate PACs also pursue access-oriented goals when they contribute to Senate candidates; however, the unusually large number of open seats (fourteen of the thirty-four up for election) had a strong impact on the flow of corporate PAC money in 1996. Corporate PACs distributed 53 percent of their Senate contributions to incumbents and 38 percent to open-seat candidates that year (see Table 5-4), whereas in 1994 they had distributed 73 percent and 18 percent to these groups of candidates. The access orientation of corporate PACs is further revealed by their contributing only 10 percent of their 1996 and 8 percent of their 1994 Senate dollars to challengers. Similarly, trade association PACs were generous to House and Senate incumbents, invested few resources in challenger races, and spent considerable sums to help Senate candidates in open-seat contests.

TABLE 5-3

The Allocation of PAC Contributions to House Candidates in the 1996 Elections

	Corporate	Trade, membership, and health	Labor	Non-connected
Democrats				
Incumbents				
In jeopardy	11%	12%	22%	12%
Shoo-ins	16	16	27	11
Challengers				
Hopefuls	1	4	25	13
Likely losers	—	—	6	2
Open-seat candidates				
Prospects	1	3	10	4
Long shots	1	2	3	1
Republicans				
Incumbents				
In jeopardy	25%	24%	3%	24%
Shoo-ins	36	29	4	15
Challengers				
Hopefuls	2	3	—	7
Likely losers	—	1	—	1
Open-seat candidates				
Prospects	5	5	—	8
Long shots	2	2	—	2
Total House contributions ($, thousands)	$46,118	$40,054	$35,781	$3,718

Source: Compiled from Federal Election Commission data.

Notes: Figures are for general election candidates in major-party contested races, excluding a small number of atypical races that were decided in runoffs or won by independents. Dashes = less than 0.5 percent. The categories and numbers of candidates are the same as those in Table 4-2. Some columns do not add to 100 percent because of rounding.

Labor PACs have consistently pursued highly partisan, mixed strategies. In 1996 they contributed virtually all their money to Democrats. Labor contributions to House Democrats favored candidates in competitive races, but labor PACs distributed over one-fourth of their funds to Democratic shoo-ins. Labor committees gave 83 percent of their Senate contributions to Democratic candidates in close races and only 4 percent to Senate shoo-ins. Whereas labor con-

TABLE 5-4

The Allocation of PAC Contributions to Senate Candidates in the 1996
Elections

	Corporate	Trade, membership, and health	Labor	Non-connected
Democrats				
Incumbents				
In jeopardy	6%	8%	19%	11%
Shoo-ins	2	2	4	2
Challengers				
Hopefuls	1	3	15	5
Likely losers	—	—	2	—
Open-seat candidates				
Prospects	9	12	47	13
Long shots	2	3	7	2
Republicans				
Incumbents				
In jeopardy	32%	28%	2%	24%
Shoo-ins	13	10	2	8
Challengers				
Hopefuls	9	7	—	8
Likely losers	—	—	—	—
Open-seat candidates				
Prospects	23	22	1	23
Long shots	4	4	—	3
Total Senate contributions ($, thousands)	$16,547	$10,982	$6,316	$6,292

Source: Compiled from Federal Election Commission data.

Notes: Figures are for general election candidates in major-party contested races. Dashes = less than 0.5 percent. The categories and numbers of candidates are the same as those in Table 4-2. Some columns do not add to 100 percent because of rounding.

tributions in House races appear to have been motivated by both access-oriented and election-oriented goals, labor activity in Senate races focused almost exclusively on influencing electoral outcomes.

Nonconnected PACs follow highly ideological strategies. In 1996 over two-thirds of their House spending went to candidates in close races, as did three-quarters of their spending in Senate elections. These PACs contributed a relatively small portion of their funds to incumbent shoo-ins and a large portion to hopeful challengers and open-seat prospects. As a group, nonconnected PACs treated Republicans somewhat better than Democrats in 1996, allocating 57 percent of their House and 66 percent of their Senate contributions to GOP candidates. This represents a reversal of previous patterns.[28] The Republican takeover of Congress spurred many conservatives into action, resulting in the formation of some new conservative PACs and record fund-raising and spending by others.

CAMPAIGN SERVICES

Although most of the journalistic reporting on PACs has focused on contributions and independent expenditures, some PACs also carry out activities that have traditionally been conducted by political parties.[29] Some PACs (mainly ideological committees), including CWAVE PAC and various PACs on both sides of the abortion rights issue, recruit candidates to run for Congress.[30] Others provide candidates with in-kind contributions of polls, campaign ads, issue research, fund-raising assistance, and strategic advice. AMPAC and COPE, for example, contribute polls to some candidates.[31] Rep. Fred Heineman was among the candidates who received an AMPAC-commissioned poll in 1996. The National Federation of Independent Business's SAFE Trust PAC, whose name stands for Save American Free Enterprise, hosts campaign training schools and produces media advertisements for many of the candidates it supports.[32] CWAVE PAC helps its congressional, state, and local candidates frame environmental issues. The NCEC provides Democratic House and Senate candidates and party committees with precinct-level demographic profiles, targeting assistance, and technical advice.[33] These and other PACs furnish campaign assistance in lieu of cash contributions because they want to influence how candidates' campaigns are run or leave a more enduring impression than one can get from simply handing over a check.

One of the most important forms of assistance that a PAC can give to a candidate, particularly a nonincumbent, is help with fund-raising. Lead PACs, such as BIPAC, COPE, and the NCEC, brief other PACs about the campaigns on their watch lists, using techniques similar to those used by the Hill committees. Even some smaller PACs, such as the Federal Managers Association PAC (representing federal employees) and the AAP PAC (representing publishers), help congressional candidates raise money by cosponsoring fund-raising events or serving on candidates' fund-raising committees.[34] The maturation of the Washington PAC community has led to the development of several networks of PACs, or PAC "families," which assist each other in selecting candidates for support.[35]

EMILY's List, whose name stands for "Early Money Is Like Yeast" and whose motto is "It makes the dough rise," is an example of a PAC that gives candidates fund-raising assistance. This nonconnected committee supports pro-choice Democratic women candidates, helping them raise money in the early, critical stage of the election. EMILY's List requires its members to donate $100 to the PAC and to make minimum contributions of $100 to each of two candidates whom the PAC has designated for support. Members are instructed to write these checks to the candidates and then send them to the PAC, which in turn forwards the checks to the candidates with a letter explaining the PAC's role in collecting the money. Under this procedure, commonly referred to as "bundling," the PAC acts as a clearinghouse for individual campaign contributions. Bundling enables a PAC to direct more money to candidates than it is legally allowed to contribute. Bundling works well with individuals who wish to have a candidate acknowledge both their and the group's political support. In addition to direct contributions of $218,000 in cash and in-kind contributions, EMILY's List bundled roughly $6.2 million to women running in the 1996 congressional elections. It also spent roughly $4 million on a project designed to mobilize women voters.[36]

Organized interests besides PACs also provide candidates with help in congressional elections. Think tanks, such as the Heritage Foundation, provide issue research. Labor unions and church-based organizations in African American and ethnic communities have long histories of political activism and have made decisive contributions to Democratic candidates' field activities. Business leaders have traditionally assisted Republicans. The National Chamber Alliance for Politics (NCAP), a PAC sponsored by the U.S. Chamber of Commerce, distributes watch lists to pro-business PACs, and AIPAC provides information about candidates to PACs that support Israel.[37] Despite the fact that they carry out activities similar to those of lead PACs and the Hill committees, neither NCAP nor AIPAC gives cash contributions to congressional candidates.[38] Environmental groups and the Christian Coalition are relative newcomers to electoral politics, but their voter guides and voter mobilization efforts have played important roles in recent congressional elections.

INDEPENDENT EXPENDITURES AND ISSUE ADVOCACY

Independent expenditures usually take the form of direct communications from a PAC to voters that explicitly call for the election or defeat of one or more candidates. Issue advocacy campaigns waged by interest groups can be intended to harm or help a candidate's prospects, but they cannot expressly advocate a candidate's election or defeat. As noted in the last chapter, independent expenditure efforts must be made with hard money and reported to the FEC, whereas issue advocacy campaigns can be waged with either hard or soft money. Moreover, when issue advocacy campaigns are not coordinated with a federal candidate's campaign committee, they do not have to be reported to the FEC. Because they are not subject to federal laws requiring public disclosure it is impossible to learn precisely how much money interest groups spend on issue advocacy in a given election year, or the source of that money. Issue advocacy occupies a black hole in the campaign finance system.

Nevertheless, most estimates suggest that the amounts spent on issue advocacy and independent expenditures are impressive. The most visible expenditures of both kinds take the form of television, radio, or newspaper advertisements that are directed toward the general public. However, some consist of direct mail, advertisements in trade magazines, or telephone calls made to designated groups of voters.

The vast majority—roughly 90 percent—of the almost $8.8 million in independent expenditures made in the 1996 congressional elections were undertaken by nonconnected and trade PACs. Independent expenditures are consistent with the ideological or mixed strategies that these PACs follow. Moreover, because ideological PACs do not have organizational sponsors, and because trade PACs are established to advance the political views of organizations that frequently have tens of thousands of members, these committees rarely worry about the retribution of an angry member of Congress or the negative publicity that might result from an independent expenditure. Unlike corporate PACs and labor committees, nonconnected and trade PACs are relatively safe from either outcome because they lack a single sponsor whose interests can be directly harmed.

PACs allocated $2.9 million in independent expenditures in the 1996 primaries and general elections to advocate the election of individual House candidates and another $1.6 million calling for their defeat. They spent an additional $3.2 million advocating the election of Senate candidates and $924,000 calling for their defeat.[39] Most independent expenditures are made in connection with close election contests. In 1996, PACs spent just under $3.9 million on House incumbents in jeopardy, hopeful challengers, and open-seat prospects (see Table 5-5). PACs spent a mere $350,000 in uncompetitive House races. Incumbent-challenger contests were the focus of most PAC independent expenditures and, on balance, these favored challengers.

The overall partisan balance of PAC independent expenditures had a Republican tilt. PACs focused a disproportionate amount of their independent expenditures—over 60 percent—on contests featuring first-term House Re-

TABLE 5-5

PAC Independent Expenditures in the 1996 House Elections

	Democrats		Republicans	
	For	Against	For	Against
Incumbents				
In jeopardy	$94,556	$59,529	$1,330,686	$1,239,872
Shoo-ins	64,946	24,855	88,076	331
Challengers				
Hopefuls	354,028	12,231	289,586	31,890
Likely losers	18,721	0	53,246	1
Open-seat candidates				
Prospects	48,501	1,444	391,860	12,278
Long shots	28,414	1,523	66,699	4,034
Total	$609,166	$99,582	$2,220,153	$1,288,406

Source: Compiled from Federal Election Commission data.

Notes: Figures are for general election candidates in major-party contested races, excluding a small number of atypical races that were decided in runoffs or won by independents. The categories and numbers of candidates are the same as those in Table 4-2.

publicans, spending an average of $18,100 in ways designed to help the prospects of GOP freshmen and another $18,900 in ways intended to harm them.[40] The race in Washington State's 9th congressional district featured the heaviest independent spending: PACs spent $194,341 to help Republican freshman representative Randall Tate and $217,730 to defeat him. Tate ultimately lost by 6 percent of the vote. In contrast, another freshman, Rep. Helen Chenoweth, R-Idaho, had a barrage of nearly $205,000 in PAC spending against her and only $8,400 in her favor. Yet, she managed to hold her seat by a two-point margin.

PAC independent expenditures in Senate contests are similar to those for the House in that most of the activity—a total of more than $3,432,000 in 1996— takes place in competitive races (see Table 5-6). Other similarities can be seen in the intention to influence the outcomes of incumbent-challenger races and the overall tilt in favor of Republicans. The record for independent expenditures in a 1996 Senate contest was set in Texas, where PACs spent almost $1.2 million to help Sen. Phil Gramm retain his seat and a mere $1 against him. Much of this spending was motivated by a desire to improve Gramm's standing in the polls after his poor showing in the campaign for the Republican presidential nomination.

TABLE 5-6

PAC Independent Expenditures in the 1996 Senate Elections

| | Democrats | | Republicans | |
	For	Against	For	Against
Incumbents				
In jeopardy	$63,841	$97,835	$1,434,304	$538,253
Shoo-ins	0	0	5,193	6,097
Challengers				
Hopefuls	14,398	4,863	375,599	11,546
Likely losers	0	0	7,661	0
Open-seat candidates				
Prospects	35,399	8,465	883,936	188,488
Long shots	0	0	5,462	0
Total	$113,638	$111,163	$2,712,155	$744,344

Source: Compiled from Federal Election Commission data.

Notes: Figures are for general election candidates in major-party contested races. The categories and numbers of candidates are the same as those in Table 4-2.

The 1996 elections also set new records for issue advocacy campaigns. The most extensive and widely discussed campaign was carried out by the AFL-CIO.[41] Under its new president, John Sweeney, the AFL-CIO took major steps to reassert the influence of the labor movement in electoral politics. Under the guise of Labor '96, the AFL-CIO and affiliated unions spent $35 million to help the Democrats try to retake Congress. The AFL-CIO originally targeted seventy-five House Republicans for defeat. Thirty races were added, including some open-seat contests, at the request of affiliated unions. Candidates in several other districts and states received varying amounts of attention from the unions. The unions carried out a five-part program designed to inject organized labor's issue priorities into the election agenda, organize union voters and their families, and get them to vote.

The first part of Labor '96 consisted of training nearly 175 union members to organize fifty-four targeted congressional districts. An additional 3,200 union activists were trained in issue education sessions and get-out-the-vote (GOTV) activities. Fifty Senate and House challengers and twenty-five of their campaign managers attended an issues seminar to familiarize them with labor's priority issues.

The second part of the program was a grass-roots voter education effort. Labor '96 distributed 11.5 million voter guides that compared the Democratic and Republican candidates' issue stands on labor's priorities in 114 House, 15 Senate, and 2 gubernatorial contests. The guides bore the heading "What's at Stake for Working Families in the 1996 Elections?" and used a side-by-side format to ease comparisons. Union members also distributed leaflets at work sites, organized public events, and made more than 5.5 million telephone calls to educate labor voters.

The most widely publicized aspect of Labor '96 was its media campaign. Labor '96 aired 27,000 television commercials in forty districts, distributed voter video guides in twenty-four, and aired radio ads in several others.[42] These ads focused on labor's core issues, including Republican-proposed cuts in Medicare and Medicaid, education, health insurance portability, and environmental protections. Another part of the media campaign organized press conferences, protests, and other events to attract free media coverage for labor's cause.

The fourth part of Labor '96 involved voter registration and mobilization. The AFL-CIO took advantage of the increased opportunities for voter registration created by the "motor voter" law to register union members and their families.[43] It also distributed $2 million to nonpartisan voter registration groups in targeted districts. In the closing days of the election, more than one hundred labor organizers in forty-eight locations headed GOTV drives.

The last element of Labor '96 consisted of building coalitions with other groups. The AFL-CIO worked with Citizen Action, the Interfaith Alliance, Project '96, the A. Philip Randolph Institute, Rock the Vote, the Women's Vote Project, and dozens of other groups to organize rallies, literature drops, phone banks, and other grass-roots activities.

The AFL-CIO's 1996 campaign demonstrates that labor can be a major force in congressional elections. It is credited with setting the agenda in dozens of House races and several Senate contests. Labor '96 helped increase union voter turnout by 2.32 million from that in 1992 in an election in which 8 million fewer voters nationwide turned up at the polls. Most important, Labor '96 appeared to affect the outcomes of several elections. Forty-five of 105 AFL-CIO targets were defeated, including 11 House freshmen and 15 candidates who were the targets of AFL-CIO television ads or voter guides.

Various elements of the business community responded to the AFL-CIO's campaign. Perhaps none more so than the National Federation of Independent Business (NFIB). In October 1995 it sponsored a seminar in Washington, D.C., to give instruction in running for office, campaign management, grass-roots organizing, and forming coalitions with other small businesses to endorse candidates through local advertisements. In April 1996 the group held satellite conferences in eighteen cities in ten states to train five hundred NFIB members in political action. Over the course of the election cycle, the NFIB mailed 197,051 letters to recruit volunteers to help organize 103 congressional districts. It carried out a telemarketing campaign for the same purpose. The NFIB also mailed nearly 240,000 campaign voter guides urging its members to vote for specific candidates. These guides, like those sent out by the AFL-CIO, were not subject to FEC spending limits and reporting requirements because they were considered internal communications mailed to members rather than posters intended to influence the voting decisions of the general public.[44]

The NFIB's political activities went well beyond the efforts of SAFE Trust PAC and the more than $1.1 million it spent on internal communications and training sessions. Together with the U.S. Chamber of Commerce, the National Association of Manufacturers, the National Restaurant Association, and the National Association of Wholesaler-Distributors, the NFIB created the Coalition—Americans Working for Real Change. The Coalition spent $5 million in thirty-seven House races to counter the AFL-CIO's issue advocacy ads. These funds enabled the group to purchase six thousand television commercials and seven thousand radio ads, and mail two million letters to the groups' members. Both AFL-CIO and the NFIB spent more on issue advocacy campaigns than they did on direct contributions and independent expenditures in 1996.

The efforts by the NFIB and the Coalition demonstrate that organized business, like organized labor, can have a significant influence on congressional elections. Seventy percent of the 275 congressional candidates who received NFIB support won their elections, as did 54 percent of the 113 candidates who were designated for "major involvement." Included among this latter group are 5 Senate and 25 House candidates who had victory margins of six points or less. Sixty-seven percent of the 36 Republican candidates whose districts were targeted for Coalition television ads were also reelected.[45]

Noneconomic groups also carry out issue advocacy campaigns. The Sierra Club and the National Rifle Association are among the many noneconomic groups that spent money outside of the federal campaign finance system to influence the outcomes of congressional elections in 1996. Like the AFL-CIO and NFIB, these groups used voter guides, television and radio ads, and grassroots activities to influence the campaign agenda in many races.[46] The Christian Coalition has a well-established lead over all other groups in the distribution of voter guides. Its efforts helped GOP candidates win many close contests, including several in the South.[47] The Christian Coalition helped the Republicans win control of Congress in 1994 and maintain control two years later. In 1996 alone the group distributed more than 54 million guides using church-based networks throughout the nation.[48]

Some of the groups that carry on issue advocacy campaigns are tax-exempt organizations that are not supposed to engage in partisan political activity. A few appear to be little more than fronts for more partisan organizations, including party committees. These groups collect funds from interest groups, party committees, and the individuals that parties and other groups refer to them. Their tax-exempt status enables the groups' contributors to deduct their donations from their federal taxes and enables the groups to avoid disclosing the sources of their funds to the FEC.[49] The Coalition for Our Children's Future is a tax-exempt group with a declared mission to promote a balanced budget amendment to the Constitution. Yet in the 1996 election it spent an estimated $700,000 in Louisiana and California on highly partisan television ads, radio commercials, direct mail, and telephone banks designed to help Republican candidates.[50] Three weeks before the 1996 election, the group spent an estimated $300,000 on ads denouncing Rep. Cal Dooley, D-Calif., for his positions on such issues as the death penalty and welfare reform, which bear little relation to a balanced budget.

Other tax-exempt groups that appear to have engaged in political activities are Project '96, the union-sponsored coalition that mobilized labor voters; Vote Now '96, which spent $3 million to register individuals who belong to traditionally loyal Democratic groups; Americans for Tax Reform, which mobilized conservative pro-Republican voters; and GOPAC, the Abraham Lincoln Opportunity Foundation, and the Progress and Freedom Foundation, which were used by Speaker Newt Gingrich to recruit Republican candidates and disseminate a pro-GOP message.[51] Tax-exempt groups have become a tool for skirting federal campaign finance laws. They have no political accountability, disseminate primarily negative communications, and have been known to impart misleading information to voters.

THE IMPACT OF INTEREST GROUP ACTIVITY

Congressional candidates and their campaign aides generally evaluate the help they get from PACs and other interest groups less favorably than the assistance they get from party committees.[52] They indicate that PACs and other groups play bigger roles in the campaigns of Democrats than Republicans. Democratic candidates, for example, report receiving significantly more help than their GOP counterparts with mobilizing voters and recruiting volunteers from labor unions and other partisan groups. Senate candidates and campaign aides of both parties find PACs and other groups to be helpful in fund-raising but not as helpful as the DSCC or NRSC. House campaigners, however, appraise the fund-raising assistance of organized interests somewhat more favorably than the help they get from the DCCC or NRCC. The information provided by both House and Senate campaigners indicates that interest group activity tends to be more heavily focused in competitive contests and more important to the election efforts of hopeful challengers and open-seat prospects than incumbents. As the testimonies of candidates who were targeted by the AFL-CIO, the Coalition, the Christian Coalition, and other groups attest, PAC contributions, campaign services, independent expenditures, interest group issue advocacy advertisements, and grass-roots efforts can change the dynamic of an election, sometimes spelling the difference between victory and defeat.

In the absence of legal change, interest group–sponsored issue advocacy advertisements will probably become more important in setting the political agenda and mobilizing voters. Interest group and party spending in these areas will probably not do away with candidate-centered congressional elections, but they may result in election agendas in some races being set by organizations other than candidates' campaign committees. Also, it may become more common for Washington-based interest groups and party committees to outspend the candidates themselves in individual House and Senate races.

CHAPTER 6

Campaigning for Resources

Vice President Hubert Humphrey described fund-raising as a "disgusting, degrading, demeaning experience."[1] This is a sentiment with which few politicians would disagree. Yet, spending money on political campaigns predates the Constitution. In 1757 George Washington purchased twenty-eight gallons of rum, fifty gallons of spiked punch, forty-six gallons of beer, thirty-four gallons of wine, and a couple of gallons of hard cider to help shore up his political base and pry loose the support of enough uncommitted voters to get elected to the Virginia House of Burgesses.[2] Population growth, technological advancements, suburbanization, and the other changes associated with the emergence of a modern mass democracy in the United States have driven up the costs of campaigning since George Washington launched his political career. By the end of the millennium, candidates for Congress and other political offices will have spent billions of dollars to get elected.

As shown in previous chapters, the FECA restructured the campaign finance system by instituting disclosure requirements and regulating campaign contributions and expenditures made in direct connection with federal elections. Most of the FECA's loopholes concern issue advocacy campaigns and other soft money expenditures that are carried out by parties and interest groups. Candidate campaign activities continue to be heavily regulated by the FECA.

Raising the funds needed to run for Congress has evolved into a campaign in and of itself. Part of this campaign takes place in the candidate's state or district, but many candidates are dependent on resources that come from party committees and PACs located in and around Washington, D.C., and from wealthy individuals who typically reside in major metropolitan areas.

The campaign for resources begins earlier than the campaign for votes. It requires a candidate to attract the support of sophisticated, goal-oriented groups and individuals who have strong preconceptions about what it takes to win a congressional election. Theoretically, all congressional candidates can turn to the same sources and use the same techniques to gather campaign funds and services. In fact, however, candidates begin and end on uneven playing fields. The level of success that candidates achieve with different kinds of contributors or fund-raising techniques depends largely on whether they are incumbent, challenger, or open-seat candidates. It also depends on the candidates' party affiliation and on whether they are running for the House or the Senate. In this chapter I analyze the fund-raising strategies and successes of different kinds of candidates.

The 1996 congressional elections broke almost all records for campaign spending. Expenditures in House campaigns soared by 18 percent over record-breaking 1994 levels to reach $477.8 million.[3] Ninety-four House candidates each spent more than $1 million, and nine spent in excess of $3 million. House Speaker Newt Gingrich, whose expenditures reached nearly $5.6 million, spent the most. His unsuccessful opponent, Michael Coles, the millionaire cookie manufacturer, came in second, spending $3.3 million—most of it his own money.[4]

Senate spending fell roughly 10 percent from the heights reached in 1994 to $287.5 million in 1996. Fifty-six of the sixty-eight major-party candidates each spent more than $1 million, including twenty-eight who spent more than $3 million, and nine who spent above $6 million. The two biggest spenders were Democrats Mark Warner of Virginia, who spent $11.6 million of mostly his own money in an unsuccessful campaign against Republican incumbent John Warner, and Sen. John Kerry of Massachusetts, who spent nearly $11 million in an attempt to defeat Gov. William Weld. Still, none of these candidates came close to breaking the record set by former representative Michael Huffington, R-Calif., who spent almost $30 million—nearly $28.4 million of it his own money—in an unsuccessful attempt to win an open seat in the Senate in 1994.

INEQUALITIES IN RESOURCES

Significant inequalities exist in the resources, including money and party coordinated expenditures, that different kinds of candidates are able to raise. The typical House incumbent involved in a two-party contest raised just under $750,000 in cash and party coordinated expenditures in 1996, which is over two and one-half times more than the typical House challenger. Open-seat candidates also gathered significant resources, accruing an average of $690,000 in two-party contests.

FIGURE 6-1

Average Campaign Resources Raised in Competitive House Elections
in 1996

$, thousands

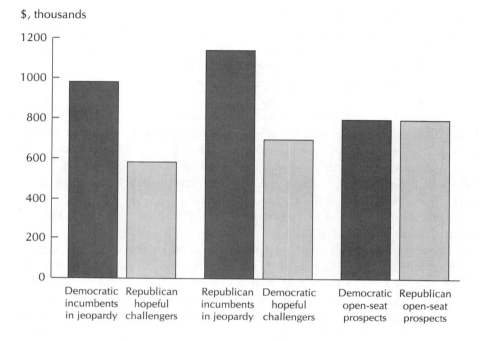

Democratic Republican   Republican Democratic   Democratic Republican
incumbents   hopeful   incumbents   hopeful   open-seat   open-seat
in jeopardy challengers   in jeopardy challengers   prospects   prospects

Source: Compiled from Federal Election Commission data.

Notes: Figures include receipts and party-coordinated expenditures for all two-party contests
that were decided by margins of 20 percent of the vote or less, excluding a small number of
atypical races that were decided in runoffs or won by independents. The categories and numbers
of candidates are the same as in Table 4-2.

The resource discrepancies in competitive House races are great. Incumbents in jeopardy raised over 65 percent more in cash and party coordinated expenditures than did hopeful challengers during the 1996 elections (see Figure 6-1). Perceiving themselves as vulnerable, the incumbents followed the standard practice of gathering enough resources to swamp their opponents. Republican House freshmen in close contests raised especially large sums, averaging $1.2 million, 72 percent more money than their opponents. Competitive open-seat contests were much more equal in regard to the amount raised.

The resource discrepancies in uncompetitive House contests are even greater than those in competitive ones. Incumbents, who begin raising funds early

FIGURE 6-2
Average Campaign Resources Raised in Uncompetitive House Elections
in 1996

$, thousands

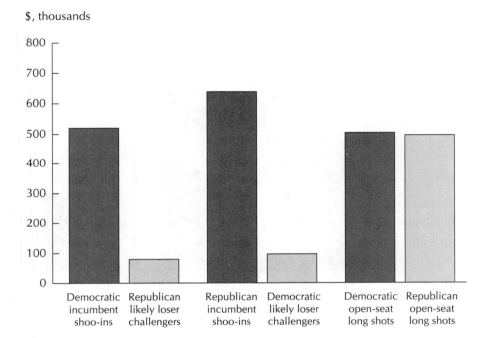

Source: Compiled from Federal Election Commission data.

Notes: Figures include receipts and party-coordinated expenditures for all two-party contests that were decided by margins over 20 percent of the vote, excluding a small number of atypical races that were decided in runoffs or won by independents. The categories and numbers of candidates are the same as in Table 4-2.

(often before they know whom they will face in the general election), raise much more money than their opponents (see Figure 6-2). Incumbent shoo-ins raised over six and one-half times more than likely loser challengers in 1996. The spread among Democratic and Republican open-seat candidates in uncompetitive races is usually much smaller, amounting to less than $8,000 in 1996.

The typical Senate incumbent raised about $1.5 million more than the typical challenger during the 1996 election (see Figure 6-3). Open-seat Senate contests were fairly well funded, with the average contestant spending just over $3.5 million. The differences in the amounts spent by Democratic and Republican candidates were relatively small, favoring GOP contenders by about

FIGURE 6-3

Average Campaign Resources Raised in the 1996 Senate Elections

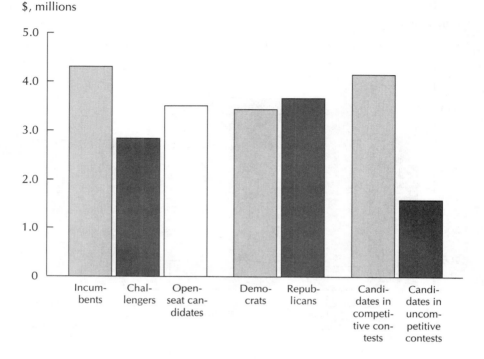

$, millions

Source: Compiled from Federal Election Commission data.

Notes: Figures include receipts and party-coordinated expenditures for all two-party contested races. N = 68.

$230,000. Finally, electoral competitiveness was important in attracting campaign resources. Candidates who defeated their opponents by 20 percent of the two-party vote or less spent 50 percent more than candidates involved in one-sided races.

HOUSE INCUMBENTS

Incumbents raise more money than challengers because they tend to be visible, popular, and willing to exploit the advantages of officeholding. This is reflected both in how incumbents solicit contributions and in whom they turn to for cash. Incumbents rarely hesitate to remind a potential donor that they are in a

position to influence public policy and will more than likely s
position when the next Congress convenes.

Sources of Funds

Individuals who make contributions of less than $200, many of whom reside
in a candidate's state or district, are an important source of funds for House
incumbents (see Figure 6-4). In 1996 they accounted for $138,688, or 18 per-
cent, of the average incumbent's campaign war chest.[5] Symbolically, they are
often viewed as an indicator of grass-roots support.

Individuals who contributed $200 or more accounted for almost $260,000,
or 35 percent, of the typical incumbent's funds. Many make contributions across

FIGURE 6-4
Sources of House Incumbents' Campaign Receipts in the 1996 Elections

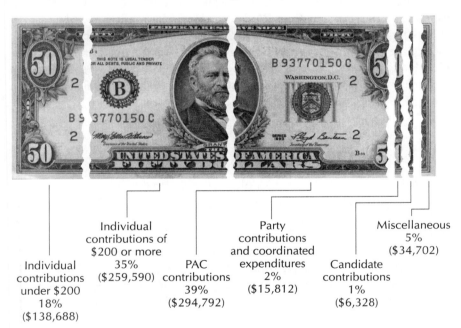

| Individual contributions under $200 18% ($138,688) | Individual contributions of $200 or more 35% ($259,590) | PAC contributions 39% ($294,792) | Party contributions and coordinated expenditures 2% ($15,812) | Candidate contributions 1% ($6,328) | Miscellaneous 5% ($34,702) |

Source: Compiled from Federal Election Commission data.

Notes: The dollar values in parentheses are averages. Candidate contributions include loans
candidates made to their own campaigns. Miscellaneous includes interest from savings accounts
and revenues from investments. Figures are for general election candidates in major-party contested elections, excluding a small number of atypical races that were decided in runoffs or won
by independents. N = 356.

district or state lines. Individuals living in just one town—Great Neck, New York, a wealthy suburb of New York City—donated just under $4.7 million to House and Senate candidates across the United States. These contributions, along with the millions distributed by Washington-based parties and PACs, have helped to form a national market for campaign contributions.[6]

PACs provided nearly $295,000, or 39 percent, of a typical incumbent's bankroll in 1996. Parties delivered much less, accounting for a mere 2 percent of the typical incumbent's total resources. House members contributed even less of their own money to their campaigns. Finally, they raised almost $35,000 from miscellaneous sources, including contributions from other candidates and retired members and interest and revenues from investments.

Prior to the Republican takeover of Congress in 1994, Democratic House members collected a greater portion of their funds from PACs than did Republicans, who relied more heavily on individual contributors.[7] The Democrats' procedural control of the House gave them greater influence over the substance and scheduling of legislation, which provided them with an overwhelming advantage in raising money from PACs. The 1996 elections witnessed considerable change in this regard. Republican incumbents increased substantially the money they raised from PACs, although they continued to rely more on individuals than did their Democratic counterparts (see Table 6-1). Republican freshmen were among the most successful in collecting PAC money, raising on average $87,000 more than other Republican House members.

Fund-Raising Activities

Incumbents routinely complain about the time, effort, and indignities associated with raising funds. Their lack of enthusiasm for asking people for money figures prominently in how they raise campaign contributions. A fear of defeat and a disdain for fund-raising have two principal effects: they encourage incumbents to raise large amounts of money and to place the bulk of their fundraising in the hands of others, mainly professional consultants.

Most incumbents develop permanent fund-raising operations. They hire direct-mail specialists and PAC fund-raising experts to write direct-mail appeals, update contributor lists, identify and solicit potentially supportive PACs, script telephone solicitations, and organize fund-raising events. These operations enable incumbents to limit their involvement to showing up at events and telephoning potential contributors who insist on having a direct conversation with them prior to giving.

Incumbents raise small contributions by making appeals through the mail, over the telephone, or at fund-raising events. Direct mail can be a relatively

TABLE 6-1
Sources of Support for House Incumbents in the 1996 Elections

	Democrats		Republicans	
	In jeopardy	Shoo-ins	In jeopardy	Shoo-ins
Individual contributions under $200	$176,138 (18%)	$64,927 (12%)	$259,608 (23%)	$119,043 (19%)
Individual contributions of $200 or more	$265,587 (27%)	$189,214 (36%)	$419,861 (37%)	$224,374 (35%)
PAC contributions	$447,990 (46%)	$234,114 (45%)	$350,280 (31%)	$261,942 (41)
Party contributions and coordinated expenditures	$29,546 (3%)	$3,964 (1%)	$48,962 (4%)	$1,704 (—)
Candidate contributions	$8,952 (1%)	$2,427 (—)	$20,871 (2%)	$175 (—)
Miscellaneous	$55,119 (6%)	$25,343 (5%)	$42,658 (4%)	$31,129 (5%)
(N)	(44)	(112)	(75)	(125)

Source: Compiled from Federal Election Commission data.

Notes: Figures are averages for general election candidates in major-party contested races, excluding a small number of atypical races that were decided in runoffs or won by independents. Dashes = less than 0.5 percent. Candidate contributions include loans candidates made to their own campaigns. Miscellaneous includes interest from savings accounts and revenues from investments. Some columns do not add to 100 percent because of rounding.

reliable method of fund-raising for an incumbent because solicitations are usually made from lists of previous donors that indicate which appeals garnered earlier contributions.[8] Most direct mail generates contributions of less than $100 and is targeted at the candidate's constituents. However, many prominent House members, including Speaker Gingrich and Minority Leader Richard Gephardt, have huge direct-mail lists that include hundreds of thousands of individuals who reside across the United States and even a few from abroad. A significant portion of these individuals contribute large sums. In 1996 Gingrich raised roughly $1.2 million in individual contributions of $200 or more from outside of Georgia, and Gephardt raised just under $1 million in individual large contributions from outside Missouri.

Traditional fund-raising events are another popular means for raising small contributions. Cocktail parties, barbecues, and picnics with admission costs ranging from $10 to $50 that are held in the candidate's district are useful ways to raise money. They are also helpful in generating favorable press coverage, energizing political activists, and building goodwill among voters.

Incumbents can ensure the success of local fund-raising events by establishing finance committees comprised of business executives, labor officials, civic leaders, and political activists who live in their districts. These committees often begin with a dozen or so supporters who host "low-dollar" receptions (where individuals usually contribute from $20 to $100) in their homes and make telephone solicitations on the candidate's behalf. Guests at one event are encouraged to become the sponsors of others. In time, small finance committees can grow into large pyramid-like fund-raising networks, consisting of dozens of finance committees, each of which makes a substantial contribution to the candidate's reelection efforts. Most House and Senate incumbents have fund-raising networks that extend from their district or state to the nation's capital.

Individual large contributions and PAC money are also raised at fund-raising events and through networks of supporters. Events that feature the president, congressional leaders, sports heroes, or other celebrities help attract individuals and groups who are willing to contribute anywhere from a few hundred to several thousand dollars. Some of these are held in the candidate's state, but most are held in such political, financial, and entertainment centers as Washington, New York City, and Hollywood.

Traditional fund-raising events can satisfy the goals of a variety of contributors. They give individuals who desire proximity to power the opportunity to speak with members of Congress and other political elites. Persons and groups that contribute for ideological reasons get the opportunity to voice their specific issue concerns. Individuals and organizations that are motivated by material gain, such as a tax break or federal funding for a project, often perceive these events as opportunities to build a relationship with members of Congress.[9]

In raising individual large contributions House members have advantages over challengers that extend beyond the prestige and political clout that come with incumbency and an ability to rely on an existing group of supporters. Incumbents also benefit from the fact that many wealthy individuals have motives that are similar to those of party committees and PACs. Moreover, information that parties and PACs mail to their big donors often focuses on

incumbents' campaigns, further leading some wealthy individuals to contribute to incumbents who are in jeopardy rather than to hopeful challengers. More
than one-quarter of all individuals who donated $200 or more to each of four
congressional candidates or $4,000 or more to two candidates in 1990, for
instance, gave all their contributions to incumbents. Another 45 percent of
these individuals gave between 67 percent and 99 percent of their funds to
incumbents.[10] The rise of Washington-based cue-givers and the FECA's ceilings
on campaign contributions have led to the replacement of one type of fat cat
with another. Individuals and groups that directly gave candidates tens or hundreds of thousands of dollars have been replaced by new sets of elites that help
candidates raise these sums rather than directly contribute them.[11]

Incumbents consciously use the influence that comes with holding office to
raise money from PACs and wealthy individuals who seek political access. Legislators' campaigns first identify potential donors who are most likely to respond favorably to their solicitations. These include PACs that supported the
incumbent in a previous race, lobbyists who agree with an incumbent's positions on specific issues, and others who are affected by legislation that the incumbent is in a position to influence.

Members of Congress who hold party leadership positions, serve on powerful committees, or are recognized entrepreneurs in certain policy areas can easily
raise large amounts of money from many wealthy interest group constituencies.
It is no coincidence that the five House incumbents who raised more than $1
million in PAC contributions in 1996 all held leadership positions.[12] Rep. Bill
McCollum, R-Fla., raised most of his PAC money from a fairly narrow constituency. McCollum capitalized on his vice chairmanship of the Financial Institutions and Consumer Credit Subcommittee of the House Banking and
Financial Services Committee to collect almost $232,000 (53 percent of his total
PAC dollars) from finance, insurance, and real estate PACs.[13] He raised another
$79,400 in contributions of $200 or more from individuals who work in these
economic sectors (20 percent of his total individual large contributions).[14]

Once an incumbent has identified his or her interest group constituency, the
next step is to ask for a contribution. The most effective solicitations describe the
member's background, legislative goals, accomplishments, sources of influence
(including committee assignments, chairmanships, or party leadership positions),
the nature of the competition they face, and the amount of money they need.
Incumbents frequently assemble this information in PAC kits they mail to PACs.

Some PACs require a candidate to meet with one of their representatives,
who personally delivers a check. A few require incumbents to complete questionnaires on specific issues, but most PACs rely on members' prior roll-call
votes or interest group ratings as measures of their policy proclivities. Some

PACs, particularly ideological committees, want evidence that a representative or senator is facing serious opposition before giving a contribution. Party leaders and Hill committee staff are sometimes called to bear witness to the competitiveness of an incumbent's race.

Parties are another source of money and campaign services. The most important thing incumbents can do to win party support is demonstrate that they are vulnerable. The Hill committees have most of the information they need to make such a determination, but incumbents can give details on the nature of the threat they face that might not be apparent to a party operative who is unfamiliar with the nuances of a member's seat. The NRCC gives incumbents who request extra party support the opportunity to make their case before a special Incumbent Review Board composed of NRCC House members. Once a Hill committee has made an incumbent a priority, it will go to great efforts to supply the candidate with money, campaign services, and assistance in collecting resources from others.

The financing of Rep. Connie Morella's 1996 reelection effort in Maryland's 8th congressional district is typical of that of most safe incumbents. The Morella campaign raised nearly $10,000 (23 percent of its total receipts) in small contributions using campaign newsletters, direct-mail solicitations, and many low-dollar fund-raising events held in the district. It collected another $83,365 (roughly 20 percent of its receipts) in individual contributions of $200 or more at high-dollar events. Just over one-quarter of these funds was raised from individuals who reside outside of Maryland.

The Morella campaign raised approximately $198,000 (48 percent of its money) from PACs.[15] About 74 percent of this money was contributed by corporate, trade, and other business-related committees.[16] About $36,000, or 18 percent, was raised from labor PACs, which constitutes a very large amount for a Republican and reflects her support among the 8th district's unionized federal workforce. She collected another 7 percent from nonconnected committees. Her PAC money was raised at events held in the district or nearby Washington and through solicitations coordinated by the candidate's campaign staff. Morella had little difficulty raising money from these groups because as the chair of the Technology Subcommittee of the House Science Committee, she plays a major role in authorizing federal projects. Finally, the campaign accepted no money from party committees. According to her campaign manager, Morella chose not to request party funds in order to underscore her political independence and because she felt the money would be better spent on Republicans involved in competitive races. Like most congressional incumbents, Morella contributed none of her own money to her reelection effort.

With only two-year terms, House incumbents usually begin raising money almost immediately after they are sworn into office. Sometimes they have debts to retire, but often they use money left over from previous campaigns as seed money for the next election. One-third of all House incumbents began the 1996 election cycle with more than $100,000 left over from their previous campaigns. More than 42 percent of those who were successful completed their 1996 campaigns with more than $100,000 in the bank. Much of this money will be used as seed money to jump-start fund-raising for later election bids.

Early fund-raising is carried out for strategic reasons. Incumbents build substantial war chests early in the election cycle to try to deter potential challengers.[17] An incumbent who had to spend several hundreds of thousands or even millions of dollars to win by a narrow margin in the last election will have a greater compulsion to raise money early than someone whose previous election was a landslide victory. Once they have raised enough money to reach an initial comfort level, however, incumbents appear to be driven largely by the threat posed by an actual challenger.[18] Incumbents under duress seek to amass huge sums of money regardless of the source, while those who face weak opponents may weigh other considerations, such as developing a "diversified portfolio of contributors."[19]

A typical incumbent's campaign—one waged by a candidate who faces stiff competition in neither the primary nor the general election—will generally engage in heavy fund-raising early and then allow this activity to taper off as it becomes clear that the candidate is not in jeopardy. The 1996 Morella campaign exemplifies this pattern. Morella raised $413,371 during the 1996 election, substantially less than the typical House incumbent. Between January 1 and December 31, 1995, her campaign raised $142,326 (34 percent of its total funds). All this money was raised before Don Mooers, Morella's general election opponent, had filed for candidacy with the state of Maryland. During the year that followed, the Morella campaign continued to raise money at a leisurely pace. Between January 1 and June 30 of 1996, it raised $100,042, (24 percent of its funds). In the next three months, it raised another $82,684 (20 percent). During this same three months, the Mooers campaign raised nearly $93,000. The Morella team barely responded to Mooers's fund-raising success. It raised another $87,769 (21 percent) between October 1 and election day, which is considerably less than it had collected before Mooers declared his candidacy.[20] According to Morella's campaign manager, the campaign never felt pressured to raise a great deal of money, particularly when it became apparent that Mooers's candidacy did not pose a serious challenge.[21]

Morella's 1996 campaign finances demonstrate that a good deal of incumbent fund-raising is challenger-driven. Early money is raised to deter a strong opponent from entering the race. If a strong challenger materializes, then an incumbent's fund-raising activities will usually increase. If none emerges, they will remain steady or slow down.

The 1996 Fazio campaign also supports the generalization that incumbent fund-raising is heavily influenced by the nature of the threat a challenger poses. The campaign collected a total of $2,412,373, making it the seventh most expensive House campaign waged that year. It raised $1,347,660 (56 percent of its total receipts) from PACs and another $825,412 (34 percent) in individual contributions of $200 or more, of which one-third was collected from individuals residing outside of California. The campaign collected $189,098 (8 percent) in individual contributions of less than $200. The Democratic Party provided $30,050 in contributions and coordinated expenditures. Democratic members of Congress contributed $48,928, retirees donated $4,500, and leadership PACs gave another $4,700.

Fazio began to solicit contributions early and aggressively because he recognized that his marginal seat and four-point victory in 1994 made him appear vulnerable in 1996. Between January 1 and June 30, 1995, Fazio's campaign amassed a treasury of more than $289,392 (roughly 12 percent of its total funds). Between July 1 and December 31 of that same year, it collected another $372,540 (15 percent of its funds). All this money was raised despite the fact that Fazio faced only weak opposition in the Democratic primary and a Republican had yet to officially step forward to challenge him.[22]

Following Republican Tim Lefever's declaration of candidacy, Fazio knew he would be in a tough race. Lefever was the candidate who had barely lost to him in 1994, and the votes siphoned off by the Libertarian candidate Ross Crain would have been sufficient to have given Lefever a victory. Lefever's declaration encouraged the Fazio campaign to keep up the pace of its fund-raising. By March 31, 1996, the campaign had raised an additional $335,865 (14 percent of its receipts). Lefever's $388,000 in receipts encouraged the Fazio campaign to press its fund-raising efforts further. Between April 1 and October 15 Fazio collected another $1.06 million (about 44 percent of his funds). The campaign raised $337,938 (14 percent) between October 16 and November 23 and collected just over $19,000 by the end of the year to help close out its debts.

The Fazio campaign's fund-raising was driven by the threat the candidate had anticipated and the one that eventually arose. Just as a lack of competition enabled Morella to raise less money than the typical incumbent, stiff competition encouraged Fazio to set a personal fund-raising record.

HOUSE CHALLENGERS

Challengers have the greatest need for money, but they encounter the most difficulties in raising it. The same factors that make it difficult for challengers to win votes also harm their ability to collect campaign contributions. A lack of name recognition, limited campaign experience, a relatively untested organization, and a high probability of defeat discourage most contributors, especially those who give large amounts in pursuit of access, from supporting challengers. The fact that their opponents are established Washington operators who possess political clout does not make challengers' quests for support any easier.

Sources of Funds

Challengers raise less money than incumbents, and their mix of funding sources differs from that of incumbents. House challengers raise a greater portion of their funds from individuals. Challengers competing in the 1996 elections raised an average of $61,784, or 22 percent of their campaign budgets, in individual contributions of less than $200 (see Figure 6-5). Challengers collected nearly the same portion of their funds as incumbents in the form of individual large contributions ($200 or more), but the average $88,712 that they raised was only one-third the amount raised by a typical incumbent. Challengers garnered 19 percent of their money from PACs, trailing incumbents by a ratio of 1:5.5 in PAC dollars. Party money, in contrast, played a greater role in challenger than in incumbent campaigns. Challengers, on average, received $5,000 more in party contributions and coordinated expenditures than did incumbents. Finally, challengers dug far deeper into their own pockets than did incumbents. The typical challenger contributed or loaned the campaign a little more than $44,000, which is about seven times the amount contributed or loaned by the typical incumbent.

Democratic challengers, especially Democratic hopefuls, raised more money from PACs than did their Republican counterparts (see Table 6-2). Republican challengers collected more money from individuals who made large contributions. Republican hopefuls received more party support than did Democrats. Democrats, however, invested substantially more in their own campaigns, reflecting the greater career orientation that many Democratic politicians have toward politics.

Fund-Raising Activities

Most competitive challengers start raising early money at home. They begin by donating or loaning their campaigns the initial funds that are needed to solicit contributions from others. They then turn to relatives, friends, professional colleagues, local political activists, and virtually every individual whose name is in their Rolodex or on their holiday card list. Some of these people are asked to

FIGURE 6-5

Sources of House Challengers' Campaign Receipts in the 1996 Elections

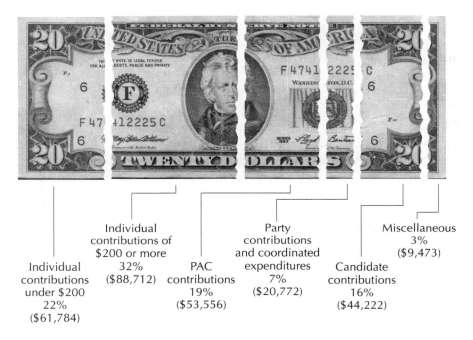

| Individual contributions under $200 22% ($61,784) | Individual contributions of $200 or more 32% ($88,712) | PAC contributions 19% ($53,556) | Party contributions and coordinated expenditures 7% ($20,772) | Candidate contributions 16% ($44,222) | Miscellaneous 3% ($9,473) |

Source: Compiled from Federal Election Commission data.

Notes: The dollar values in parentheses are averages. Candidate contributions include loans candidates made to their own campaigns. Miscellaneous includes interest from savings accounts and revenues from investments. Figures are for general election candidates in major-party contested elections, excluding a small number of atypical races that were decided in runoffs or won by independents. Percentages do not add to 100 percent because of rounding. N = 356.

chair fund-raising committees and host fund-raising events. Candidates who have previously run for office are able to turn to past contributors for support. Competitive challengers frequently obtain lists of contributors from members of their party who have previously run for office or from private vendors. In some cases, challengers receive lists from party committees or PACs; however, most of these organizations mail fund-raising letters on behalf of selected candidates rather than physically turn over their contributor lists. In 1996 House challenger Don Mooers received donor lists from several local Democratic politicians who were not up for reelection.[23]

Only after enjoying some local fund-raising success do most nonincumbents set their sights on Washington. Seed money raised from individuals is espe-

TABLE 6-2

Sources of Support for House Challengers in the 1996 Elections

	Democrats		Republicans	
	Hopefuls	Likely losers	Hopefuls	Likely losers
Individual contributions under $200	$148,979 (21%)	$21,817 (23%)	$126,565 (22%)	$22,553 (28%)
Individual contributions of $200 or more	$197,912 (28%)	$24,911 (26%)	$226,027 (39%)	$32,847 (40%)
PAC contributions	$170,761 (24%)	$19,514 (20%)	$71,917 (12%)	$5,849 (7%)
Party contributions and coordinated expenditures	$42,583 (6%)	$8,281 (19%)	$58,680 (10%)	$5,214 (7%)
Candidate contributions	$117,023 (17%)	$17,527 (18%)	$82,106 (14%)	$10,384 (13%)
Miscellaneous	$20,446 (9%)	$4,831 (5%)	$20,469 (3%)	$2,985 (4%)
(N)	(75)	(125)	(44)	(112)

Source: Compiled from Federal Election Commission data.

Notes: Figures are averages for general election candidates in major-party contested races, excluding a small number of atypical races that were decided in runoffs or won by independents. Candidate contributions include loans candidates made to their own campaigns. Miscellaneous includes interest from savings accounts and revenues from investments. Some columns do not add to 100 percent because of rounding.

cially helpful in attracting funds from PACs, particularly for candidates who have not previously held elective office.[24] The endorsements of local business, labor, party, or civic leaders have a similar effect. If it can be obtained, the assistance of congressional leaders or members of a candidate's state delegation can be very helpful to challengers who hope to raise money from their party's congressional campaign committee, PACs, or individual large contributors.[25]

When powerful incumbents organize luncheons, attend "meet-and-greets," and appear at fund-raising events for nonincumbents, contributors usually respond favorably. Unfortunately for most challengers, their long odds of success make it difficult for them to enlist the help of incumbents. House members prefer to focus their efforts on candidates who have strong electoral prospects and may someday be in a position to return the favor by supporting the member's leadership aspirations or legislative goals in Congress.

A knowledge of how party leaders and PAC managers make contribution decisions can improve challengers' fund-raising prospects. Political experience and a professional campaign staff are often helpful in this regard.[26] Candidates who put together feasible campaign plans, hire reputable consultants, and can present polling figures indicating that they enjoy a reasonable level of name recognition can usually attract the attention of party officials, PAC managers, individuals who make large contributions, and the inside-the-beltway journalists who handicap elections. Political amateurs who wage largely volunteer efforts, in contrast, usually cannot.

During the 1996 congressional elections, House challengers who had previously held elective office raised, on average, $35,300 from party committees and $10,700 in party-connected money from other candidates, retired members of Congress, and leadership PACs. Unelected politicians raised an average of $24,000 from party committees and $7,800 in party-connected dollars, whereas political amateurs raised an average of only $15,200 and $3,500 from these sources. Experienced challengers also typically receive more election services from their party's congressional campaign committee.[27] Challengers who rely on paid staffers or consultants to manage and carry out their campaigns typically receive more party support than those who wage less professional bids for office.[28] Tim Lefever, who had a great deal of political experience and ran a professional campaign, received close to the legal maximum in party support—more than $66,500 in NRCC and RNC contributions and coordinated expenditures and $950 in support from the Republican Central Committee of Colusa County. Donald Mooers, who ran a largely volunteer effort, by contrast, received $22,535 in contributions and coordinated expenditures from the DCCC and another $2,000 from the Montgomery County Central Democratic Committee.

One way in which challengers can increase their chances of success in raising money from PACs is for them to identify the few committees that are likely to give them support. For Democrats, this includes labor groups. Challengers can improve their prospects of attracting labor PAC money by showing they have strong ties to the labor community, have previously supported labor issues in the state legislature, or support labor's current goals.[29] Competitive Democratic challengers who were able to make this case in 1996 did quite well with the labor community, raising an average of $120,000 from labor PACs.

Challengers of both parties may be able to attract support from PACs, particularly ideological committees, by convincing PAC managers that they are committed to the group's cause. A history of personal support in behalf of that cause is useful. Challengers, and in fact most nonincumbents, typically demonstrate this support by pointing to roll-call votes they cast in the state legislature, to the backing of PAC donors or affiliated PACs located in their state or district, or to the support of Washington-based organizations that share some of the PAC's views. Nonincumbents who make a PAC's issues among the central elements of their campaign message and communicate this information in their PAC kits enhance their odds of winning a committee's backing. Properly completing a PAC's questionnaire or having a successful interview with a PAC manager is extremely important. Political experience and professional expertise can help a nonincumbent accomplish these objectives. In 1996, challengers who had previously held office raised an average of $123,100 in PAC money, roughly $64,300 more than the typical unelected politician and $92,600 more than the typical amateur. Challengers who field professional campaign organizations also raise substantially more than those who rely mostly on volunteers.[30]

Ideological causes were in the forefront of many candidates' PAC fund-raising strategies during the last few decades. Women challengers were able to capitalize on their gender and attract large amounts of money and campaign assistance from EMILY's List, the WISH List (the Republican counterpart of EMILY's List), and other pro-women's groups.[31] Challengers who take a stand on either side of the abortion issue are frequently able to raise money from PACs that share their positions. By taking a side on such emotionally laden issues as handgun control or support for Israel some challengers are able to attract the support of ideological PACs.

A perception of competitiveness is critical to challenger fund-raising, and a scandal involving an incumbent can help a challenger become competitive. The 1992 election cycle was the last to include a large number of legislators implicated in some form of scandal. Clearly not every incumbent who was reported to have bounced a check at the House bank had to worry about being accused of committing a major ethical transgression, but any House member who wrote twenty-five or more bad checks or was the subject of some other highly publicized investigation probably had good reason to show concern. These incumbents typically drew strong opponents who raised an average of $33,000 more than challengers who did not run against an incumbent implicated in a scandal, including nearly $5,000 more from parties and almost $10,000 more from PACs.

The experiences of Don Mooers and Tim Lefever demonstrate the effect that perceptions of competitiveness have on challenger fund-raising. Almost from the beginning, Mooers's campaign to unseat Connie Morella was in trouble. Mooers had announced that he intended to run an aggressive, well-financed campaign, but his fund-raising records told a different story. Mooers began collecting money about eleven months after Morella, which is typical in most incumbent-challenger races. Between December 1, 1995, and June 30, 1996, the Mooers campaign raised about $55,535 (28 percent of its total funds), including a few thousand dollars that came out of the candidate's pocket. The campaign then had a significant burst of fund-raising activity, collecting $92,773 (46 percent of its funds) between July 1 and September 30. As election day came closer, however, the political reality of Morella's hold over the 8th district came into focus, and the stream of contributions Mooers had enjoyed earlier slowed to a trickle, with the candidate raising only $46,852 (22 percent of his money) between October 1 and November 25. Between November 26 and December 31 Mooers raised another $8,435 (4 percent of his funds) for debt retirement.

Mooers's fund-raising troubles typify those of most House challengers, including virtually all those who lose by large margins. The candidate got a late start fund-raising, disliked asking people for money, and had no professional fund-raising operation to solicit contributions for him. As such, the campaign had trouble raising PAC money (he collected only $20,187 from PACs, most of which came from labor committees) and putting the squeeze on individual donors, many of whom had already contributed to other candidates. These problems were compounded by the 8th district's proximity to Washington. Many of the district's federal employees, and others who do business with the government, were solicited for contributions by members of Congress who had political clout over individuals who depend on the government for their livelihood. This left the well close to dry for Mooers and other Washington-area candidates who were challenging safe incumbents. These same challengers also had slim prospects of attracting funds from outside the area. Mooers raised only $18,600 in out-of-state contributions, most of which came from the District of Columbia and Virginia.[32]

As a result of his previous bid for Congress, Tim Lefever had established fund-raising networks at home and in Washington, and he raised significant funds using both. His campaign fund-raising exemplifies that of most hopeful challengers in that money was solicited from a broad array of individuals and groups by a variety of techniques. Experience, a professional organization, and a good strategy enabled Lefever to raise a total of $663,127 in his 1996 congressional race against Vic Fazio, including almost $109,000 from PACs and $13,700 in individual contributions from outside of California.

The Lefever campaign, unlike the Mooers organization, began collecting money for the 1996 contest soon after the 1994 election. The campaign's initial solicitations were successful. It raised $129,135 (roughly 19 percent of its funds) between June 28 and December 31, 1995, and it collected an additional $67,626 (10 percent of its receipts) in January, February, and March, 1996. The campaign's fund-raising picked up dramatically between April 30 and September 30, during which it collected another $328,932 (50 percent of its funds). An additional $131,532 (20 percent of its total money) was raised in the remaining three weeks before election day. Following his defeat, Lefever raised $6,604 (1 percent of its resources) to help retire his campaign debts.

The growing competitiveness of the race helped Lefever attract the support of party committees, PACs, and individuals who were captivated by the opportunity to defeat a Democratic House leader. Unfortunately for Lefever, Fazio's supporters also responded to the competitiveness of the race, enabling the incumbent to raise $3.64 for every $1.00 the challenger collected. The dynamics of the race were similar to those in many close incumbent-challenger contests: a hopeful challenger was able to raise enough funds to run a competitive campaign, but the incumbent was able to collect many times more money and win.

CANDIDATES FOR OPEN HOUSE SEATS

Candidates for open seats possess few of the fund-raising advantages of incumbents but also lack the liabilities of challengers. Open-seat candidates rely on many of the same fund-raising strategies as challengers but usually have considerably more success. Because most open-seat contests are competitive, they receive a great deal of attention from parties, PACs, and other informed contributors. This places open-seat candidates in a position to convince Washington insiders that their campaigns are worthy of support.

Sources of Funds

The campaign receipts of open-seat candidates resemble those of both incumbents and challengers. Open-seat candidates raise about the same amount of money as incumbents. Like challengers, however, they usually collect more of their resources from parties, about 7 percent in 1996 (see Figure 6-6). The typical open-seat candidate's PAC receipts lie between those collected by incumbents and challengers. One of the major differences in funding between the three types of campaigns is that open-seat candidates depend more on their own money.

FIGURE 6-6
Sources of House Open-Seat Candidates' Campaign Receipts in the 1996
Elections

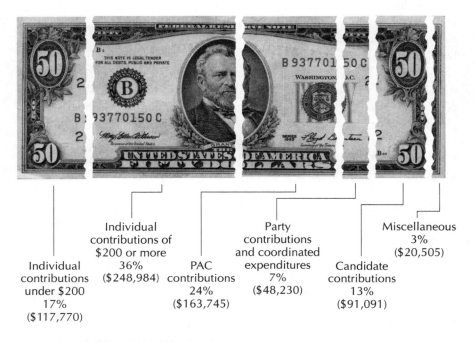

	Individual contributions of $200 or more		Party contributions		Miscellaneous 3%
	36%		and coordinated		($20,505)
Individual	($248,984)	PAC	expenditures	Candidate	
contributions		contributions	7%	contributions	
under $200		24%	($48,230)	13%	
17%		($163,745)		($91,091)	
($117,770)					

Source: Compiled from Federal Election Commission data.

Notes: The dollar values in parentheses are averages. Candidate contributions include loans candidates made to their own campaigns. Miscellaneous includes interest from savings accounts and revenues from investments. Figures are for general election candidates in major-party contested elections, excluding a small number of atypical races that were decided in runoffs or won by independents. N = 100.

Republican open-seat candidates collected more PAC money in 1996 than they had in elections held before the Republican takeover of Congress. Republican candidates relied more on party support and large individual contributions than did their Democratic counterparts (see Table 6-3). Democrats, in contrast, bankrolled larger portions of their own campaigns than did Republicans.

Fund-Raising Activities

Open-seat candidates can help their cause by informing potential contributors of the experience and organizational assets they bring to the race, but these

TABLE 6-3

Sources of Support for House Open-Seat Candidates in the 1996 Elections

	Democrats		Republicans	
	Prospects	Long shots	Prospects	Long shots
Individual contributions under $200	$117,479 (15%)	$72,484 (14%)	$166,409 (21%)	$77,107 (16%)
Individual contributions of $200 or more	$237,110 (34%)	$167,063 (33%)	$299,348 (38%)	$198,479 (40%)
PAC contributions	$194,919 (24%)	$138,019 (27%)	$172,303 (22%)	$118,839 (24%)
Party contributions and coordinated expenditures	$49,670 (6%)	$16,515 (3%)	$72,130 (9%)	$34,893 (7%)
Candidate contributions	$139,877 (18%)	$101,879 (20%)	$62,977 (8%)	$43,554 (9%)
Miscellaneous	$23,101 (3%)	$8,252 (2%)	$23,186 (3%)	$23,378 (5%)
(N)	(32)	(18)	(32)	(18)

Source: Compiled from Federal Election Commission data.

Notes: Figures are averages for general election candidates in major-party contested races, excluding a small number of atypical races that were decided in runoffs or won by independents. Candidate contributions include loans candidates made to their own campaigns. Miscellaneous includes interest from savings accounts and revenues from investments. Some columns do not add to 100 percent because of rounding.

factors have less effect than others, such as the partisan makeup of the district, on the fund-raising abilities of open-seat candidates. Unelected politicians raised the most party money in 1996, averaging almost $52,800, about $2,200 more than the typical elected official and approximately $11,100 more than the typical amateur. Elected politicians, however, raised the most party-connected money, averaging $18,500, roughly $1,100 more than the typical unelected official and $4,000 more than the typical amateur. Mounting a professional campaign

also helps open-seat candidates to attract more party support.[33] Open-seat contestants who have political experience and have assembled professional campaign organizations are better able to meet the campaign objectives that Hill
committee staffers set. As a result, they are among the top recipients of party
money, campaign services, and fund-raising assistance. Getting the endorsement of their state's congressional delegation and other incumbents can also
help an open-seat contestant attract party funds.

Winning support from PACs can be a little more challenging. Although
open-seat candidates use the same techniques as challengers to identify interest
group constituencies and to campaign for PAC support, they usually have greater
success. Because their odds of victory are better, open-seat candidates have an
easier time gaining an audience with PAC managers and are able to raise more
PAC money. Similarly, open-seat candidates point to the same kinds of information as do challengers to make the case that their campaigns will be competitive. Experienced open-seat contestants collect more PAC money than amateurs.
In 1996, open-seat candidates who had previously held elective office, raised,
on average, almost $206,600, nearly $45,600 more than the typical unelected
politician and $104,000 more than the typical amateur. Open-seat candidates
who wage professional campaigns also collect substantially more PAC money
than those who wage largely volunteer efforts.[34]

The fund-raising experiences of Democrat Jay Hoffman and Republican John
Shimkus who ran in Illinois's 20th district exemplify those of open-seat candidates in competitive races. Both candidates had contested primaries and both
built up considerable war chests. Hoffman raised about $815,300. He col-
lected roughly $365,100 (45 percent of his money) from PACs, using his posi-
tion as a state representative to leverage significant PAC dollars. Labor committees
gave Hoffman $225,300. Trade association PACs and corporate committees
furnished him with an additional $77,530 and $16,000, respectively. Liberal
ideological committees gave Hoffman an additional $42,858.

Shimkus had not served in the state legislature, but his position as county
treasurer, an earlier competitive bid for Congress, and the Republicans' control
of the House made him an appealing candidate to many contributors. He raised
approximately $653,500, collecting $225,000 (34 percent of his money) from
PACs. Shimkus received $168,950 from corporate and trade committees and
$48,819 from conservative PACs that agreed with his pro-business views and
wanted to help the Republicans keep control of the House. Shimkus collected
nothing from organized labor, which is typical for a Republican nonincumbent.

Both candidates raised significant sums through the mail and at low-dollar
receptions. Hoffman collected about $113,700 and Shimkus about $200,200

in contributions of less than $200. These figures accounted for 14 and 31 percent of the respective candidates' campaign funds. Hoffman raised almost $242,100 (about 30 percent of his funds) in individual contributions of $200 or more, including $21,700 from contributors who were not residents of Illinois. Shimkus raised nearly $172,900 (26 percent of his money) in individual large contributions, of which approximately $28,600 came from out of state.

Shimkus, however, received more party support than Hoffman. The Republican collected $20,000 in party contributions and nearly $59,000 in coordinated expenditures, whereas his Democratic opponent got only $7,650 in contributions and slightly more than $5,400 in coordinated expenditures. Shimkus raised an additional $15,000 from Republican members of Congress and $27,356 from GOP-sponsored leadership PACs. Hoffman collected only $11,500 from Democratic members and $5,500 from leadership PACs. Because both candidates were able to collect the money needed to wage a competitive campaign from others, neither invested large amounts of their own money. Shimkus committed $2,752 in personal funds to the race and Hoffman spent $200.

The fact that Illinois's 20th congressional district had been occupied by only one incumbent for fourteen years injected a degree of uncertainty into its future once the seat became open. The district drew a great deal of attention from prospective candidates, party committees, PACs, and other contributors. This enabled both Hoffman and Shimkus to raise large amounts of money quickly. Between July 1 and December 31 of 1995, Hoffman collected $112,317 and Shimkus raised $74,030. These sums represented approximately 14 percent of each of the candidates' receipts. Between January 1 and March 31, the period which includes Illinois's March 19 primary, the Democrat raised another $112,114 and the Republican amassed another $98,507, which accounted again for approximately 14 percent of each candidate's total funds.

After their primary victories, the candidates' fund-raising soared, as contributors began to focus their attention on the two nominees. Between April 1 and June 30, Hoffman raised $143,057 (18 percent of his total funds) and Shimkus collected $85,569 (13 percent of his funds). In the three months that followed, the closeness of the election encouraged more money to flow into the district; Hoffman raised an additional $205,868 and Shimkus collected $161,573 (representing 25 percent of each candidate's funds). From October 1 to election day, Hoffman raised another $241,065 (30 percent of his funds) and Shimkus another $227,154 (35 percent of his funds). The candidates' late fund-raising spurts reflected the uncertainty surrounding their race and is common in competitive open-seat contests.

SENATE CAMPAIGNS

The differences in the campaigns that Senate and House candidates wage for resources reflect the broader differences that exist between House and Senate elections. Candidates for the Senate need more money and start requesting support earlier. They often meet with party officials, PAC managers, wealthy individuals, and other sources of money or fund-raising assistance three years before they plan to run. Most Senate candidates also attempt to raise money on a more national scale than do House contestants. The monumental size of the task requires Senate candidates to rely more on others for fund-raising assistance. Nonincumbent Senate candidates are more likely than their House counterparts to hire professional consultants to manage their direct-mail and event-based individual and PAC solicitation programs.

Senate candidates raised on average almost $1.4 million in individual large contributions in 1996, which accounted for 39 percent of their campaign resources (see Figure 6-7). Individual small contributions and donations from PACs each accounted for another 36 percent, and party contributions and co-ordinated expenditures accounted for 8 percent. The candidates themselves provided roughly 12 percent of the money spent directly in Senate campaigns. Compared with candidates for the House, candidates for the upper chamber rely more heavily on individuals and party committees and less on PACs to build up their war chests.

Party affiliation affects fund-raising for the upper chamber of Congress less than it does for the lower chamber. Republican Senate candidates raised more PAC money in the 1996 elections than did the Democrats (see Table 6-4). This reversal of the patterns exhibited in previous elections was caused by the GOP's winning the majority in 1994. Republicans also rely more heavily on their party for campaign resources. Democrats are willing to spend more personal assets than are their GOP opponents.

The differences between incumbent, challenger, and open-seat candidates are significant, especially in regard to the total dollars the candidates raise. Senate incumbents rely more on PAC money than do challengers and open-seat contestants, but the differences are smaller than those for the House. Senate incumbents depend less on personal funds than do Senate challengers. Open-seat contestants collect fewer of their resources in individual contributions of under $200. Senate challengers are more likely than their House counterparts to win the backing of PACs because their races are generally more competitive. The fact that many of them are current officeholders also helps Senate challengers leverage money from PACs and wealthy individuals whose contributions are motivated by political access. The greater visibility and competitiveness

FIGURE 6-7
Sources of Senate Candidates' Campaign Receipts in the 1996 Elections

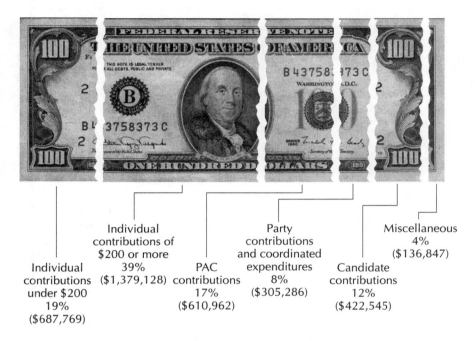

	Individual contributions of $200 or more 39% ($1,379,128)		Party contributions and coordinated expenditures 8% ($305,286)	Miscellaneous 4% ($136,847)
Individual contributions under $200 19% ($687,769)		PAC contributions 17% ($610,962)		Candidate contributions 12% ($422,545)

Source: Compiled from Federal Election Commission data.

Notes: The dollar values in parentheses are averages. Candidate contributions include loans candidates made to their own campaigns. Miscellaneous includes interest from savings accounts and revenues from investments. Figures are for general election candidates in major-party contested elections. Percentages do not add to 100 percent because of rounding. N = 68.

of their races also give Senate challengers advantages in raising money from individuals or groups that pursue ideological goals.

This is not to imply that incumbency does not provide members of the Senate with fund-raising advantages. Senators, like House members, often begin their quest for reelection with significant sums left over from their previous campaigns and start raising funds early. Twenty senators had in excess of $100,000 left over after their 1994 campaigns, and twelve had this much left after 1996. Sixteen of the thirty senators up for reelection in 1998 had raised in excess of $1 million by December 31, 1996. Sen. Alfonse D'Amato, R-N.Y., led the pack, having raised nearly $9.7 million.

TABLE 6-4
Sources of Support for Senate Candidates in the 1996 Elections

	Party		Status			Competitiveness	
	Democrats	Republicans	Incumbents	Challengers	Open-seat candidates	Competitive	Uncompetitive
Individual contributions under $200	$718,318 (21%)	$657,219 (18%)	$1,100,730 (26%)	$591,046 (21%)	$461,884 (13%)	$824,228 (20%)	$244,276 (15%)
Individual contributions of $200 or more	$1,307,760 (38%)	$1,450,495 (40%)	$1,668,077 (39%)	$1,111,201 (39%)	$1,364,110 (39%)	$1,590,142 (38%)	$693,331 (43%)
PAC contributions	$439,595 (13%)	$782,330 (21%)	$959,284 (22%)	$247,886 (9%)	$621,501 (18%)	$656,018 (16%)	$482,082 (30%)
Party contributions and coordinated expenditures	$271,945 (8%)	$338,626 (9%)	$287,472 (7%)	$243,411 (9%)	$362,207 (10%)	$341,128 (9%)	$75,879 (5%)
Candidate contributions	$531,814 (16%)	$313,277 (9%)	$135,784 (3%)	$644,808 (23%)	$468,615 (13%)	$544,375 (13%)	$26,596 (2%)
Miscellaneous	$159,213 (5%)	$114,481 (3%)	$152,531 (4%)	$204 (—)	$223,246 (6%)	$155,801 (4%)	$75,250 (5%)
(N)	(34)	(34)	(20)	(20)	(28)	(52)	(16)

Source: Compiled from Federal Election Commission data.

Notes: Figures are averages for general election candidates in major-party contested races. Dash = less than 0.5 percent. Candidate contributions include loans candidates made to their own campaigns. Miscellaneous includes interest from savings accounts and revenues from investments. Some columns do not add to 100 percent because of rounding.

Senators are able to raise these large sums early because they have a great deal of political clout, which few challengers possess. For example, Sen. John Warner, R-Va., was able to use his memberships on the Senate Rules, Agriculture, Armed Services, Environment and Public Works, and Small Business Committees to raise approximately $183,800 from agriculture PACs, $230,900 from defense PACs, $258,700 from construction and transportation industry PACs, and $405,300 from finance, insurance, real estate, and miscellaneous business PACs for his 1996 reelection campaign (more than 67 percent of his total PAC dollars).[35] He also raised more than $617,700 from individuals employed in these industries, which represented nearly 28 percent of the individual contributions he raised in amounts of $200 or more.[36]

The in-state fund-raising of Senate candidates differs from that of House candidates in scope and professionalism but not in goals or techniques. Senate candidates merely send out more direct-mail solicitations and hold more fund-raising events than House contestants. Yet fund-raising for Senate campaigns is more national in scope than fund-raising for the House. Most candidates for the upper chamber need to tap into fund-raising networks that extend from Washington to New York, Hollywood, and other wealthy areas. Senator Warner, for example, raised more than $790,000 (35 percent) of his individual large contributions outside of Virginia in 1996. To succeed in winning the financial support of the PACs and wealthy individuals located in these places, Senate candidates must not only make the case that they can put together the kind of campaign that can win, they must also be conversant about the national issues that are of concern to these donors. Incumbents and challengers and open-seat candidates who have considerable political experience are able to convey to national donors as well as voters within their home states that they are knowledgeable about the issues.

Candidates who appear uninformed about national issues or do not give the impression they have the ability to mount a successful statewide campaign often find themselves unable to raise much money. Art Trujillo, the Democratic nominee who opposed Republican senator Pete Domenici in New Mexico is an example of an experienced politician who was unable to successfully tap into the pools of major donors located across the country. Trujillo, a former Santa Fe mayor trounced attorney Eric Treisman by a margin of 41 percentage points in the state's June 4 primary. When the primary was over, however, his failure to make the case that he could beat Domenici caused most potential donors to take pause and contribute elsewhere. Trujillo's inability to transform a low-intensity primary victory into a spirited general election campaign, and Domenici's tremendous popularity in New Mexico, resulted in Trujillo's raising less than $164,000 to mount his campaign. Individuals, the vast majority of whom resided in the candidate's state, contributed nearly 83 percent of these funds. Labor PACs contributed another $10,800 (7 percent of his funds), but PACs connected with corporations and other business-related interests contributed nothing. Party committees provided a mere $5,000 (including coordinated expenditures) and Democratic members of Congress and Democratic-sponsored leadership PACs gave only $2,000.

A final difference between House and Senate elections concerns how candidates obtain support from their Hill committees. All four Hill committees rely on members of Congress to help them raise funds, but candidate assistance in fund-raising is also an informal criterion for senatorial campaign committee support. The DSCC and NRSC have special accounts for elections in different regions. The DSCC also has the Democratic Women's Council to provide support to women candidates for the Senate. These accounts give Senate candidates incentives to participate in fund-raising events held for their region—and for women, in the case of female candidates—making it possible for the senatorial campaign committees to meet, or come close to meeting, the high ceilings that the FECA sets for coordinated expenditures in Senate elections.

CHAPTER 7

Campaign Strategy

The campaign for votes involves voter targeting, communications, and mobilization. During the heyday of the parties, party organizations formulated and executed campaign strategies. Party leaders, candidates, and activists talked with neighbors to learn about their concerns, disseminated campaign communications that addressed those concerns, and turned out the vote on election day. The predisposition of voters to support their party's candidates tended to be strong and was occasionally reinforced with government jobs, contracts, and other forms of patronage.

Contemporary campaigns also involve targeting, communicating with, and mobilizing voters. Successful candidates craft a message with broad appeal, set the agenda that defines voters' choices, and get their supporters to the polls on election day. In the years in which presidential elections are held, many candidates do not have the opportunity to fully define the campaign agenda themselves. Thus, the candidates who stake out positions that correspond to the national political agenda have the advantage.

In this chapter I focus on how voters decide to cast their ballots in congressional elections and on the strategies and tactics that campaigns use to affect those decisions. The primary topics are voting behavior, strategy, targeting, and message.

VOTING BEHAVIOR

Traditional democratic theory holds that citizens should make informed choices when voting in elections. It contends that they should be knowledgeable about the candidates, be aware of the major issues, and take the time to discern which candidate is more likely to represent their views and govern in the nation's best interests. The weight of the evidence, however, suggests that the vast majority of voters in congressional elections fall short of these expectations.[1]

Most voters make their congressional voting decisions on the basis of relatively little information. In a typical House contest between an incumbent and a challenger, for example, only about 20 percent of all voters can recall the names of the two major-party candidates. In open-seat House contests, about one-third of all voters can remember the candidates' names. Voters tend to possess more information about contestants in Senate elections: roughly 30 percent can recall the names of both candidates in contests involving an incumbent and a challenger, and about two-thirds can identify both candidates in open-seat races.[2]

When put to the less-stringent test of merely recognizing the candidates' names, just over half of all voters recognize the names of both major-party contestants in incumbent-challenger House races, and almost 80 percent recognize the names of both candidates in open-seat contests. The levels of name recognition are higher in Senate contests: roughly 80 percent recognize the names of both the incumbent and challenger, and more than 90 percent recognize the names of candidates in open-seat races.[3] Thus, the name recognition test, which demands roughly the same, minimal amount of knowledge from voters as does actually casting a ballot, shows that a substantial portion of the electorate lacks the information needed to make what scholars refer to as "an informed vote choice."

The inability to recall or recognize the candidates' names is indicative of the overall lack of substantive information in congressional elections. Most House election campaigns are low-key affairs that do not convey much information about the candidates' ideological orientations or policy positions.[4] Information on House challengers, most of whom wage underfunded campaigns, is usually scarce. Campaign communications, voters' assessments of the issues, and candidates' qualifications become important only in hard-fought contests.[5]

Incumbency and Voter Information

By and large, the candidates who suffer most from voter disinterest are House challengers. Whereas more than 90 percent of all voters recognize their House member's name, slightly more than half usually recognize the name of the challenger. Incumbents also tend to be viewed favorably. About half of those voters who recognize their representative's name indicate they like something about that person; only 14 percent mention something they dislike. The corresponding figures for House challengers are 29 percent and 15 percent.[6] As the high reelection rates for House members indicate, the name recognition and voter approval ratings of most incumbents are difficult for opponents to overcome. Only those challengers who can break through the name recognition barrier and overcome their "invisibility problem" stand a chance of winning.

Senate challengers tend to be less handicapped by voter inattentiveness. They enjoy better name recognition because of their political experience, skill, and superior campaign organizations, and the newsworthiness of their campaigns attracts media attention and voter interest. Voters learn more about the ideological orientations and issue positions of Senate challengers than of their House counterparts.[7] Even though the name recognition of Senate challengers is lower than the near-universal recognition enjoyed by Senate incumbents, it is high enough to make the typical incumbent-challenger race competitive. This helps explain why there is more electoral turnover in the upper than in the lower chamber of Congress.

The inequalities in candidate information that characterize most incumbent-challenger races generally do not exist in open-seat contests. The major-party candidates in an open-seat race for a marginal seat begin the campaign with similar opportunities to increase their name recognition and convey their messages to voters. The greater competitiveness of these contests results in more extensive press coverage, which in turn helps both candidates become better known to voters. Thus, more voters make informed choices in open-seat races than in incumbent-challenger contests.

Voting Decisions

Given their lack of knowledge of the candidates and issues, how do most voters make a decision on election day? Only those voters who know something about the background, political qualifications, party affiliation, and issue stances of both candidates are in a position to sift through the information, weigh the benefits of voting for one candidate over another, and cast their ballots in accordance with classical democratic theory.[8] Nevertheless, voters who fall short of the level of awareness idealized by democratic theory may respond to the campaign information that candidates and the media disseminate. Competitive, high-intensity elections that fill the airwaves, newspapers, and voters' mailboxes with campaign information provide some voters, especially those with an interest in politics, with enough information to form summary judgments about the candidates. And these voters often tend to rely on those judgments when deciding which candidate to support.[9]

In the absence of spirited, high-intensity elections, most voters use "voting cues"—shortcuts that enable them to cast a ballot without engaging in a lengthy decision-making process. The most frequently used voting cue is incumbency.

Knowing only an incumbent's name is sufficient for an individual to cast an adequately informed vote, some scholars argue. Reasoning that the incumbent should be held accountable for the government's performance, the state of the economy, the nation's foreign involvements, or other issues, these voters quickly determine whether to support the status quo and vote for the incumbent or to advocate change and cast their ballot for the challenger.[10]

Other voters pin the responsibility for the state of the nation on the president. When these voters are satisfied with how things are being run in Washington, they support the congressional candidate who belongs to the president's party. When they are dissatisfied with the state of the nation's affairs, as in 1994, they vote for the candidate whose party does not occupy the White House. The connection between presidential and congressional voting, which began increasing in the early 1990s, can help a congressional candidate when a popular president is running for reelection, but belonging to the president's party usually has more harmful than beneficial effects in midterm elections.[11] The party cue, like the incumbency cue, enables voters to make retrospective voting choices without having much knowledge about the candidates or their positions on the issues. Under conditions of unified government, party cues are stronger because voters can more readily assign credit or blame for the state of the nation to the party that controls both the executive and legislative branches.[12] The power-sharing arrangements of divided government, in contrast, obscure political responsibility because they enable politicians to blame others in power.

The party cue also enables voters to speculate about a candidate's ideological orientation and issue positions. Republicans are generally identified as more conservative than Democrats and are associated with free market economics, deregulation, lower taxes, family values, hawkish foreign policy, and the wealthier elements of society. Most Republicans profess to be for limited government and some campaign as though they are antigovernment. Democrats are often viewed as the party of government. They are associated with greater economic intervention, environmental protection, education, a more dovish foreign policy, and protecting the interests of senior citizens, minorities, the poor, and working people. Some voters project the parties' images to candidates and use these projections to guide their congressional voting decisions. Others habitually support a party's nominees regardless of their credentials, issue positions, or opponents.

Partisanship and incumbency can affect the voting decisions of individuals who possess even less political information than do those individuals described above. The voting behavior of individuals who go to the polls out of a sense of civic responsibility or out of habit and who lack much interest in or knowledge about politics can in many ways be equated with the behavior of shoppers at a supermarket. Individuals in both situations select a product—either a consumer good or a congressional candidate—with little relevant information. Except for first-time shoppers and newly enfranchised voters, these individuals have made similar selections before. Previous decisions and established preferences often strongly influence their current decisions. Shoppers, lacking a good reason to try a new product, such as a sale or a two-for-one giveaway, are likely to purchase the same brand-name product that they previously purchased. Voters are likely to cast a ballot for the candidates or party that they supported in previous elections.[13] If a voter recognizes one candidate's name, which is almost always the incumbent's, that candidate usually gets the individual's vote. If the voter recognizes neither candidate but tends to be favorably predisposed toward one party, then most often the person votes for that party's candidate. Situations in which voters have little information, then, usually work to the advantage of incumbents and of candidates who belong to the district's or state's dominant party.

However, if the recognized candidate or favored party is associated with scandal or a domestic or foreign policy failure, many relatively uninformed voters, as well as some who are informed, break old habits and cast their ballots against that candidate or party. During the elections held in the 1990s, for example, many challengers, with the support of Washington-based party committees and interest groups, sought to make control of Congress itself a major campaign issue. This strategy is credited with enabling the Republicans to take over Congress and end forty uninterrupted years of Democratic control of the House. Attacking Congress contributed to the electoral success of challengers of both parties in 1994 and 1996.

VOTERS AND CAMPAIGN STRATEGY

Candidates and political consultants generally do not plan election campaigns on the basis of abstract political theories, but they do draw on a body of knowledge about how people make their voting decisions. Politicians' notions about voting behavior have some ideas in common with the findings of scholarly research. Among these are the following: (1) most voters have only limited information about the candidates, their ideologies, and the issues; (2) voters are generally more familiar with and favorably predisposed toward incumbents than challengers; and (3) voters tend to cast their ballots in ways that reflect their party identification and previous voting behavior. Candidates and consultants also believe that a campaign sharply focused on issues can be used to motivate supporters to show up at the polls and to win the support of undecided voters.

They try to set the campaign agenda so that the issues that politically informed voters use as a basis for casting their ballots are the most attractive issues for their candidate.

Politicians' beliefs account for some of the differences that exist among the campaigns waged by incumbents, challengers, and open-seat candidates as well as many of the differences that exist between House and Senate campaigns. Generally, members of Congress use strategies that capitalize on the advantages of incumbency. They discuss the services and the federal projects they have delivered to their constituencies.[14] They focus on elements of their public persona that have helped make them popular with constituents and draw on strategies they have used successfully in previous campaigns.[15]

Some incumbents capitalize on their advantages in name recognition and voter approval by virtually ignoring their opponents. They deluge the district with direct mail, radio advertisements, television commercials, yard signs, or other communications that make no mention of their opponent in order to minimize the attention the challenger gets from the local media and voters. An alternative strategy is to take advantage of a challenger's relative invisibility by attacking his or her experience, qualifications, or positions on the issues early in the campaign. Incumbents who succeed in defining their opponents leave them in the unenviable position of being invisible to most voters and negatively perceived by others. The Morella campaign pursued the former strategy in 1996, treating Mooers as if his candidacy would have no impact on the outcome of the election.[16] The Fazio campaign followed the latter approach, attacking Lefever and making him defend the record of the Republican Congress—a strategy that was popular in 1996 with Democratic incumbents and nonincumbents in the House and Senate alike.[17]

House challengers are in the least enviable position of any candidates. Not only are they less well known and less experienced, but they are also without the campaign resources of their opponents. In order to win, challengers need to force their way into voters' consciousness and to project a message that will give voters a reason to cast a ballot for a little-known quantity.

Many challengers make the election a referendum on some negative aspect of the incumbent's performance. They portray the incumbent as incompetent, corrupt, or out of touch with the district. They magnify the impact of any unpopular policy or scandal with which the incumbent can be associated. Challengers often try to link the current officeholder to unpopular policies or trends and to tout themselves as agents of change, often using negative or comparative ads to do so.

Lacking the advantages of an incumbent or the disadvantages of a challenger, both candidates in an open-seat race face the challenge of making themselves familiar to voters and becoming associated with themes and issues that will attract electoral support. They also both have the opportunity to define their opponents. Some open-seat candidates seek to define themselves and their opponents on the basis of issues. Others, particularly those running in districts that favor their party, emphasize partisan cues.

GAUGING PUBLIC OPINION

Campaigns use many different instruments to take the public's pulse. Election returns from previous contests are analyzed to locate pockets of potential strength or weakness. Geodemographic analysis enables campaigns to identify individuals who voted in previous elections and to classify them according to their gender, age, ethnicity, race, religion, and economic background. By combining geodemographic information with polling data and election returns, candidates are able to identify potential supporters and to formulate messages that will appeal to them.

Polls are among the most commonly used means of gauging public opinion. Virtually every Senate campaign and roughly 85 percent of all House campaigns have used some form of polling to learn about voters. Benchmark polls, which are taken early in the election cycle, inform candidates about the issue positions, partisanship, and initial voting preferences of people living in their state or district. House campaigns commonly commission benchmarks a year prior to the election, and Senate candidates have been known to commission them as early as three years before election day.[18] Benchmark polls also measure the levels of name recognition and support that the candidates and their opponents or prospective opponents enjoy. They help campaigns learn about the kinds of candidates voters prefer, the types of messages that are likely to attract support, and to whom specific campaign advertisements should be directed.

Campaigns also use benchmark polls to generate support. Challenger and open-seat candidates disseminate favorable benchmarks to attract press coverage and the support of campaign volunteers and contributors. Incumbents typically publicize benchmarks to discourage potential challengers. When poll results show a member of Congress to be in trouble, however, the incumbent uses them to convince parties, PACs, and other potential contributors that he or she needs extra help to win.

Trend polls are taken intermittently throughout the campaign season to discover changes in voters' attitudes. Some senators use them to chart their public approval throughout their six-year terms. These polls are more narrowly focused than benchmarks. They feature detailed questions designed to reveal whether a campaign has been successful in getting voters to associate their candidate with a specific issue or theme. Trend polls help campaigns determine whether they have been gaining or losing ground with different segments of the electorate. They can reassure a campaign that its strategy is working or indicate that a change in message is needed.

Just as trend and benchmark polls present "snapshots" of public opinion, tracking polls provide campaigns with a "motion picture" overview. Tracking polls ask small samples of voters to discuss their reactions to a few key advertisements, issue statements, or campaign events. Each night a different group of voters is interviewed. The interviews are pooled into "rolling averages" that usually consist of the responses from the three most recent nights. Changes in rolling averages can be used to reformulate a campaign's final appeals. Because tracking polls are expensive, most House campaigns wait until the last three weeks of the campaign to use them.

Candidates may supplement their polling with focus groups. Focus groups usually consist of one to two dozen participants and a professional facilitator, who meet for two to three hours. The participants are selected not to be a scientifically representative sample but to represent segments of the population whose support the campaign needs to reinforce or attract. Campaigns use focus groups to learn how voters can be expected to respond to different messages or to pretest actual campaign advertisements. Some high-priced consultants, such as Wirthlin Worldwide, a prominent Republican firm, employ computerized audience response techniques to obtain a precise record of how focus group participants react to specific portions of campaign advertisements.[19] These techniques enable an analyst to plot a line that represents the participants' reactions onto the ad itself, pinpointing exactly which portions participants liked or disliked. Focus group research is useful in fine-tuning the visuals and narratives in television communications.

Finally, candidates learn about public opinion through a variety of approaches that do not require the services of public opinion experts. Newspaper, magazine, radio, and television news stories provide information about voters' positions on major issues. Exchanges with local party leaders, journalists, political activists, and voters can also help candidates get a sense of the public mood.

When asked about the significance of different forms of information, House candidates and campaign aides typically rank direct contact with voters first, indicating that they consider it to be very important to extremely important (see Table 7-1). Voter contact is followed by public opinion polls, which are generally considered to be moderately helpful to very helpful in learning about voters' opinions. News stories come next, followed by discussions with local party activists and mail from voters. Although they play a bigger role than

TABLE 7-1

Campaigners' Perceptions of the Importance of Different Sources
of Information for Gauging Public Opinion in House Campaigns

	All	Incumbents		Challengers		Open-seat candidates	
		In jeopardy	Shoo-ins	Hope-fuls	Likely losers	Pros-pects	Long shots
Candidate contact with voters	4.37	4.23	4.41	4.44	4.44	4.16	4.59
Public opinion surveys	3.53	4.23	3.54	3.68	2.88	3.96	3.09
Newspaper, radio, TV	3.05	2.69	3.13	3.08	3.27	2.86	3.17
Local party activists	2.63	2.78	2.74	2.69	2.41	2.45	2.80
Mail from voters	2.45	2.65	3.43	2.19	1.99	2.00	2.29
National party publications	2.28	1.83	1.96	2.39	2.75	2.12	2.65
National party leaders	2.14	1.80	1.94	2.31	2.32	2.20	2.30
(N)	(325)	(48)	(70)	(52)	(82)	(49)	(24)

Source: The 1992 Congressional Campaign Study.

Notes: Candidates and campaign aides were asked to assess the importance of each source on the following scale: 1 = not important or not used; 2 = slightly important; 3 = moderately important; 4 = very important; 5 = extremely important. The values listed are the arithmetic means of the scores. Figures include responses from House general election candidates and campaign aides in major-party contested races, excluding a small number of atypical races.

PACs and other interest groups, national party officials and the materials they publish are less important than local information sources.

Incumbents and candidates for open seats make greater use of surveys than do challengers. Candidates in competitive contests of all types make greater use of them than do those in lopsided races. Challengers and open-seat candidates in one-sided contests often cannot afford to buy polls and must rely heavily on news reports, party publications, and the advice of national party leaders. Incumbents, who are often sensitized to issues by the constituent mail that floods their offices, consider letters to be a more significant indicator of public sentiment than does any other group of candidates. Incumbents in safe seats show a greater preference than others for learning about public opinion through the mail and other forms of unmediated voter contact.

VOTER TARGETING

Campaigns are not designed to reach everyone. Targeting involves categorizing different groups of voters, identifying their political preferences, and designing appeals to which they are likely to respond. It is the foundation of virtually every aspect of campaign strategy. Candidates and campaign managers consider many factors when devising targeting strategies, including the underlying partisan and candidate loyalties of the groups that reside in the district, the size and turnout levels of those groups, and the kinds of issues and appeals that will attract their support.[20] Using this information, they formulate a strategy designed to build a winning coalition.

Partisanship is an important consideration in the voter targeting of roughly three-fifths of all campaigns (see Table 7-2). Most campaigns focus on indi-

TABLE 7-2

The Partisan Component of Targeting Strategies in House Campaigns

	All	Incumbents		Challengers		Open-seat candidates	
		In jeopardy	Shoo-ins	Hope-fuls	Likely losers	Pros-pects	Long shots
Members of own party	8%	6%	12%	6%	7%	8%	8%
Members of opposing party	3	6	—	2	6	2	—
Independents	3	2	3	6	2	6	—
Members of both parties	3	4	1	6	2	4	6
Members of own party and independents	37	42	28	49	34	41	36
Members of opposing party and independents	5	6	1	4	7	10	—
All voters	40	33	54	28	41	29	50
(N)	(334)	(52)	(71)	(55)	(81)	(49)	(26)

Source: The 1992 Congressional Campaign Study.

Notes: Figures include responses from House general election candidates and campaign aides in major-party contested races, excluding a small number of atypical races. Dashes = less than 0.5 percent. Some columns do not add to 100 percent because of rounding.

viduals who identify with their party and independent voters. Challengers and open-seat candidates are somewhat more likely than incumbents to focus on independents, but candidates in competitive contests focus their efforts on independents and members of their own party, regardless of incumbency. Rep. Fred Heineman, who was locked in a tough rematch with Democrat David Price, concentrated on independents and shoring up his Republican base.[21] Connie Morella, a Republican who has represented Maryland's strongly Democratic-leaning 8th district since 1986, by contrast, is typical of most safe incumbents in that she has built a measure of bipartisan support over the years. Like many incumbents, she routinely sends out letters to congratulate constituents who recently registered to vote in her district. Unlike most other incumbents, however, she often sends letters of congratulation to voters who have registered in the opposing party, in this case as Democrats.[22]

Nonincumbents in uncompetitive races are the least likely to focus their efforts on a combination of independents and members of their own party. These underdogs also need to pursue votes from members of the opposing party. In some cases, such candidates do not have the resources needed to carry out even a basic party-oriented targeting strategy. Lacking a poll or a precinct-by-precinct breakdown of where Republican, Democratic, and independent voters reside, some amateurs resort to unorthodox strategies, such as focusing on precincts that had the highest turnout levels in the previous election.[23]

Other factors that campaigns consider when designing targeting strategies include demography and issues. Sixty-two percent of all House campaigns target demographic, geographic, or occupational groups: 34 percent concentrate on specific ethnic, racial, religious, gender, or age groups; 16 percent focus on counties, suburbs, cities, or other geographic locations; and 12 percent target union members, blue-collar workers, small-business owners, or voters involved in particular industries (see Table 7-3). Issues and political attitudes, including voting intentions and partisanship, play a central role in the targeting strategies of roughly one-third of all campaigns.

Group-oriented and issue/attitudinal-oriented targeting strategies each offer campaigns some distinct advantages. The group-oriented, or geodemographic, approach is based on the idea that there are identifiable segments of the population whose support the campaign needs to attract and that specific communications can be tailored to win that support. Just as soliciting money from a readily identifiable fund-raising constituency is important in the campaign for resources, communicating a message to identifiable groups of supporters and undecided voters is important in the campaign for votes. Campaigns that use group-based targeting strategies emphasize different aspects of their message, depending on the intended audience for a particular campaign advertisement.

TABLE 7-3

The Geodemographic and Attitudinal Components of Targeting Strategies in House Campaigns

	All	Incumbents		Challengers		Open-seat candidates	
		In jeopardy	Shoo-ins	Hope-fuls	Likely losers	Pros-pects	Long shots
Demography	34%	35%	35%	36%	26%	29%	56%
Geography	16	19	40	9	9	11	12
Occupation	12	11	5	17	14	13	6
Issues	15	14	10	19	20	8	14
Party affiliation	12	8	5	13	15	19	6
Persuadable voters	4	3	2	4	—	16	—
Miscellaneous	8	10	2	2	16	5	6
(N)	(332)	(48)	(72)	(54)	(83)	(50)	(25)

Source: The 1992 Congressional Campaign Study.

Notes: Figures include responses from House general election candidates and campaign aides in major-party contested races, excluding a small number of atypical races. Dashes = less than 0.5 percent. Some columns do not add to 100 percent because of rounding.

By tailoring their messages to attract the votes of specific population groups, these campaigns hope to build a winning coalition. During the 1990s, many campaigns stressed the effect of the economy on children and families in literature that was mailed to women, whereas they emphasized tax cuts and economic growth issues in literature that was mailed to business executives and upper-class and upper-middle-class voters.

Candidates focus on many groups, reflecting the diverse segments of the population represented by the two major parties, especially the Democrats.[24] More Democrats than Republicans target senior citizens, and Democratic candidates target women more than any other segment of the population. The 1996 contest between Heineman and Price gives some insights into the dynamics of geodemographic targeting. The race was held in a central North Carolina district that includes many rural communities as well as Raleigh, Chapel Hill, and other portions of the more urban and suburban "Research Triangle." Price focused most of his efforts on Democrats, independents, senior citizens, African Americans, and Republican women. He also targeted voters in Wake County, whose lack of support cost him reelection in 1994.[25] Heineman focused on Republicans, independents, women, and Wake County voters. An overlap in targets is typical of a close election because both campaigns go after the same swing voters.

The issue/attitudinal strategy is based on the premise that issues and ideas should drive the campaign. Campaigns that target on the basis of specific policies or a broad ideology, such as conservatism or progressivism, hope to win the support of single-issue or ideological voters who favor these positions. In many cases, one or two specific issues are emphasized in order to attract the support of swing voters whose ballots a candidate believes will be a deciding factor in the election outcome. Some candidates targeted pro-life or pro-choice voters in the 1990s, believing their ballots would be decisive. Others targeted pro-environment or anti–gun control voters. Republicans who employed these strategies focused primarily on voters who were concerned about the deficit, taxes, the size of government, government regulation, and crime. Democrats who employed them focused on voters who cared about public education, the environment, health care, and the protections and services that government provides for the elderly, children, and underprivileged groups.

Targeting strategies that are based on issues or voter attitudes more readily lend themselves to the communication of a coherent campaign message than do group-oriented strategies. They are especially effective at mobilizing single-issue voters and political activists who have strong ideological predispositions. Yet they run the risk of alienating moderate voters who agree with the candidate on most policy matters but disagree on the issues the campaign has chosen to emphasize. Campaigns waged by policy amateurs and ideologues are the most likely to suffer from this problem. Often these candidates become boxed in by their own message, are labeled "ultra-liberals" or "right wingers" by their opponents, and ultimately lose.

Incumbents target demographic, geographic, and occupational groups more than do challengers and open-seat candidates. Many challengers target on the basis of issues in order to peel away support from their opponent. Occupation, which is often related to issues, plays a greater role in the strategic planning of challengers than any other targeting component. Open-seat candidates in competitive races are the most likely to go after independents. Often referred to as "persuadable" or "swing" voters, independents can make the difference between winning and losing in elections in which neither candidate has a huge base of support.

THE MESSAGE

The message delivered by a candidate gives substance to a campaign and helps to shape the political agenda, mobilize backers, and win votes. In a well-run campaign, the same coherent message pervades every aspect of the candidate's communications—from paid television advertisements to impromptu remarks. Campaign messages can be an essential ingredient to victory in close elections because they have a strong influence on the decisions of persuadable voters.

Campaign messages rely heavily on imagery. The most successful campaigns weave the candidate's persona and policy stances into thematic messages. These form the core of the image the candidate seeks to project. According to Joel Bradshaw, president of the Democratic consulting firm Campaign Design Group, good campaign messages are clear and easy to communicate, short, convey a sense of emotional urgency, reflect voters' perceptions of political reality, establish clear differences between the candidate and the opponent, and are credible.[26]

The precise mix of personal characteristics, issues, and broad themes that candidates project depends on their political views, the groups they target, and the messages they anticipate their opponents will communicate. Good strategic positioning results in the transmission of a message that most voters will find appealing; when both candidates achieve this result an election becomes what strategists refer to as a "battle for the middle ground."[27] In designing a message, campaign decision makers consider a variety of factors, which Fred Hartwig of Peter Hart and Associates refers to as "the Seven P's of Strategy": performance, professional experience, positioning, partisanship, populism, progressivism, and positivity.[28] Ladonna Lee, a leading Republican political strategist, emphasizes the importance of consistency. The different components of the message must add up to a coherent public image or persona.[29]

Campaigns endeavor to create a favorable image for their candidates by identifying them with decency, loyalty, honesty, hard work, and other cherished values.[30] Campaign communications interweave anecdotes about a candidate's personal accomplishments, professional success, family, or ability to overcome humble origins to portray him or her as the living embodiment of the American dream—someone whom voters should be proud to have represent them in Washington. Campaigns frequently emphasize elements of their candidate's persona that point to an opponent's weakness. Veterans who run against draft dodgers, for example, commonly emphasize their war records.

Incumbents frequently convey image-oriented messages. They seek to reinforce or expand their base of support by concentrating on those aspects of their persona that make them popular with constituents.[31] Their messages convey images of competent, caring individuals who work tirelessly in Washington to improve the lives of the folks they represent back home. Incumbents' campaign communications often describe how they have helped constituents resolve problems, brought federal programs and projects to the district, and introduced or cosponsored popular legislation. Some discuss their efforts to prevent a military base or factory from closing. Those whose districts have experienced the ravages of floods, earthquakes, riots, or other disasters almost always highlight their roles in bringing federal relief to victims.

Many challengers and open-seat contestants also seek to portray themselves as caring, hard-working, and experienced. Nonincumbents who have previously held elective office frequently contrast their accomplishments with those of their opponent. During the elections held in the early and mid-1990s, many challengers who were state legislators blamed their opponents for contributing to the federal deficit while pointing to their own budget-cutting efforts.

Political amateurs usually discuss their successes in the private sector, seeking to make a virtue of their lack of political experience. Many blame the "mess in Washington" on the "career politicians" and discuss how someone who has succeeded in the private sector is needed to make government work for the people again. Still, a challenger who focuses on experience rarely wins. As one consultant explained, "By virtue of their being the current officeholder, an incumbent can 'out-experience' a challenger to death."

Issues

Most House candidates and campaign aides maintain that the bulk of their messages focus on policy concerns rather than the candidate's personality—a claim that has been borne out by examinations of their campaign materials.[32] Roughly 47 percent of all House campaigns make issues the primary focus of their message; 25 percent, mostly incumbent campaigns, emphasize candidate imagery (see Table 7-4). Nonincumbents in uncompetitive contests run the most issue-oriented campaigns, reflecting the fact that many are policy amateurs who were drawn to the election in order to advance specific causes.[33] Challengers run the most opposition-oriented campaigns. They point to incumbents' ethical lapses, congressional roll-call votes that are out of sync with constituents' views, or federal policies that have harmed local voters or the national interest. More than one-third of all challengers try to make their opponent or their opponent's actions in office a defining campaign issue. Some incumbents holding marginal seats respond in kind by pointing to unpopular aspects of their challenger's background or issue positions. Significant numbers of open-seat candidates in close contests also make their opponent the central focus of their message.

Almost all candidates take policy stands that identify them with "valence" issues, such as a strong economy, job creation, domestic tranquility, and international security, which are universally viewed in a favorable light. Some make

TABLE 7-4

The Major Focus of Advertising in House Campaigns

	All	Incumbents		Challengers		Open-seat candidates	
		In jeopardy	Shoo-ins	Hope-fuls	Likely losers	Pros-pects	Long shots
Candidate's image	25%	35%	46%	25%	5%	18%	25%
Candidate's issue positions	47	41	47	31	56	47	67
Candidate's image and issue positions	2	—	3	4	2	4	—
Opponent's image	12	9	1	21	10	22	4
Opponent's issue positions	11	13	3	14	21	6	4
Opponent's image and issue positions	2	—	—	4	4	2	—
All of the above	1	2	—	2	2	—	—
(N)	(338)	(46)	(70)	(52)	(84)	(49)	(24)

Source: The 1992 Congressional Campaign Study.

Notes: Figures include responses from House general election candidates and campaign aides in major-party contested races, excluding a small number of atypical races. Dashes = less than 0.5 percent. Some columns do not add to 100 percent because of rounding.

these the centerpiece of their campaign. They either ignore or soft-pedal "position" issues (sometimes referred to as "wedge" issues), which have two or more sides.[34] When both candidates campaign mainly on valence issues, the dialogue can be likened to a debate between the nearly identical Tweedledee and Tweedledum.

When candidates communicate dissimilar stands on position issues, however, political debate becomes more meaningful. Issues such as gun control, abortion, and civil rights, have for several years had the potential to draw the attention of voters and affect elections. Prayer in school, family values, social entitlement programs, senior citizens' concerns, illegal immigration, U.S. policy toward Cuba, and environmental issues also have the ability to influence elections.

Challengers are especially likely to benefit from emphasizing position issues. By stressing points of disagreement between themselves and the incumbent, challengers can help their images crystallize, attract media attention, and strip away some of their opponent's support.[35] Incumbents may not derive the same electoral benefits from running on position issues because they are usually evaluated in personal terms.[36] Candidates who campaign on position issues hope to attract the support of single-issue or ideological voters or to overcome some weakness in their image. Some liberal Democrats emphasize crime to project "tougher" images. Some conservative Republicans discuss health care. Both groups of candidates seek to convince centrist voters that they share their concerns.

Candidates try to anticipate the issues their opponents will emphasize before taking a strong policy stance. Candidates who run against police officers rarely mount "law-and-order" campaigns because of the obvious disparities in credibility that they and their opponents have on crime-related issues. In the 1994 and 1996 elections in North Carolina's 4th district, David Price decided not to focus on crime-related issues, whereas Fred Heineman, a former police chief, made them a major focus of his campaigns. Price instead emphasized education, capitalizing on his background as a college professor.[37]

Candidates who learn that their opponent holds an unpopular position on a salient issue generally try to make it the central focus of the campaign in order to win the support of independents and pry voters from their opponent's camp. Democrats and some moderate Republicans lure women's votes by making abortion rights a major part of their campaign platforms. In 1992 and 1996, Democrats who adopted this position got the added benefit of being able to coordinate their message with the Clinton-Gore campaign. Divisions within the Republican Party made abortion an issue to avoid for many GOP candidates. Women who are running against men are the most likely to campaign as pro-choice and to run on women's issues in general, but some male candidates also stake out pro–abortion rights positions to attract the support of women and liberal voters.[38]

Economic issues—whether they be inflation, unemployment, taxes, jobs, the federal budget, or the national deficit—have been the number one concern of voters in most elections since the Great Depression. Virtually every candidate in the 1980s and 1990s made some aspect of the economy part of their campaign.[39] Democratic candidates often discuss the economy as a fairness issue. In 1992 many Democrats followed the Clinton-Gore campaign's lead in pointing to the increased tax burdens that Reagan-Bush policies placed on the middle class and the tax breaks they gave to wealthy Americans. In 1996 many Democratic candidates again adopted the Clinton-Gore campaign's message, pointing to alleged attempts by Republicans to cut Social Security, Medicare, and other popular middle-class programs in order to give a tax break to the rich.[40]

Republican candidates usually focus on economic growth and the deficit. Throughout the 1980s and 1990s they sought to blame the economic woes of the country on wasteful government subsidies, excessive regulation, and profligate pork-barrel spending approved by the Democratic-controlled Congress. Their message gained supporters in 1994, as Republican candidates proclaimed that tax cuts were the crown jewel of their vaunted Contract with America. In addition to tax relief, Republicans campaigned for a balanced budget amendment, line-item veto, deregulation, and product liability and tort reform, which they argued would lead to the reinvigoration of the American economy.[41]

Political reform was also an important issue for both Republicans and Democrats in the 1990s, reflecting the anti–Washington establishment mood of the country. Many House challengers concentrated on term limits, campaign finance reform, and "reinventing government," often contrasting their reform positions with their opponent's vote for a congressional pay raise and dependence on PAC contributions. Incumbents address political reform differently. Some seek to defend Congress, while others try to impress upon voters that they are part of the solution and not the problem. One House member said he "neutralized" the reform issue by arguing that he "was constructively working to improve government from the inside, while [his opponent] was content to merely lob stones from a distance."[42] Another popular incumbent strategy is to campaign for reelection to Congress by attacking the institution itself.[43] The Republicans' success in making political corruption a campaign issue in 1994 and their lengthy investigations of the Clinton administration and Democratic fund-raising activities in 1996 suggest that calls for political reform will play a prominent role in future congressional elections.

Most candidates prefer themselves to be the ones whom voters associate with valence issues, not their opponents, but candidates can also find it profitable to take strong stands on position issues. This is especially true when their policy stances on these issues are welcomed by voters in their district or occupy a prominent place on the national agenda. The 1996 national campaign agenda was dominated by the clash between the Clinton administration and the Republican-controlled Congress over federal policies and programs. Democratic and Republican congressional candidates took opposing positions on many national issues. The clearest partisan divisions concerned the Republican budget package and reductions in the growth of Medicare; virtually all candidates adopted their party's position on these issues (see Table 7-5).

Most of the other position issues on the 1996 campaign agenda also divided the candidates along partisan lines, but the candidates exhibited some systematic divisions within partisan ranks. Democratic incumbents were overwhelmingly opposed to term limits, but 54 percent of the party's challengers and 44

TABLE 7-5

Percentage of House Candidates Who Supported Selected Position Issues

	All	Democrats			Republicans		
		Incumbents	Challengers	Open-seat candidates	Incumbents	Challengers	Open-seat candidates
Republican budget	51	1	3	—	100	96	92
Reduce Medicare growth	48	1	—	3	98	90	91
Term limits	61	16	54	44	84	88	93
Reduce B-2 bomber funding	54	70	78	77	37	30	32
Family and medical leave	66	95	100	100	25	32	37
Ban on partial-birth abortions	63	36	25	34	93	92	96
Handgun control	55	76	85	83	34	15	14
U.S. troops in Bosnia-Herzegovina	45	90	89	81	18	17	30
NAFTA	50	19	28	37	70	74	62
Aid for Russia	64	86	80	57	60	28	42
Welfare reform	57	3	22	14	98	100	96
(N)	(606)	(146)	(133)	(28)	(171)	(102)	(26)

Source: Compiled from *Time*/Congressional Quarterly 1996 Congressional Candidate Survey.

Notes: Figures represent the percentage of candidates in major-party contested elections who supported each issue position; they combine with the responses of candidates who opposed each position to total 100 percent. The average N at the bottom of each column is the average number of respondents who answered all the questions. Figures are for general election candidates in major-party contested races, excluding a small number of atypical races. Dashes = less than 0.5 percent.

percent of its open-seat candidates took the opposition position. A smaller but significant division existed between Republican House members and nonincumbents on this issue. A greater proportion of Republican incumbents than nonincumbents opposed family and medical leave. Virtually all the Democratic incumbents opposed the Republicans' Welfare Reform bill, whereas 22 percent of all Democratic challengers and 14 percent of all Democratic open-seat candidates supported it. The B-2 stealth bomber, the North American Free Trade Agreement, handgun control, and U.S. aid for Russia were not as partisan as the previous issues, but they, too, caused splits to develop between incumbents and nonincumbents of one or both parties.

The differences in issue stances reflect the differences in the perspectives held by incumbents, challengers, and open-seat candidates. The greater opposition of House members to term limits reflects their appreciation of the time it takes to become an effective legislator and a recognition that term limits have the potential to shorten their own congressional careers. Differences in the Republicans' stances on cuts in the B-2 bomber program probably reflect the incumbents' experience with the budget process and their understanding in a palpable way that federal money saved in one area can be spent in another. Differences in the Democrats' stances over the NAFTA treaty are at least in part due to the history of the issue. Many Democratic incumbents, including several of the party's top leaders, vigorously opposed the treaty when it was being negotiated by President Bush and voted on in the House. The opposition they voiced toward the treaty in 1996 reflects their earlier positions. The positions of most Democratic nonincumbents, in contrast, were more recently formulated and were in line with President Clinton's pro-NAFTA stance.

Just as membership in Congress and having a voting record to defend influence incumbents' positions on issues, the knowledge that their opponents are constrained by their records influences the positions that challengers stake out. Open-seat candidates, particularly those who have not previously held a major elective office, have the most freedom in selecting issue positions.

Differences between the perspectives of incumbents and nonincumbents can blunt some of the partisanship of congressional elections and are a hurdle that must be overcome for elections to become fully nationalized. Local political culture can also lead candidates of the same party to hold different positions. Fewer southern than northern Republicans supported family and medical leave. More southern than northern Democratic candidates were pro-NAFTA. Fewer southern than northern candidates of both parties supported B-2 funding cuts, handgun control, and the continuance of partial-birth abortions. These issues serve as reminders that the South is one of the nation's most conservative regions and that locally reinforced ideological divisions pose considerable obstacles to the nationalization of congressional elections.

Partisanship, Populism, and Progressivism

Candidates who run in districts that are made up overwhelmingly of people who identify with their party normally emphasize partisan themes and messages. They frequently mention their party in speeches and campaign literature. They also run "tag lines" at the end of their television or radio advertisements stating, "This ad was paid for by 'Candidate X,' Democrat [or Republican] for Congress." Campaigns that are run in "hostile" or divided districts typically use nonpartisan strategies, avoiding any mention of party affiliation.

Progressive strategies have become increasingly popular with Democrats who run as agents of change. These candidates avoid the term *liberal* because voters associate it with government regulations and high taxes, which are unpopular.[44] They instead choose to call themselves progressives or "new" Democrats.

Populist strategies are commonly used by candidates of both parties. Republican populists, like Newt Gingrich, rail against the government, taxes, and special interests in Washington. Democratic populists also champion the cause of ordinary Americans. Rather than oppose big government, however, these candidates run against big business. For example, Byron Dorgan, who was elected North Dakota's at-large representative in 1980 and its junior senator in 1992, earned his populist credentials when, as state tax commissioner, he sued out-of-state corporations doing business in North Dakota to force them to pay taxes there.[45]

Negative Campaigning

Negative campaigning has always been and will probably always be a part of American elections. Just as positive campaigning attempts to build up a candidate, negative campaigning endeavors to tear down an opponent. Negative campaigning is a legitimate form of campaign communication that has the potential to enhance the electoral process. Campaign ads that question a candidate's qualifications or point to unpopular, wasteful, or unethical practices bring a measure of accountability to the political system.[46] Still, much negative campaigning amounts to little more than character assassination and mudslinging that turns off voters and discourages them from participating in elections.[47] From the point of view of the candidates this is unimportant. What matters is that more of their supporters than their opponent's show up at the polls.

Negative campaigning is used by one or both candidates in almost three-quarters of all House and virtually every Senate election. As elections get closer, the probability that they feature negative ads goes up.[48] The sense of urgency that pervades a close contest encourages the contestants to figuratively tar and feather each other because it is easier to discredit an opponent than to build loyalty.[49]

Attack ads can be an important component of challenger campaigns because they can help break voters of the habit of casting their ballots for the incumbent. However, some incumbents have made negative advertising a central element of their strategies in recent years, using early attacks to define their challengers for voters before the challengers can define themselves.[50] Because of their competitiveness, open-seat campaigns tend to be the most negative of all.

The most effective negative ads are grounded in fact, document their sources, focus on some aspect of the opponent's policy views rather than personality, use ridicule, are delivered by a surrogate, and avoid discussing the plight of unfortunate citizens.[51] Many negative ads feature actors depicting incumbents' voting themselves pay raises or attending lavish parties with lobbyists. Some show opponents flip-flopping on the issues. Ridicule is a powerful weapon in politics because it is difficult for people to vote for a candidate at whom they have just laughed.

Campaign attacks that do not adhere to the preceding guidelines tend to be less effective and can backfire, making the candidate who levies the charges look dishonest or mean-spirited. Republican challenger Tim Lefever learned this lesson in his 1996 rematch against Vic Fazio. Lefever ran a television ad that accused Fazio of having built his "entire political career defending people like Richard Allen Davis [who murdered twelve-year-old Polly Klaas] from the Death Penalty." Lefever was widely denounced in the media by other politicians and even by the father of Davis's victim.[52]

Opposition research provides the foundation for negative campaigning. Campaigns begin with a thorough examination of an opponent's personal and professional background. Current members of Congress are qualified to serve in the House or Senate by virtue of their incumbency, although the elections held between 1992 and 1996 demonstrated that incumbency can be used as a weapon against them. The backgrounds of challengers and open-seat candidates are usually more open to question, especially if the candidates have no political experience or have pursued a career that most constituents would view with skepticism. Junk bond traders and dog catchers, for example, are at risk of being attacked as unqualified because of their professions.

The candidate's public record is the next thing that is usually explored. Challengers often study their opponent's attendance records, roll-call votes, and floor speeches. Incumbents and open-seat candidates usually study their opponent's political record. If an opponent has never held office, then a campaign will usually turn to newspaper or trade magazine accounts of speeches made to civic organizations, trade associations, or other groups.

Virtually all campaigns search for activities that can be construed as illegal or unethical. Federal indictments for influence peddling, the Keating Five scandal in the Senate, and the banking and Post Office scandals in the House provided many challengers with grist for the attack portions of their campaigns in the 1990s. Sometimes proximity to scandal can threaten an incumbent who has not been shown to have done any wrong. The chair of the House ethics committee, Rep. Nancy Johnson, R-Conn., learned this lesson when Democratic challenger Charlotte Koskoff charged her with perpetrating a cover-up for Speaker Gingrich and came within 1,587 votes of defeating her.

Similarly, most contestants routinely search for unethical business transactions, evidence of tax dodging, and other questionable activities that could be used to discredit their opponents. Sometimes ex-spouses, estranged children, former friends, colleagues, and neighbors are interviewed to find examples of improper behavior or character flaws. Other times, investigations of military records, drivers' licenses, and campaign finance reports reveal that an opponent has lied about his or her service in the armed forces, is vulnerable to charges of having lived in the state or district for only a few years, or can be charged with being a tool of some wealthy special interest.

Most opposition research is tedious. Researchers scour the *Congressional Record,* records of the floor proceedings of state legislatures, newspapers, and other public sources to be able to show that a candidate is out of touch with the district, has flip-flopped on an issue, has taken an inordinate number of government-financed trips, or has committed some other questionable act. Opposition researchers often pore over campaign finance reports so a candidate can claim that an opponent is too beholden to PACs and wealthy individuals who live out of state to represent the views of constituents.

The widespread use of negative advertising has encouraged most campaigns to search for their own candidate's weaknesses. As one campaign manager explained, "We need to be prepared for the worst. We have to spend a lot of time looking at the things our opponent may try to pin on us."[53] Campaigns investigate their own candidates in anticipation of attacks they expect to be levied against them.

Some campaigns discuss a potential liability with members of the press before an opponent has had a chance to raise it. Preemption is an effective tactic for "inoculating" a candidate against an attack. Another strategy is to hire one of the consulting firms that stakes its reputation on its ability to prepare a televised response to an attack in less than one day. A few well-financed Senate and House contenders have gone so far as to record television commercials that present responses to particular charges before their opponent makes them. Rep. Scott Klug, R-Wis., went a step further in his 1996 reelection campaign. Anticipating that his opponent, Paul Soglin, the mayor of Madison, might try to link him to Gingrich, Klug preempted him. The congressman ran an ad in which his face "morphed" into Gingrich's. Then Klug's face reappeared and he stated, "I rank as the ninth most independent congressman, so if people tell you I'm Newt Gingrich, you tell them they've got the wrong picture."

Many of the most effective negative campaigns run in the last few elections blamed incumbents for economic stagnation, supporting tax increases, causing government gridlock and corruption, or losing touch with their districts. In the early and middle 1990s many challengers added congressional pay raises, political scandal, congressional perks, and the acceptance of PAC contributions to that list. Some personalized their attacks by counting the number of checks a member bounced at the House bank or the number of junkets he or she had taken at taxpayer or corporate expense. In 1994 many Republican House challengers attacked Democratic incumbents for being part of a corrupt, unresponsive Washington establishment. By linking their opponents to President Clinton, who had a low standing in the polls, the Republicans were able to defeat many senior House Democrats. Two years later, many Democratic candidates attacked Republican incumbents for voting to pass legislation that would pay for tax breaks for upper-income citizens by diminishing funding for future Medicare benefits and other programs that enjoy broad support. The Democrats defeated many House Republican freshmen by comparing their congressional voting records with Gingrich's and exhorting voters to elect a member of Congress who would represent their views, not those of some politician from Georgia.[54] One of the lessons to be drawn from the congressional elections of the 1990s is that negative campaigning is a potent weapon that can be used against members of both parties.

CHAPTER 8

Campaign Communications

Campaign communications range from sophisticated television advertisements to old-fashioned knocking on doors. The resources at a candidate's disposal, the types of media available, and the competitiveness of the election are the factors that most strongly influence how campaigns reach voters. In this chapter I examine the techniques that campaigns use to disseminate their messages and get their supporters to the polls.

Campaign communications are meant to accomplish six objectives: to improve a candidate's name recognition, project a favorable image, set the campaign agenda, exploit the issues, undermine the opponent's credibility and support, and defend the candidate against attacks. These objectives, of course, are designed to advance the campaign's broader goals of shoring up and expanding its bases of support and getting its supporters sufficiently interested in the election to vote.

Campaign communications usually proceed through four short phases that begin in late summer and continue until election day. In the first, often called the biography phase, candidates introduce themselves to voters by highlighting their experience and personal backgrounds. Next, candidates use issues to attract the support of uncommitted voters, energize their supporters, and further define themselves to the public.

The attack phase often begins after one candidate learns that he or she is slipping in the polls or failing to advance on an opponent. At this time, candidates contrast themselves with their opponent, point to inconsistencies between an opponent's rhetoric and actions, try to exploit unpopular positions that the opponent has taken, or just plain sling mud at one another. In the final weeks of the campaign, most successful candidates pull their message together by reminding voters who they are, why they are running, and why they are more worthy of being elected than their opponent. At this final, or summation, phase they commonly emphasize phrases and symbols that were presented earlier in the campaign.

TELEVISION ADVERTISING

Virtually every household in the United States possesses at least one television set, and the average adult watches more than three and one-half hours of television per day.[1] More than half of all voters maintain that television is their most important source of information in senatorial and other statewide races. Roughly half cite television as their most important source of information on House candidates.[2]

Television is the best medium for conveying image-related information to voters. It is also extremely useful in setting the campaign agenda and associating a candidate with popular issues.[3] Television ads enable candidates to transmit action-oriented videos that demonstrate such desirable qualities as leadership. Pictures of candidates meeting with voters or attending groundbreaking ceremonies convey more powerfully than do written or verbal statements the message that these individuals are actively involved in community affairs and have close ties to voters. Visuals are what make television an important campaign medium. As Republican strategist Robert Teeter explains, "80 or 90 percent of what people retain from a TV ad is visual. . . . If you have the visual right, you have the commercial right. If you don't, it almost doesn't matter what you're saying."[4] Television advertisements have the added advantage of enabling the campaign to control its message. Unlike interactive modes of communication, such as debates and speeches, paid advertisements do not allow an opponent or disgruntled voter to interrupt. Message control makes TV a potent weapon for increasing name recognition.[5]

Roughly nine out of ten Senate campaigns and 70 percent of all House campaigns use television, and these numbers would be higher if the costs were not so high.[6] Campaigns must pay the same rates as commercial advertisers for nonpreemptible advertising slots. These are most often prohibitively expensive, especially during prime time. Democratic representative José Serrano or Rodney Torres, his Republican opponent, would have had to spend $40,000 to broadcast one thirty-second prime-time advertisement to reach voters living in New York's 16th congressional district during the 1996 election. The cost of broadcasting an ad to this South Bronx district is exorbitant because the district is in a media market that spans the entire New York metropolitan area. Candidates in Texas's 11th district, which includes Waco, in contrast, paid only $260 to air a thirty-second prime-time television ad that blanketed virtually the entire district.[7]

Some campaigns save money by forgoing the certainty that their ads will be broadcast during prime time. Those who purchase preemptible broadcast time are guaranteed a television station's lowest unit rate by federal law but run the risk of their ads being aired at some less desirable time. That is a risk few campaigns take. Some campaigns, including many in major metropolitan areas, save money and improve targeting by substituting cable TV for broadcast stations.[8]

High costs and the mismatch between media markets and the boundaries of congressional districts discourage House candidates in the highly urbanized areas of the Middle Atlantic, West Coast, and southern New England from using television advertising. The distribution of media markets and relatively low advertising rates in most southwestern states and many rural areas, however, enable many House candidates to use television extensively.[9] Senate candidates tend to make greater use of television than candidates for the House because the configuration of state borders and media markets make television a relatively cost-efficient communications medium in statewide contests. The greater funding levels of Senate campaigns and the expectation that Senate candidates will use television also contribute to its greater use in contests for the upper chamber.

Televised campaign advertisements have come a long way since the days when candidates appeared as talking heads that spouted their political experiences and issue positions. Six trends define the evolution of the modern television campaign commercial. They are a movement toward greater emphasis on imagery, the use of action-oriented themes and pictures, the employment of emotionally laden messages, a decrease in the length of ads, an increase in negative advertising, and a reduction in the amount of time required to create an ad. Gimmicky, ten- and fifteen-second spots punctuated by twenty or so words have recently become popular with congressional candidates. An ability to counterattack within twenty-four hours has become a major selling point for many media firms.[10]

During the biography stage of the campaign, incumbents' ads typically depict them as experienced leaders who know and care about their constituents. Challengers and candidates for open seats also try to present themselves as capable and honorable by pointing to their accomplishments in politics, family life, or the private sector. All candidates broadcast advertisements that repeatedly mention and display their names, and end their commercials with the line "Vote for [candidate's name] for Congress."

Candidates who have led remarkable lives or have histories of public service often broadcast what are called "mini-docudramas" to showcase their war record, community activism, or road to professional success. The thirty-second biographical ad designed by Greg, Stevens, and Company for Sen. John Warner's 1996 Republican primary in Virginia highlighted Warner's exceptional military service and pictured him with prominent Republican leaders, thereby strengthening his credibility with GOP conservatives. It helped him defeat his more conservative opponent, James C. Miller III, former budget director in the Reagan administration.

The opening shot is of childhood photographs of John Warner with his father and mother. A small tag line at the bottom of the screen reads, "Paid for by friends of John Warner." A male narrator states:

> He learned about the values of duty and honor early in life. He left school to serve his country not once, but twice.

The black-and-white photographs that accompany this monologue show Warner first in a sailor's uniform and then in an airman's uniform. The words "duty," "honor," "World War II," and "Korean War" fade in and out as the pictures change. The narrator continues:

> He fought to rebuild America's military and worked at Ronald Reagan's side to help end the cold war, winning the respect of conservative leaders.

At this point, a black-and-white photograph of Warner with two naval officers appears on the screen with the words "Secretary of the Navy" superimposed near the bottom. Next, a color photograph appears of Warner in the Oval Office with Ronald Reagan. Following this photograph, in quick succession, are color pictures of Warner with Colin Powell in front of an American flag, with Dan Quayle, and with Margaret Thatcher. Text appears on the screen that reads: "95% Conservative Coalition rating." The narrator continues:

> Now he's the leader in the Senate's fight against crime and terrorism—leadership that's helped every corner of the state he loves. Committed to restoring common sense conservative values. Senator John Warner.

During this part of the narration, the visuals switch from still photos to video showing Warner walking into a Capitol Hill office. Text appears on the screen that reads: "Senior member, Armed Services Committee." Then Warner is shown meeting with various groups of constituents from Virginia, including workers, farmers, blacks, whites, a family, and a group of well-dressed youths. The ad ends with a picture of John Warner and the text: "Senator John Warner, Common Sense Conservative Leadership." Not many candidates have records of public service that are as impressive as Senator Warner's, but most candidates can use television to make the point that they are resourceful leaders whose personal experiences underlie their commitment to conservative or liberal causes.

Some incumbents, and a few nonincumbents with political experience, use "community action" spots to show that their efforts have constituents. In 1996 Sen. Mitch McConnell, R-Ky., broadcast a TV ad showcasing his efforts to help a small Kentucky town after part of a bluff in the town fell into the Mississippi River. McConnell is shown meeting with citizens, while a former Democratic mayor credits him with saving the town because he got the Army Corps of Engineers to repair the bluff. The ad closes with McConnell telling an elderly women, "If they don't do any of this right, you let me know."

"Feel good" ads are virtually devoid of substance and are designed to appeal to the electorate's sense of community pride or nationalism. They feature visuals of a candidate marching in parades, on horseback in the countryside, or involved in some other popular local activity. "Passing the torch" ads manipulate symbols to show that the candidate is the right person for the job. The most effective of these spots in recent years was broadcast by a presidential rather than a congressional candidate. It featured a teenage Bill Clinton shaking hands with President John F. Kennedy on the grounds of the White House.

During the issue phase, campaign ads communicate general policy positions on valence or position issues. The television and radio ads that John Shimkus aired in 1996 focused almost exclusively on his opposition to taxes. They stated that Jay Hoffman, his opponent, had raised taxes and that Shimkus wanted to cut them.[11] Hoffman's ads sought to link Shimkus with Gingrich. They focused on Republican proposals to cut funding for Medicare, education, and other popular federal programs.[12] Other candidates focused on such popular issues as crime, abortion, or the deficit. Although most voters have only a limited interest in any single issue, ads that focus on position issues can help candidates pick up crucial support among single-issue voters or emphasize certain elements of their images.[13]

In the attack phase of the campaign, candidates use televised advertisements that often feature fancy graphics to point to their opponent's shortcomings. Television is ideally suited to comparative ads because it enables candidates to present pictures of themselves and their opponent side-by-side and to roll lists of issues down the screen showing themselves on the popular and the opponent on the unpopular sides of salient policies. Sometimes the opponent's head is reduced in size, "phased out," or distorted to keep voters' attention and to subtly imply that faulty issue positions are only one of an opponent's weaknesses. Television is also an effective medium for portraying inconsistencies in an opponent's positions. Advertisements that feature images of the opponent somersaulting back and forth across the screen or debating him or herself are useful in highlighting inconsistencies among an opponent's speeches, campaign positions, or congressional roll-call votes.

Television can also be used to deliver the message that an incumbent has failed to represent constituents' views in Congress. In 1996 former representative David Price broadcast an ad in which he used humor to paint his opponent, Rep. Fred Heineman, as out of touch with voters in North Carolina's 4th district. The video shows a flight through space, passing by planets, stars, and moon. As the narration begins, Earth zooms by and a voice, mimicking NASA Control, states:

> Earth to Fred. Come in Congressman.

A small tag line reads, "Paid for by the Price for Congress Committee." The ad continues with a narrator stating:

> It's amazing. Fred Heineman actually said middle-class people make between $300,000 and $750,000 a year.

The text of the statement appears on the screen along with information revealing the source of the Heineman quotation as the November 13, 1995, edition of *Business Week.* As the flight through space continues past Jupiter, the voice imitating NASA control asks, "Fred, are you there?" The narrator continues:

> And Heineman claims his $180,000 a year income makes him—quote—lower middle class.

At this point, text appears on the screen revealing that this quote is from the March 29, 1996, edition of *USA Today.* The voice then interjects: "Earth, to, uhm, Fred, over," and the narrator continues:

> Fred Heineman. He's out of touch with average families here. Way out.

Finally, the voice states: "Earth to Fred. Come in!" and the flight through space goes forward until the Milky Way Galaxy is left behind.

Challengers often use televised ads to criticize an incumbent's performance. Some present pictures of empty desks with voice-overs decrying poor attendance records. Pictures of airplanes or beaches are used to make the case that legislators have been vacationing at the public's or some interest group's expense rather than performing their jobs in Washington. Video footage of lavish parties staged in fancy ballrooms make great backdrops for challenger ads claiming that an incumbent has spent so much time partying with lobbyists in Washington that he or she has lost touch with the concerns of ordinary constituents. Both congressional campaign committees create generic ads to help challengers exploit voter frustration with Congress.

One attack ad often begets another, and television is ideal for alternative, often theatrical, strategies. An ad in which a candidate criticizes an opponent for dragging the race into the mud can effectively answer negative charges while enhancing a candidate's image of sincerity as he or she appears to take the high road. Humorous ads can also be effective at disarming opponents' attacks. In 1996 Democratic Senate candidate Tom Bruggere used an ad featuring three children playing near a swing set to criticize his opponent, Sen. Gordon Smith, R-Ore., for waging a negative campaign. After two of the children state what they want to do when they grow up, one of them, a young girl, asks: "Gordy, what do you want to be?" To which a boy playing the part of young Smith replies, "a politician," and then scoops up a handful of mud and throws it on the girl's blouse. The ad then gives Bruggere's positions on several issues. It closes with the mudslinger being dragged away by his mother, who exclaims, "Gordon Smith just wait until I get you home!"

In the summation stage of the campaign, eleventh-hour television blitzes are used to solidify a candidate's message in the minds of voters. Key phrases and visuals from earlier commercials are repeated as candidates who are ahead shore up support and those running behind appeal to undecided voters.

RADIO ADVERTISING

Radio is an extremely popular medium for congressional campaign communications. More than 90 percent of all House candidates and virtually every Senate contestant purchase radio ads.[14] Inexpensive to record and broadcast, radio commercials are ideal for building a candidate's name identification. Another advantage is that some candidates—whether they are intimidated by the television camera, not telegenic, novices to the spotlight, or products of the pretelevision era—perform better on radio. For many incumbents, taping radio commercials is an easy extension of the radio shows they regularly send back to stations in their districts. Like television, radio is an excellent vehicle for emotion-laden messages.[15]

Radio allows candidates to target voters with great precision. Radio stations broadcast to smaller, more homogeneous audiences than television, enabling campaigns to tailor their messages to different segments of the population.

Campaigns can reach Hispanic voters in the Southwest, Florida, or the inner cities of the Northeast by advertising on Spanish-language stations. "Golden oldies" stations, which feature music from the 1960s and 1970s, are ideal for reaching middle-aged voters. Radio talk programs, such as the *Rush Limbaugh Show,* are excellent vehicles for reaching voters who are committed to particular ideologies. Commuting hours furnish near-captive audiences of suburbanites who travel to work. Democratic representative George Brown Jr., who is not reputed to be a fan of country and western music, places campaign ads on a station that plays such music to reach the hundreds of thousands of music enthusiasts who commute to and from work in his California district.[16]

NEWSPAPER ADVERTISING

Newspaper advertisements dominated campaign communications for much of American history but fell in importance with the decline of the partisan press in the late 1800s.[17] Congressional campaigns still purchase newspaper ads, but they are not as widely used as radio and many other media. Seventy percent of all House and 80 percent of all Senate campaigns purchase ads in local or state-wide newspapers.[18]

Newspapers have shortcomings as a campaign medium. They do not lend themselves to emotional appeals, are not as good as television for portraying imagery, and cannot be used to deliver a personalized message. Only a few congressional districts and states have large enough minority communities to sustain independent newspapers that can be used to target communications to these groups. The effectiveness of campaign advertisements that appear in newspapers is also limited[19]

If such shortcomings exist, why do most campaigns place ads in newspapers? One reason is that they are inexpensive. Newspaper advertisements cost less than ads transmitted via television, radio, mail, or virtually any other media. Newspaper ads can also be useful in announcing the times and locations of campaign events. Finally, some candidates and campaign aides believe that purchasing advertising space from a local newspaper can help them secure the paper's endorsement.

DIRECT-MAIL ADVERTISING

Mail can be used to raise money, convey a message, or encourage people to vote, but the key to success in all three areas is a good mailing list. A good fund-raising list is made up of previous donors or persons who have a history of contributing to like-minded candidates; a good advertising list includes supporters and persuadable voters; and a good voter mobilization list includes only the candidate's supporters.

Direct mail (sometimes referred to as persuasion mail) is one of the most widely used methods of campaign advertising in congressional elections. It is used by more than nine out of ten House and nearly all Senate candidates.[20] Mail is a one-way communications tool that offers significant advantages in message control and delivery. Precise targeting is its main advantage. Campaigns can purchase lists that include such information as a voter's name, address, gender, age, race or ethnicity, employment status, party registration, voting history, and estimated income.[21] This information enables campaigns to tailor the candidate profiles, issue positions, and photographs they include in their mailings to appeal to specific segments of the population. This ability makes mail an excellent medium for staking out position issues and for campaigning in heterogeneous states or districts. Campaigns waged in highly diverse areas, such as New York's 12th district, which is 58 percent Hispanic and includes most of Chinatown, often use the mail to campaign in more than one language.

A second advantage of mail is that it is relatively inexpensive. Letters that are produced using personal computers and laser printers can be mailed to voters for little more than the price of a first-class stamp. Campaigns can also take advantage of post office discounts for presorted mailings.

Nevertheless, direct mail is not without its disadvantages, including the fact that it is often tossed out as junk mail. Another disadvantage is that it rests principally on the power of the printed word. Whereas television and radio enable campaigns to embellish their messages with visual images or sound effects, mail depends primarily on written copy to hold voters' attention and get a message across. This makes it a less effective medium for communicating image-related information.

Direct-mail experts rely on many different techniques to combat the weaknesses of their medium. Personalized salutations, graphs, and pictures are often used to capture and hold voters' attention. Other gimmicks include the use of postscripts that are designed to look as though they were handwritten.

Direct mail is an especially powerful medium for challengers and candidates who have strong ideological positions because it is ideal for negative advertising or making appeals that stir voters' emotions. Yet mail also offers some advantages to incumbents. Many members of Congress send out letters early in the election cycle to reinforce voter support without mounting a highly visible campaign.[22] These mailings often include messages reinforcing those that incumbents communicate in congressionally franked mass mailings to constituents, which are prohibited ninety days before a primary or general election for House members and sixty days before an election for senators.[23]

Direct mail plays a prominent role in many congressional elections. Democratic challenger Loretta Sanchez, who defeated the arch-conservative Robert Dornan, the nine-term representative from California's 46th district, made mail the centerpiece of her communication efforts. Sanchez could not afford to air any television advertisements because the 46th district is located in the prohibitively expensive Los Angeles media market.[24] Instead, she spent 43 percent of her $823,000 budget to send sixteen separate mailings to an average of 40,000 voters. These were targeted to Democrats, female independent voters, young Republican women, Hispanics, and voters who did not show up at the polls regularly. The objective of the campaign was to maximize voter turnout among these groups; if enough of them voted, it was thought, Sanchez would win in what has historically been a low turnout district. Her direct mail emphasized that the 1996 election would be critical to stopping the Republican agenda in Congress and stressed the importance of every person's vote. Members of Sanchez's campaign team believe that direct mail was critical in producing their candidate's razor-thin victory margin.[25]

FREE MEDIA

One of the major goals of any campaign is to generate free, or "earned," media—radio, television, newspaper, or magazine coverage that candidates receive when news editors consider their activities newsworthy. Earned media has other advantages besides free advertising. Because it is delivered by a neutral observer, it has greater credibility than campaign-generated communications.[26] The major disadvantage of free media is that campaigns cannot control what news correspondents report. Misstatements and blunders are more likely to appear in the news than are issues raised in major policy speeches.

News coverage of congressional elections consists of stories based on press releases issued by campaigns; stories about events, issues, or time that a reporter has spent with a candidate; and analytical or editorial stories about a candidate or campaign.[27] Most analysis focuses on the "horse-race" aspect of the election. Those stories that get beyond handicapping the race usually discuss candidates' political qualifications, personal characteristics, or campaign organizations. Fewer stories focus on the issues.[28] Coverage by television and radio tends to be shorter, more action-oriented, and less detailed and features less editorializing than print journalism.

Most journalists strive to cover politics objectively, but this does not mean that all candidates are treated the same. Reporters follow certain norms when pursuing leads and researching and writing their stories—norms that usually work to the advantage of incumbents.[29] Moreover, editorials are largely exempt from the norms of objectivity that apply to news stories. Newspaper owners and their editorial boards make no bones about voicing their opinions on editorial pages. Radio and television stations also air programs that feature pundits discussing the virtues and foibles of specific candidates. Most readers have come to expect newspaper editors and political talk show hosts to endorse specific candidates shortly before the election. Media endorsements and campaign coverage can have a significant impact on elections.

Attracting Coverage

Attracting media coverage requires planning and aggressiveness. Besides issuing streams of press releases, campaign offices distribute copies of the candidate's schedule to correspondents, invite them to campaign events, and bend over backward to grant interviews. Candidates also submit themselves to interrogations by panels of newspaper editors with the goal of generating good press coverage or winning an endorsement.

Successful campaigns carefully play to the needs of different news media. Press releases that feature strong leads, have news value, provide relevant facts, and contain enough background information for an entire story are faxed to print reporters.[30] Advance notice of major campaign events, including information about predicted crowd size, acoustics, and visual backdrops, is given to television and radio correspondents with the hope that the event will be one of the few they cover.[31] Interpretive information is provided to all journalists, regardless of the media they work in, to try to generate campaign stories with a favorable news spin. News organizations routinely report stories based on materials distributed by campaigns; because few news organizations have adequate resources to research or even verify this information, most free press is uncritical.

Newspapers and radio stations are more likely than television stations to give candidates free media coverage. Television stations devote little time to covering congressional elections, particularly House races. Television news shows occasionally discuss the horse-race aspect of campaigns, cover small portions of campaign debates, or analyze controversial campaign ads, but few are willing to give candidates air time to discuss issues. Radio stations are more generous with air time. Many invite candidates to participate in call-in talk shows and public forums. Newspapers usually give the most detailed campaign coverage. Small, understaffed newspapers frequently print portions of candidates' press releases and debate transcripts verbatim.

Senate candidates attract more free media than do House candidates. Incumbents and open-seat contestants usually get more—and more favorable—press coverage than do challengers, regardless of whether they are running for the House or the Senate. Inequities in campaign coverage are due to the professional norms that guide news journalists and to the inequalities that exist among candidates and campaign organizations. The preoccupation of journalists with candidates' personalities, qualifications, campaign organizations, and probable success are to the advantage of incumbents because they are almost always better known, more qualified, in possession of more professional organizations, and more likely to win than their opponents.[32]

Press coverage in House contests between an incumbent and a challenger is so unequal that veteran Democratic political adviser Anita Dunn believes "the local press is the unindicted co-conspirator in the alleged 'permanent incumbency.'"[33] As Dunn explains,

> A vicious circle develops for challengers—if early on, they don't have money, standing in the polls, endorsements, and the backing of political insiders, they—and the race—are written off, not covered, which means the likelihood of a competitive race developing is almost nonexistent.[34]

The 1996 contest between the Republican incumbent Connie Morella and the Democratic challenger Don Mooers in Maryland's 8th district demonstrates this point. The *Washington Post* (the major newspaper serving the area) mentioned Mooers in a total of twenty-one stories before the election, and all of them implied he had little chance of winning. The headline of one of the *Post*'s stories on the Democratic primary was "Lots of Foes, Little Hope." It described all the Democratic candidates as having "little campaign experience" and stated that their "lack of polish was evident." It also quoted one of the contestants as saying, "Heaven help whoever gets the nomination. They're going to need it."[35]

The *Post*'s early coverage of the general election stated that Mooers faced "an uphill struggle against a skilled politician who is experienced, popular and well-financed—three attributes he still is cultivating." It went on to say that he was "infused with an earnest 1960s idealism" but had poor prospects because he was without a campaign staff and his "campaign coffers hold a scant $4,642 compared with Morella's $388,858."[36] Mid-summer general election coverage described Mooers as "a political newcomer . . . who came out ahead in a crowded Democratic primary beating eight relatively unknowns in a race that drew scant attention from the media or the voters." It pointed out that a confident Morella responded to a challenge by Mooers to limit her campaign spending to $1 per voter by stating, "I'm cheap. I may even spend less than that."[37] Finally, a story published a week before the election called Morella "always up to the challenge," and featured a likeness of her flattening six previous Democratic opponents and about to flatten Mooers. The caption above the picture reads, "Caught under the Morella steamroller."[38] Not surprisingly, the paper provided little coverage of Morella's victory, simply stating that she won by "a comfortable margin."

Although many challengers can usually count on getting only four stories—their announcement, coverage of their primary victory, a candidate profile, and the announcement of their defeat—it is still worth pursuing free media coverage. Those few challengers who are able to make the case to journalists that they have the capacity to mount a strong campaign are able to attract significant media coverage, often enough to become known among local voters. Challengers who have held elective office or had significant unelective political experience, assembled professional campaign organizations, and raised substantial funds are in a better position to make this case than are those who have not. They typically receive extra press coverage, which in turn helps them raise more money, hire additional help, become more competitive, and attract even greater attention from the media.[39] A similar set of relationships exists for open-seat candidates, except that it is usually easier for them to make the case that they are involved in a close contest.

Scandal can also help candidates attract more media coverage. Even underdogs are taken more seriously when their opponents have been accused of breaking the law or ethical misconduct. Former Republican representative Peter Torkildsen of Massachusetts, who defeated a seven-term incumbent, Nicholas Mavroules, in 1992, is an example of an experienced challenger who took advantage of the heightened media exposure that resulted from scandal. Torkildsen, who had served six terms as a state representative and two years as the Massachusetts commissioner on labor and industries, mounted a highly professional and well-funded campaign effort. Under normal circumstances, neither he nor any Republican challenger in Massachusetts would have received much media coverage in a race against a long-time Democratic incumbent in a safe Democratic district. However, when Mavroules was indicted on federal charges of bribery, extortion, and tax evasion in August 1992, all normalcy left the election. News correspondents began to devote significant coverage to the Republican congressional primary—an event usually ignored in the state's Democrat-dominated politics—and later to Torkildsen's general election campaign to unseat Mavroules. The Torkildsen campaign fanned the flames of voter outrage over Mavroules's seventeen-count federal indictment by issuing press releases that contrasted Mavroules's dependence on PAC money with Torkildsen's refusal to accept it. These releases generated a great deal of free press. Torkildsen's ability to capitalize on the media opportunities provided by incumbent scandal enabled him to battle to a ten-point general election victory.[40]

Campaign Debates

Debates are among the few campaign activities that receive extensive press coverage and can place a challenger on equal footing with an incumbent. The decision to participate in a debate is a strategic one. Front-runners, who are usually incumbents, generally prefer to avoid debating because they understand that debates have the potential to do them more harm than good. Nevertheless, incumbents recognize that the public expects them to debate; to avoid being blasted for shirking their civic responsibility, they do so. Candidates who are running behind, usually challengers, have the most to gain from debating. They prefer to engage in as many debates as possible and to hold them when they will attract the most media coverage.

Before debates are scheduled, the candidates or their representatives negotiate certain matters in regard to them. In addition to the number and timing of debates, candidates must agree on whether independent or minor-party candidates will participate, on the format that will be used, and on where the debate or debates will be held. All these factors can influence who, if anyone, is considered the winner. Negotiations about debates can become heated but are almost always successfully resolved. Well over 90 percent of all House and Senate contestants debate their opponents.[41] Those few who refuse, usually enjoy insurmountable leads or lack verbal agility. For example, Sen. Strom Thurmond, R-S.C., who turned ninety-three during the early days of his 1996 reelection campaign, was precisely in this situation and opted not to debate his opponent, Elliot Close, a quick-witted Democrat. Whether or not the candidates debate is one of the few questions in congressional elections that is usually decided in favor of challengers and candidates who are running behind. The Thurmond-Close race was an exception to the rule.

Media Bias

Most House challengers and incumbents agree that the media do not provide equal coverage to House campaigns (see Table 8-1).[42] Incumbent shoo-ins and likely loser challengers are more apt to perceive an incumbent bias, reflecting the one-sided nature of press coverage in elections for safe seats. Not surprisingly, challengers, particularly those in uncompetitive contests, are the most likely to complain that the media did not cover their campaigns fairly.[43] To some extent these perceptions are a product of the norms that guide journalists

TABLE 8-1

Campaigners' Perceptions of the Distribution of Media Coverage in House Campaigns

| | | Incumbents | | Challengers | | Open-seat candidates | |
	All	In jeopardy	Shoo-ins	Hope-fuls	Likely losers	Pros-pects	Long shots
Gave more coverage to own campaign	29%	34%	63%	24%	6%	24%	17%
Gave more coverage to opponent's campaign	34	19	4	40	60	37	44
Covered campaigns equally	37	47	33	36	33	39	39
(N)	(328)	(47)	(73)	(53)	(83)	(49)	(23)

Source: The 1992 Congressional Campaign Study.

Notes: Figures include responses from House general election candidates and campaign aides in major-party contested races, excluding a small number of atypical races. Some columns do not add to 100 percent because of rounding.

and the distribution of media endorsements—which favor incumbents, especially those who hold safe seats.[44]

Some partisan differences also exist in the perception of media coverage. More Democratic campaigners than Republicans maintain that the press gives equal or fair coverage to both campaigns, reflecting a widely shared opinion among Republican politicians and voters that the media corps is made up of members of a liberal establishment. Nevertheless, the 41 percent of candidates and campaign aides of both parties who believe that the media are biased against them reflect the adversarial relationship that exists between politicians and the press.[45]

FIELD WORK

Field work involves voter registration and get-out-the-vote drives, literature drops, and the distribution of yard signs and bumper stickers. It also includes candidate appearances at town meetings and in parades, speeches to Rotary Clubs and other civic groups, door-to-door campaigning, and other grass-roots activities. Field work is an important means of campaign communication and voter mobilization.

Field activities were the key to campaigning during the golden age of parties, and they continue to play a role in modern congressional elections. Sophisticated targeting plans, similar to those used in direct mail, guide many field activities. Field work remains one of the most labor intensive, volunteer-dependent aspects of congressional elections.[46] Candidates, their supporters, and local party workers knock on doors to learn whether citizens intend to vote, whom they support, and if they have any specific concerns they would like the candidate to address. Supporters and potential supporters who express an interest in an issue, need to register to vote, need help in getting to the polls, or are willing to work in the campaign typically receive follow-up calls.

Person-to-person communication is a highly effective means of political persuasion, especially when it takes place directly between the candidate and a voter. It also provides a campaign with useful feedback. Candidates routinely draw on conversations with individuals they meet along the campaign trail to develop anecdotes that humanize issues.

Field activities are relatively inexpensive because they can be carried out by volunteers. Local party activists, union members, and other volunteers are often called on to deliver campaign literature, register voters, or drive them to the polls. The development of the coordinated campaign has allowed many congressional candidates to rely in part on party organizations to carry out their field work.[47] Forty percent of all House campaigns report that local party committees played a moderately important-to-extremely important role in their registration and get-out-the-vote drives, and over half of the campaigns maintain that local parties were a moderately important-to-extremely important source of campaign volunteers.[48]

THE IMPORTANCE OF DIFFERENT COMMUNICATIONS TECHNIQUES

Congressional campaigns disseminate their messages through a variety of media, each having its advantages and disadvantages. Door-to-door campaigning is inexpensive but time consuming. Television advertising requires little commitment of the candidate's time, but it is rarely cheap. Radio advertising and direct mail require accurate targeting to be effective.

Most campaigners believe that television is the best medium for disseminating their messages (see Table 8-2). Those involved in close contests rely on television the most. Incumbents find television more important than challengers do, reflecting the fact that more incumbents can afford to broadcast television commercials. But it is open-seat candidates who most consistently evaluate

TABLE 8-2

Campaigners' Perceptions of the Importance of Different Communications Techniques in House Campaigns

Perception	All	Incumbents		Challengers		Open-seat candidates	
		In jeopardy	Shoo-ins	Hope-fuls	Likely losers	Pros-pects	Long shots
Television (paid or free)	4.18	4.34	4.01	4.13	3.81	4.71	4.54
Radio (paid or free)	3.76	3.78	3.70	3.70	3.73	3.86	3.88
Newsletters and direct mail	3.68	3.72	3.80	3.76	3.33	3.88	3.86
Press releases and free media	3.67	3.57	3.76	3.94	3.62	3.34	3.83
Literature drops	3.50	3.27	3.26	3.54	3.72	3.40	4.00
Speeches and rallies	3.46	3.00	3.44	3.26	3.78	3.31	4.04
Candidate visits to shopping centers, factories, etc.	3.10	2.93	3.41	3.27	2.95	2.68	3.52
Door-to-door canvassing	3.10	2.63	2.93	3.55	3.06	3.14	3.61
Debates	3.06	2.70	2.70	2.98	3.17	3.48	3.77
Newspaper ads	3.00	3.09	2.87	3.16	2.97	2.90	3.04
Billboards and buttons	2.62	2.13	2.72	2.83	2.62	2.41	3.30
Surrogate cam-paigning	2.54	2.13	2.44	2.73	2.73	2.42	2.91
(N)	(325)	(47)	(70)	(54)	(81)	(49)	(24)

Source: The 1992 Congressional Campaign Study.

Notes: Candidates and campaign aides were asked to assess the importance of each technique on the following scale: 1 = not important or not used; 2 = slightly important; 3 = moderately important; 4 = very important; 5 = extremely important. The values listed are the arithmetic means of the scores. Figures include responses from House general election candidates and campaign aides in major-party contested races, excluding a small number of atypical races.

television as extremely important, if not essential, to their campaigns. As shown in Chapter 6, the overwhelming majority of open-seat candidates can afford the high cost of broadcast time, and their races are usually competitive enough to warrant purchasing it.

TABLE 8-3

The Impact of Geography and Targeting Strategies on the Importance
of Different Communications Techniques in House Campaigns

	District geography			Targeting strategy	
	Urban	Rural	Suburban or mixed	Geodemo- graphic	Issue- or attitude- based
Television (paid or free)	4.17	4.50	4.13	4.25	4.12
Radio (paid or free)	3.77	3.72	3.76	3.78	3.75
Newsletters and direct mail	3.80	3.60	3.58	3.90	3.49
Press releases and free media	3.54	3.88	3.80	3.81	3.59
Literature drops	3.64	3.04	3.40	3.62	3.43
Speeches and rallies	3.46	3.48	3.44	3.47	3.44
Candidate visits to shopping centers, factories, etc.	3.02	3.25	3.22	3.12	3.08
Door-to-door canvassing	3.25	2.89	3.17	3.08	3.11
Debates	3.07	3.12	3.03	3.14	3.00
Newspaper ads	2.99	3.32	2.94	2.99	3.00
Billboards and buttons	2.71	2.68	2.50	2.69	2.57
Surrogate cam- paigning	2.54	2.40	2.57	2.60	2.50
(N)	(172)	(25)	(125)	(113)	(209)

Source: The 1992 Congressional Campaign Study.

Notes: Districts are defined as urban (or rural) if 60 percent or more of the population lives in an urban (or rural) area; all others are classified as suburban or mixed. Targeting strategies are defined as geodemographic if campaigns focused on voters in specific geographic locations or demographic or occupational groups; targeting strategies are defined as issue- or attitude-based if they focused on issues, voters' party affiliations, persuadable voters, Perot supporters, or miscellaneous factors. Candidates and campaign aides were asked to assess the importance of each technique on the following scale: 1 = not important or not used; 2 = slightly important; 3 = moderately important; 4 = very important; 5 = extremely important. The values listed are the arithmetic means of the scores. Figures include responses from House general election candidates and campaign aides in major-party contested races, excluding a small number of atypical races.

Most House candidates and campaign aides also assess radio, direct mail, and free media as very important. Campaign literature and speeches are rated slightly lower, except by likely losers and long shots, but both are still thought to be moderately important-to-very important ways of reaching voters. Likely loser challengers and open-seat long shots tend to rely more heavily on campaign literature and speeches, reflecting their inability to purchase more expensive media and the overall low-key nature of their campaigns.

Campaigns use candidate visits to shopping malls and workplaces, door-to-door canvasses, campaign debates, and newspaper advertisements to help get out their message, but most see these as only moderately important communication techniques. Neighborhood canvasses, billboards, surrogate campaigning, and other grass-roots activities are viewed less favorably by incumbents because they can use television, direct mail, and other, more expensive forms of campaign advertising. Incumbents in jeopardy, who are often involved in the most expensive campaigns, place the lowest value on grass-roots campaign activities.

District characteristics and campaign strategy also affect media usage patterns. Television is a more important communications medium for House campaigns in rural districts than it is for those conducted in urban and suburban settings, reflecting cost considerations and the mismatch between media markets and House seats in metropolitan areas (see Table 8-3). Greater population density allows campaigns waged in urban and suburban districts to make greater use of field activities, including distributing campaign literature and canvassing door-to-door, than campaigns waged in rural areas. Campaigns that target individuals who live in particular neighborhoods, work in certain occupations, or belong to specific segments of the population (such as women, the elderly, or members of an ethnic group) make greater use of direct mail than do campaigns that focus their efforts on less easily identifiable groups, such as single-issue voters.

CHAPTER 9

Candidates, Campaigns, and Electoral Success

During the golden age of parties, party identification was the most important determinant of voting behavior, and partisan tides were extremely important in congressional elections. The decline of voter partisanship in the 1960s and 1970s paved the way for incumbency to have a greater effect on election outcomes. Incumbent success rates climbed to better than 90 percent, as members of Congress began to make better use of the resources that the institution put at their disposal.[1] Although challenger victories were rare, the type of campaign mounted by individual candidates, especially open-seat contestants, could determine the difference between victory and defeat.

The election of 1994 was unusual in that it was one of the few recent contests in which one party was able to nationalize congressional elections at the expense of another. Although the 1996 congressional elections were more nationalized than those held in the last few decades, they largely represented a return to normalcy in that incumbency, money, district partisanship, and other factors pertaining to individual candidates and their campaigns were the major determinants of congressional election outcomes.

What separates winners from losers in contemporary congressional elections? How great an impact do candidate characteristics, political conditions, campaign strategy, campaign effort, party and interest group activities, and media coverage have on the percentage of the votes that House candidates receive? Do these factors affect incumbents, challengers, and open-seat contestants equally, or do these candidates need to do different things to win elections? This chapter addresses these questions. It also contains a discussion of the differences in the opinions of winners and losers over what determines the outcomes of elections.

INCUMBENT CAMPAIGNS

Incumbency is highly important in regard to the kinds of campaigns that candidates mount, and it is the most important determinant of congressional election outcomes.[2] Virtually all incumbents begin the general election campaign with higher name recognition and voter approval levels, greater political experience, more money, and better campaign organizations than their opponents. Incumbents also benefit from the fact that most constituents and political elites in Washington expect them to win and act accordingly. For the most part, voters cast ballots, volunteers donate time, contributors give money, and news correspondents provide coverage in ways that favor incumbents. Most strategic politicians also behave in ways that contribute to high incumbent success rates. These individuals usually wait until a seat becomes open rather than take on a sitting incumbent.

The big leads that most incumbents enjoy at the beginning of the election season make defending those leads the major objective of their campaigns. Incumbent campaigns tend to focus more on reinforcing and mobilizing existing bases of support than winning new ones. As the campaign manager for Connie Morella, a shoo-in House member, explained,

> Our candidate has a great personal story and a strong record. . . . Our goals were to remind voters of her commitment to the district and how she has served as an independent voice that represents them in Congress. We targeted federal employees and retirees, women's groups, teachers, the high-tech sector, Republicans, and independents . . . the same groups that supported us before.[3]

The overwhelming advantages that members of Congress possess make incumbency an accurate predictor of election outcomes in roughly nine out of ten House and three-quarters of all Senate races in which incumbents seek reelection.

Of course, not every incumbent is a shoo-in, and a few challengers have realistic chances of winning. Incumbents who are implicated in a scandal, have cast roll-call votes that are out of sync with voters, or possess other liabilities need to mount more aggressive campaigns. They must begin campaigning early to maintain their popularity among supporters, to remind voters of their accomplishments in office, and to set the campaign agenda. They also must be prepared to counter the campaigns of the strong challengers who are nominated to run against them. Many incumbents in jeopardy face experienced challengers, some of whom amass the financial and organizational resources needed

TABLE 9-1

Significant Predictors of House Incumbents' Vote Shares

	Percent
Base vote	65.29
Partisan bias (per one-point advantage in party registration)	+0.08
Political scandal	−4.39
Significant independent or minor-party candidate	−9.65
Challenger spending on campaign communications (per $1,000)	−0.023
Party spending on behalf of challenger (per $1,000)	−0.12
Independent expenditures against incumbent (per $1,000)	−0.097
Media advantage favoring incumbent	+2.54

Sources: The 1992 Congressional Campaign Study, Federal Election Commission data, various editions of *Congressional Quarterly Weekly Report,* and other sources.

Notes: Complete regression statistics are presented in Table A-2 in the first edition of the book. The analysis includes general election candidates in major-party contested races, excluding a small number of atypical races. N = 117.

to mount a serious campaign. A few of these challengers in each election are able to capitalize on their opponent's weaknesses and win.

Usually little can be done to increase the victory margins of House incumbents who begin with big leads over their opponents. All incumbents—Democrat or Republican, Caucasian or African American, old or young, male or female—have tremendously favorable odds of winning again. Few variables—indeed only the seven identified in Table 9-1—have a significant direct effect on the percentages of the vote that incumbents win.

Such factors as gender, age, race, and occupation, which are so influential in separating House candidates from the general population, typically have no impact on the shares of the vote received by incumbents.[4] Primary challenges from within their own party also rarely harm the reelection prospects of incumbents who defeated their primary opponents. Moreover, incumbents' targeting strategies, issues, and communications expenditures have no significant effect on their shares of the vote in the general election. The campaign efforts that party committees and supportive PACs mount on an incumbent's behalf also rarely spell the difference between success and defeat.

The first figure in Table 9-1, labeled the base vote, represents the percentage of the vote that a House incumbent in a typical two-party contested race would have received if all the other factors were set to zero.[5] A hypothetical incumbent who runs for reelection in a district that has equal numbers of registered Democratic and Republican voters, who has not been implicated in a scandal, who does not face minor-party opposition, who is against a challenger who spends no money and does not benefit from party-coordinated expenditures, who is not attacked by PACs, and who is not given preferential treatment by the press would win slightly more than 65 percent of the vote.

Certain districts and states lend themselves to the election of particular kinds of candidates. Districts populated mainly by Democratic voters (often urban districts that are home to many lower-middle-class, poor, or minority voters) typically elect Democrats; those populated by members of the GOP (frequently suburban districts inhabited by more affluent voters) usually elect Republicans. The partisan bias of the district (the difference between the percentage of registered voters who belong to a candidate's party minus the percentage of registered voters who belong to the opponent's party) has a positive impact on incumbents' electoral prospects. As the second figure in the table indicates, for every 1 percent increase in the partisan advantage that incumbents enjoy among registered voters, they receive an additional 0.08 percent of the vote. A Democratic incumbent who represents a district with seventy-five registered Democratic voters for every twenty-five registered Republicans typically wins 4 percent (a fifty-point advantage in party registration multiplied by 0.08) more of the vote than a Democratic incumbent who holds a seat that is evenly split between Democratic and Republican registered voters. Partisan bias is an important source of incumbency advantage because most House members represent districts that are populated primarily by members of their party.

Those few House members who represent districts in which the balance of voter registration does not favor their party are often in danger of losing reelection. Former representative Peter Torkildsen, a Republican of Massachusetts, is an example of a House member who represented a district in which voter registration favored the opposing party. Torkildsen, it should be recalled from Chapter 8, defeated a scandal-ridden incumbent in a Democratic-leaning district.[6] Once in Congress, he used his positions on the House Armed Services and Small Business Committees to attend to the interests of constituents who depended on the district's military bases and the local defense industry for their livelihoods. He followed the lead of Massachusetts's popular governor, William Weld, by developing a fiscally conservative probusiness agenda, while championing such liberal social issues as abortion rights. His assiduous attention to his district and a strong Republican national tide enabled him to beat Democrat John Tierney, an attorney, by a margin of 4 percent in 1994.[7]

Torkildsen had to defend his seat against Tierney again in 1996. This time the incumbent was running in a political climate that favored his opponent's rather than his own party. Tierney ran against the GOP's Contract with America, and championed his own Contract with the Middle Class, Workers, and Small

Business People. Torkildsen was on the defensive for most of the race. Despite his spending advantage over Tierney ($1.1 million to $779,000), Torkildsen was unable to hold on to the support of independent-minded Democrats. He lost the race by a mere 360 votes.[8]

Members of Congress who are implicated in a scandal are also usually at risk. Those identified with salacious or highly publicized misbehavior frequently choose to retire rather than add the anguish of defeat to the humiliation associated with their ethical lapses. Nevertheless, some scandal-tainted members of Congress attempt to remain in office. Many of them suffer at the ballot box. Constituents may not possess complete information about their elected representatives, but the efforts of House challengers and the media usually enable enough voters to learn about a public official's ethical transgressions to put that person's career in jeopardy. This is a lesson that several House members who were deeply implicated in the House banking scandal or under federal indictment learned the hard way.[9] The typical incumbent who is implicated in a major scandal is penalized by almost 4.4 percent of the vote, which is enough to defeat an incumbent in a marginal district. Moreover, as the close call of the House ethics committee chairwoman Nancy Johnson in 1996 demonstrates, being associated with a major scandal can be almost as dangerous as committing the offense that leads to one.

One of the most important signs that a House incumbent might be in trouble is the emergence of a significant independent or minor-party candidate (one who garners 10 percent or more of the vote). These candidates usually run during periods of voter frustration or against incumbents who are perceived to be out of touch with their constituents or who are implicated in a scandal. Although they rarely win (Rep. Bernard Sanders of Vermont is the only one since 1955 to serve in the House), independent candidates can sometimes sufficiently alter the dynamics of a race to affect its outcome.[10] The main effect of independent and minor-party candidacies is to take away votes from incumbents. House members who must defeat both a major-party opponent and significant additional opposition average almost 10 percent fewer votes than those who do not.

Because most House members begin the general election campaign well known and liked by their constituents, few elements of incumbent campaigning have much influence on election outcomes. The targeting approaches that incumbents use, the themes and issues they stress, and whether or not they bash their opponents do not significantly affect the typical incumbent's vote margin.[11] Nor do the dollars incumbents spend on direct-mail, television, radio, and newspaper advertising, field work, or other communications make a significant contribution to the percentage of the votes they win.[12]

Incumbent spending in 1996 followed the usual pattern of increasing in direct response to the closeness of the race.[13] Shoo-ins, such as Connie Morella, who ran against underfunded challengers undertook fairly modest reelection efforts by incumbent standards, assembling relatively small organizations and spending moderate sums of money. Those who were pitted against well-funded challengers, however, followed Vic Fazio's lead and mounted extensive campaigns.

Although the communications expenditures and other campaign activities of incumbents are not significantly related to higher vote margins, they are not inconsequential. A more accurate interpretation is that incumbent campaigning generally works to reinforce rather than expand a candidate's existing base of support. Incumbents who are in the most trouble—because they represent marginal districts, have been implicated in a scandal, failed to keep in touch with voters, or cast too many legislative votes that were out of line with constituents' views—usually spend the most. Most of these candidates either succeed in reinforcing their electoral bases or watch their shares of the vote dip slightly from previous years. Others watch their victory margins become perilously low. The high-powered campaigns these incumbents wage might make the difference between winning and losing. In some cases, probably no amount of incumbent spending would make a difference. Scandal, poor performance, and some other factors simply put reelection beyond the reach of a few House members. Regardless of whether an incumbent in a close race wins or loses, that individual would undoubtedly have done worse absent an extensive campaign effort.

House challengers' expenditures, however, significantly reduce incumbents' vote shares. The typical challenger spent roughly $190,000 on voter contact in 1996, reducing the average incumbent's vote share to about 63 percent. Hopeful challengers spent an average of $456,000 on campaign communications, which drove down the votes won by the typical incumbent in jeopardy to about 52 percent.[14]

Party and interest group activities in House elections do more to harm than help incumbents' prospects. The coordinated expenditures that parties make on behalf of incumbents and the independent expenditures that PACs make to help them do not significantly improve most incumbents' already high prospects of reelection. The same is probably true of the issue advocacy efforts that parties and interest groups make to portray incumbents in a positive light.

The efforts that parties, PACs, and groups make on behalf of challengers, by contrast, do influence congressional elections. For every $10,000 a party spends on behalf of a challenger, it deprives the incumbent of 1.2 percent of the vote. Given that coordinated expenditures for challengers averaged about $16,000 in 1996, these expenditures cost the typical incumbent nearly 2 percent of the vote. Those challengers for whom a party spent $61,800 in coordinated expenditures (the legal maximum) cut into their opponents' shares of the vote by about 7 percent. Similarly, for every $10,000 in independent expenditures that PACs make to defeat an incumbent, they deprive that incumbent of nearly 1 percent of the vote.

Media coverage is important in incumbents' reelection efforts. Incumbent campaigns that receive more free media than their opponents or are the sole beneficiaries of media endorsements win roughly 2.5 percent more of the vote than incumbents who do not enjoy such positive relations with the fourth estate. The efforts that House candidates and their press secretaries make to cultivate news correspondents are clearly worthwhile.

CHALLENGER CAMPAIGNS

Most challengers begin the general election at a disadvantage. Lacking a broad base of support, these candidates must build one. Challengers need to mount aggressive campaigns in order to become visible, build name recognition, give voters reasons to support them, and overcome the initial advantages of their opponents. Challenger campaigns must also communicate messages that will not only attract uncommitted voters but also persuade some voters to abandon their proincumbent loyalties in favor of the challenger. The typical House challenger is in a position similar to that of a novice athlete pitted against a world-class sprinter. The incumbent has experience, talent, professional handlers, funding, equipment, and crowd support. The challenger has few, if any, of these assets and has a monumental task to accomplish in a limited amount of time. Not surprisingly, most challengers end up eating their opponents' dust. Still, not every novice athlete or every congressional challenger is destined to suffer the agony of defeat. A strong challenger, who is able to assemble the money and campaign organization needed to devise and carry out a good game plan, may be able to win if the incumbent stumbles.

Even though the vast majority of challengers ultimately lose, the experience and resources that they bring to their races can have an impact on their ability to win votes. In short, challenger campaigning matters. The data in Table 9-2 reveal that challengers' targeting strategies, issue positions, and campaign expenditures, as well as the amounts of party and interest group support they attract, affect their shares of the votes in a small but meaningful way. These generalizations hold regardless of a particular challenger's age, race, gender, or occupation.

A challenger who runs in a district that is evenly split between registered

TABLE 9-2

Significant Predictors of House Challengers' Vote Shares

	Percent
Base vote	27.99
Partisan bias (per one-point advantage in party registration)	+0.13
Contested primary	+4.77
Group-based targeting	+1.95
Campaigned on position issues	+2.76
Challenger spending on campaign communications (per $1,000)	+0.009
Incumbent spending on campaign communications (per $1,000)	+0.005
Party spending on behalf of challenger (per $1,000)	+0.107
Media advantage favoring challenger	+3.28

Sources: The 1992 Congressional Campaign Study, Federal Election Commission data, various editions of *Congressional Quarterly Weekly Report,* and other sources.

Notes: Complete regression statistics are presented in Table A-4 in the first edition of the book. The analysis includes general election candidates in major-party contested races, excluding a small number of atypical races. N = 129.

Republicans and Democrats, who is handed a major-party nomination without a primary fight, who does not use a group-based targeting strategy, who does not campaign on position issues, whose race is bereft of all candidate or party campaign spending, and who does not get more favorable media coverage than the incumbent will typically end the election with almost 28 percent of the vote—a far cry from victory.[15]

Challengers who run under more favorable circumstances fare better. In most cases the partisan composition of the district works to the advantage of the incumbent, but a few challengers are fortunate enough to run in districts that include more members of their party than the incumbent's party. Challengers who run in districts in which the balance of registered voters favor their party by 10 percent win roughly 1.3 percent more votes than those who run in neutral districts. Those few challengers who run in districts that favor their party by 20 percent win 2.6 percent more votes than others.

Contested primaries, which only rarely have negative consequences in the general election for the incumbents who survive them, give challengers who emerge from them victorious important electoral advantages over challengers who do not have to compete for the nomination. It should be recalled from Chapter 2 that opposing-incumbent primaries are often hotly contested when an incumbent is perceived to be vulnerable and are usually won by strategic candidates who know how to wage strong campaigns. The organizational effort, campaign activities, and media coverage associated with contested primaries provide the winners with larger bases of support and higher levels of name recognition than they would have enjoyed had the primary not been contested. The momentum that House challengers get from contested primaries, and the incumbent weaknesses that give rise to those primaries in the first place, give those challengers who had to defeat one or more opponents in the primary nearly 5 percent more of the general election vote than challengers who are merely handed their party's nomination.

Political experience and campaign professionalism have indirect effects on the ability of challengers to win votes. As seen in Chapter 3, challengers with officeholding or significant unelective political experience are more likely than political amateurs to assemble organizations that are staffed by salaried professionals and purchase campaign services from political consultants. Political experience and campaign professionalism help challengers raise money and attract free media, as shown in Chapter 6. They also help challengers attract free media. Challenger campaigns that are well staffed with experienced people are also presumably better at targeting, communications, and grass-roots activities than are those staffed by amateur volunteers.[16]

House challengers who use group-based targeting strategies win almost 2 percent more votes than those who target on the basis of issues or voter attitudes. Challengers who campaign on position, or wedge, issues, which presumably appeal to the groups they target, win nearly an additional 2.8 percent. The 20 percent or so of all House challengers who are typically endorsed by the press or receive the lion's share of free media coverage win over 3 percent more of the vote than the approximately 80 percent who are not treated so favorably by the local media. The combined effects of good campaign targeting, message selection, and press relations—three hallmarks of a strong nonincumbent campaign—help boost challengers' vote margins by roughly 8 percent.

Campaign spending also has a significant impact on the shares of votes received by challengers. For every $100,000 that House challengers spend on television, radio, newspaper, or direct-mail advertising or on campaign field work, they win an additional 0.9 percent of their base vote.[17] For every $10,000 a party spends on behalf of a challenger, that candidate wins an additional 1 percent. Incumbent spending on campaign communications, which is largely a function of the closeness of the race and the efforts of strong challengers and their supporters, is also positively related to challengers' vote shares. Large communications expenditures by both candidates are strongly associated with closely decided incumbent-challenger races. Torkildsen and Tierney spent approximately $800,000 and $560,000, respectively, on campaign communications in a 1996 race that was decided by a whisker-thin margin.[18] Tim Lefever spent an estimated $490,000 to communicate with voters and came within twelve percentage points of defeating Vic Fazio, who spent an estimated $1.6 million.[19] The fact that the typical House challenger spent only $193,000 on campaign communications in 1996 helps to explain why so few of them won that year and why challengers generally fare poorly.

How best to allocate scarce financial resources is a nearly constant concern for strategists in challenger campaigns. Are radio or television commercials more effective than newspaper ads? How effective is direct mail at influencing voters compared with less precisely tailored and less-well-targeted forms of advertising? Is it worthwhile to invest any money in get-out-the-vote drives, handbills, or the grass-roots activities commonly referred to as campaign field work?

Direct mail is one of the most cost-effective campaign activities. Every $1,000 that challenger campaigns spend on mail is associated with a 0.03 percent increase in the votes they win.[20] The typical challenger campaign spent about $33,000 on mail in 1996, which helped it win an additional 1 percent of the vote.[21] Some campaigns, however, spend considerably more and reap greater rewards. Rep. Loretta Sanchez, D-Calif., spent approximately $350,000 on fourteen pieces of persuasion mail (excluding fund-raising letters) in 1996, which helped put her campaign over the top.[22]

Television commercials are considerably more expensive and bring somewhat lower returns. The typical House challenger campaign spent $68,000 on television ads in 1996, which was associated with an increase of one-half of 1 percent of the vote.[23] Of course, campaigns that spent more on television, such as Price's, attracted considerably more votes.

Radio and newspaper advertisements play important roles in some challenger campaigns, but they do not significantly affect the number of votes that the typical challenger wins.[24] Field work, which refers to get-out-the-vote drives, billboards and yard signs, campaign events, and the distribution of handbills and other literature, is a labor-intensive rather than capital-intensive form of electioneering. Thus, the money that the typical challenger spends on field work does not perfectly represent the candidate's field operations. Nevertheless, personal contact between candidates and voters and other field activities that are often carried out by volunteers rather than professional consultants play a substantial role in contemporary congressional elections.

In sum, most House challengers lose because the odds are so heavily stacked against them. Those few who run in competitive districts, target specific population groups, campaign on position issues, assemble the resources needed to communicate with voters, spend their money wisely, benefit from party and interest group campaigning, and curry favor with the media attract more votes than others, but they rarely win enough votes to defeat an incumbent. The pre-election activities that incumbents undertake to cultivate the support of constituents and their successes in warding off talented and well-funded challengers are critical in determining the outcome of most incumbent-challenger races.

Yet, politics is a game that is often played at the margins. Not all House incumbents begin the general election as shoo-ins and go on to win. The few incumbents who hold competitive seats, commit ethical transgressions, draw both a strong major-party opponent and significant independent or minor-party opposition, are targeted for defeat by the opposing party and independent-spending PACs, or receive less than favorable treatment from the media often find themselves in a precarious position. Many of these candidates spend huge sums of money, sometimes to no avail. If the challengers who run against these incumbents are able to capitalize on the opportunities before them by assembling the money and organizational resources needed to wage a strong campaign, they can put their opponents on the defensive. Challengers who set the campaign agenda, carefully target groups of actual and potential supporters, tailor their messages to appeal to these groups, and communicate these messages through paid advertisements, free media, and strong field operations have a reasonable prospect of winning. A victory by a challenger is typically the result of both incumbent failure and a strong challenger campaign. During the 1996 general election, 119 House incumbents were in jeopardy, yet challengers defeated only 20 of them.

OPEN-SEAT CAMPAIGNS

Elections for open seats are usually won by far smaller margins than incumbent-challenger races. Once a seat becomes open, a whole series of factors comes into play. The partisanship of the district and the skills and resources that candidates and their organizations bring to the campaign have a greater influence on elections when there is no incumbent who can draw on voters' personal loyalties. Because voters lack strong personal loyalties to either candidate, factors that are outside the control of campaigns, such as national political trends, redistricting, and the mass media, can also have an important effect on open-seat elections. The factors that significantly affect the outcome of open-seat House races are listed in Table 9-3.

National partisan tides clearly helped most Democratic open-seat contestants in 1996 notwithstanding President Clinton's short coattails (the Democrats enjoyed a net gain of only ten House seats and suffered a net loss of two Senate seats despite winning the White House).[25] Voters who were dissatisfied with the changes introduced by the Republican Congress, uneasy about the

TABLE 9-3

Significant Predictors of House Open-Seat Candidates' Vote Shares

	Percent
Base vote	43.76
National partisan tide	+3.31
Partisan bias (per one-point advantage in party registration)	+0.20
Media advantage favoring candidate	+3.70
Candidate spending on campaign communications:	
$100,000	+16.37
$200,000	+18.83
$300,000	+20.28
$400,000	+21.29
$500,000	+22.09
Opponent spending on campaign communications:	
$100,000	−15.02
$200,000	−17.28
$300,000	−18.60
$400,000	−19.54
$500,000	−20.27

Sources: The 1992 Congressional Campaign Study, Federal Election Commission data, various editions of *Congressional Quarterly Weekly Report,* and other sources.

Notes: The candidate and opponent spending figures are calculated from a regression equation that estimates the impact of the natural log of campaign spending on candidates' vote shares. Complete regression statistics are presented in Table A-6 in the first edition of the book. The analysis includes general election candidates in major-party contested races. N = 70.

future of Social Security and Medicare, and displeased with Newt Gingrich's congressional leadership appeared to be willing to give Clinton and some of his fellow Democrats a second chance at governance. Democratic open-seat candidates were uniquely situated to benefit from partisan trends in two important respects. First, they could run as political outsiders and attack the Republican Congress using the same themes that were being trumpeted by the Clinton campaign and in the AFL-CIO's issue advocacy ads. Second, they did not have to defeat an incumbent to win.

The partisan bias of open seats is important. Candidates who run for open seats where the balance of voter registration favors their party do much better than others. Those who run for open seats where the balance of party registration favors their party by 20 percent end up winning, on average, an additional 4 percent of the vote.

The mass media also play an important role in open-seat House races. Experienced politicians who have strong campaign organizations and run for open seats in districts that are made up mostly of voters who belong to their party usually receive better treatment from the media than do their opponents. Open-seat candidates who attract more media coverage than their opponents and win the endorsements of the local press pick up almost 4 percent of the vote on top of their base. They also enjoy some indirect benefits from their preferential treatment by the media. An open-seat candidate who is labeled the front-runner by the media early in a race usually raises more money, is able to spend more on campaign communications, achieves higher levels of name recognition, and gathers more momentum than his or her opponent.

Candidates in open-seat elections stand to make large gains in name recognition and voter support through their campaign communications. In contrast to incumbent-challenger races, the communications expenditures made by both campaigns in open-seat elections significantly affect the numbers of votes the candidates receive. A campaign's initial expenditures are particularly influential because they help voters become aware of a candidate and his or her message. Further expenditures, although still important, have a lower rate of return; as more voters learn about the candidates and their issue positions the effects of campaign spending diminish. An open-seat candidate who faces an opponent who spends no money gains, on average, an additional 16.37 percent above the base vote of 43.76 percent for the first $100,000 spent communicating with voters. That same candidate gains an additional 2.46 percent (a total increase of 18.83 percent) for the next $100,000 spent on campaign communications, and an additional 1.45 percent of the vote (a total increase of 20.28 percent) for the next $100,000. But such lopsided spending is unusual in open-seat contests; more often, these elections feature two well-funded campaigns. In situations in which the campaigns spend nearly the same amount on voter contact, their expenditures largely offset one another. Once the candidates have completely saturated the airwaves, the quality and timing of their messages and other elements of their campaigns may have a bigger influence on the outcome of the election than the total dollars that each campaign ultimately spends. In the 1996 race in Illinois's 20th district, for example, Hoffman outspent Shimkus $815,300 to $653,500, but Shimkus won by 1,238 votes.

The amounts that open-seat campaigns spend on field work and direct-mail, radio, television, and newspaper advertising are all positively related to the shares of the vote that candidates receive, but the effect of each of these expenditures on election outcomes is difficult to evaluate because of the electoral and financial competitiveness of these races. It is possible, however, to make some generalizations about the relative importance of each kind of campaign communication.[26] Newspaper ads are the best value, followed by field work. However, because campaigns budget relatively small amounts on these activities and because their impact diminishes as spending on them goes up, it is impossible to predict how great an effect very large expenditures on newspaper advertising or field work would have on an open-seat candidate's share of the votes. Of those media that claim the largest portions of the typical open-seat campaign's communications budget, direct mail has the greatest impact on vote share, followed by radio and television.

CLAIMING CREDIT AND PLACING BLAME

Once the election is over, candidates and their campaign staffs have a chance to reflect on their contests. Their main interest, naturally, is what caused their election to turn out as it did. Winners and losers have very different ideas about what factors influence congressional election outcomes. Some differences are obvious. With the exception of incumbents, losing candidates almost always obsess about money. If they had had more funds they would have reached more voters and received more votes, virtually all agree. The almost three-to-one overall spending advantage that victorious House incumbents had over losing challengers in 1996 supports this point (see Figure 9-1). The 32 percent spending advantage that successful open-seat candidates had over their opponents is not as large, but it also lends credence to the point that money matters. The fact that the winning challenger with the lowest campaign expenditures in 1996, Rep. James Maloney, D-Conn., spent more than $614,400 further suggests that challengers must cross a high spending threshold to be competitive. Indeed, successful challengers in normal two-party races spent an average of $1,075,007 in 1996.[27]

Once one gets beyond the obvious factor of money, there are other differences of opinion. Winners have a strong tendency to credit their victories to attributes of the candidate and to factors that were largely under their campaign's control. They believe that the candidate's image was the most important determinant of their election (see Table 9-4). Successful incumbents credit their record in office next and often claim that the anti-incumbency mood that gripped the nation depressed their victory margins.

Winners rank issues next, with their stances on national issues taking priority over local concerns. Many Democratic winners in the 1990s believed that they benefited from focusing on Medicare, education, the environment, and the other issues that formed the core of their parties' national political agenda. Successful Republicans believed that they benefited from focusing on tax cuts,

FIGURE 9-1
Average Campaign Expenditures of House Winners and Losers in 1996

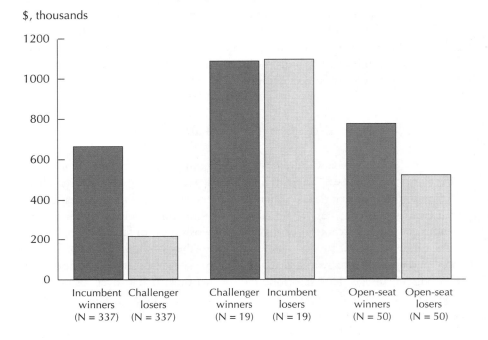

$, thousands

Incumbent winners (N = 337) | Challenger losers (N = 337) | Challenger winners (N = 19) | Incumbent losers (N = 19) | Open-seat winners (N = 50) | Open-seat losers (N = 50)

Source: Compiled from Federal Election Commission data.

Note: Includes all general election candidates in major-party contested House races, excluding a small number of atypical races.

crime, and cutting government waste—core issues from the Contract with America. Candidates of both parties rate the partisan loyalties of voters in their districts as moderately important. Successful incumbents recognize the importance of officeholding, acknowledging the fund-raising, media relations, and name identification advantages it bestowed on them. Finally, winners believe that campaign debates, newspaper endorsements, negative campaigning, scandals, and presidential and other elections are much less important in the outcome of their contests.

The winners' opinions reflect a tendency to attribute their victories to their own efforts and the wisdom of voters.[28] These beliefs stand in stark contrast to political science theories that suggest that congressional election outcomes are primarily a function of national conditions and events.[29]

TABLE 9-4

Winners' and Losers' Opinions of the Determinants
of House Elections

	Winners	Losers
Candidate's image	4.48	3.34
Party loyalty	3.28	3.86
Local issues	2.89	2.49
National issues	3.69	3.20
Debates	2.24	2.16
Endorsements	2.40	2.55
Negative campaigning	2.36	2.58
Incumbent's record	4.13	2.70
Incumbency advantages	3.26	4.70
Anti-incumbency	3.31	2.16
Incumbent scandal	1.53	1.58
Presidential election	2.54	3.43
Perot campaign	2.07	2.54
U.S. Senate election	1.73	2.09
State or local elections	1.71	2.12
(N)	(160)	(164)

Source: The 1992 Congressional Campaign Study.

Notes: Candidates and campaign aides were asked to assess the importance of each factor on the following scale: 1 = not important; 2 = slightly important; 3 = moderately important; 4 = very important; 5 = extremely important. The values listed are arithmetic means of the scores. Figures for incumbent's record, incumbency advantages, anti-incumbency, and incumbent scandal exclude responses from candidates and campaign aides from open seats. Figures include responses from House general election candidates and campaign aides in major-party contested races, excluding a small number of atypical races.

Losers have a very different view of what caused their candidacies to end as they did. First and foremost, losing challengers point to the incumbent's perquisites of office, which they believe to have been extremely important. Next, most losers blame voters' partisanship and the presidential election for their defeat. In 1996 many Republican losers linked their losses to that of the Dole-Kemp ticket. Losers of both parties believe that candidate imagery, issue positions, and debates are less important than these other factors. They prefer to rationalize their defeats by blaming them on factors over which neither they nor their campaigns had any control.[30] The losers' views bear similarities to political science theories that downplay the importance of individual candidates and campaigns.[31]

SENATE CAMPAIGNS

The small number of Senate elections that occur in a given election year and the differences in the size and politics of the states in which they take place make it difficult to generalize about Senate campaigns. Nevertheless, a few generalizations are possible. Not surprisingly, chief among them is that incumbents possess substantial advantages over challengers. The advantages that incumbency conveys in Senate elections are similar to those in House elections. Incumbents enjoy fund-raising advantages and higher levels of name recognition as well as greater political experience, particularly in running a statewide campaign.

Yet, the advantages that senators enjoy are not as great as those that House members have over their opponents. Most Senate challengers and open-seat candidates have previously served in the House, as governor, or in some other public capacity, and are more formidable opponents than their House counterparts. Their previous political experience helps Senate challengers assemble the financial and organizational resources and attract the media coverage that are needed to run a competitive campaign.[32]

One of the most important differences between Senate and House contests is the effect of incumbent expenditures on election outcomes. Although increased challenger spending has a negative effect on incumbents' margins in both Senate and House elections, it is only in Senate races that spending by incumbents is positively related to the number of votes they receive. Incumbent expenditures on campaign communications are not as important as are challenger expenditures, but the amounts spent by both sides are influential in determining the victor in Senate elections.

This difference is due to two major factors. First, because Senate challengers are usually better qualified, Senate elections tend to be closer than House contests. Second, senators tend to have weaker bonds with their constituents than do representatives; senators' larger constituencies prevent them from establishing the kinds of personal ties that House members have with voters.[33] Senators' six-year terms and greater responsibilities in Washington also discourage them from meeting as frequently with constituents as do House members. The greater diversity of their constituencies also means that senators are more likely to offend some voters when carrying out their legislative activities. As a result of these differences, campaign spending and campaigning in general are more likely to affect the electoral prospects of Senate than House incumbents.

The dynamics of Senate elections bear other similarities to and differences from House contests. Scandal and the partisan bias of the state influence the results of elections for both the upper and lower chambers. The quality of the opposition that an incumbent faces both in the primary and the general election has a bigger impact on the outcomes of Senate elections than House contests. Competitive primary contests are also harmful to the general election prospects of Senate incumbents.[34]

Senate candidates have a somewhat different view of the causes of their election outcomes than do House contestants. Both the winners and losers in Senate contests emphasize factors that are largely under their control. Contestants across-the-board believe that the images they projected to the voters were the number one determinant of the outcome of their elections. Winners typically maintain that candidate imagery was extremely important, whereas losers believe it was moderately important. Winners are more likely to emphasize the importance of issues, ranking them second only to imagery. Losing challengers, in contrast, believe that the advantages of officeholding are substantially more important. Winning and losing incumbents are equally likely to view incumbency as a two-edged sword, agreeing that the anger that many voters direct at Washington reduces their vote margins.

Incumbents place greater emphasis on the importance of their record in the Senate than do challengers, but both sets of candidates acknowledge that job performance was at least a moderately important determinant of the outcome of Senate elections. Both winners and losers also place moderate importance on the partisan loyalties of state voters and the presidential election. Senate candidates attribute less influence to such factors as debates, negative campaigning, local issues, and state and local elections than do House contestants.

CHAPTER 10

Elections and Governance

"The election is over, and now the fun begins." Those were the words of one new House member shortly after being elected to Congress. Others had more sober, if not more realistic, visions of what lay ahead. Although getting elected to Congress is difficult, especially for those who have to topple an incumbent, staying there also requires great effort. The high reelection rates enjoyed by members of Congress are not a guarantee of reelection; they are the result of hard work, the strategic deployment of the resources that Congress makes available to its members, and the campaign dynamics discussed in previous chapters.

This chapter is an examination of the efforts that members of Congress make in order to stay in office, including the resources and strategies they use to shore up their electoral coalitions. Also reviewed is the impact of elections on Congress as a policy-making institution. First, I discuss the goals and activities of members of Congress and their congressional staffs. I then discuss the committees, issue caucuses, party organizations, and other groups that influence congressional activity. Finally, I comment on the policy-making process.

THE PERMANENT CAMPAIGN

As locally elected officials who make national policy, members of Congress almost lead double lives. The main focus of their existence in Washington, D.C., is framing and enacting legislation, overseeing the executive branch, and carrying out other activities of national importance. Attending local functions, ascertaining the needs and preferences of constituents, and explaining their Washington activities are what legislators do at home. Home is where members of Congress acquire their legitimacy to participate in the legislative process and their individual mandates to act. The central elements of legislators' lives both at home and in Washington are representing the voters who elected them, winning federally funded projects for their state or district, and resolving difficulties that constituents encounter when dealing with the federal government. The two aspects of members' professional lives are unified by the fact that much of what representatives do in Washington is concerned with getting reelected, and a good deal of what they do at home directly affects the kinds of policies and interests they seek to advance.[1] In a great many respects, the job of legislator resembles a permanent reelection campaign.

Members of Congress develop home styles that help them to maintain or expand their bases of electoral support. One element of these home styles concerns the presentation of self. Members build bonds of trust between themselves and voters by demonstrating that they are capable of handling the job, care about their constituents, and are living up to their campaign promises.[2]

A second component of home style is concerned with discussing the Washington side of the job. Members describe, interpret, and justify what they do in the nation's capital to convey the message that they are working relentlessly on their constituents' behalf.[3] Many respond to the low opinion that people have of Congress by trying to separate themselves from the institution in the minds of voters. Members frequently portray themselves as protectors of the national interest locked in combat with powerful lobbyists and feckless colleagues.

Legislators and their staffs spend immense amounts of time, energy, and resources advertising the legislator's name among constituents, claiming credit for favorable governmental actions, and taking strong but often symbolic issue positions to please constituents.[4] Their offices provide them with abundant resources for these purposes. House members receive an average of $819,000 for staff, $195,000 for general office expenses, one or more state or district offices, a postage account of $108,000, a travel budget of up to $67,000, and virtually unlimited long-distance telephone privileges.[5] Members who are assigned to certain committees, occupy committee chairs, or hold party leadership positions receive extra staff, office space, and operating funds. Senators are allowed even greater budgets, reflecting their larger constituencies and the greater responsibilities associated with representing an entire state. Senators' staffs, office space, and budget allocations are determined by their state's population and by their committee assignments.

Although few legislators consume all the resources they are allocated, many come close. The average House member hires approximately fifteen staff assistants; the average senator hires about thirty-five. Among these aides are administrative assistants, legislative assistants, legislative correspondents, computer operators, schedulers, office managers, caseworkers, press secretaries, receptionists, staff assistants, and interns. Each performs a different set of functions, but nearly all are somehow related to building political support among constituents. Legislative correspondents, legislative assistants, and computer operators are highly conscious of the electoral connection when they send franked mail to constituents.[6] Caseworkers help constituents resolve problems with the federal bureaucracy, knowing that their performance can directly affect the reelection prospects of the legislator for whom they work. Receptionists, staff assistants, and schedulers are well aware that the tours they arrange for visitors to Washington contribute to the support their member maintains in the district. Those who forget that constituents come first are quickly reminded of this by the member's administrative assistant, who is responsible for making sure that the office runs smoothly and frequently serves as the member's chief political adviser.

The most reelection-oriented staffers tend to be congressional press secretaries. Most members of Congress have at least one press secretary, and some have two or three deputy press assistants.[7] The press secretary is the chief public relations officer in a congressional office. Press secretaries write newsletters and press releases and are heavily involved in crafting the targeted congressional letters that legislators send to constituents. They also produce copy for radio and television spots, which they arrange to have aired over local stations. Press secretaries help to organize town meetings, arrange interviews with the local correspondents, and disseminate to the news media transcripts and videotapes of their boss's floor and committee speeches. A good press secretary is often able to arrange for local media outlets to print or air a legislator's remarks verbatim or with minimal editing.[8]

The election of highly media-conscious members in the mid-1970s, increased television coverage of politics, the opening of Congress to greater media scrutiny, the growth in the size of the congressional press corps, and the availability of new communications led to the emergence of the press secretary as a key congressional aide. These changes created both pressures and opportunities to increase the public relations side of congressional offices.[9] Members of Congress, who work in a resource rich institution, responded by allowing themselves to hire specialized staff who could help them advance their political careers.

Congress has also allowed its members to exploit new computer technologies to firm up their relations with voters. Legislators use computerized databases to target large volumes of mail to specific audiences. Constituents who write or telephone their legislator about an issue are routinely entered into a computerized list that records their name, address, and the reason for their contact. They are then sent periodic communications that update them on what their legislator is doing in this area. Other constituents contact members' offices via electronic mail or by accessing their Internet Web sites.

Subsidized House and Senate recording studios and party-owned recording facilities also help legislators reach out to voters. Many members use the studios to record radio shows and television briefings or to edit floor speeches that they deliver to local media outlets. Some make use of satellite technology to hold live "town meetings" with constituents located on the other side of the country.

A DECENTRALIZED CONGRESS

The candidate-centered nature of congressional elections provides the foundation for a highly individualized, fragmented style of legislative politics. Members are largely self-recruited, are nominated and elected principally as a result of their own efforts, and know they bear the principal responsibility for ensuring they get reelected. Local party organizations, Washington-based party committees, PACs, and other groups and individuals may have helped them raise money and win votes, but politicians arrive in Congress with the belief that they owe their tenure to their own efforts.

Reelection Constituencies

Legislators' first loyalties are to their constituents, and most staff their offices, decide which committee assignments to pursue, and choose areas of policy expertise with an eye toward maintaining voter support. Campaign contributors, including those who live outside a legislator's district or state, form another important constituency. Local elites and interest groups that provide campaign support or political advice routinely receive access to members of Congress, further encouraging legislators to respond to forces outside of the institution rather than within.[10] Other personal goals, including advancing specific policies, accruing more power in the legislature, or positioning themselves to run for higher office, also have a decentralizing effect on the legislative process.[11] Much of the work done to advance these goals—policy research, disseminating press releases, bill drafting, attending committee meetings, bureaucratic oversight, and meeting with constituents, campaign contributors, and lobbyists—is borne by staffers who owe their jobs and their loyalties to individual legislators more than to the institution.[12] This, in turn, makes their bosses less dependent on congressional leaders and encourages members to march to their own drums.

Congressional Committees

The dispersal of legislative authority among nineteen standing committees and eighty-four subcommittees in the House, sixteen standing committees and sixty-nine subcommittees in the Senate, four joint committees, and a small number of select committees in each chamber adds to the centrifugal tendencies that originate from candidate-centered elections. Each committee and subcommittee is authorized to act within a defined jurisdiction. Each is headed by a chair and ranking member who are among the majority and minority parties' senior policy experts. Each also has its own professional staff, office, and budget to help it carry out its business.

The committee system originally was designed to enable Congress to function more efficiently. It allows Congress to investigate simultaneously a multitude of issues and to oversee a range of executive branch agencies. Although committees and subcommittees are Congress's main bodies for making national policy, much of what they do revolves around local issues, the distribution of federal grants and programs, and the reelection of individual legislators. Most legislators serve on at least one committee or subcommittee with jurisdiction over policies of importance to their constituents. Members use their committee assignments to develop expertise in policy areas, to actively promote their constituents' interests, to build reputations as champions of popular issues, and to attract campaign support.

Congressional committees can be categorized according to the objectives they enable members to pursue: reelection, prestige, and policy.[13] "Reelection committees," such as the House Transportation and Infrastructure Committee and the Senate Environment and Public Works Committee, enable their members to work directly on the policy areas that are most important to constituents. Reelection committees usually rank high among the assignments sought by new members of Congress. More than half of all first-term House members seek appointment to one or more of them.[14]

"Prestige committees" give their members influence over legislative activities that are of extraordinary importance to their congressional colleagues. The House and Senate Appropriations Committees are the ultimate prestige, or power, committees. They are responsible for funding federal agencies and programs and have the ability to initiate, expand, contract, or discontinue the flow of federal money to projects located across the country. This gives their members the power to affect the lives of those who are the beneficiaries of these programs and the ability to influence the reelection prospects of legislators who represent them. The House Ways and Means and Senate Finance Committees' jurisdiction over tax-related matters, and particularly their ability to give tax breaks to various interests, give members of these panels sway with their colleagues. Members of prestige committees can help their constituents by acting directly or, by wielding their clout with other legislators, indirectly. Membership on one of the appropriating or tax-writing committees is particularly helpful when it comes to raising campaign funds from individuals and PACs associated with a wide array of economic interests.

In contrast with reelection and prestige committees, "policy committees," such as those that deal with criminal justice, education, or labor issues, are sought by legislators who have a strong interest in a particular policy area. These committees are among the most divisive because they are responsible for some highly charged issues, such as education, health insurance, and welfare reform, and many members use them to stake out conservative or liberal stands. Ambitious legislators who seek a career beyond Congress often use policy committees as platforms for developing a national reputation on salient issues.

Thus the committee system gives expression to the differing goals and viewpoints of representatives, senators, and their constituents. By so doing, it decentralizes Congress.

Congressional Caucuses

Congressional caucuses—informal groups of members who share legislative interests—have a similar but less powerful effect on Congress. Even though caucuses were prohibited from having their own congressional staffs and office space when the House adopted its rules for the 104th Congress, they continue to function as competing policy centers, alternative suppliers of information, and additional sources of legislative decision-making cues.[15] Groups such as the Congressional Black Caucus and the Women's Caucus are recognized as advocates for specific segments of the population. The Sunbelt Caucus, Western States Senate Coalition, and other geographically based groups seek to increase the clout of legislators from particular regions. The Steel, Mushroom, and Textile Caucuses have ties to outside industries and work to promote their interests in Congress. Although they do not hold any formal legislative powers, caucuses further add to the fragmentation of Congress.

Interest Groups

Privately funded interest groups, which form an important part of the political environment with which Congress interacts, also have decentralizing effects on the legislative process. Like caucuses, interest groups are sources of influence that compete with congressional leaders for the loyalty of legislators on certain issues. Roughly eighty thousand people work for trade associations, legal firms, and consulting agencies in the Washington area.[16] Not all these people are lobbyists, but in one way or another they work to advance the political interests of some group, and Congress is their number one target.[17]

Interest groups work to influence the legislative process in many ways. Some groups advertise on television, on radio, in newspapers, or through the mail to influence the political agenda or stimulate grass-roots support for or opposition to specific pieces of legislation. Their efforts often resemble election campaigns. The advertisements purchased by the health care and insurance industries in opposition to President Clinton's health care reform package in 1994 exemplify such efforts, as do the advertising campaigns waged by unions and other groups in support of or in opposition to the minimum wage bill in 1996.

Most interest groups also advocate their positions in less visible ways, designed to play to the legislative and electoral needs of individual members of Congress. Representatives of interest groups testify at committee hearings and meet with legislators at their offices and informally at social events. Lobbyists use a variety of forums to provide members and their staffs with technical information, impact statements of how congressional activity (or inactivity) can affect their constituents, and insights into where other legislators stand on the issues. Sometimes they go so far as to draft a bill or help design a strategy to promote its enactment.[18]

Many groups supplement these "insider" techniques with approaches that focus more directly on the electoral connection. Trade and business groups ask local association members to contact their legislators. Unions, churches, and other groups with large memberships frequently organize telephone and letter-writing campaigns. These communications show members of Congress that important blocs of voters and their advocates are watching how they vote on specific pieces of legislation.[19] The recent increase in interest group–sponsored issue advocacy advertising in connection with the legislative process and elections has resulted in some groups contributing to the permanent campaigns that consume a significant portion of the professional lives of most members of Congress.

Interest groups, congressional subcommittee members, and executive-branch officials form collegial decision-making groups, which are frequently referred to as "iron triangles," "issue networks," or "policy subgovernments."[20] These issue experts often focus on the minutiae of arcane, highly specialized areas of public policy. Because they form small governments within a government, they further contribute to the decentralization of Congress.

POLITICAL PARTIES: CENTRALIZING AGENTS

Unlike the structural, organizational, and political factors that work to decentralize Congress, political parties act as a glue—albeit sometimes a weak one—to bond members together. They socialize new members, distribute committee assignments, set the legislative agenda, disseminate information, and carry out other tasks that are essential to Congress's law-making, oversight, and representative functions. Although they are not the central actors in elections, party committees do help individual candidates develop their campaign messages. Party campaign efforts on behalf of individual candidates and election agenda-setting efforts encourage legislators to vote for bills that are at the core of their party's agenda when Congress is in session.[21] Party issue advocacy that takes place outside of the campaign season is meant to increase or reduce support for specific bills or damage the reputations of members who voted against them. Issue advocacy ads, such as those that the Republicans aired against Senate Democrats who voted for or against the balanced budget amendment in 1997 and are up for reelection in 1998, have given party organizations, especially those in the nation's capital a greater role in the permanent campaign.

The congressional parties' leadership organizations are structured similarly to those of legislative parties in other countries. The Democrats and Republicans are each headed by one leader in each chamber—the Speaker and minority leader in the House and the majority and minority leaders in the Senate. Each party has several other officers and an extensive whip system to facilitate communications between congressional party leaders and rank-and-file legislators. Legislative parties convene caucuses and task forces to help formulate policy positions and legislative strategy. Providing campaign assistance, giving out committee assignments and other perks, setting the congressional agenda, structuring debate, and persuading legislators that specific bills are in the best interests of their constituents and the nation are tools that congressional leaders use to build coalitions.

Nevertheless, party leaders have less control over the policy-making process than do their counterparts in other democracies.[22] The persuasive powers of party leaders are usually insufficient to sway members' votes when party policy positions clash with those of legislators' constituents and campaign supporters. Recognizing the primacy of the electoral connection, party leaders generally tell legislators to respond to constituents rather than "toe the party line" when the latter could endanger their chances of reelection. The efforts of congressional party leaders are probably less of a factor in explaining how party members cast their roll-call votes than are commonalities in political outlook or similarities among legislators' constituents.[23] Party leaders are most able to overcome the forces that fragment Congress when they seek to enact policies that possess widespread bipartisan support or when the majority party possesses many more seats than the opposition and proposes popular legislation that advances its core principles. As the 104th Congress showed, a change in party control can also act as a catalyst for party unity. Members of the new House and Senate majorities were aware that their accomplishments as a party would directly influence their individual reelection campaigns and their party's ability to maintain control of Congress.

RESPONSIVENESS, RESPONSIBILITY, AND PUBLIC POLICY

In representative democracies, elections are the principal means of ensuring that governments respond to the will of the people and promote their interests. Voters, through elections, hold public officials accountable for their actions and for the state of the nation as a whole. Elections are a blunt but powerful instrument of control that allows people to inform their individual representatives or the government as a collectivity of how political action or inaction has affected the quality of their lives. Other avenues of influence, such as contacting members of Congress or giving campaign contributions, are usually used to advance narrower goals, are more demanding, and are in practice less democratic.

Individuals whose public service is contingent on getting reelected often straddle the fuzzy line that demarcates responsiveness and responsibility in government. On some occasions, legislators are highly responsive, functioning as delegates who advance their constituents' views. On others, they take the role of trustee, relying on their own judgment to protect the welfare of their constituents or the nation.[24] Responsible legislators must occasionally vote against their constituents' wishes in order to best serve the interests of the nation.

Election Systems and Public Policy

The type of election system we have in the United States has a great effect on the responsiveness and responsibility of elected officials and entire governments because the system determines to whom public officials are accountable. Parliamentary systems, such as that in Great Britain, which feature party-focused elections, tend to hold elected officials accountable to national political majorities.[25] Members of Parliament (MPs) perform casework and are attentive to their constituents, but they are inclined to vote for legislation that is fashioned to please national rather than local constituencies. MPs support party initiatives because they know that their prospects for reelection are closely tied to their party's ability to enact its legislative program. The candidate-centered nature of the American system, in contrast, encourages elected officials to be responsive to the desires of constituents and organized groups that support their campaigns, sometimes in opposition to their party's leadership.

The separation of powers reinforces legislators' predispositions to support district voters first and campaign supporters second when making public policy. Even when one party controls the White House and both chambers of Congress, it may find it difficult to unify legislators because they can disagree with one another without fear of losing control of the government. Members of the majority party in Congress cast roll-call votes secure in the knowledge that they will remain in office for their full two- or six-year terms even if their party suffers a major legislative defeat. In parliamentary systems, majority party members understand that a major policy defeat may be interpreted as a vote of no confidence in their party and may force an election that could turn them out of office in less than a month. The separation of powers also affects the behavior of legislators who are in the minority party. They have little incentive to vote against legislation that could benefit their constituents just because it was sponsored by the majority party, since even a smashing legislative defeat would not force a snap election.

President Clinton's close victory on the North American Free Trade Agreement demonstrates the difficulties that congressional parties face when they try to overcome the centrifugal forces influencing members of Congress. NAFTA was opposed by many congressional Democrats whose constituents thought they would lose manufacturing jobs as a result of the relaxation of trade barriers with Canada and Mexico. The treaty forced many legislators to choose between remaining loyal to their party's national leaders and pleasing their constituents. Most members, regardless of seniority, placed their constituents' interests and their own views above those of party leaders, who were themselves divided. Among those who opposed NAFTA were Reps. Richard Gephardt, D-Mo., and David Bonior, D-Mich., two of the House Democrats' top three leaders. These leaders, who were selected by their congressional colleagues to advance core party policies, used the prestige, staff, and other resources of their leadership offices to oppose a policy that was advanced by President Clinton, their party's titular leader.

The separation of powers, bicameralism, federalism, and a fixed-date system of elections make it difficult for legislators to enact long-term, nationally focused policies. Members of Congress who believe that their individual images, policy positions, and public records were decisive in their election are less likely than legislators in party-centered democracies to sacrifice the short-term interests of constituents or to compromise on salient issues to enact policies advocated by party leaders. House members, who must run for reelection every two years, respond particularly strongly to parochial concerns.

The effects of parochialism are most apparent in distributive politics, which provide tangible benefits to private individuals or groups. Building coalitions in support of spending on roads, bridges, universities, museums, and other projects is relatively simple in a decentralized legislature such as the U.S. Congress. Bill sponsors can add new programs and projects in order to win enough legislative supporters to pass their plan.[26] A farm advocate who is hoping to subsidize northern sugar beets, for example, might build support for this cause by expanding the number of subsidized crops in a bill to include sugar cane, rice, corn, wheat, and even tobacco, thereby expanding support that began with representatives from Minnesota to include colleagues from Hawaii, Massachusetts, virtually every southern state, and the states of the Midwest.[27] Subsidies for ostrich farmers can be left out because they will not draw many legislative votes, but food stamps can be added to attract the support of legislators from poor urban districts.[28] Trading subsidies for votes is a simple example of logrolling. Other deals are cut over tax breaks, budget votes, and even appointments to the federal judiciary.[29]

Logrolling and other forms of compromise usually do not allow individual legislators to get all the federal "pork" they would like for their constituents. Nevertheless, these compromises enable most legislators to insert enough pork into a bill to claim credit for doing something to help their constituents. A broadly supported distributive bill is an easy candidate for congressional enactment because, like a Christmas tree decorated by a group of friends, everyone can see his or her handiwork in it and find something to admire in the finished product.

Distributive politics are problematic because they are practiced with both eyes focused on short-term gains and little attention to long-range consequences. Broadening programs that were originally intended to provide benefits to one group to include others usually causes the programs to become ineffectively targeted, watered down, and overly expensive. When large sums are spent to benefit many groups, overall spending is increased, and fewer funds remain available to help the group that was originally targeted for assistance. This does little to promote the original goals of a bill and leads to deficit spending.[30] Pork-barrel spending and logrolling, which are at the heart of distributive politics, have contributed heavily to the national debt of more than $5.3 trillion that the U.S. government reported in February 1997. Distributive politics are a prime example of what happens when independently elected officials seek to promote the interests of their constituents and campaign supporters without giving much thought to the effect of their collective actions on the nation.

Recent congresses, especially those elected in 1994 and 1996, have taken steps to reduce government spending, but constant wrangling over tax cuts, military spending, and other federal programs have hindered their attempts at deficit reduction.

Policy Gridlock and Political Cycles

Parochialism also leads to a reactive style of government and incremental policy making. Congress is better at making short-term fixes than at developing long-term initiatives. Congressional leaders often find it difficult to develop a vision for the future. During the 1980s, House Democrats took steps to outline, publicize, and act on a partisan agenda. Parts of this effort were successful, but much of it was not. Differences in legislators' political philosophies, the diversity of their constituencies, and the limited resources available to party leaders made it difficult to develop and implement a Democratic game plan for the nation's future.[31] House Republicans also tried on several occasions in the 1980s to develop a partisan agenda, but prior to the Contract with America, they, too, enjoyed only limited success.[32]

Under most circumstances, election outcomes, constituent demands, interest group pressures, and White House initiatives support the continuation of the status quo or suggest only small changes in public policies. When pressure for change exists, Congress generally initiates limited reform, but only after a period of some delay. On some occasions, however, the federal government does enact comprehensive programs that significantly affect people's lives.

Major policy change is most likely to occur during periods of crisis and is frequently associated with partisan realignments. Realignments traditionally occur when a critical event polarizes voters on a major issue, the two major parties take clear and opposing stands on that issue, and one party succeeds in capturing the White House and large majorities in both the House and Senate. The ascendant party then has an electoral mandate to enact major policy change.[33]

The events leading up to and continuing through Franklin Roosevelt's presidency exemplify federal policy making during a period of crisis. The seeds of Roosevelt's New Deal programs were sewn in the Great Depression of the 1930s. Republicans controlled the White House, the House of Representatives, and the Senate when the stock market crashed in 1929. The Democrats made the Republicans' failure to initiate economic reforms to reverse the depression a major campaign issue. After winning the White House and both chambers of Congress, the Democrats used their mandate to replace laissez-faire economics with Keynesian policies, which relied on government intervention to revive the economy. Other partisan and policy realignments took place during the late 1820s, the Civil War era, and the 1890s.

Some major policy changes have been instituted in the absence of partisan realignments, but most of these were less sweeping than those that followed critical elections. The civil rights and Great Society programs of the 1960s and the American withdrawal from Vietnam are examples of major policy changes that occurred in the absence of a partisan realignment. Historical perspective is needed before scholars can conclude that the 1994 congressional elections constituted a full-scale realignment in favor of the Republicans, but Democratic hegemony over Congress has clearly ended.[34] Regardless of whether a realignment was constituted in 1994, the GOP was able to use its stunning electoral success to institute major changes in public policy and shift the national policy debate. Under Speaker Gingrich's leadership, the GOP-controlled Congress passed legislation reducing federal mandates on the states, cutting federal regulations, and changing the welfare system from a federally mandated program to one run by each state independently with a block grant from the federal government.[35] Many of the programs that were revamped had been enacted sixty years earlier, during the New Deal.

The Republicans also shifted the policy debate from how to improve the efficiency and performance of the federal government to how to decrease its scope. For the first time since the New Deal, the subject of reducing entitlement benefits dominated public debate. Politicians, commentators, and policy analysts discussed whether reducing current or future per capita outlays for Social Security, Medicare, Medicaid, and other entitlement programs was an acceptable way to cut the size and cost of government, reduce the federal deficit, and pay for tax cuts. Other debates raged over issues such as a presidential line-item veto, a balanced budget amendment, and term limits. The first of these changes was passed; the latter two were not.

Republican House leaders also restructured some major aspects of how the House did business. The GOP cut the number of House committees, subcommittees, and committee staffs, enacted term limits for committee chairs and the Speaker, and made other formal changes aimed at strengthening the hands of the majority party leadership. The Republicans eliminated legislative study organizations, which had formerly enhanced the representation of specific (mostly Democratic) constituencies. Republican leaders also bypassed the normal committee process in writing several important pieces of legislation, relying instead on task forces, which facilitate coalition building within the majority party but greatly reduce minority party input.[36]

The 1994 elections and the revolutionary 104th Congress that followed showed that contemporary elections can lead to major policy and institutional change. The influx of a large number of new House members who were committed to the policy proposals outlined in the Contract with America, and the indebtedness that many other Republican legislators felt toward Gingrich for leading the charge to take over the House, set the stage for the changes that followed the GOP takeover. The Clinton administration's temporary abdication of leadership on domestic policy issues immediately following the election enabled Republican leaders to set the political agenda and pass many of their policy proposals in the House. The Senate, which also witnessed the election of a Republican majority, adopted many of the legislative initiatives created by the House but left its unique stamp on the bills that were ultimately signed into law. It also rejected some of the House bills, including the House Republicans' much-heralded balanced budget amendment.

The 1994 elections show that the elections of individual members of Congress can collectively lead to great political change. Elections that result in a shift in partisan control and the swearing in of many new members can help the legislative branch overcome its normal state of decentralization, especially when there is a widespread consensus for change among the American people. These conditions help the majority party in Congress act programmatically. When this occurs, congressional parties in the United States resemble both parliamentary parties in other countries and an idealized system of responsible party government.[37] However, as the final days of the 104th and most of the 105th session of Congress demonstrated, once public support for sweeping change erodes, the centrifugal forces that customarily dominate Congress reassert themselves, and the legislature returns to its normal, incremental mode of policy making. The parochialism of members of Congress, bicameralism, the internal decentralization of the House and the Senate, and other centrifugal forces promote political cycles marked by long periods of incremental policy making followed by short periods of major policy change.

CHAPTER 11

Campaign Reform

Congress has come under assault in recent years for its inability to solve some of the nation's most pressing problems, its perceived shortcomings in representing the general public, and its failure to keep its own house in order. Gridlock, deficit spending, scandal, the foibles of its members, and the operations of Congress itself have led many to champion congressional reform.[1] Reformers have called for a variety of changes, ranging from a balanced budget amendment to term limits, which would restructure the political careers of members and would-be members and drastically transform the way in which Congress operates. Campaign reform falls somewhere in between these two extremes. In this chapter I identify aspects of the system that should be considered for reform, present some reform proposals, and discuss the prospects for meaningful reform to be enacted.

THE CASE FOR REFORM

Numerous arguments can be made for reforming Congress: some focus on the outcomes of congressional elections and others on the processes that produce those outcomes. Arguments that fall in the first category, most notably those for term limits, dwell on the fact that incumbents almost always win. They frequently discount or ignore that incumbents' successes are largely the result of legislators' efforts to serve their constituents prior to the election season, the weak competition they encounter once the campaign has begun, and inequalities in the campaign resources available to different kinds of candidates. They also ignore that many incumbents choose to retire rather than face a strong challenge.

Many of those who build their case for reform on the outcomes of congressional elections are willing to embrace fairly radical changes because they are frustrated with their economic situation, rising crime, increased taxes, and reduced government services and because they believe the desires of the average taxpayer are being sacrificed by a government that panders to special interests. Reform movements are often headed by defeated congressional challengers and other frustrated politicians, some of whom have even served in Congress. Some reform efforts draw financial support from private groups that have strong ties to a political party. Despite their lofty rhetoric, which is designed to tap into Americans' traditional ambivalence toward politics and distrust of politicians, the heads of reform groups usually stand to receive some kind of benefit if their objectives are achieved.

Advocates of term limits argue that a regular rotation of public-spirited amateur legislators in and out of Congress would result in the enactment of laws that would solve the nation's most pressing problems. This position is naive and based on a superficial understanding of the political process. Term limits might encourage greater rotation among national legislators, but those nonincumbents with the best prospects of getting elected would continue to be experienced politicians and wealthy individuals who have the ability to assemble the organizational and financial resources needed to communicate to voters, not the public-spirited "citizen legislators" that some reformers have in mind. Putting a cap on the number of terms a legislator can serve would also strengthen the congressional and executive branch aides and "inside-the-beltway" lobbyists who are part of the permanent Washington establishment. Turning members of Congress into lame ducks at the end of a fixed number of terms would encourage even the most popular and effective legislators to become more concerned with courting new employers than responding to constituent interests or governing responsibly. Congressional term limits would also probably reduce electoral competition and incumbent accountability because most strategic nonincumbents who are capable of waging strong campaigns would wait until a seat in Congress became open rather than challenge an incumbent.

The fact that over half the members of the 105th Congress were sworn into office after the 1992 elections makes questionable the premise from which advocates of term limits proceed—that there is not enough turnover in the federal legislature. This is a point that was not lost on members of the House and Senate, who failed to provide the two-thirds votes needed to pass a term limits amendment to the Constitution in both the 104th and 105th Congresses. Ironically, term limits for state legislators, which were passed in more than twenty states, might enhance competition in congressional elections by encouraging state legislators serving their last term to run for Congress.[2]

Term limits are one of many "shot gun" proposals for reform that are advocated by those who have failed to achieve their goals through normal political channels. A balanced budget amendment and many of the initiatives and referenda on state and local ballots are others.[3] These shortcuts and bypasses to regular elections and legislative processes are no substitute for the political will of citizens and their elected representatives. If enacted, they would probably do more harm than good, despite reformers' best intentions.

Reform proposals designed to make congressional elections more competitive have the potential to improve the political system. Rather than altering the principles of republican government, which are the foundation of American democracy, these proposals have the potential to improve the system's capacity to live up to those principles. Real campaign reform must increase the competitiveness of congressional elections, improve the accountability of the electoral process, enhance representation in Congress, and endeavor to increase the legitimacy of the election system in the eyes of citizens.

The first step toward increasing competition in congressional elections is to encourage a larger number of talented candidates to run for office, especially in races against incumbents. The best way to accomplish this goal is to provide all candidates with access to adequate campaign resources. More qualified challengers will run if they know they will be competing on a more level playing field. The fact that most incumbents begin and end both the campaign for resources and the campaign for votes far ahead of their opponents discourages many of the best would-be challengers from running. Others are discouraged by the prospect of having to compete against wealthy opponents who can spend almost unlimited personal funds on campaigning. The advantages associated with incumbency and millionaire candidacies cannot be completely eliminated by campaign reform, but campaign reform should ensure that nonincumbents have access to adequate resources. This will encourage better challengers to run and give those who decide to enter the fray a fighting chance.

Merely imposing limits on campaign spending by incumbents, challengers, or open-seat contestants is not the solution. Even though reformers raise the issue of campaign costs more often than they discuss electoral competition, the complaint that campaigns cost too much has little foundation in reality. The amount of money spent on congressional elections has risen in recent years but not inordinately so when one takes into consideration the rate of inflation and the growth in advertising costs imposed by television, radio, and direct-mail companies. The price that candidates pay for political campaigns is minuscule compared with the price that corporations pay to advertise consumer products. The state of American advertising is such that companies such as Coca-Cola, which spend billions of dollars a year repeating the names of products that are already household terms, drown out candidate communications. This is particularly harmful to House challengers. As Will Robinson, a veteran Democratic media consultant, has commented: "Our challengers not only have to compete with an incumbent congressman, they also have to compete with that damned 'Energizer Bunny!' They need more, not less, money."[4] The resources—not necessarily cash—committed to educating citizens about candidates and issues are critical to the functioning of a representative democracy, and if anything, the sums available to some candidates—mainly nonincumbents—ought to be increased. Increasing election resources would potentially enhance the knowledge that voters have about candidates, issues, and campaigns. And the more information individuals possess about elections, the more likely they are to vote.[5] Spending and contribution limits should be imposed on candidates only in combination with reforms that substitute public resources for private cash.

Another solution in search of a problem is the imposition of limits on the funds that candidates can raise outside of their district or state. The emergence of national fund-raising constituencies reflects both the uneven geographic distribution of wealth in the United States and the uneven distribution of power in Congress. When it comes to congressional fund-raising, candidates go where the money is, and most of the money flows to those who are in positions of power or those who have the best chances of attaining power. Where candidates get their contributions from should not be a major concern because members of Congress, including congressional leaders, remain highly responsive—perhaps too much so—to their constituents despite the fact that they currently reach beyond district or state boundaries when raising money. Furthermore, as national policy makers, members of Congress should pay at least some attention to representatives of organized interests that are affected by congressional action, even if those interests are not located in their states or congressional districts. Interest group representatives may be among the few knowledgeable sources of information that members have about the views of individuals and interests who reside outside of their districts or states.

Ceilings on the amounts that candidates can raise from nonconstituents are not likely to improve representation in Congress, but they will make fund-raising more difficult, particularly for congressional challengers whose ability to collect needed campaign money is usually limited. Moreover, most voters are probably not overly concerned about the contributions that legally flow across state borders. A vigilant media and a reasonably funded opponent can hold a candidate publicly accountable for those. What voters do care about are the huge soft money contributions that seem to flow effortlessly from millionaires' pockets and corporate, union, and trade association treasuries into the campaign accounts of their elected representatives. Although congressional candidates are barred from accepting soft money contributions, most members of the general public are too unfamiliar with the nuances of campaign finance law to recognize that soft money flows to party committees and interest groups rather than candidates.

The real problem of campaign spending, as it relates to electoral competition, is not how much money is spent but who spends it. Congressional elections can be improved by taking steps to broaden the distribution of campaign resources, not reduce them. If ceilings on campaign expenditures are set too low, challengers will have less opportunity to communicate with voters and elections will become less competitive. Critics of spending limits are probably correct in their assertion that legislation limiting the amounts that challengers can spend would be tantamount to an incumbent protection act.[6] Spending limits in open-seat races and incumbent-challenger contests would also work to the advantage of candidates who belong to the majority party in their state or district, thereby deterring competition in those places.

Related to the issue of costs are concerns about who makes large campaign contributions and how they are raised. Complaints that wealthy and well-organized elements of society play too big a role in funding campaigns have been around for a long time and have been addressed by various pieces of legislation.[7] The FECA bans businesses and unions from making contributions directly to candidates and limits individuals to contributions of $1,000 and PACs to contributions of $5,000 per candidate during each phase of the election. The law has not eliminated the role of wealthy individuals in campaign finance. Rather, it has forced candidates to turn to a broader array of financial sources and encouraged some individuals and groups to spend money outside of the federal campaign finance system through independent voter mobilization programs and issue advocacy campaigns.

An unintended side effect of the FECA has been to increase the amount of time and money that candidates spend chasing contributions. Nearly 40 percent of the members of the House and Senate report spending a moderate to a great deal of time raising money for their next campaign—time that they would prefer to devote to learning about pending legislation, attending floor debates, meeting with constituents, and other important congressional duties.[8] Of course, the demands made by fund-raising on incumbents are minuscule compared with those on challengers and open-seat candidates. Fund-raising imperatives reduce the time that all candidates have to communicate with voters.

A second unanticipated consequence of the law is that it has increased the role of soft money in elections. Soft money is the "black market" economy of campaign finance. Ceilings on individual contributions to federal candidates and the parties' federal campaign accounts have encouraged wealthy individuals to look for alternative ways to spend money in elections. Prohibitions against corporations, trade associations, and unions contributing or spending funds from their treasuries have had similar effects.

Court rulings prompted by the efforts of enterprising contributors, politicians, party officials, political consultants, and interest group leaders expanded the activities on which soft money can be spent to include nationally directed voter mobilization programs and issue advocacy campaigns that can influence the outcome of federal elections. These rulings have made soft money a more attractive vehicle for wealthy contributors. The popularity of soft money has also been increased by the premiums routinely offered to contributors, including private audiences with presidents, cabinet members, and congressional leaders.

Skyrocketing soft money transactions have drastically changed the financing of federal elections, and they pose unique problems. So much soft money flows outside the normal, federally regulated areas of congressional campaign finance that the FECA is more loophole than law. The 1990s witnessed the growth of a national economy of soft money contributions and expenditures that almost rivals in size the campaign finance economy that is regulated by federal law.

Soft money contributions and expenditures, some of which exceed $1 million, greatly increase the influence that wealthy elements of society have on the financing of campaigns. Individuals and groups located in the Capitol Hill community defined by Washington, D.C.'s 20003 ZIP code, alone, contributed at least $33.2 million—$31.8 million of it in soft money—over the course of the 1996 elections.[9] Contributors in the Washington metropolitan area contributed in excess of $117.4 million.[10] Citizens should be concerned when such huge sums of unregulated campaign money are collected in large denominations from such a small area, particularly an area that is home to both the U.S. Capitol and the nation's top lobbying firms. Revelations that large amounts of soft money have been raised from noncitizens and foreign corporations and spent by tax-exempt organizations have added new twists to the soft money problem.

Nevertheless, not all soft money is the same. Party soft money is used to help a large, rather than a small, group of candidates. Because party soft money is given to and spent by party committees, which are umbrella organizations that represent a broad range of interests, it does not create such strong policy-oriented IOUs between contributors and legislators as those created by narrowly focused interest groups that spend soft money to help only a few candidates. Party leaders and fund-raisers may urge House members and senators to support legislation that is important to the party's financial benefactors, but the argument that "we owe it to a group of wealthy donors to pass this bill" is unlikely to carry much sway with legislators who oppose passage because of constituent interests or their own views. More important is the fact that party committees and candidates are held accountable for their soft money finances because national party soft money transactions are publicized by the FEC. As both parties, but especially the Democrats, learned in the closing weeks of the 1996 elections and after, the odor of tainted money can cost a party votes and hinder future fund-raising efforts.

Soft money raised and spent by interest groups is another matter. Some of these groups, such as those that spent $2.3 million on issue advocacy ads featuring Sen. Alfonse D'Amato promoting a New York State environmental bond, carry out political activities designed to advance the careers of one or a small group of politicians.[11] By spending millions of undocumented dollars on activities intended to influence congressional elections, these groups create relationships between candidates and wealthy donors that are hidden from the public.[12] Some groups make it difficult to discern their true policy agendas by adopting nondescript names, such as Citizens for Reform, the Coalition for Our Children's Future, the National Policy Forum, and Vote Now '96. Some groups have strong ties to one of the major parties, as noted in Chapter 4. Most soft money groups, including those that have strong ties to congressional candidates, party committees, or interest groups, are little more than subterfuges that enable wealthy individuals, organizations, and party committees to skirt federal campaign finance statutes. These groups have little or no public accountability. They should be barred from spending soft money in ways that are intended to affect the outcomes of federal elections or, at the very least, required to report all their election-related activity to the FEC.

A third unintended consequence of the FECA is its contribution to the decline in public trust in Congress. This lessening of confidence manifests itself in attitudes toward the institution, declining levels of voter turnout, feelings of political apathy and alienation, and a disapproval of politics and politicians. The FECA's disclosure requirements improved campaign finance reporting; more information than ever before became available about the flow of political money. Yet, public awareness of the role of money in politics has done little to increase citizen confidence in the political system. It has probably had the opposite effect. Many would probably agree with the statement that Sen. Max Cleland, D-Ga., made before the Senate Governmental Affairs Committee on the opening day of the 1997 campaign finance hearings: "Our democracy has become an auction, not an election."[13]

Some maintain that a fourth unintended consequence of the FECA is its creation of a system of campaign contributions that enables wealthy contributors to have a greater influence than others on elections. In situations where money matters, primarily in close races, reformers are correct in their assertion that those who make large contributions have a greater effect on elections than those who do not. By providing their preferred candidates with some of the money needed to communicate with voters, wealthy individual contributors and PACs, like the hundreds of thousands of professionals and volunteers who work on campaigns, increase their influence on the electoral process.

It is unclear, however, exactly what campaign contributors receive for their efforts. The sums that any one individual or one PAC can legally contribute directly to a candidate—in contrast to soft money transactions involving parties and other groups—are too small to determine the outcomes of elections, given the hundreds of thousands of dollars that are spent in most House contests and the millions of dollars spent in many Senate and some House campaigns. What individuals and groups usually get for their contributions is the opportunity to meet with members of Congress and their staffs, not the power to tell them how to govern.[14] Representatives and senators consider an array of factors when making policy decisions, including the views of constituents, committee chairs, party leaders, other legislators, and executive branch officials.[15] Legislators also strive to keep their roll-call votes consistent with those they have cast on related issues.[16]

Reformers who focus on the role of money underestimate the importance of these other factors. Despite public perceptions, campaign contributions ranging from one to several thousand dollars in most races probably do not seriously skew the representation in Congress. The lobbying efforts that groups make have a greater effect on members' voting decisions than their campaign contributions.[17] Moreover, these contributions certainly have a smaller effect than the hundred thousand dollar donations that were common during the pre-FECA era and the multimillion dollar expenditures that have become commonplace in the era of soft money. Public perceptions that individual and PAC contributions can buy votes in Congress are probably inaccurate, but the role of money in politics has undoubtedly contributed to the decline in public support for Congress.

The growing disconnection between the campaign for votes and the campaign for resources is a big part of the problem. During the golden age of parties, when local party activists were among the most important campaign resources, there was an intimate connection between the two campaigns. Elections were neighborhood affairs, and campaigns involved personal contact between candidates, party activists, other volunteers, and voters. Personal contact between voters and campaigners existed before, during, and after the election season. Parties provided ordinary voters and campaigners with ongoing relationships with members of Congress and others involved in the political system. Often these relationships revolved around jobs, contracts, social clubs, and opportunities to improve oneself or one's neighborhood.[18] Such relationships humanized government for voters and built bonds of trust between people and political institutions.

Contemporary campaigns encourage fewer meaningful ties to develop between voters and candidates. Campaigns for votes are more impersonal, consisting of television, radio, direct-mail ads, and the free media they generate. Fleeting contacts occasionally take place between citizens, candidates, and party and campaign activists, but they rarely result in the development of enduring personal relationships. Moreover, campaigns for resources are increasingly focused away from ordinary voters and toward national party organizations, PACs, and wealthy individuals who are in a position to provide the wherewithal needed to mount a contemporary campaign. Corporations, unions, and other organizations that finance independent television, direct mail, radio ads, and other communications and mobilization efforts have also become important targets in the campaign for resources.

Many voters believe that the elite "special interests" that contribute large sums to campaigns, rather than individuals who vote in them, possess the strongest and most beneficial relationships with members of Congress and others in government.[19] Because members of Congress and the organizations that elect them have relatively little patronage, few preferments, and hardly any opportunities for social advancement to distribute to their constituents, many voters have come to believe that these "goodies" are being distributed instead to wealthy campaign contributors in Washington and the nation's other financial centers. Transformations in the way that campaigns are conducted at home and in Washington have contributed to the public's belief that the operation of the federal government has changed in ways that favor special interests in Washington over the folks back home.

Low voter turnout is a serious shortcoming of congressional elections that is raised less frequently by reformers than the shortcomings of the FECA and the role of money in politics. Less than 50 percent of all eligible Americans turned out to vote in 1996. Turnout-related issues are important because the political legitimacy of elected officials who receive the votes of less than half of all eligible voters can be questioned. Congress sought to address this issue in 1993 when it enacted the motor-voter bill, which mandated that Americans be able to sign up to vote when registering their cars or transacting other business with national, state, or local governments. More efforts should be taken to encourage people to vote and to participate in other areas of politics.

The content of campaign messages is another aspect of congressional elections that is rarely discussed by reformers, but 84 percent of the general public is bothered by what politicians say to get elected.[20] Candidates campaign in slogans and sound bites mainly because short communications are cheaper than long ones. Candidates and political consultants also believe that repetition is preferable to detail because their audiences have limited attention spans. Meeting the needs of the journalists who cover campaigns and controlling the flow of campaign information are two other objectives that encourage candidates to disseminate short, symbolic statements. The fact that most voters cast their ballots on the basis of candidate imagery and qualifications rather than on a detailed understanding of the issues further encourages many candidates, particularly incumbents, to campaign on valence issues rather than focus on concrete solutions to major problems. Reforms that provide candidates with free or subsidized postage, radio time, or television time could improve the quality of campaign communications.

The fact that many candidates from the major parties campaign on similar positions is a complaint raised by radicals and supporters of minor parties, who comprise a small part of the population. They argue that the narrow range of positions is caused by the way elections are financed; Democrats and Republicans, they say, raise money from similar sources. Although their charge is undeniable, their explanation is wrong. The narrow breadth of dialogue in American elections is caused by candidates and parties responding to the fundamental agreement that exists among most voters on the issues. Ballot access or campaign finance reforms designed to strengthen minor parties or increase their number might slightly influence the nation's political debate, but it is doubtful that these changes would break the consensus that exists on major issues. Moreover, minor parties divide political opposition, which can help unpopular incumbents get reelected and impede majority rule.[21]

Reformers should not be overly optimistic about the effect that campaign reform would have on voters' confidence in their elected representatives, Congress as an institution, or the entire political system. Congress has never been looked upon with much favor by the American public, and changing the way that its members finance their campaigns is unlikely to alter this viewpoint.

RECOMMENDATIONS

Campaign reform should be founded on an understanding that elections are primarily fought between candidates. Candidates and their campaign organizations devise strategies, accumulate and distribute resources, publicize issue positions, communicate images, and carry out grass-roots activities in order to win voter support. Party committees, PACs, and other groups play important supporting roles in the election process—roles that have grown as a result of the weakening of the FECA. Reformers need to appreciate the different goals and resources that individuals and groups bring to elections and need to consider how their proposals will affect these groups.

Campaign reform should be predicated on the assumption that highly participatory, competitive elections are desirable because they are the best way to hold elected officials accountable to voters, enhance representation, and build trust in government. Reform should make congressional elections more competitive by encouraging more qualified candidates to run and by improving the ability of candidates, particularly nonincumbents, to communicate with voters. Campaign reform should also seek to increase the number of people who vote and give campaign contributions. It should attempt to minimize the amount of unregulated money spent to influence federal elections. The recommendations that follow are not a comprehensive reform package but are a series of proposals that would make congressional elections more participatory and more competitive and instill greater public confidence in the political system.

Free or Subsidized Communications

Free or subsidized campaign communications—whether they come in the form of postage, television or radio time, or communications vouchers—would give candidates, particularly challengers, the opportunity to present their messages to the public. The promise of free or heavily discounted communications resources would probably encourage better candidates to run for Congress because it would give them the knowledge that should they win their party's nomination they would be guaranteed access to some of the resources needed to campaign.[22] By encouraging the entry of better candidates and providing those who win a nomination with resources, this reform would lead to more competitive congressional elections.

The availability of resources for communications also might indirectly encourage greater electoral competition. Congressional challengers and open-seat candidates who used these resources effectively would be in a position to attract the attention of local journalists, thereby helping the candidates communicate more effectively with voters and helping voters cast their ballots on the basis of more information. Because campaign communications help stimulate public interest in elections, reforms that ensured both candidates adequate communications resources would probably also increase voter turnout.[23] A perception of greater competitiveness might also encourage some PACs and wealthy individuals to contribute to challengers, although most would likely continue to employ access or mixed strategies, which dictate contributing primarily to incumbents.

Free or subsidized mailings would give candidates opportunities to present targeted, detailed information about their qualifications, issue positions, and political objectives. Giving congressional candidates free postage for three or four first-class mailings—including postage for one or two newsletters of six to ten pages—is a simple reform that would improve the quality of the information that voters receive and increase electoral competitiveness.

Parties should also be offered free postage to mobilize current supporters and attract new ones. Minor parties and their candidates, as well as candidates who run as independents, could be given free postage if they persuaded a threshold number of voters to register under their label prior to the current election or if their candidates received a minimum number of votes in the previous contest. Minor parties and their candidates and independent candidates could also be reimbursed retroactively for postage if they reached some threshold level of votes in the current election. Extending free postage to candidates and parties is justified by the fact that it would contribute to the education of citizens—the same argument that is used to justify congressionally franked mail and reduced postage for party committees and nonprofit educational groups.

Giving candidates access to radio and television broadcast time would be more complicated because of disparities in rate charges and because congressional districts and media markets often do not match one another.[24] One solution is to require local broadcasters to provide Senate candidates with free television time and to require local radio stations to give free radio time to both House and Senate candidates. Congress could require broadcasters to issue back-to-back, prime-time segments to opposing candidates. Candidates could be issued five-minute blocks of time early in the campaign season, which they could use to air "infomercials" similar to those that Ross Perot popularized during the 1992 presidential election. These time slots would be lengthy enough for candidates to communicate some information about their personal backgrounds, political qualifications, issue positions, and major campaign themes. Later in the campaign season, two- or one-minute time slots could be distributed so that candidates could reinforce the images and campaign themes they introduced earlier. Thirty- or fifteen-second time slots could be made available during the summation stage of the election for candidates to pull together their campaign messages and rally their supporters.

This system of structured, free media time would give candidates the opportunity to communicate positive, substantive messages. It would also encourage voters to compare those messages. The differences in requirements for each chamber reflect the fact that television is an efficient and heavily used medium in virtually all Senate elections but is less practical and less frequently used in House contests, especially those held in major metropolitan areas.

The Democratic and Republican national committees should also be given free blocks of time on the national networks so that each can have the opportunity to remind voters of their party's accomplishments, philosophies, and objectives. Giving parties resources they can use to influence the national political agenda during (and after) an election could introduce more collective responsibility into the political system.[25] Minor parties and candidates should be given free blocks of radio and television time on terms similar to those for free postage.

Requiring local broadcasters to provide free political advertisements is justifiable because the airwaves are public property and one of the conditions of using them is that broadcasters "serve the public interest, convenience, and necessity."[26] The United States is the only major industrialized democracy that does not require broadcasters to contribute air time to candidates for public office—a distinction that should be eliminated.[27] Cable television operators should also be required to distribute advertising time to House and Senate candidates and parties with the justification that much of what is viewed on cable television passes through the public airwaves or over publicly maintained utility poles.

An alternative to providing candidates and parties with communications resources is government distribution of communications vouchers. This would allow campaigners to exercise more freedom in designing their communication strategies. Campaigns that felt the need to allocate more resources to setting the agenda could use their vouchers to purchase mass media ads. Campaigns that wished to focus on mobilizing specific population groups could devote a greater portion of their vouchers to direct mail. One of the trade-offs of the voucher option is that it imposes fewer costs on broadcasters and greater costs on taxpayers. One way to ease the burden on the public treasury would be to require all radio, television, and cable companies to sell candidates and parties prime-time advertising space at highly discounted rates.[28] Another way to lessen the onus of campaign costs on taxpayers would be to require all candidates who accept communications vouchers to turn over any portion of their campaign treasury that remained after the election to a federal election campaign fund that would be used to help provide vouchers in the next election.[29]

The preceding proposals would not provide communications resources to primary candidates or general election contestants from parties lacking widespread political support. This denial would serve as both a cost-saving measure and a way to discourage the declaration of trivial candidacies. Reforms that placed free or subsidized communications resources at the disposal of candidates and parties would potentially reduce the importance of money in politics as well as lower campaign costs and increase the competitiveness of congressional elections.

Contributions and Coordinated Expenditures

The amounts that individuals and groups can contribute to campaigns should be reviewed periodically in light of the roles that each set of contributors plays in the electoral process. The limits on individual contributions to candidates should be raised to $3,000 for the primary and the same amount for the general election to account for inflation and increases in campaign costs that have taken place since the limits were first set in 1974. PAC contributions should be raised to $10,000 for each phase of the election—a sum that reflects inflation and increased campaign costs but takes into consideration public skepticism about PAC money. The aggregate limit for individual contributions to all federal candidates and party committees and PACs that participate in federal elections should be raised from $25,000 to $75,000 per year to match the rate of inflation. This change would increase the amount of hard money that parties spend in federal elections without greatly increasing the influence of wealthy individuals on any one congressional race. These changes, which should be coupled with limits on the contribution of soft money, would encourage wealthy individuals and groups to increase their hard money contributions.

Expenditures by House and Senate candidates' campaign organizations should remain unlimited, unless large communications subsidies are made available to them. Money is essential to communicating with voters under the current cash-based campaign system. Spending limits could reduce the communications that candidates have with citizens, deprive voters of the information they need to cast informed ballots, and increase the influence of interest groups, parties, and the media. Independent expenditures and issue advocacy campaigns financed by wealthy individuals, parties, PACs, corporations, unions, and other groups are no substitute for the unfiltered communications that candidates disseminate to voters. The same is true of field activities carried out by party committees and news stories published in local newspapers or over the airwaves.

Party coordinated expenditures on behalf of candidates should be increased twofold to account for increased campaign costs and to allow party organizations to play a bigger role in congressional elections. Increasing the level of party activity in elections could enhance their competitiveness because parties strive to focus most of their resources on close contests, including those of challengers. Greater party expenditures would indirectly affect the competitiveness of some campaigns in that they would help candidates attract resources and attention from other contributors and the press. By enabling parties to pledge more support to potential candidates, this reform could help the parties to encourage strategic politicians who are undecided about entering a race for Congress to decide in favor of running.

Candidate Contributions and Incumbent War Chests

The amounts that candidates contribute to their own campaigns or carry over from previous elections should be limited. If, because of constitutional challenges, limits cannot be imposed, the impact of these resources should be minimized. Personal funds and existing war chests give incumbents and millionaires great advantages in congressional elections, not the least of which is discouraging talented potential opponents from running against them. These funds should be limited by offering candidates who adhere to ceilings of $150,000 access to subsidized campaign resources. In addition, a challenger who faces an incumbent with a huge existing war chest or any candidate who faces an opponent who makes personal contributions to his or her own campaign in excess of $150,000 should be allowed to raise contributions from individuals, parties, and PACs that are twice as large as normally allowed.

Tax Incentives

Tax incentives should be used to broaden the base of campaign contributors and to offset the impact of funds collected from wealthy and well-organized segments of society. Prior to the tax reforms introduced in 1986, individuals were able to claim a tax credit of $50 if they contributed $100 or more to federal candidates. (Couples who contributed $200 could claim a tax credit of $100.) Although a significant number of taxpayers took advantage of these credits, the credits themselves were not sufficient to encourage many citizens to give campaign contributions.[30]

A system of graduated tax credits similar to those used in some other Western democracies might accomplish this goal.[31] Individuals who are eligible to claim a 100 percent tax credit for up to $100 in campaign contributions would be more likely to make them. Credits of 75 percent for the next $100 and 50 percent for the following $100 would encourage further contributions. Tax credits would encourage candidates and parties to pursue small contributions more aggressively and would increase the number of taxpayers who give them. Using taxpayer dollars to increase the number of individuals who give money to federal candidates is an expensive proposition, but it would probably be the most effective way to increase the number of people who participate in the financing of congressional elections. Increasing the base of small contributors is the best way to offset the influence of individuals and groups that make large contributions while maintaining a tie between a candidate's level of popular and financial support.

Soft Money

Soft money contributions and expenditures need to be better regulated. Individuals and groups should be allowed to continue to make soft money contributions, but a ceiling of $75,000 (equal to the proposed hard money limit) should be set on the amounts raised from any one source by party organizations that make expenditures designed to influence federal elections. This ceiling would enable party committees to continue to spend soft money while forcing them to broaden their base of soft money donors. So the public can be more fully apprised of soft money campaign activities, disclosure rules should be changed to require that all funds spent to directly or indirectly influence federal elections, including all soft money, be reported to the FEC. This change would bring party soft money directly under the FECA's regulatory umbrella.

Party soft money expenditures should be limited to party-building efforts, grass-roots efforts, and generic campaign advertising. Voter mobilization and election agenda setting are activities that parties have traditionally financed with soft money. These activities are important for several reasons. First, they contribute to the competitiveness of elections. Second, they register and mobilize new voters, unlike candidate voter mobilization efforts, which mainly target citizens who have a previous voting history.[32] Third, they stimulate local political activism, thereby strengthening state and local party organizations and improving the farm teams from which congressional candidates emerge. Fourth, they help build bridges among elected officials who serve in different branches and levels of government. And fifth, they encourage voters to discern differences between the parties and to reward or punish politicians for their performance in office or the substance of their platforms.

Parties should be prohibited from spending soft money on television, radio, and direct-mail issue advocacy advertisements that include the names or likenesses of federal candidates. These are not traditional party activities. The very fact that an ad makes a direct reference to one or more federal candidates is justification for classifying it as a federal election activity that should be regulated under federal campaign finance law.

Interest groups should be allowed to make soft money contributions of up to $75,000 to parties. Barring an outright ban on interest group expenditures intended to influence federal elections, a ceiling should be placed on the amount of soft money that interest groups can spend in a given state, depending on the size of its population. Interest groups, like parties, should also be banned from spending soft money on issue advocacy ads that directly name or present the likeness of a federal candidate.

Given recent Supreme Court rulings, it would take a constitutional amendment to ban election-related interest group soft money expenditures, but Congress ought to attempt to alter the tax code to discourage the formation of the groups that make these expenditures. Privately run, nonparty groups and their backers are currently the least regulated organizations in congressional elections, and they are not subject to the same kind of public accountability or institutional checks as are parties, PACs, and candidates. At a minimum, Congress should require interest groups that engage in any election-related spending to detail the substance of their political activities, including issue advocacy, to both the FEC and the Internal Revenue Service.

The Federal Election Commission

The Federal Election Commission should be strengthened. The commission is currently unable to investigate many of the complaints brought before it, has a backlog of cases that is several years old, and has been criticized for its failure to dispense quickly with frivolous cases and pursue more important ones. Some of these shortcomings are caused by the fact that it is often micromanaged by its oversight committees in Congress and is severely underfunded. Other shortcomings are due to the FEC's structure—it has three Democratic and three Republican commissioners—which lends itself to indecision and stalemate.

It is essential that the FEC be restructured so that it operates in a more decisive fashion. Only strong enforcement by the FEC, with backup from the Justice Department and a specially appointed independent counsel on appropriate cases, can discourage unscrupulous politicians from violating the law. Recent failures by the FEC to enforce the law adequately have encouraged members of Congress to spend tens of millions of dollars on partisan investigations. Such investigations, which may be useful for embarrassing political opponents, are an inadequate substitute for the fair and impartial administration of the law.

Voter Turnout Initiatives

Campaign reform should address low voter turnout in elections. Citizen apathy and disenchantment with the political system are probably responsible for some voter abstention, but voter registration laws are believed to depress turnout by about 9 percent.[33] The motor-voter law, enacted in 1993, has eased some barriers to voter registration. Barriers could be further eased by requiring all states to include a check-off box on their tax forms that enables citizens to register to vote when they file their tax returns.

Measures that make it easier for voters to exercise the franchise should also be considered. Making election day a national holiday is one possibility. Making wider use of mail-in ballots, such as those Oregon used for its 1996 Senate special election, is another. "Early," "countywide," and "mobile" voting procedures should also be considered. Such procedures currently allow voters in Texas to cast their ballots over a seventeen-day period commencing twenty days before an election at any of the numerous locations in the county in which they are registered to vote. These locations include mobile units that are dispatched to parks and other popular locations on weekends. Measures that make it easier to register to vote or cast a ballot will not cause a groundswell in voter turnout, but they should increase it, especially when combined with candidate and party voter mobilization efforts.[34]

PROSPECTS FOR REFORM

It would not be easy to enact legislation that improves the quality of candidates for Congress, enhances the ability of candidates—especially nonincumbents— to communicate with voters, and enables campaigns to turn out more of their supporters. Campaign reform is a highly charged issue. Candidates and parties often try to portray themselves as reformers while advocating changes that reflect their own self-interest. Incumbents are heavily preoccupied with protecting elements of the system that work to their advantage. Challengers are just as vocal about doing away with those advantages, at least until they become incumbents. Republicans advocate an increase in existing limits on party spending, which would enable them to take advantage of their party's superior fund-raising prowess. Democrats are more favorably disposed toward public subsidies coupled with spending limits, which would reduce the Republicans' financial advantages.

Interchamber differences in regard to reform also exist, with members of the Senate advocating the elimination of PAC contributions and House members defending PACs. These differences reflect the greater dependence of members of the lower chamber on PAC funds. Other differences of opinion reflect the demands that campaigning makes on different kinds of candidates from varied districts. Women, African Americans, ethnic minorities, and members of other traditionally underrepresented groups, who depend on large national donor networks, have preferences that differ from those of most white male candidates. Candidates' opinions about campaign reform also vary according to the characteristics of their constituencies. Candidates from wealthy urban seats tend to have fund-raising opportunities, spending needs, and views on reform dif-

ferent from those from poor rural states or districts. Of course, not all differences are grounded in personal or partisan advantage. Philosophical differences
also divide politicians and parties.

The diversity of views and the complexity of the issue make it difficult to
find the common ground needed to pass meaningful campaign reform. The
sometimes questionable recommendations and inflammatory public relations
campaigns of reform groups have made it difficult for members of Congress to
move beyond public posturing and engage in serious reform efforts. Since the
late 1970s, House members and senators of both parties have introduced comprehensive packages that they knew would never be adopted by their respective
chambers, survive a conference committee, and be signed into law by the president. Their efforts have been geared largely to providing political cover for
themselves rather than to enacting campaign finance reform.

Members of the 104th Congress proposed about seventy campaign finance
reform bills, most of which were all but ignored after they were introduced.
Two bills—House Resolution 3820, which was stewarded by Rep. Bill Thomas, R-Calif., chairman of the House Oversight Committee, and Senate Resolution 1219, cosponsored by Sens. John McCain, R-Ariz., and Russell Feingold,
D-Wis.—received serious consideration. Although they are very different, both
bills contained useful provisions, including some of the recommendations discussed in the previous section. The fate of each gives some insight into the
difficulties in enacting comprehensive campaign reform.

House Resolution 3820 focused primarily on the financing of House elections. It sought to increase the amounts that individuals could contribute to
House candidates and party committees to account for inflation. It would have
required candidates to raise a majority of their funds from within their congressional districts. The bill proposed to allow parties to spend unlimited sums to
communicate with registered party voters or individuals who voted in a party's
last primary. It would have increased PAC contributions to national and state
party committees to $40,000 each.

The bill also sought to lower PAC contributions to candidates to $2,500,
ban leadership PACs, prohibit PACs and lobbyists from bundling campaign
contributions, and make it easier for corporate PACs and more difficult for
labor PACs to collect contributions. Finally, the bill would have allowed candidates whose opponents spent more than $150,000 in personal funds to accept
individual and party contributions in excess of the ceilings for individual and
party contributions until those contributions equaled the opponent's personal
expenditures. Parties could also match, in contributions to its nominee, any
funds that an opposing incumbent carried over from a previous election.

House Resolution 3820 was blasted by House Democrats as a partisan bill that favored the Republicans and their supporters. Yet the GOP was also divided over it. After the Republicans on the Rules Committee and other GOP leaders expressed ambivalence about the bill, it suffered a crushing 162-259 vote defeat on the floor of the House.

Senate Resolution 1219 proposed a trade-off for congressional candidates: those who accepted spending limits based on the size of their states' voting age population would receive thirty minutes of free broadcast time, a discount of 50 percent off the lowest unit rate on other broadcasts, and the ability to send pieces of mail to each voting age resident at the third-class bulk rate.[35] The bill would have banned PAC contributions, restricted bundling, prohibited incumbents from using franked mass mailings in the calendar year of an election, imposed new limits and disclosure requirements on soft money contributions and expenditures, and required candidates to raise 60 percent of their campaign funds from their state.[36] Finally, by allowing a complying candidate whose opponent exceeded the limit to raise individual contributions in amounts of $2,000 (twice the normal limit), it would have discouraged candidates from contributing more than $250,000 in personal funds to their own campaigns.

Although it was heralded as a bipartisan bill, was praised by President Clinton, and received favorable press attention, Senate Resolution 1219 was never scheduled for debate nor did it receive a floor vote in the 104th Congress. Its sponsors and a few other legislators held several press conferences about the bill to encourage their colleagues to support bringing it to the floor during the 105th Congress.

Reformers might have been wiser to have shunned comprehensive packages, such as House Resolution 3820 and Senate Resolution 1219, in favor of an incremental approach to reform. More progress would probably have been made if Congress had first enacted changes that enjoyed widespread support and then worked to build bipartisan coalitions on the less consensual issues. Incrementalism offers the additional advantage of enabling Congress to adjust the law to offset the unintended consequences that routinely emerge as the result of regulatory change.

Reform often occurs in response to the public outcry for change that follows a major political scandal. The Federal Election Campaign Act of 1974, the most important piece of campaign finance legislation enacted in American history, was passed after the Watergate scandal focused public attention on the break-in at Democratic National Committee headquarters and the financing of presidential elections. The Keating Five, House Post Office, and House banking scandals and the general frustrations that many Americans vented at the

103rd and 104th Congresses did not generate enough pressure to result in reform. Public disapproval of campaign contributions made by foreign interests also may fall short of inspiring Congress to act on this important issue.

Moreover, a massive overhaul in the campaign finance system will not serve as a panacea for the nation's problems. Campaign finance reform may improve elections, but it will not remedy other shortcomings in the political system. Reform is an ongoing process that requires continuous vigilance. Many politicians, party officials, and interest group leaders discovered avenues for campaign spending that bypassed the contribution and spending limits imposed by the FECA; they or others will undoubtedly find new ways to circumvent future campaign reforms.

CONCLUSION

The rules and norms that govern congressional elections resemble those that structure any activity: they favor some individuals and groups over others. In recent years the number of Americans who believe that the electoral process is out of balance and provides too many advantages to incumbents, interest groups, wealthy individuals, and other "insiders" has grown tremendously. Their views are reflected in the growing distrust that citizens have of government, the sense of powerlessness expressed by many voters, and the public's willingness to follow the leads of insurgent candidates and reformers without scrutinizing their qualifications or objectives. These are signs that the prestige and power of Congress are in danger. They are also signs that meaningful campaign reform is in order.

Campaign reform should make congressional elections more competitive and increase the number of citizens who participate in them, both as voters and as financial contributors. Campaign reform should enable candidates to spend less time campaigning for resources and more time campaigning for votes. Reform should seek to enhance representation, accountability, and trust in government. The campaign finance reform legislation that has been debated by Congress during the last few years would succeed in accomplishing some, but not all, of these goals.

Without major campaign reform, incumbency will remain the defining element of most congressional elections. Challengers, particularly those who run for the House, will continue to struggle to raise campaign funds and attract the attention of voters. The dialogue that occurs in House incumbent-challenger contests will remain largely one-sided, whereas that in open-seat contests and Senate races will continue to be somewhat more even. Huge sums of soft money that are intended to influence the outcomes of congressional elections will continue to flow outside the federal campaign finance system and, in some cases, overshadow the election activities of candidates. Congress, elections, and other institutions of government will remain targets for attack both by those who have a sincere wish to improve the political process and those seeking short-term partisan gain.

Elections are the most important avenues of political influence that are afforded to the citizens of a representative democracy. They give voters the opportunity to hold public officials accountable and to reject politicians with whom they disagree. Respect for human rights and political processes that allow for citizen input are what make democratic systems of government superior to others. Yet all systems of government have their imperfections, and some of these are embodied in their electoral processes. There are times when these imperfections are significant enough to warrant major change. Such change should bring the electoral process closer in line with broadly supported notions of liberty, equality, and democracy as well as the other values that bind a nation. The current state of congressional elections, and campaign finance in particular, demonstrates that change is warranted in the way in which Americans elect those who serve in Congress.

Notes

1. THE STRATEGIC CONTEXT

1. Leon D. Epstein, *Political Parties in Western Democracies* (New York: Praeger, 1967), chap. 8.

2. James G. Gimpel, *Fulfilling the Contract: The First 100 Days* (Boston: Allyn and Bacon, 1996); Robin Kolodny, "The Contract with America in the 104th Congress," in *The State of the Parties,* ed. John C. Green and Daniel M. Shea (Lanham, Md.: Rowman and Littlefield, 1996), 314–327.

3. Kenneth Martis, *The Historical Atlas of U.S. Congressional Districts, 1789–1983* (New York: Free Press, 1982), 5–6.

4. See, for example, Frank J. Sorauf, "Political Parties and Political Action Committees: Two Life Cycles," *Arizona Law Review* 22 (1980): 445–464.

5. Jerrold B. Rusk, "The Effect of the Australian Ballot Reform on Split Ticket Voting: 1876–1908," *American Political Science Review* 64 (December 1970): 1220–1283.

6. See, for example, V. O. Key, *Politics, Parties, and Pressure Groups* (New York: Thomas Y. Crowell, 1964), 371.

7. Ibid., 389–391.

8. Committee on Political Parties, American Political Science Association, "Toward a More Responsible Two-Party System," *American Political Science Association,* supp. 44 (1950): 21.

9. The Federal Election Campaign Act of 1974 had a predecessor that was enacted in 1971 but had little effect on congressional elections. For an overview of the FECA and the campaign finance system that existed prior to it, see Herbert E. Alexander, *Financing Politics: Money, Elections, and Political Reform* (Washington, D.C.: CQ Press, 1992), esp. chaps. 2 and 3.

10. The only subsidy the FECA gives to the parties is a grant to pay for their presidential nominating conventions. As nonprofit organizations, the parties also receive a discount for bulk postage.

11. Karl-Heinz Nassmacher, "Comparing Party and Campaign Finance in Western Democracies," in *Campaign and Party Finance in North America and Western Europe,* ed. Arthur B. Gunlicks (Boulder, Colo.: Westview Press, 1993), 233–263.

12. Arthur B. Gunlicks, "Introduction," in *Campaign and Party Finance,* 6.

13. Sorauf, "Political Parties and Political Action Committees," 445–464.

14. Paul S. Herrnson, *Party Campaigning in the 1980s* (Cambridge, Mass.: Harvard University Press, 1988), 82.

15. The term *soft money* was coined by Elizabeth Drew in *Politics and Money: The New Road to Corruption* (New York: Macmillan, 1983), esp. 15. See also Herbert E. Alexander and Anthony Corrado, *Financing the 1994 Election* (Armonk, N.Y.: M. E. Sharpe, 1995), chap. 6.; Robert Biersack, "The Nationalization of Party Finance," in *The State of the Parties,* 108–124.

16. Federal Election Commission, "Political Parties' Fundraising Hits 881 Million," press release, January 10, 1997.

17. See Anthony Corrado, *Creative Campaigning: PACs and the Presidential Selection Process* (Boulder, Colo.: Westview Press, 1992), 80–84.

18. Charles R. Babcock, "Use of Tax-Exempt Groups Integral to Political Strategy," *Washington Post,* January 7, 1997; Rebecca Carr, "Tax-Exempt Groups Scrutinized as Fundraising Clout Grows," *Congressional Quarterly Weekly Report,* February 22, 1997; and Charles R. Babcock and Ruth Marcus, "For Their Targets, Mystery Groups' Ads Hit Like Attacks from Nowhere," *Washington Post,* March 9, 1997.

19. *FEC v. Massachusetts Citizens for Life, Inc.* 479 U.S. 248 (1986); *Colorado Republican Federal Campaign Committee v. FEC,* 116 S.Ct. 2309 (1996).

20. As is explained in Chapter 4, the FEC has ruled that a portion of the party money that is spent on issue advocacy must be hard money.

21. Louis Hartz, *The Liberal Tradition in America* (New York: Harcourt, Brace, 1955).

22. See, for example, Robert A. Dahl, *Democracy in the United States: Promise and Performance* (Chicago: Rand McNally, 1967), 252; Herbert McClosky and John Zaller, *The American Ethos: Public Attitudes toward Democracy* (Cambridge, Mass.: Harvard University Press, 1984), 62–100.

23. See Rusk, "The Effect of the Australian Ballot."

24. Key, *Politics, Parties, and Pressure Groups,* 342, 386; Nelson W. Polsby, *The Consequences of Party Reform* (Oxford: Oxford University Press, 1983), 72–74; William J. Crotty, *American Parties in Decline* (Boston: Little, Brown, 1984), 277–278.

25. Lee Ann Elliot, "Political Action Committees—Precincts of the '80s," *Arizona Law Review* 22 (1980): 539–554; Kay Lehman Schlozman and John T. Tierney, *Organized Interests and American Democracy* (New York: Harper and Row, 1986), 75–78.

26. John R. Petrocik, *Party Coalitions: Realignments and the Decline of the New Deal Party System* (Chicago: University of Chicago Press, 1981), chaps. 8 and 9; Paul Allen Beck, "A Socialization Theory of Partisan Realignment," in *Controversies in American Voting Behavior,* ed. Richard G. Niemi and Herbert F. Weisberg (Washington, D.C.: CQ Press, 1984), 396–411; Martin P. Wattenberg, *The Decline of American Political Parties, 1952–1988* (Cambridge: Harvard University Press, 1990), chap. 4.

27. Austin Ranney, *Channels of Power: The Impact of Television on American Politics* (New York: Basic Books, 1983), 110; Doris Graber, *Mass Media and American Politics,* 4th ed. (Washington, D.C.: CQ Press, 1993), 250–252.

28. Jack Dennis, "Support for the Party System by the Mass Public," *American Political Science Review* 60 (September 1966): 605.

29. CBS News/*New York Times* poll, October 1986, cited in Bruce E. Keith, David B. Magleby, Candice J. Nelson, Elizabeth Orr, Mark C. Westlye, and Raymond E. Wolfinger, *The Myth of the Independent Voter* (Berkeley: University of California Press, 1992), 8.

30. Keith et al., *The Myth of the Independent Voter,* table 1.1 and chaps. 4 and 5.

31. See ibid., n. 8, p. 19.

32. This group includes independents who lean toward one of the two parties. See ibid.

33. Sorauf, "Political Parties and Political Action Committees," 447.

34. Robert Agranoff, "Introduction/The New Style of Campaigning," in *The New Style in Election Campaigns,* ed. Robert Agranoff (Boston: Holbrook Press, 1972), 3–50; Larry J. Sabato, *The Rise of the Political Consultants: New Ways of Winning Elections* (New York: Basic Books, 1981).

35. See Ranney, *Channels of Power,* 110; and Graber, *Mass Media,* 250.

36. Agranoff, *The New Style in Election Campaigns.*

37. Sorauf, "Political Parties and Political Action Committees."

38. Cornelius P. Cotter and John F. Bibby, "Institutional Development and the Thesis of Party Decline," *Political Science Quarterly* 95 (1980): 1–27; David Adamany, "Political Parties in the 1980s," in *Money and Politics in the United States: Financing Elections in the 1980s,* ed. Michael J. Malbin (Washington, D.C.: American Enterprise Institute, 1984), 70–121; Herrnson, *Party Campaigning,* chaps. 3 and 4; Stephen E. Frantzich, *Political Parties in the Technological Age* (New York: Longman, 1989), 81–90, 182–186.

39. In addition to the thirty-four House Democrats who were defeated in the general election in 1994, another four lost in the primaries.

40. Norman J. Ornstein, Thomas E. Mann, and Michael J. Malbin, *Vital Statistics on Congress, 1995–1996* (Washington, D.C.: Congressional Quarterly, 1996), table 2-8, and various issues of *Congressional Quarterly Weekly Report.*

41. See, for example, Key, *Politics, Parties, and Pressure Groups,* 421.

42. David R. Butler and Bruce Cain, *Congressional Redistricting: Comparative and Theoretical Perspectives* (New York: Macmillan, 1992), 10, 87; Michael Lyons and Peter F. Galdersi, "Incumbency, Reapportionment, and U.S. House Redistricting," *Political Review Quarterly* 49 (1995): 857–873. For another view, see Richard Niemi and Alan I. Abramowitz, "Partisan Redistricting and the 1992 Elections," *Journal of Politics* 56 (1994): 811–817.

43. David R. Mayhew, *Congress: The Electoral Connection* (New Haven, Conn.: Yale University Press, 1974); Morris P. Fiorina, *Congress: Keystone of the Washington Establishment* (New Haven, Conn.: Yale University Press, 1978), 19–21, 41–49, 56–62; Diane E. Yiannakis, "The Grateful Electorate: Casework and Congressional Elections," *American Journal of Political Science* 25 (1981): 568–580; Bruce Cain, John Ferejohn, and Morris Fiorina, *The Personal Vote* (Cambridge, Mass.: Harvard University Press, 1987), 103–106; Gary C. Jacobson, *The Politics of Congressional Elections,* 4th ed. (New York: Longman, 1997), 28–33; George Serra and Albert Cover, "The Electoral Consequences of Perquisite Use: The Casework Case," *Legislative Studies Quarterly* 17 (1992): 233–246.

44. Harrison W. Fox and Susan Webb Hammond, *Congressional Staffs: The Invisible Force in American Lawmaking* (New York: Free Press, 1977), 88–99, 154–155.

45. Herrnson, *Party Campaigning,* chap. 4; Frank J. Sorauf, *Inside Campaign Finance* (New Haven, Conn.: Yale University Press, 1992), 80–84.

46. Donald Ostdiek, "Congressional Redistricting and District Typologies," *Journal of Politics* 57 (1995): 533–543.

47. Bruce I. Oppenheimer, James A. Stimson, and Richard W. Waterman, "Interpreting U.S. Congressional Elections: The Exposure Thesis," *Legislative Studies Quarterly* 11 (1986): 227–247; James E. Campbell, "The Presidential Surge and Its Midterm Decline in Congressional Elections, 1868–1988," *Journal of Politics* 53 (1991): 478–487.

48. Michael S. Lewis-Beck and Tom W. Rice, *Forecasting Elections* (Washington, D.C.: CQ Press, 1992), chaps. 4–6.

49. Jerome M. Clubb, William H. Flanigan, and Nancy H. Zingale, *Partisan Realignment: Voters, Parties, and Government in American History* (Beverly Hills, Calif.: Sage Publications, 1980), 258–260.

50. On coattail effects see esp. Walter Dean Burnham, "Insulation and Responsiveness in Congressional Elections," *Political Science Quarterly* 90 (1975): 411–435; Randall L. Calvert and John A. Ferejohn, "Coattail Voting in Recent Presidential Elections," *American Political Science Review* 77 (1983): 407–419; Richard Born, "Reassessing the Decline of Presidential Coattails: U.S. House Elections, 1952–1980," *Journal of Politics* 46 (1980): 60–79; James E. Campbell, "Predicting Seat Gains from Presidential Coattails," *American Journal of Political Science* 30 (1986): 397–418; Gary C. Jacobson, *Electoral Origins of Divided Government, 1946–1988* (Boulder, Colo.: Westview Press, 1990), 80–81.

51. Edward R. Tufte, "Determinants of the Outcomes of Midterm Congressional Elections," *American Political Science Review* 69 (1975): 812–826; Lewis-Beck and Rice, *Forecasting Elections,* 60–75.

52. Morris P. Fiorina, *Retrospective Voting in American National Elections* (New Haven, Conn.: Yale University Press, 1981), 165; Eric M. Uslaner and M. Margaret Conway, "The Responsible Electorate: Watergate, the Economy, and Vote Choice in 1974," *American Political Science Review* 79 (1985): 788–803.

53. The Republicans picked up an additional five House and two Senate seats as a result of Democratic incumbents who switched parties following the election.

54. Gerald Kramer, "Short-Term Fluctuations in U.S. Voting Behavior," *American Political Science Review* 65 (1971): 131–143; Gary C. Jacobson and Samuel Kernell, *Strategy and Choice in Congressional Elections* (New Haven, Conn.: Yale University Press, 1983), chap. 6; Jacobson, "Does the Economy Matter in Midterm Elections?" *American Journal of Political Science* 34 (1990): 400–404. For another interpretation see Robert S. Erikson, "Economic Conditions and the Vote: A Review of the Macro Level Evidence," *American Journal of Political Science* 34 (1990): 373–399.

55. John F. Bibby, *Parties, Politics, and Elections in America* (Chicago: Nelson Hall, 1987), 239–240.

56. Norman Nie and Kristi Andersen, "Mass Belief Systems Revisited: Political Change and Attitude Structure," *Journal of Politics* 36 (1974): 540–591; Crotty, *American Parties in Decline,* 49–50.

57. Richard A. Brody and Benjamin I. Page, "The Assessment of Policy Voting," *American Political Science Review* 66 (1972): 450–458; Norman H. Nie, Sidney Verba, John R. Petrocik, *The Changing American Voter* (New York: Twentieth Century Fund, 1979), esp. chap. 18.

58. *Thornburg v. Gingles,* 478 U.S. 30 (1986).

59. Juliana Gruenwald, "Supreme Court Orders Panel to Review Chicago District," *Con-*

gressional Quarterly Weekly Report, November 16, 1996, 3286; and Ronald D. Elving, "Virginia Unlikely to Appeal Ruling against 3rd," *Congressional Quarterly Weekly Report,* February 15, 1997; "N.Y. to Redraw District in City," *Washington Post,* February 28, 1997.

60. Richard F. Fenno Jr., *Home Style: House Members in Their Districts* (Boston: Little, Brown, 1978), 164–168.

61. The estimate for the savings and loan cleanup is from Barbara Miles and Thomas Woodward, "The Savings and Loan Cleanup: Background and Progress," CRS Issue Brief, Washington, D.C.: Library of Congress, updated March 10, 1994.

62. David B. Magleby, Kelly D. Patterson, and Stephen H. Wirls, "Fear and Loathing of the Modern Congress: The Public Manifestation of Constitutional Design" (paper presented at the annual meeting of the Midwest Political Science Association, Chicago, April 1994), 14–16; see also Gary C. Jacobson, "The 1994 House Elections in Perspective," in *Midterm: The Elections of 1994 in Context,* ed. Philip A. Klinkner (Boulder, Colo.: Westview Press, 1996); and John R. Hibbing and Elizabeth Theiss-Morse, *Congress as Public Enemy: Public Attitudes toward American Political Institutions* (Cambridge: Cambridge University Press, 1995), 31–33, 69–71, 96–100.

63. On the 1994 elections, see the essays in Klinkner, *Midterm.*

64. Gimpel, *Fulfilling the Contract.*

65. Twenty percent is an appropriate victory margin given the heightened level of uncertainty in contemporary congressional elections. A narrower margin, such as 15 percent, would have eliminated campaigns that were competitive for part of the election season but were ultimately decided by more than 15 percent of the vote. Slightly changing the boundaries for the competitiveness measure does not significantly change the results. For a fuller discussion of the classification scheme see the appendix to the first edition of this book.

66. Gary C. Jacobson, *The Politics of Congressional Elections,* 23–24.

67. Campbell was elected as a Democrat in 1992 but switched parties in March 1995.

2. CANDIDATES AND NOMINATIONS

1. E. E. Schattschneider, *Party Government* (New York: Holt, Rinehart, and Winston, 1942), 99–106.

2. Thomas A. Kazee, "The Emergence of Congressional Candidates," in *Who Runs for Congress? Ambition, Context, and Candidate Emergence,* ed. Thomas A. Kazee (Washington, D.C.: Congressional Quarterly, 1994), 1–14; L. Sandy Maisel, Linda L. Fowler, Ruth S. Jones, and Walter J. Stone, "Nomination Politics: The Roles of Institutional, Contextual, and Personal Variables," in *The Parties Respond: Changes in the American Party System,* 2nd ed., ed. L. Sandy Maisel (Boulder, Colo.: Westview Press, 1994), 145–168.

3. Joseph A. Schlesinger, *Ambition and Politics: Political Careers in the United States* (Chicago: Rand McNally, 1966), 11–12, 16–19, 198–199; Jacobson and Kernell, *Strategy and Choice in Congressional Elections,* chap. 3; William T. Bianco, "Strategic Decisions on Candidacy in U.S. Congressional Districts," *Legislative Studies Quarterly* 9 (1984): 360–362; Kazee, "The Emergence of Congressional Candidates"; David T. Canon, *Actors, Athletes, and Astronauts: Political Amateurs in the United States* (Chicago: University of Chicago Press, 1990), 76–79.

4. L. Sandy Maisel, Linda L. Fowler, Ruth S. Jones, and Walter J. Stone, "The Naming of Candidates: Recruitment or Emergence?" in *The Parties Respond: Changes in the American Party System,* 1st ed., ed. L. Sandy Maisel (Boulder, Colo.: Westview Press, 1990); Linda L. Fowler and Robert D. McClure, *Political Ambition: Who Decides to Run for Congress* (New Haven: Yale University Press, 1989), 231.

5. Gary C. Jacobson and Samuel Kernell, "National Forces in the 1986 U.S. House Elections," *Legislative Studies Quarterly* 15 (1990): 65–87; Canon, *Actors, Athletes, and Astronauts,* 106–108.

6. See, for example, John Alford, Holly Teeters, Daniel S. Ward, and Rick Wilson, "Overdraft: The Political Cost of Congressional Malfeasance," *Journal of Politics* 56 (1994): 788–801.

7. Timothy Groseclose and Keith Krehbiel, "Golden Parachutes, Rubber Checks, and Strategic Retirements from the 102nd House," *American Journal of Political Science* 38 (1994): 75–99; Gary C. Jacobson and Michael Dimock, "Checking Out: The Effects of Bank Overdrafts on the 1992 House Election," *American Journal of Political Science* 38 (1994): 601–624.

8. See n. 3.

9. Mayhew, *Congress*; Fiorina, *Congress*. The value of congressional allowances is from Roger H. Davidson and Walter J. Oleszek, *Congress and Its Members*, 5th ed. (Washington, D.C.: CQ Press, 1997), 149.

10. See Fenno, *Home Style.*

11. Peverill Squire, "Preemptive Fundraising and Challenger Profile in Senate Elections," *Journal of Politics* 53 (1991): 1150–1164; Janet M. Box-Steffensmeier, "A Dynamic Analysis of the Role of War Chests in Campaign Strategy," *American Journal of Political Science* 40 (1996): 352–371. But see Jonathan S. Krasno and Donald Philip Green, "Preempting Quality Challengers in House Elections," *Journal of Politics* 50 (1988): 920–936.

12. Sara Fritz and Dwight Morris, *Gold-Plated Politics: Running for Congress in the 1990s* (Washington, D.C.: Congressional Quarterly, 1992), esp. chap. 2.

13. On redistricting, see Richard G. Niemi and Laura R. Winsky, "The Persistence of Partisan Redistricting Effects in Congressional Elections, *Journal of Politics* 54 (1992): 565–571.

14. Stephen E. Frantzich, "De-Recruitment: The Other Side of the Congressional Equation," *Western Political Quarterly* 31 (1978): 105–126; Michael K. Moore and John R. Hibbing, "Is Serving in Congress Fun Again? Voluntary Retirements from the House Since the 1970s," *American Journal of Political Science* 36 (1992): 824–828; Eric M. Uslaner, *The Decline of Comity in Congress* (Ann Arbor: University of Michigan Press, 1993), esp. chap. 2.

15. Frantzich, "De-Recruitment," 105–126; Joseph Cooper and William West, "The Congressional Career in the 1970s," in *Congress Reconsidered,* ed. Lawrence Dodd and Bruce Oppenheimer (Washington, D.C.: CQ Press, 1981); and John R. Hibbing, "Voluntary Retirement from the U.S. House: The Costs of Legislative Service," *Legislative Studies Quarterly* 8 (1982): 57–74.

16. Another prominent Republican whose decision to retire in 1996 was influenced by his failure to gain a leadership position was Rep. Robert Walker, R-Pa., who finished a distant second in his bid to become majority whip.

17. Steven G. Livingston and Sally Friedman, "Reexamining Theories of Congressional Retirement: Evidence from the 1980s," *Legislative Studies Quarterly* 18 (1993): 231–254; John B. Gilmour and Paul Rothstein, "Early Republican Retirement: A Cause of Democratic Dominance in the House of Representatives," *Legislative Studies Quarterly* (1993)

18:345–365; D. Roderick Kiewiet and Langche Zeng, "An Analysis of Congressional Career Decisions, 1947–1986," *American Political Science Review* (1993): 928–941; Richard L. Hall and Robert P. Van Houweling, "Avarice and Ambition in Congress: Representatives' Decisions to Run or Retire from the U.S. House," *American Political Science Review* 89 (1995): 121–136.

18. "Cooley Convicted of Lying," *Congressional Quarterly Weekly Report*, March 22, 1997.

19. For a comprehensive assessment of these factors, see Canon, *Actors, Athletes, and Astronauts*, 103–110.

20. Some of the data used in Figures 2-2 through 2-6 and Tables 2-1 through 2-4 come from various editions of *Who's Who in American Politics* (New Providence, N.J.); *Who's Who among African Americans* (Detroit: Gale Research); "Election '96: Republican National Convention," *AsianWeek*, August 9–15, 1996; "Election '96: Democratic National Convention," *AsianWeek*, August 23–29, 1996; the Joint Center for Political and Economic Studies; and the National Association of Latino Elected and Appointed Officials.

21. On ambitious, policy, and experience-seeking or hopeless amateurs see Canon, *Actors, Athletes, and Astronauts*, xv, 26–32; and Canon, "Sacrificial Lambs or Strategic Politicians? Political Amateurs in U.S. House Elections," *American Journal of Political Science* 37 (1993): 1119–1141.

22. Jacobson and Kernell, *Strategy and Choice*, 94–96, 102.

23. Ibid., 77–78.

24. On the decision making of quality challengers, see Gary W. Cox and Jonathan N. Katz, "Why Did the Incumbency Advantage in U.S. House Elections Grow?" *American Journal of Political Science* 40 (1996): 478–497.

25. Throughout this chapter seats are categorized according to their status (open or incumbent-occupied) at the beginning of the election cycle. Seats that began the election cycle as incumbent-occupied but featured two nonincumbents in the general election are classified as open from Chapter 3 forward.

26. An exception to this rule occurs in Texas, where an individual can appear on the ballot for two offices simultaneously.

27. Harold D. Lasswell, *Power and Personality* (Boston: W. W. Norton, 1948), 39–41.

28. The generalizations that follow are drawn from responses to question 18 of the 1992 Congressional Campaign Study (see the appendix to the first edition of this book and the publisher's Web site: http://books.CQ.com [navigate to the "Free Resources" area]). See also Louis Sandy Maisel, *From Obscurity to Oblivion: Running in the Congressional Primary* (Knoxville: University of Tennessee Press, 1982), 31–32; Herrnson, *Party Campaigning*, 86; and Kazee, "The Emergence of Congressional Candidates."

29. Thomas A. Kazee and Mary C. Thornberry, "Where's the Party? Congressional Candidate Recruitment and American Party Organizations," *Western Political Quarterly* 43 (1990): 61–80; Steven H. Haeberle, "Closed Primaries and Party Support in Congress," *American Politics Quarterly* 13 (1985): 341–352.

30. Herrnson, *Party Campaigning*, 51–56.

31. See, for example, Fowler and McClure, *Political Ambition*, 205–207.

32. On WISH List, see Craig A. Rimmerman, "New Kids on the Block: Wish List and the Gay and Lesbian Victory Fund," in *Risky Business? PAC Decisionmaking in Congressional Elections*, ed. Robert Biersack, Paul S. Herrnson, and Clyde Wilcox (Armonk, N.Y.: M. E.

Sharpe, 1994), 214–223; Mark J. Rozell, "WISH List: Pro-Choice Women in the Republican Congress," in *After the Revolution: PACs and Lobbies in the New Republican Congress,* ed. Robert Biersack, Paul S. Herrnson, and Clyde Wilcox (Boston: Allyn and Bacon, forthcoming).

33. Caryn R. Sagal, "1992: The Year of the Challenger or the Year of the Incumbent? The Showdown in California's 3rd Congressional District" (independent honors thesis, University of Maryland, 1994); Phil Duncan, ed., *Politics in America, 1996: The 104th Congress* (Washington, D.C.: Congressional Quarterly, 1995), 87–88.

34. Sagal, "1992: The Year of the Challenger?"

35. Fenno, *Home Style,* 176–189.

36. See Paul S. Herrnson, "National Party Organizations and the Postreform Congress," in *The Postreform Congress,* ed. Roger H. Davidson (New York: St. Martin's Press, 1992), 48–70.

37. Paul S. Herrnson and Robert M. Tennant, "Running for Congress under the Shadow of the Capitol Dome: The Race for Virginia's Eighth District," in *Who Runs for Congress?* 67–81.

38. Ibid., 73.

39. See, for example, Schlesinger, *Ambition and Politics,* 99; and Canon, *Actors, Athletes, and Astronauts,* 50–53, 56–58; L. Sandy Maisel, Elizabeth J. Irvy, Benjamin D. Ling, and Stephanie G. Pennix, "Re-exploring the Weak-Challenger Hypothesis: The 1994 Candidate Pools," in *Midterm.*

40. Robert Marshall Wells, "FEC Cites Collins for Violations," *Congressional Quarterly Weekly Report,* June 8, 1996.

41. Ibid.

42. Ibid.

43. See Herrnson and Tennant, "Running for Congress."

44. Michael Dizon, "9 Vie to Succeed Durbin in House," *Chicago Tribune,* February 16, 1996.

45. Ibid.

46. Donald R. Matthews, "Legislative Recruitment and Legislative Careers," *Legislative Studies Quarterly* 9 (1984): 551.

47. Glenn R. Simpson, "One-Fifth of Congress Now Millionaires as Number in House Climbs to 13 Percent," *Roll Call,* June 30, 1994, 1, 12.

48. R. Darcy, Susan Welch, and Janet Clark, *Women, Elections, and Representation* (New York: Longman, 1987), 93–108.

49. Ibid., 138–140; Robert A. Bernstein, "Why Are There So Few Women in the House?" *Western Political Quarterly* 29 (1986): 155–164; Linda L. Fowler, *Candidates, Congress, and the American Democracy* (Ann Arbor: University of Michigan Press, 1993), 127–136.

50. Barbara Burrell, "Women Candidates in Open-Seat Primaries for the U.S. House: 1968–1990," *Legislative Studies Quarterly* 17 (1992): 493–508.

51. On the effect of race on candidate selection, see Fowler, *Candidates, Congress, and the American Democracy,* 136–142.

52. Kevin A. Hill, "Does the Creation of Majority Black Districts Aid Republicans? An Analysis of the 1992 Congressional Elections in Eight Southern States," *Journal of Politics* 57 (1995): 384–401; Charles Cammeron, David Epstein, and Sharyn O'Halloran, "Do Majority-Minority Districts Maximize Substantive Black Representation in Congress," *American Political Science Review* 90 (1996): 794–812.

53. Former representative Cleo Fields, who chose not to run for reelection after his district was obliterated was the only House member who had occupied a majority-minority district who was not reelected. On racial redistricting, see David T. Canon, Matthew M. Schousen, and Patrick Sellers, "The Supply Side of Congressional Redistricting: Race and Strategic Politicians, 1972–1992," *Journal of Politics* 58 (1996): 846–862.

54. Amy Keller, "The Roll Call Fifty," *Roll Call,* January 20, 1997.

55. Alan Ehrenhalt, *The United States of Ambition: Politicians, Power, and the Pursuit of Office* (New York: Random House, 1991), 225–226.

56. It should be noted that some members of Congress list more than one occupation. Percentages are compiled from Ornstein, Mann, and Malbin, *Vital Statistics on Congress, 1993–1994* (Washington, D.C.: Congressional Quarterly, 1994), table 1-11, and various issues of *Congressional Quarterly Weekly Report.*

57. "Characteristics of Congress," *Congressional Quarterly Weekly Report,* February 22, 1997.

58. See, for example, David Ian Lublin, "Quality, Not Quantity: Strategic Politicians in U.S. Senate Elections, 1952–1990," *Journal of Politics* 56 (1994): 228–241.

59. This generalization is drawn from responses to question 18 of the 1992 Congressional Campaign Study.

3. THE ANATOMY OF A CAMPAIGN

1. See, for example, Edie N. Goldenberg and Michael W. Traugott, *Campaigning for Congress* (Washington, D.C.: CQ Press, 1984), 19–24.

2. Committee on Political Parties, "Toward a More Responsible Two-Party System"; Agranoff, "Introduction," 3–50; Sabato, *The Rise of the Political Consultants.*

3. The figure includes office furniture, supplies, rent, salaries, taxes, bank fees, lawyers, accountants, telephone, automobile, computers, other office equipment, and food but excludes campaign travel. Gingrich's legal and accounting fees were extraordinarily high because he was under investigation by the House ethics committee. Figures provided by the Campaign Study Group.

4. Ibid., 18–19.

5. There have been important exceptions to this generalization in recent years. See Canon, *Actors, Athletes, and Astronauts,* 3, 36.

6. This generalization is based on responses to further breakdowns of question 19 of the 1992 Congressional Campaign Study.

7. This finding supports Fenno's observation that the explanatory power of challenger quality and political experience is largely the result of the quality of the candidates' campaign organizations. See Richard F. Fenno Jr., *Senators on the Campaign Trail: The Politics of Representation* (Norman: University of Oklahoma Press, 1996), 100.

8. William C. Miller Jr., Representative Morella's campaign manager and the chief of staff of her congressional office, interview, March 14, 1997.

9. Mooers had to leave the State Department in order to run because of Hatch Act prohibitions against partisan activity by federal employees.

10. Donald Mooers, interview, March 13, 1997.

11. Ibid.

12. David E. Price, *The Congressional Experience* (Boulder, Colo.: Westview Press, 1992), 1–3.

13. Phil Duncan, ed., *Politics in America, 1996: The 104th Congress* (Washington, D.C.: Congressional Quarterly, 1995), 978–979.

14. James McLaughlin, Fabrizio McLaughlin Associates, General Consultant to Fred Heineman's campaign, interview, March 10, 1997.

15. Ibid.

16. Joe Goode, Price's campaign manager, interview, March 3, 1997.

17. Ibid.

18. Ibid.

19. Ibid.

20. Mary Ellen Madonia, finance director for the Shimkus campaign and district caseworker in Shimkus's congressional office, interview, March 17, 1997; Jay Hoffman, interview, March 24, 1997.

21. The estimates are for budgetary allocations made during the campaign season. Studies that examine the money collected and spent over the course of an entire two-year House or six-year Senate election cycle report lower expenditures for voter contact and higher expenditures on overhead, research, and other activities that take place before the campaign season. See Fritz and Morris, *Gold-Plated Politics*; Goldenberg and Traugott, *Campaigning for Congress*, 85–92; Stephen Ansolabehere and Alan Gerber, "The Mismeasure of Campaign Spending: Evidence from the 1990 U.S. House Elections," *Journal of Politics* 56 (1994): 1106–1108.

22. McLaughlin interview; Goode interview.

23. Miller interview; Mooers interview.

24. Complete data for the 1996 elections were not available. Figures provided by the Campaign Study Group.

25. Figures provided by the Campaign Study Group.

4. THE PARTIES CAMPAIGN

1. Sorauf, "Political Parties and Political Action Committees," 447.

2. See, for example, Agranoff, "Introduction," 3–50.

3. Sorauf, "Political Parties and Political Action Committees"; Herrnson, *Party Campaigning*, chaps. 2 and 3.

4. Joseph A. Schlesinger, "The New American Political Party," *American Political Science Review* 79 (1985): 1151–1169; Paul S. Herrnson, "Political Leadership and Organizational Change at the National Committees," in *Politics, Professionalism, and Power*, ed. John Green (Lanham, Md.: University Press of America, 1993), 186–202.

5. Herrnson, *Party Campaigning*, chap. 2.

6. Paul S. Herrnson, Kelly D. Patterson, and John J. Pitney Jr., "From Ward Heelers to Public Relations Experts: The Parties' Response to Mass Politics," in *Broken Contract? Changing Relationships between Citizens and Government in the United States*, ed. Stephen C. Craig (Boulder, Colo.: Westview Press, 1996), 251–267.

7. Richard K. Armey, Jennifer Dunn, and Christopher Shays, *It's Long Enough: The Decline of Popular Government under Forty Years of Single Party Control of the U.S. House of Representatives* (Washington, D.C.: Republican Conference, U.S. House of Representatives, 1994). Richard K. Armey, *Under the Clinton Big Top: Policy, Politics, and Public Relations in the President's First Year* (Washington, D.C.: Republican Conference, U.S. House of Representatives, 1993).

8. Gimpel, *Fulfilling the Contract*; Kolodny, "The Contract with America in the 104th Congress."

9. Even though the reports that candidates filed with the FEC indicate that some received large national committee contributions and coordinated expenditures, this spending is almost always dictated by a congressional or senatorial campaign committee's election strategy. As is explained later in this chapter, national committee spending in congressional elections is often the result of a "money swap."

10. The term *Hill committees* probably originates from the fact that the congressional and senatorial campaign committees were originally located in congressional office space on Capitol Hill.

11. These figures include "hard" dollars, which can be spent directly on individual federal campaigns, and soft money, which can be spent on issue advocacy advertisements, party building, and voter mobilization activities. Federal Election Commission, "FEC Reports Major Increase in Party Activity for 1995–96," press release, March 19, 1997.

12. These figures do not include staff employed by the candidates' campaign organizations.

13. Prior to the 1992 elections, both the DCCC and the NRCC created redistricting divisions, which will probably be resurrected to help the committees focus on the decennial redrawing of House districts prior to the 2002 elections.

14. Gary C. Jacobson, "Party Organization and Campaign Resources in 1982," *Political Science Quarterly* 100 (1985–1986): 604–625.

15. Herrnson, "Political Leadership and Organizational Change"; Brooks Jackson, *Honest Graft: Big Money and the American Political Process* (New York: Alfred A. Knopf, 1988), 286–290.

16. Jacobson and Kernell, *Strategy and Choice in Congressional Elections*, 39–43, 76–84.

17. The information on committee strategy, decision making, and targeting is from numerous interviews conducted before, during, and after the 1992, 1994, and 1996 election cycles with several high-ranking officials of the congressional and senatorial campaign committees.

18. Gruenwald, "Supreme Court Orders Panel"; Elving, "Virginia Unlikely to Appeal Ruling."

19. On the 1990 election, see Les Frances, "Commentary," in *Machine Politics, Sound Bites, and Nostalgia,* ed. Michael Margolis and John Green (Lanham, Md.: University Press of America), 58; on the 1994 election see Paul S. Herrnson, "Money and Motives: Spending in House Elections," in *Congress Reconsidered,* 6th ed., ed. Lawrence C. Dodd and Bruce I. Oppenheimer (Washington, D.C.: CQ Press, 1996), 106–107; on the 1980s, see Herrnson, *Party Campaigning,* chap. 3.

20. Paul S. Herrnson, "Campaign Professionalism and Fundraising in Congressional Elections," *Journal of Politics* 54 (1992): 859–870.

21. Robert Biersack and Paul S. Herrnson, "Political Parties and the Year of the Woman,"

in *The Year of the Woman? Myths and Realities,* ed. Elizabeth Adell Cook, Sue Thomas, and Clyde Wilcox (Boulder, Colo.: Westview Press, 1994), 173–174.

22. Presentation to students in the University of Maryland's Capitol Hill Internship Program, October 18, 1992.

23. In 1996, for the first time in several elections, the DCCC's regional coordinators operated primarily out of the committee's Washington headquarters, visiting specific campaigns less frequently than in the past. The DCCC made this change to conserve resources so that it could spend more money directly in House races.

24. These are considered separate elections under the FECA. Party committees usually give contributions only to general election candidates.

25. The coordinated expenditure limit for states with only one House member was originally set at $20,000 and reached $61,820 in 1996.

26. Herrnson, *Party Campaigning,* 43–44.

27. Anthony Corrado, "The Politics of Cohesion: The Role of the National Party Committees in the 1992 Elections," in *The State of the Parties,* ed. John C. Green and Daniel M. Shea (Lanham, Md.: Rowman and Littlefield, 1996), 79–80; Diana Dwyre, "Spinning Straw into Gold: Soft Money and U.S. House Elections," *Legislative Studies Quarterly* 21 (1996): 411; James A. Barnes, "New Rules for the Money Game," *National Journal,* July 6, 1996.

28. Party committees can also give "in-kind" services in lieu of cash contributions; however, they are more likely to use the coordinated expenditure route.

29. Money swaps among the Republican national party organizations, which involved in excess of $22.8 million, were also important considerations.

30. In 1982, for example, the Republicans spent $10.5 million on House elections, and the Democrats spent $1.9 million. Herrnson, *Party Campaigning,* 66. See also Sorauf, *Inside Campaign Finance: Myths and Realities* (New Haven: Yale University Press, 1992), 112–116.

31. The figures include spending by all party organizations, including national, congressional, senatorial, state, and local party committees because, as noted earlier, the national parties coordinated a national spending strategy on federal elections in 1996.

32. On 1992, see the first edition of this book, 84–86.

33. On the distribution of party funds in 1982 see Jacobson, "Party Organization and Campaign Resources," 604–625; on the distribution of party funds in 1984, see Paul S. Herrnson, "National Party Decision Making, Strategies, and Resource Distribution in Congressional Elections"; on the distribution of funds in 1992, see the first edition of the book, 85–86; on the distribution of party funds in 1994, see Herrnson, "Money and Motives."

34. NRCC staff identified Republican freshmen in jeopardy using criteria similar to those they used to identify other incumbents in jeopardy. They are defined in the analysis as those GOP freshmen who lost or whose contests were decided by 20 percent or less of the two-party vote. This generalization is based on a further breakdown of the distribution of party money than is presented in Table 4-2.

35. Herrnson, "National Party Decision-Making," 301–323.

36. As will be noted later, every Democratic general election candidate received a $20,000 credit at the Harriman Communications Center. Incumbents were more likely than nonincumbents to take advantage of the credits because of the center's Washington location.

37. Herrnson, "Money and Motives," 108–109.

38. Ibid., 109.

39. The coverage of these topics draws heavily from Herrnson, *Party Campaigning,* chaps. 4 and 5.

40. In some cases, the congressional campaign committees require candidates to use the services of one of their preferred consultants as a precondition for committee support. Although these cases are rare, they can arouse the ire of both candidates and political consultants. See Herrnson, *Party Campaigning,* 56–57; Stephen E. Frantzich, *Political Parties in the Technological Age* (New York: Longman, 1989), 82, 87–88; and Barbara G. Salmore and Stephen A. Salmore, *Candidates, Parties, and Campaigns: Electoral Politics in America,* 2nd ed. (Washington, D.C.: CQ Press, 1989), 240–241.

41. Haley Barbour, "Memorandum to Republican Leaders," November 4, 1996.

42. Ed Brookover, political director, NRCC, interview, January 2, 1997.

43. Don Fowler, national chairman, DNC, interview, February 23, 1997.

44. Peter Carey, research director, DCCC, interview, February 5, 1997.

45. Gail Stoltz, political director, DSCC, interview, February 1, 1997.

46. The allocable costs of the polls vary by their type, size, and when they are released to candidates. FEC regulations specify that candidates must pay 100 percent of the costs if they receive the poll results within 15 days of when the poll was completed, 50 percent if they receive them between 16 and 60 days, and 5 percent if the results are received between 61 and 180 days. After 180 days, a poll can be given to a candidate free of charge. General Services Administration, *Title 11—Federal Elections,* sec. 2 U.S.C. 106.4, pp. 77–78.

47. Figures provided by the Campaign Study Group.

48. Stoltz interview.

49. Paul S. Herrnson, "The National Committee for an Effective Congress: Ideology, Partisanship, and Electoral Innovation," in *Risky Business?*

50. Blast-faxes are ordinary faxes that are simultaneously sent to many individuals instead of one.

51. Carey interview.

52. Brookover interview.

53. Information provided by the National Republican Congressional Committee.

54. Brookover interview.

55. Anonymous DCCC official, interview, February 5, 1997.

56. Todd Glass, deputy press secretary, Democratic National Committee, interview, January 10, 1997.

57. PAC kits typically include information about the candidate's personal background, political experience, campaign staff, support in the district, endorsements, issue positions, and campaign strategy.

58. David Maraniss and Michael Weisskopf, "Speaker and His Directors Make the Cash Flow Right," *Washington Post,* November 27, 1995.

59. Herrnson, *Party Campaigning,* 75.

60. Maraniss and Weisskopf, "Speaker and His Directors."

61. See, for example, Larry J. Sabato, *PAC Power: Inside the World of Political Action Committees* (New York: W. W. Norton, 1984), 144–149; Herrnson, *Party Campaigning.*

62. This generalization is drawn from responses to questions 29, 31, 32, 33, 34, and 36 of the 1992 Congressional Campaign Study. See also Herrnson, *Party Campaigning,* chap. 4.

63. Cornelius P. Cotter, James L. Gibson, John F. Bibby, and Robert J. Huckshorn, *Party Organizations in American Politics* (Pittsburgh: University of Pittsburgh Press, 1989), 20–25.

64. Ibid.; Herrnson, *Party Campaigning,* 102–106; Robert Huckfeldt and John Sprague, "Political Parties and Electoral Mobilization: Political Structure, Social Structure, and the Party Canvass," *American Political Science Review* 86 (1992): 70–86; Gregory A. Caldeira, Samuel C. Patterson, and Gregory A. Markko, "The Mobilization of Voters in Congressional Elections," *Journal of Politics* 47 (1985): 490–509; Michael A. Krassa, "Context and the Canvass: The Mechanisms of Interactions," *Political Behavior* 10 (1988): 233–246; Peter W. Wielhower and Brad Lockerbie, "Party Contacting and Political Participation, 1952–90," *American Journal of Political Science* 38 (1994): 211–229.

65. Exceptions exist: in 1996 NRSC chair Sen. Alfonse D'Amato, R-N.Y., spent nearly $1 million of the committee's funds (mostly soft money) in New York despite the fact the state had no Senate race. The money was ostensibly used to help state and local Republican candidates and build support for the GOP, but the expenditures were also probably motivated by D'Amato's desire to create a climate that would help his 1998 reelection campaign. See Jonathan D. Salant, "D'Amato: Well Funded, if Not Loved," *Congressional Quarterly Weekly Report,* February 22, 1997; and Marc Humbert, "Democrats Also Piped Money into New York," *Washington Post,* March 9, 1997.

66. Fowler interview.

67. Glass interview.

68. Neil Reiff, deputy general counsel, Democratic National Committee, interview, January 10, 1997.

69. Barbour, "Memorandum"; Mary Meade Crawford, press secretary, RNC, interview, January 10, 1997. On the roles of tax-exempt groups in electoral politics, see Charles R. Babcock, "Use of Tax Exempt Groups Integral to Political Strategy," *Washington Post,* January 7, 1997; Rebecca Carr, "Tax-Exempt Groups Scrutinized as Fundraising Clout Grows," *Congressional Quarterly Weekly Report,* February 22, 1997.

70. The ratio of soft to hard money that a national party can spend in a state, including funds spent on issue advocacy, is determined by the number of state and federal elections held in the state in a given election year. See Dwyre, "Spinning Straw into Gold," 411; and Barnes, "New Rules for the Money Game."

71. Anthony Corrado, *Creative Campaigning: PACs and the Presidential Selection Process* (Boulder, Colo.: Westview Press, 1992), 80–81.

72. See n. 70.

73. The vast majority of independent expenditures were made by the NRSC and the DSCC. Only state and local parties in Louisiana, Maine, and Texas made independent expenditures in connection with Senate races in their states. Two of the candidates against whom the NRSC made independent expenditures, Mary Landreiu and Richard Ieyoub, were candidates in Louisiana.

74. The GOP spent $424,000 in the Rhode Island Senate race in which the Democratic representative Jack Reed defeated the state treasurer, Nancy Mayer, by 27 percent of the vote.

75. Brookover interview; Crawford interview; Rob Engel, political director, DCCC, interview, February 5, 1997.

76. Fowler interview; Brooks Jackson, "Financing the 1996 Campaign: The Law of the Jungle," in *Toward the Millennium: The Elections of 1996* (Boston: Allyn and Bacon, 1997), 238.

77. Anonymous DCCC official, interview, February 5, 1997.

78. Stoltz interview; Brian Svoboda, director of nonfederal expenditures, DSCC, interview, February 3, 1997.

79. Crawford interview.

80. For reasons of cost, the ads were broadcast on radio rather than television in the Los Angeles and Philadelphia media markets. They were also broadcast on radio rather than television in Portland, Maine, where the television airwaves were already saturated with campaign ads.

81. Brookover interview.

82. The RNC contributed $8 million toward this ad campaign.

83. It should be noted that prior to the Supreme Court's decision in the *Colorado case,* after which the NRSC set up its independent expenditure division, the committee's political division broadcast a few issue advocacy ads. Jo Anne Barnhart, political director, NRSC, interview, February 4, 1997; anonymous NRSC official, interview, January 23, 1997.

84. Anonymous NRSC official, interview.

85. Ibid.

86. Ibid.

87. This generalization is drawn from responses to questions 29 through 36 of the 1992 Congressional Campaign Study.

88. Juliana Gruenwald, "Redistricting: Minority Districts' Fate Uncertain Following Supreme Court Ruling," *Congressional Quarterly Weekly Report,* June 15, 1996.

89. Juliana Gruenwald, "Texas: New Districts to Stay in Place; Tougher Races for Candidates," *Congressional Quarterly Weekly Report,* September 7, 1996.

90. These generalizations are drawn from responses to questions 29 through 36 of the Senate version of the 1992 Congressional Campaign Study and from similar studies of Senate campaigns that were conducted in the 1984 and 1986 election cycles. See Herrnson, *Party Campaigning,* chap. 4.

5. THE INTERESTS CAMPAIGN

1. See, for example, Alexander, *Financing Politics,* 10–17.

2. Although it was referred to as a political action committee from its inception, COPE operated somewhat differently from modern (post-1974) PACs until the enactment of the FECA. See Clyde Wilcox, "Coping with Increasing Business Influence: The AFL-CIO's Committee on Political Education," in *Risky Business?*

3. PACs that do not meet these requirements are subject to the same $1,000 contribution limit as individuals.

4. FEC Advisory Opinion 1975-23 (December 3, 1975).

5. *Buckley v. Valeo,* 424 U.S. 1 (1976).

6. Federal Election Commission, "PAC Activity Increases in the 1995–96 Election Cycle," press release, April 22, 1997. It should be recalled that a small but important subset of nonconnected PACs consists of the leadership PACs discussed in Chapter 4.

7. Recipients of PAC money in 1996 include candidates up for election in future years (e.g., 1998 Senate candidates). Others are candidates who are retiring debts from 1994 and earlier elections. The 1974 figure is from Jacobson, *The Politics of Congressional Elections,* 56; the 1996 figure is from FEC, "PAC Activity Increases in the 1995–96 Election Cycle."

8. Removing the 700 defunct PACs from the calculation reduces the number of inactive PACs to 21 percent of the total, but it does not affect the generalization that a small portion of the PAC community accounts for the overwhelming majority of all PAC expenditures.

9. See, for example, Theodore J. Eismeier and Philip H. Pollock III, *Business, Money, and the Rise of Corporate PACs in American Elections* (New York: Quorum Books, 1988), 27–30; J. David Gopoian, "What Makes PACs Tick? An Analysis of the Allocation Patterns of Economic Interest Groups," *American Journal of Political Science* 28 (May 1984): 259–281; Craig Humphries, "Corporations, PACs, and the Strategic Link between Contributions and Lobbying Activities," *Western Political Quarterly* 44 (1991): 353–372; Sorauf, *Inside Campaign Finance,* 64–65, 74–75; and the case studies in *Risky Business?*

10. Laura Langbein, "Money and Access: Some Empirical Evidence," *Journal of Politics* 48 (1986): 1052–1062; Richard Hall and Frank Wayman, "Buying Time: Moneyed Interests and the Mobilization of Bias in Congressional Committees," *American Political Science Review* 84 (1990): 797–820.

11. John Frendreis and Richard Waterman, "PAC Contributions and Legislative Behavior: Senate Voting on Trucking Deregulation," *Social Science Quarterly* 66 (1985): 401–412; Janet M. Grenzke, "PACs and the Congressional Supermarket: The Currency Is Complex," *American Journal of Political Science* 33 (February 1989): 1–24; John Wright, "Contributions, Lobbying, and Committee Voting in the U.S. House of Representatives," *American Political Science Review* 84 (1990): 417–438; Kevin B. Grier and Michael C. Munger, "Comparing Interest Group PAC Contributions to House and Senate Incumbents, 1980–1986," *Journal of Politics* 55 (August 1993): 615–643; Thomas Romer and James M. Snyder Jr., "An Empirical Investigation of the Dynamics of PAC Contributions," *American Journal of Political Science* 38 (1994): 745–769.

12. Jacobson and Kernell, *Strategy and Choice,* esp. chap. 4.

13. Theodore J. Eismeier and Philip H. Pollock III, "The Tale of Two Elections: PAC Money in 1980 and 1984," *Corruption and Reform* 1 (1986): 189–207; Sorauf, *Inside Campaign Finance,* 67–77; Jackson, *Honest Graft,* 69–70, 77–81, 90–93.

14. See, for example, Ornstein, Mann, and Malbin, *Vital Statistics on Congress, 1995–1996,* table 3-14.

15. Herrnson, "Money and Motives," 122–124.

16. Sorauf, *Inside Campaign Finance,* 61–71.

17. See the case studies in *Risky Business?* and *After the Revolution.*

18. Clyde Wilcox, "Organizational Variables and the Contribution Behavior of Large PACs: A Longitudinal Analysis," *Political Behavior* 11 (1989): 157–173.

19. John Wright, "PACs, Contributions, and Roll Calls: An Organizational Perspective," *American Political Science Review* 79 (1985): 400–414.

20. Sabato, *PAC Power,* 44–49; Robert Biersack, "Introduction," in *Risky Business?*

21. The information on the Realtors PAC is from Anne H. Bedlington, "The National Association of Realtors PAC: Rules or Rationality?," in *Risky Business?*

22. On AT&T's PAC, see Robert E. Mutch, "AT&T PAC: A Pragmatic Giant," in *Risky Business?*; and Mutch, "AT&T PAC: The Perils of Pragmatism," in *After the Revolution.* On AMPAC, see Michael K. Gusmano, "The AMA in the 1990s: Surviving in a Crowded Policy Network," in *After the Revolution.*

23. The information on the CVC is from Ronald G. Shaiko, "Le PAC, C'est Moi: Brent Bozell and the Conservative Victory Committee," in *Risky Business?*

24. The information on Washington PAC is from Barbara Levick-Segnatelli, "WASHPAC: One Man Can Make a Difference," in *Risky Business?*

25. The information on the AAP PAC is from Julia Stronks, "The Association of American Publishers," in *Risky Business?*

26. The information on FHP PAC is from John J. Pitney, "FHP Health Care PAC," in *Risky Business?*

27. On lead PACs see the introduction to part I in *Risky Business?*, 17–18. On the NCEC, see Herrnson, "The National Committee for an Effective Congress"; on BIPAC see Candice J. Nelson, "The Business-Industry PAC: Trying to Lead in an Uncertain Climate," in *Risky Business?* and on COPE see Wilcox, "Coping with Increasing Business Influence," and Robin Gerber, "Building to Win, Building to Last: The AFL-CIO COPE Takes on the Republican Congress," in *After the Revolution.*

28. On the flow of PAC money in the 1992 elections, see the first edition of the book; on the flow of PAC money in the 1994 elections, see Paul S. Herrnson, "Money and Motives," 110–113; and Herrnson, "Interest Groups, PACs, and Campaigns," in *The Interest Group Connection: Electioneering, Lobbying, and Policymaking in Washington,* ed. Paul S. Herrnson, Clyde Wilcox, and Ronald G. Shaiko (Chatham, N.J.: Chatham House, 1997).

29. Theodore J. Eismeier and Philip H. Pollock III, "Political Action Committees: Varieties of Organization and Strategy," in *Money and Politics in the United States: Financing Elections in the 1980s,* ed. Michael J. Malbin (Washington, D.C.: American Enterprise Institute, 1984), 122–141; Margaret Ann Latus, "Assessing Ideological PACs: From Outrage to Understanding," in *Money and Politics in the United States,* 150–160; Sabato, *PAC Power,* 93–95.

30. On CWAVE PAC see Robyn Hicks, "Grassroots Organization in Defense of Mother Nature: Clean Water Action Vote Environment," in *Risky Business?*; on abortion rights PACs see, for example, Sue Thomas, "NARAL PAC: Reproductive Choice in the Spotlight," in *Risky Business?*

31. Fowler and McClure, *Political Ambition: Who Decides to Run for Congress,* 205–207.

32. Ronald G. Shaiko and Marc A. Wallace, "From Wall Street to Main Street: The National Federation of Independent Business and the Republican Majority," in *After the Revolution*; James G. Gimpel, "Peddling Influence in the Field: The Direct Campaign Involvement of the Free Congress PAC," in *Risky Business?*

33. Herrnson, "The National Committee for an Effective Congress."

34. Mark Gable, PAC director, Federal Managers Association PAC, interview, April 25, 1997.

35. See, for example, Sabato, *PAC Power,* 44–49.

36. Karin Johannsen, communications director, EMILY's List, interview, February 13, 1997.

37. On the National Chamber Alliance for Politics, see Sabato, *PAC Power,* 47.

38. NCAP makes small in-kind contributions to help candidates raise money.

39. Federal Election Commission, "PAC Activity Increases in the 1995–96 Election Cycle," press release, April 22, 1997.

40. Spending intended to help Republican freshmen's prospects includes independent expenditures for them and those against their Democratic opponents; spending intended to harm their prospects includes independent expenditures against them and those for their

Democratic opponents. Figures include only freshmen involved in typical two-party contested races.

41. Much of the information on the AFL-CIO's issue advocacy campaign is drawn from Gerber, "Building to Win, Building to Last."

42. "Labor Targets," *Congressional Quarterly Weekly Report,* October 26, 1996; Jeanne I. Dugan, "Washington Ain't Seen Nothin' Yet," *Business Week Report,* May 13, 1996.

43. The "motor voter" law eases the burdens of voter registration by requiring states to distribute registration materials at most state agencies, including those that dispense driver's licenses.

44. Much of the information on the AFL-CIO's issue advocacy campaign is drawn from Shaiko and Wallace, "From Wall Street to Main Street."

45. Calculated from "Labor Targets."

46. On the Sierra Club, see David M. Cantor, "The Sierra Club Political Committee: Spreading Some Green in Congressional Elections," in *After the Revolution*; on the National Rifle Association, see Kelly D. Patterson, "Political Firepower: The National Rifle Association," in *After the Revolution*.

47. John C. Green, James L. Guth, and Kevin Hill, "Faith and Election: The Christian Right in Congressional Campaigns, 1978–1988," *Journal of Politics* 55 (1993): 80–91.

48. Ruth Marcus, "FEC Files Suit over Christian Coalition Role; Work with Republicans in Campaigns Alleged," *Washington Post,* July 31, 1996.

49. Corrado, *Creative Campaigning,* 80–84.

50. Charles R. Babcock and Ruth Marcus, "For Their Targets, Mystery Groups' Ads Hit Like Attacks from Nowhere," *Washington Post,* March 9, 1997.

51. See, for example, Jackie Koszczuk, "Widened Probe Keeps Speaker in Spotlight," *Congressional Quarterly Weekly Report,* September 28, 1996, 2733; Rebecca Carr, "Tax-Exempt Groups Scrutinized as Fundraising Clout Grows," *Congressional Quarterly Weekly Report,* February 22, 1997.

52. This generalization is drawn from responses to questions 29 through 36 of the 1992 Congressional Campaign Study.

6. CAMPAIGNING FOR RESOURCES

1. Quoted in David Adamany and George E. Agree, *Political Money: A Strategy for Campaign Finance in America* (Baltimore: Johns Hopkins University Press, 1975), 8.

2. George Thayer, *Who Shakes the Money Tree? American Campaign Finance Practices from 1789 to the Present* (New York: Simon and Schuster, 1973), 25.

3. Federal Election Commission, "Congressional Fundraising and Spending Up Again in 1996," press release, April 14, 1997.

4. The figures for House and Senate campaign contributions and expenditures include spending by all candidates involved in typical major-party contested general elections. They exclude elections that were won by an independent candidate (as in Vermont's at-large or Missouri's 8th districts), that were decided in a primary (as occurred in several Louisiana contests), or that featured a general election runoff (as did several Texas races).

5. The base used in calculating the percentages is the candidates' total receipts plus any

coordinated spending the parties made on the candidates' behalf. Coordinated expenditures are included because candidates have some control over the activities on which they are spent.

6. Sorauf, *Inside Campaign Finance,* 47.

7. See the first edition of this book, table 6-1.

8. On direct-mail fund-raising, see Kenneth R. Godwin, *One Billion Dollars of Influence: The Direct Marketing of Politics* (Chatham, N.J.: Chatham House, 1988).

9. For a discussion of these motives—often referred to as solidary, purposive, and material—see James Q. Wilson, *Political Organizations* (New York: Basic Books, 1973), chap. 6.

10. Robert Biersack, Paul S. Herrnson, Wesley Joe, and Clyde Wilcox, "The Allocation Strategies of Congressional High Rollers: A Preliminary Analysis" (paper presented at the annual meeting of the Midwest Political Science Association, Chicago, April 14–16, 1994).

11. See, for example, Sorauf, *Inside Campaign Finance,* 124–127.

12. They are the chair of the House Democratic Caucus, Vic Fazio; the minority leader, Richard Gephardt; the DCCC chair, Martin Frost; Speaker Newt Gingrich; and the majority whip, Tom DeLay.

13. Center for Responsive Politics (Web site: http:crp.org/96_open_secrets/HOFLO5014_1.htm).

14. Figures provided by the Center for Responsive Politics.

15. The remainder of Morella's campaign chest came from miscellaneous sources, including interest earned on bank accounts.

16. The figure for business-related PACs also includes $3,765 that Morella received from PACs sponsored by corporations without stock. The candidate received no money from corporations sponsored by cooperatives.

17. Some argue that preemptive fund-raising by incumbents may not discourage quality challengers from running. See Krasno and Green, "Preempting Quality Challengers"; Squire, "Preemptive Fundraising."

18. Jacobson, *Money in Congressional Elections,* 113–123; Jonathan S. Krasno, Donald Philip Green, and Jonathan A. Cowden, "The Dynamics of Fundraising in House Elections," *Journal of Politics* 56 (1994): 459–474.

19. Sorauf, *Inside Campaign Finance,* 75.

20. After the election, Morella raised an additional $550.

21. Miller interview.

22. Fazio won the primary against Rodger McAfee, by a 64 percent vote margin.

23. Mooers interview.

24. Robert Biersack, Paul S. Herrnson, and Clyde Wilcox, "Seeds for Success: Early Money in Congressional Elections," *Legislative Studies Quarterly* 18 (1993): 535–553; Krasno, Green, and Cowden, "The Dynamics of Fundraising in House Elections."

25. Herrnson, *Party Campaigning in the 1980s,* 75.

26. Paul S. Herrnson, "Campaign Professionalism and Fundraising in Congressional Elections," *Journal of Politics* 54 (1992): 859–870.

27. Experienced challengers raised, on average, $3,100 more from other congressional candidates than did political amateurs.

28. Campaign professionalism data are not available for 1996; however, in 1992, challengers who relied on paid staff or consultants to perform three or more of the nine cam-

paign activities listed in Table 3-1 raised an average of $22,600 in party money; those who relied on paid staff to perform fewer than three of those activities received an average of $5,400.

29. Clyde Wilcox, "Coping with Increasing Business Influence"; Gerber, "Building to Win, Building to Last"; Denise L. Baer and Martha Bailey, "The Nationalization of Education Politics: The National Education Association PAC and the 1992 Elections," in *Risky Business?*

30. Challengers who relied on paid staff or consultants to perform three or more of the nine campaign activities listed in Table 3-1 received an average of $29,300 in PAC contributions in 1992; those who relied on paid staff to perform fewer than three of those activities received an average of $6,800.

31. The WISH List's name is an acronym for Women in the Senate and House. See Craig A. Rimmerman, "New Kids on the Block"; Rimmerman, "The Gay and Lesbian Victory Fund Comes of Age: Reflections on the 1996 Elections," in *After the Revolution;* and Rozell, "WISH List."

32. This figure includes only out-of-state contributions of $200 or more because the FEC does not require candidates to collect information about individuals who contribute less than $200 to their campaigns.

33. Open-seat candidates who relied on paid staff or consultants to perform three or more of the nine campaign activities listed in Table 3-1 received an average of $24,400 in PAC contributions in 1992; those who relied on paid staff to perform fewer than three of those activities received an average of $17,600.

34. Open-seat candidates who relied on paid staff or consultants to perform seven or more of the nine campaign activities listed in Table 3-1 received an average of $117,000 in PAC contributions in 1992; those who relied on paid staff to perform fewer than three of those activities received an average of $39,400.

35. Center for Responsive Politics (Web site: http://207.196.113.3/96_open_secrets/58VA00107_1.htm).

36. Figure provided by the Center for Responsive Politics.

7. CAMPAIGN STRATEGY

1. Angus Campbell, Philip E. Converse, Warren E. Miller, and Donald E. Stokes, *The American Voter* (New York: John Wiley and Sons, 1960), 541–548; and Donald R. Kinder and David O. Sears, "Public Opinion and Political Action," in *Handbook of Social Psychology,* 3rd ed., ed. Gardner Lindzey and Elliot Aronson (New York: Random House, 1985), 659–741.

2. Jacobson, *The Politics of Congressional Elections,* 93–97; Alan I. Abramowitz and Jeffrey A. Segal, *Senate Elections* (Ann Arbor: University of Michigan Press, 1992), 39; Peverill Squire, "Challenger Quality and Voting Behavior," *Legislative Studies Quarterly* 17 (1992): 247–263.

3. Ibid.

4. Alan I. Abramowitz, "A Comparison of Voting for U.S. Senator and Representative in 1978," *American Political Science Review* 74 (1980): 633–640. Gerald C. Wright and Michael

B. Berkman, "Candidates and Policy in United States Senate Elections," *American Political Science Review* 80 (1986): 567–588; and Mark C. Westlye, *Senate Elections and Campaign Intensity* (Baltimore: Johns Hopkins University Press, 1992), 122–151.

5. Robert D. Brown and James A. Woods, "Toward a Model of Congressional Elections," *Journal of Politics* 53 (1991): 454–473; John R. Zaller, *The Nature and Origins of Mass Opinion* (Cambridge: Cambridge University Press, 1992), chap. 10.

6. Jacobson, *The Politics of Congressional Elections,* 96, 98. See also Abramowitz and Segal, *Senate Elections,* 42.

7. Wright and Berkman, "Candidates and Policy in United States Senate Elections," 567–588; and Westlye, *Senate Elections and Campaign Intensity,* chap. 6.

8. See, for example, Raymond E. Wolfinger and Steven J. Rosenstone, *Who Votes?* (New Haven: Yale University Press, 1980), 34–36, 58–60, 102–114.

9. Zaller, *The Nature and Origins of Mass Opinion,* chap. 10; Westlye, *Senate Elections and Campaign Intensity,* esp. chap. 5; Milton Lodge, Marco R. Steenbergen, and Shawn Brau, "The Responsive Voter: Campaign Information and the Dynamics of Candidate Evaluation, *American Political Science Review* 89 (1995): 309–326; Jon K. Dalager, "Voters, Issues, and Elections: Are the Candidates' Messages Getting Through?," *Journal of Politics* 58 (1996): 496–515.

10. See Morris P. Fiorina, *Retrospective Voting in American National Elections* (New Haven: Yale University Press, 1981); Edward R. Tufte, "Determinants of the Outcomes of Midterm Congressional Elections," *American Political Science Review* 69 (1975): 812–826; James E. Campbell, "Explaining Presidential Losses in Midterm Congressional Elections," *Journal of Politics* 47 (1985): 1140–1157; Samuel C. Popkin, *The Reasoning Voter: Communication and Persuasion in Presidential Campaigns* (Chicago: University of Chicago Press, 1991), esp. chaps. 3 and 4.

11. Alan I. Abramowitz, Albert D. Cover, and Helmut Norpoth, "The President's Party in Midterm Elections: Going from Bad to Worse," *American Journal of Political Science* 30 (1986): 562–576; Henry W. Chappell Jr. and Motoshi Susuki, "Aggregate Vote Functions for the U.S. Presidency, Senate, and House," *Journal of Politics* 55 (1993): 207–217; Gary C. Jacobson, "Reversal of Fortune: The Transformation of U.S. House Elections in the 1990s" (paper presented at the annual meeting of the Midwest Political Science Association, Chicago, April 10–12, 1997). See also the studies cited in n. 10.

12. Fiorina, *Divided Government* (Boston: Allyn and Bacon, 1996), 109–110; Stephen P. Nicholson and Gary M. Segura, "Midterm Elections and Divided Government: An Information-Driven Theory of Electoral Volatility" (paper presented at the annual meeting of the Midwest Political Science Association, Chicago, April 10–12, 1997).

13. Raymond E. Wolfinger, "Candidates and Parties in Congressional Elections," *American Political Science Review* 74 (1980): 622–629; Barbara Hinckley, "House Re-Elections and Senate Defeats: The Role of the Challenger," *British Journal of Political Science* 10 (1980): 441–460; and Jacobson, *The Politics of Congressional Elections,* 106–108.

14. Mayhew, *Congress.*

15. Fenno, *Home Style,* esp. chaps. 3 and 4.

16. Miller interview.

17. Paul Fricke, field director, Democratic Congressional Campaign Committee, personal communication, June 13, 1997. See Stephen Green, "Lefever Struggling with 'Extremist' Label," *Sacramento Bee,* October 13, 1997.

18. On polls see Salmore and Salmore, *Candidates, Parties, and Campaigns,* 116–119.

19. Bryce Bassett, director of marketing support, the Wirthlin Group, presentation to the Taft Institute Honors Seminar in American Government, June 15, 1993.

20. See, for example, Robert Axelrod, "Where the Votes Come From: An Analysis of Presidential Election Coalitions, 1952–1968," *American Political Science Review* 66 (1972): 11–20.

21. McLaughlin interview.

22. Manuel Perez-Rivas, "Opponent Tries to Make Party Label Stick to Morella," *Washington Post,* March 7, 1996.

23. See the example of Vicky Goudie discussed in the first edition of the book, 164.

24. Axelrod, "Where the Votes Come From," 11–20; Henry C. Kenski and Lee Sigelman, "Where the Vote Comes From: Group Components of the 1988 Vote," *Legislative Studies Quarterly* 18 (1993): 367–390.

25. Goode interview.

26. Joel C. Bradshaw, "Who Will Vote for You and Why: Designing Campaign Strategy and Theme" (paper presented at the Conference on Campaign Management, American University, Washington, D.C., December 10–11, 1992).

27. The logic behind the battle for the middle ground is presented in Anthony Downs, *An Economic Theory of Democracy* (New York: Harper and Row, 1957), chap. 8.

28. Fred Hartwig, vice president, Peter Hart and Associates, presentation to the Taft Institute Honors Seminar in American Government, June 15, 1993.

29. Ladonna Y. Lee, "Strategy," in *Ousting the Ins: Lessons for Congressional Challengers,* ed. Stuart Rothenberg (Washington, D.C.: Free Congress Research and Education Foundation, 1985), 18–19.

30. Kathleen Hall Jamieson, *Dirty Politics: Perception, Distraction, and Democracy* (New York: Oxford University Press, 1992), esp. chap. 2.

31. Fenno, *Home Style,* chaps. 3 and 4.

32. See Peter Clarke and Susan H. Evans, *Covering Campaigns: Journalism and Congressional Elections* (Stanford: Stanford University Press, 1983), 38–45.

33. See Canon, *Actors, Athletes, and Astronauts,* xv, 26–32; and Canon, "Sacrificial Lambs or Strategic Politicians?"

34. On the differences between valence issues and position issues, see Donald E. Stokes, "Spatial Models of Party Competition," in *Elections and the Political Order,* ed. Angus Campbell, Philip E. Converse, Warren E. Miller, and Donald E. Stokes (New York: John Wiley and Sons, 1966), 161–169.

35. See, for example, Gary C. Jacobson and Samuel Kernell, "National Forces in the 1986 U.S. House Elections," 72–85.

36. Jacobson, *The Politics of Congressional Elections,* 112–116.

37. McLaughlin interview; Goode interview.

38. This generalization is drawn from responses to question 13 of the 1992 Congressional Campaign Study. See also Philip Paolino, "Group Salient Issues and Group Representation: Support for Women Candidates in the 1992 Senate Elections," *American Journal of Political Science* 39 (1995): 294–313.

39. The 1992 elections exemplify this; see the first edition of this book, 173–174.

40. The Democrats were criticized as being inaccurate in their allegations because the Republicans proposed to reduce the benefits available to senior citizens in the future rather than to cut funding immediately.

41. Gimpel, *Fulfilling the Contract;* Kolodny, "The Contract with America."

42. Anonymous 1992 House candidate, interview, December 1992.

43. Richard F. Fenno, "If, as Ralph Nader Says, Congress Is 'The Broken Branch,' How Come We Love Our Congressmen So Much?" in *Congress in Change: Evolution and Reform,* ed. Norman J. Ornstein (New York: Praeger, 1975).

44. Hartwig presentation.

45. Phil Duncan, ed., *Politics in America, 1992: The 102nd Congress* (Washington, D.C.: Congressional Quarterly, 1991), 1133.

46. See, for example, James Innocenzi, "Political Advertising," in *Ousting the Ins,* 53–61; Salmore and Salmore, *Candidates, Parties, and Campaigns,* 159.

47. Stephen Ansolabehere, Shanto Iyengar, Adam Simon, and Nicholas Valentino, "Does Attack Advertising Demobilize the Electorate?" *American Political Science Review* 88 (1994): 829–838; and Stephen Ansolabehere and Shanto Iyengar, *Going Negative: How Attack Ads Shrink and Polarize the Electorate* (New York: Free Press, 1995), esp. chap. 5.

48. These generalizations are drawn from responses to question 28 of the 1992 Congressional Campaign Study.

49. Richard R. Lau, "Negativity in Political Perception," *Political Behavior* 4 (1982): 353–377; and Richard R. Lau, "Two Explanations for Negativity Effects in Political Behavior," *American Journal of Political Science* 29 (1985): 110–138; Jamieson, *Dirty Politics,* 41.

50. Lee, "Strategy," 22.

51. Jamieson, *Dirty Politics,* 103.

52. "Lefever's 15 Seconds of Sleeze," *Sacramento Bee,* November 6, 1996.

53. Anonymous campaign manager for a 1992 House candidate, interview, December 1992.

54. Sunil Ahuja, "Reelection of Freshmen Republicans of the 104th Congress" (paper presented at the annual meeting of the Midwest Political Science Association, Chicago, April 10–12, 1997).

8. CAMPAIGN COMMUNICATIONS

1. Nielson Rating Service annual report and 1980 census data, cited in Frank I. Luntz, *Candidates, Consultants, and Campaigns* (Oxford: Basil Blackwell, 1988), 73.

2. Luntz, *Candidates, Consultants, and Campaigns,* 73; Thomas E. Patterson, *The Mass Media Election: How Americans Choose Their President* (New York: Praeger, 1980), 77–91.

3. Darrell M. West, *Air Wars: Television Advertising in Election Campaigns, 1952–1992* (Washington, D.C.: Congressional Quarterly, 1993), esp. chap. 6.

4. Quoted in Luntz, *Candidates, Consultants, and Campaigns,* 77.

5. Darrell M. West, "Political Advertising and News Coverage in the 1992 California U.S. Senate Campaigns," *Journal of Politics* 56 (1994): 1053–1075.

6. This generalization is drawn from responses to question 22 of the 1992 Congressional Campaign Study.

7. The figures for New York and Waco are for a prime-time advertisement broadcast during *Monday Night Football.*

8. See Joe Ostrow, "Six Reasons to Buy Cable," *Campaigns and Elections,* February 1996, 37.

9. John R. Alford and Keith Henry, "TV Markets and Congressional Elections," *Legislative Studies Quarterly* 9 (1984): 665–675.

10. Luntz, *Candidates, Consultants, and Campaigns,* 76.

11. Madonia interview; Hoffman interview.

12. Hoffman interview.

13. Kim F. Kahn, Patrick J. Kenney, and Tom W. Rice, "Ideological Learning in U.S. Senate Elections" (paper presented at the annual meeting of the American Political Science Association, Washington, D.C., September 2–5, 1993). See also Jay Bryant, "Paid Advertising in Political Campaigns" (paper presented at the Conference on Campaign Management, American University, Washington, D.C., December 10–11, 1992).

14. See n. 6.

15. Luntz, *Candidates, Consultants, and Campaigns,* 108.

16. Marty Stone, California field director, DCCC, interview, February 23, 1993.

17. Frank Luther Mott, *American Journalism: A History of 250 Years, 1690 to 1940* (New York: Macmillan, 1947), 411–430.

18. See n. 6.

19. Luntz, *Candidates, Consultants, and Campaigns,* 109–110.

20. See n. 6.

21. Godwin, *One Billion Dollars of Influence,* chaps. 1–3; Jonathan Robbin, "Geodemographics: The New Magic," in *Campaigns and Elections,* ed. Larry J. Sabato (Glenview, Ill.: Scott Foresman, 1989), 105–124; and Sabato, "How Direct Mail Works," in *Campaigns and Elections,* 88–89.

22. Salmore and Salmore, *Candidates, Parties, and Campaigns,* 86–87.

23. Mass mailings consist of five hundred or more pieces of the same letter.

24. The campaign did, however, advertise on local cable TV stations, which is considerably cheaper than advertising on the other television stations.

25. Andrew Kennedy, senior vice president, M and R Research, Inc., and direct-mail consultant to the Sanchez campaign, interview, April 2, 1997.

26. Peter Clarke and Susan Evans, *Covering Campaigns: Journalism in Congressional Elections* (Stanford: Stanford University Press, 1983), chap. 6.

27. Xandra Kayden, *Campaign Organization* (Lexington, Mass.: D. C. Heath, 1978), 125.

28. Clarke and Evans, *Covering Campaigns,* 60–62; Doris A. Graber, *Mass Media and American Politics,* 4th ed. (Washington, D.C.: CQ Press, 1993), 262, 268–270.

29. Richard Born, "Assessing the Impact of Institutional and Election Forces on Evaluations of Congressional Incumbents," *Journal of Politics* 53 (1991): 764–799.

30. Sallie G. Randolph, "The Effective Press Release: Key to Free Media," in *Campaigns and Elections,* ed. Sabato, 26–32.

31. Kayden, *Campaign Organization,* 126.

32. Clarke and Evans, *Covering Campaigns,* 60–62; Goldenberg and Traugott, *Campaigning for Congress,* 127.

33. Anita Dunn, "The Best Campaign Wins: Coverage of Down Ballot Races by Local Press" (paper presented at the Conference on Campaign Management, American University, Washington, D.C., December 10–11, 1992).

34. Ibid.

35. Manuel Perez-Rivas and Deirdre M. Childress, "Lots of Foes, Little Hope," *Washington Post,* February 29, 1996.

36. Manuel Perez-Rivas, "Opponent Tries to Make Party Label Stick to Morella," *Washington Post,* April 28, 1996.

37. Manuel Perez-Rivas, "Democrat Votes the Key in Md.'s 8th District Race," *Washington Post,* July 29, 1996.

38. Karl Vick, "Always Up to the Challenge," *Washington Post,* October 27, 1996.

39. These generalizations are from an analysis that uses responses to question 25 of the 1992 Congressional Campaign Study, the political experience measure developed in Chapter 2, the measure of campaign professionalism (the total number of campaign activities performed by paid staff or consultants) developed in Chapter 3, and candidates' campaign receipts to demonstrate that political experience, campaign professionalism, and campaign receipts are positively related to the free media coverage that campaigns receive.

40. The material on the Torkildsen and Mavroules campaigns is from Gavin Sutcliffe, "The Price of Scandal: Legal Problems Defeat a Veteran Congressman in Massachusetts' Sixth District," unpublished paper, University of Maryland, 1992.

41. See n. 6.

42. See also Clarke and Evans, *Covering Campaigns,* chap. 4.

43. This generalization is drawn from responses to question 26 of the 1992 Congressional Campaign Study. See also Table 8-2 of the previous edition of this book.

44. This generalization is drawn from responses to question 27 of the 1992 Congressional Campaign Study. See also Table 8-3 of the previous edition of this book.

45. See n. 43. On media bias, see Herbert J. Gans, "Are U.S. Journalists Dangerously Liberal?" *Columbia Journalism Review* 24 (1985): 29–33. On politicians and the press, see also Lance W. Bennett, *News: The Politics of Illusion* (New York: Longman, 1983), 76–78; Ranney, *Channels of Power,* 54–55.

46. See, for example, Will Robinson, "Campaign Field Work" (paper presented at the Conference on Campaign Management, American University, Washington, D.C., December 10–11, 1992); and Robbin, "Geodemographics," 105–124.

47. Paul S. Herrnson, "National Party Organizations and the Postreform Congress," in *The Postreform Congress,* ed. Roger H. Davidson (New York: St. Martin's Press, 1992), 65–66.

48. These generalizations are drawn from responses to questions 30 and 35 of the 1992 Congressional Campaign Study.

9. CANDIDATES, CAMPAIGNS, AND ELECTORAL SUCCESS

1. Fiorina, *Congress;* John A. Ferejohn, "On the Decline of Competition in Congressional Elections," *American Political Science Review* 71 (1997): 166–177.

2. See Michael Krashinsky and William J. Milne, "Incumbency in U.S. Congressional Elections, 1950–1988," *Legislative Studies Quarterly* 18 (1993); also see the sources cited in Chapter 1, nn. 43–45.

3. Miller interview.

4. On the effect of candidate gender on voting behavior see Monika L. McDermott, "Voting Cues in Low-Information Elections: Candidate Gender as a Social Information

Variable in Contemporary United States Elections," *American Journal of Political Science* 41 (1997): 270–283.

5. Tables 9-1 and 9-2 were created using ordinary least-squares regressions. The data that are analyzed are for major-party contested general election campaigns for the House in 1992. (Campaigns that participated in incumbent-versus-incumbent races or in races won by an independent were omitted from the sample.) The full regression equations are presented in Tables A-2, A-4, and A-6 in the first edition of this book. The equations are the product of an extensive model-building process that tested the impact of numerous variables using a variety of statistical techniques. The variables that were tested in earlier versions of the models include candidates' background characteristics and political experience, party affiliations, the professionalism of their campaign organizations, party and PAC campaign services and expenditures, the percentage of current voters who lived in the district prior to redistricting (to control for the redrawing of House seats), and the ideological match between the candidate and the district. Numerous OLS regressions, two-stage least-squares regressions, and logistic regressions (which dichotomized the dependent variable as win/lose) were tested prior to selecting the final equations. Some of the models tested used information about both candidates in a particular election. Several variables transformations were also tested. The final models were selected for reasons of statistical fit, parsimony, and ease of interpretation. They are statistically robust. The models were replicated to the extent possible, given the limited availability of campaign-related data, for the 1994 and 1996 elections to verify that the basic relationships that are presented held across elections. The case studies used to update the analysis are drawn from 1996 major-party contested elections.

6. Phil Duncan, ed., *Politics in America 1994: The 103rd Congress* (Washington, D.C.: Congressional Quarterly, 1993), 731–732.

7. Phil Duncan, ed., *Politics in America 1996: The 104th Congress* (Washington, D.C.: Congressional Quarterly, 1995), 630–631.

8. Michael Barone and Grant Ujifusa, *The Almanac of American Politics, 1988* (Washington, D.C.: National Journal, 1987), 1026.

9. Members who bounced twenty-five or more checks at the House bank were considered deeply implicated; most people can sympathize with someone who bounced a few checks, but they are likely to view a member who bounced twenty-five or more as abusing their privileges at the House bank. On the effects of the check-bouncing scandal see Groseclose and Krehbiel, "Golden Parachutes"; Jacobson and Dimock, "Checking Out"; Michael Dimock and Gary C. Jacobson, "Checks and Choices: The Impact of the House Bank Scandal on Voters in 1992," *Journal of Politics* 57 (1995): 1143–1159; John Alford, Holly Teeters, Daniel S. Ward, and Rick Wilson, "Overdraft: The Political Cost of Congressional Malfeasance, *Journal of Politics* 56 (1994): 788–801.

10. Jo Ann Emerson, R-Mo., who won her deceased husband's seat in the 1996 general election, was technically an independent when she defeated both the Republican and Democratic nominees. She ran as an independent because she missed the deadline to file in the Republican primary while caring for her ill husband, but it was widely known during the campaign that she was a Republican and she took her seat in the 105th Congress as a member of the GOP. The last true third-party or independent candidate to be elected to the House prior to Sanders was Henry Reams of Ohio, who served from 1951 to 1955.

11. These generalizations are similar to those reported in Goldenberg and Traugott, *Campaigning for Congress,* chap. 3.

12. On the effect of campaign spending on congressional elections see esp. Jacobson, *Money in Congressional Elections;* Gary C. Jacobson, "The Effects of Campaign Spending in House Elections: New Evidence for Old Arguments," *American Journal of Political Science* 34 (1990): 334–362; Jonathan S. Krasno and Donald Philip Green, "Salvation for the Spendthrift Incumbent," *American Journal of Political Science* 32 (1988): 844–907; Donald Philip Green and Jonathan S. Krasno, "Rebuttal to Jacobson's 'New Evidence for Old Arguments,'" *American Journal of Political Science* 34 (1990): 363–372.

13. Jacobson, *Money in Congressional Elections,* 113–123; Krasno, Green, and Cowden, "The Dynamics of Fundraising in House Elections"; Christopher Kenney and Michael McBurdett, "A Dynamic Model of Congressional Spending on Vote Choice," *American Journal of Political Science* 36 (1992): 923–937.

14. Figures for spending on campaign communications in 1996 were not available. Based on the findings of the 1992 Congressional Campaign Study, they were estimated to be about 75 percent of challengers' total expenditures.

15. Group-based targeting and position issues are defined in Chapter 7.

16. See, for example, Richard F. Fenno Jr., *Senators on the Campaign Trail: The Politics of Representation* (Norman: University of Oklahoma Press, 1996), 100.

17. Communications expenditures exclude money spent on staff salaries, fund-raising, polling, and other forms of research. Field work includes get-out-the-vote drives; the distribution of campaign literature, billboards, and signs; and campaign travel.

18. The figure for the Torkildsen campaign was provided by Matthew LeBretton, campaign manager, and the figure for the Tierney campaign was provided by a member of the candidate's campaign staff who wished to remain anonymous.

19. These estimates are based on the percentage of the campaign budget that is typically devoted to communications: 70 percent for incumbents and 75 percent for challengers.

20. The generalizations for the effect of spending on direct mail, television, radio, newspaper ads, and field work are drawn from Table A-3 in the first edition of this book.

21. Spending figures provided by the Campaign Study Group.

22. Kennedy interview.

23. Spending figures provided by the Campaign Study Group.

24. For precise estimates of the impact that spending on these campaign activities has on challengers' vote shares, see the first edition of this book, p. 214.

25. On the impact of presidential coattails see sources cited in Chapter 1, nn. 47–50.

26. These generalizations are drawn from Table A-7 in the first edition of this book.

27. This calculation excludes Nick Lampson, whose victory in Texas's 9th district was decided in a runoff. Had Lampson been included the average would have exceeded $1.1 million.

28. See John W. Kingdon, *Candidates for Office: Beliefs and Strategies* (New York: Random House, 1968), chap. 2.

29. See the sources listed in nn. 47–52 and 54 of Chapter 1.

30. See Kingdon, *Candidates for Office,* chap. 2.

31. See n. 29.

32. Jonathan S. Krasno, *Challengers, Competition, and Reelection: Comparing Senate and House Elections* (New Haven: Yale University Press, 1994), esp. chaps. 4–7; Peverill Squire and Eric R. A. N. Smith, "A Further Examination of Challenger Quality in Senate Elections," *Legislative Studies Quarterly* 21 (1996): 231–248.

33. John R. Hibbing and John R. Alford, "Constituency Population and Representativeness in the United States Senate," *Legislative Studies Quarterly* 15 (1990): 581–598.

34. See Westlye, *Senate Elections and Campaign Intensity,* chaps. 7 and 8; Alan I. Abramowitz and Jeffrey A. Segal, *Senate Elections* (Ann Arbor: University of Michigan Press, 1992), 109–115.

10. ELECTIONS AND GOVERNANCE

1. See Roger H. Davidson and Walter J. Oleszek, *Congress and Its Members,* 5th ed. (Washington, D.C.: CQ Press, 1997), esp. chap. 1.

2. Fenno, *Home Style,* 54–61.

3. Ibid., 153.

4. Mayhew, *Congress,* 49–68.

5. The figures are for 1996. See Davidson and Oleszek, *Congress and Its Members,* 149.

6. Ibid., 148, 150.

7. Timothy E. Cook, *Making Laws and Making News: Media Strategies in the U.S. House of Representatives* (Washington, D.C.: Brookings Institution, 1989), 71.

8. See, for example, Ben H. Bagdikian, "Congress and the Media: Partners in Propaganda," *Columbia Journalism Review* 12 (1974): 5.

9. Ibid., 2, 3, 37, 90.

10. Langbein, "Money and Access"; Wright, "Contributions, Lobbying, and Committee Voting."

11. Richard F. Fenno Jr., *Congressmen in Committees* (Boston: Little, Brown, 1973), 13.

12. Fox and Hammond, *Congressional Staffs,* 121–124.

13. Fenno, *Congressmen in Committees,* 1–14.

14. Kenneth J. Cooper, "The House Freshmen's First Choice," *Washington Post,* January 5, 1993, A13.

15. Davidson and Oleszek, *Congress and Its Members,* 355–357; Hammond, "Congressional Caucuses in the 104th Congress," *Congress Reconsidered,* 274–292.

16. "80,000 Lobbyists? Probably Not, but Maybe," *New York Times,* May 12, 1993, A13.

17. Kay Lehman Schlozman and John T. Tierney, *Organized Interests and American Democracy* (New York: Harper and Row, 1986), 272.

18. Ibid., 289–310.

19. Linda L. Fowler and Ronald D. Shaiko, "The Grass Roots Connection: Environmental Activists and Senate Roll Calls," *American Journal of Political Science* 31 (1987): 484–510; James G. Gimpel, "Grassroots Organizations and Equilibrium Cycles in Group Mobilization and Access," in *The Interest Group Connection.*

20. See Gordon Adams, *The Iron Triangle* (New York: Council on Economic Priorities, 1981), 175–180; Hugh Heclo, "Issue Networks and the Executive Establishment," in *The New American Political System,* ed. Anthony King (Washington, D.C.: American Enterprise Institute, 1978), 87–124.

21. Paul S. Herrnson and Kelly D. Patterson, "Toward a More Programmatic Democratic Party? Agenda Setting and Coalition Building in the House," *Polity* 27 (1995): 607–628; Paul S. Herrnson and David M. Cantor, "Party Campaign Activity and Party Unity in the U.S. House of Representatives," *Legislative Studies Quarterly* 22 (1997): 393–415.

22. See Epstein, *Political Parties in Western Democracies,* 340–348.

23. See, for example, Herbert F. Weisberg, "Evaluating Theories of Congressional Roll Call Voting," *American Journal of Political Science* (1978): 554–577.

24. Hannah Pitkin, *The Concept of Representation* (Berkeley: University of California Press, 1967).

25. Cain, Ferejohn, and Fiorina, *The Personal Vote.*

26. R. Douglas Arnold, "The Local Roots of Democracy," in *The New Congress,* ed. Thomas E. Mann and Norman J. Ornstein (Washington, D.C.: American Enterprise Institute, 1981), 250–287.

27. Davidson and Oleszek, *Congress and Its Members,* 283–284.

28. John Ferejohn, "Logrolling in an Institutional Context: A Case Study of Food Stamp Legislation," in *Congress and Policy and Change,* ed. Gerald C. Wright Jr., Leroy N. Rieselbach, and Lawrence C. Dodd (New York: Agathon Press, 1986), 223–253.

29. Davidson and Oleszek, *Congress and Its Members,* 281–285.

30. It should be noted that in recent congresses legislation has had to stay within a set of overall budgetary limits in order to limit growth of the federal deficit. This zero-sum process requires legislators to cut spending in some areas if they wish to increase them in others.

31. Herrnson and Patterson, "Agenda Setting and Coalition Building"; Herrnson and Cantor, "Party Campaign Activity and Party Unity."

32. Herrnson, Patterson, and Pitney, "From Ward Heelers to Public Relations Experts," 251–267.

33. V. O. Key Jr., "A Theory of Critical Elections," *Journal of Politics* 17 (1955): 3–18; Walter Dean Burnham, *Critical Elections and the Mainsprings of American Politics* (New York: W. W. Norton, 1970); Everett Carll Ladd Jr., with Charles D. Hadley, *Transformations of the American Party System* (New York: W. W. Norton, 1978).

34. Alan I. Abramowitz, "The End of the Democratic Era? 1994 and the Future of Congressional Election Research," *Political Research Quarterly* 48 (1995): 873–889; Gary C. Jacobson, *The Politics of Congressional Elections,* 4th ed., 219–224.

35. Gimpel, *Fulfilling the Contract.*

36. On the evolution of and most recent changes in the legislative process, see Barbara Sinclair, *Unorthodox Lawmaking* (Washington, D.C.: CQ Press, 1997), esp. chaps. 1 and 6.

37. Committee on Political Parties, "Toward a More Responsible Two-Party System"; Leon D. Epstein, *Political Parties in the American Mold* (Madison: University of Wisconsin Press, 1986), 30–38.

11. CAMPAIGN REFORM

1. See, for example, John R. Hibbing and Elizabeth Theiss-Morse, *Congress as Public Enemy: Public Attitudes toward American Institutions* (Cambridge: Cambridge University Press, 1995), 63–71.

2. For further discussions of the detrimental impact of term limits see Jeffrey J. Mondak, "Elections as Filters: Term Limits and the Composition of the U.S. House," *Political Research Quarterly* 48 (1995): 701–727. For arguments in favor of and against term limits, see the essays in *Limiting Legislative Terms,* ed. Gerald Benjamin and Michael J. Malbin (Washington, D.C.: CQ Press, 1992).

3. On initiatives and referenda see David B. Magleby, *Direct Legislation: Voting on Ballot Propositions in the United States* (Baltimore, Md.: Johns Hopkins University Press, 1984) and Thomas E. Cronin, *Direct Democracy: The Politics of Initiative, Referendum, and Recall* (Cambridge, Mass.: Harvard University Press, 1989).

4. Will Robinson, Democratic political consultant, interview, February 2, 1993.

5. Lyn Ragsdale and Jerrold G. Rusk, "Candidates, Issues, and Participation in Senate Elections," *Legislative Studies Quarterly* 22 (1995): 305–327.

6. There is much debate over spending limits and other kinds of campaign finance reforms. See Jacobson, *Money in Congressional Elections,* 48–49, 211–214; Jacobson, "The Effects of Campaign Spending"; Krasno and Green, "Salvation for the Spendthrift Incumbent"; Robert A. Jackson, "Voter Mobilization in the 1986 Midterm Election," *Journal of Politics* 55 (1993): 1081–1099; Robert Goidel and Donald A. Gross, "Reconsidering the Myths and Realities of Campaign Finance Reform," *Legislative Studies Quarterly* 21 (1996): 129–147.

7. See, for example, Alexander, *Financing Politics,* 23–26.

8. Joint Committee of Congress, *Organization of Congress,* Final Report, H. Rept. 103-413, 103rd Cong., 1st sess., 1993, 2:231–232, 275–287. Cited in Davidson and Oleszek, *Congress and Its Members,* 133.

9. These funds do not include soft money given to state party committees and interest groups, which do not have to be reported to the FEC. Figures were provided by the FEC and the Center for Responsive Politics (Web site: http://www.crp.org/tray.com/fecinfo/bzcg.htm).

10. This figure comprises mainly soft money, but it also includes individual contributions of $200 or more. It underestimates the sums that flowed from this area because it represents only soft money contributions to national parties from ZIP codes where individuals and groups made aggregate contributions of at least $300,000.

11. Ironically, D'Amato's voting record is rarely characterized as pro-environment and he received a zero rating from the League of Conservation Voters in 1996. Blaine Harden, "D'Amato Has Reelection Recipe Simmering," *Washington Post,* February 22, 1997.

12. The FECA does not require these groups to disclose their political activities; unlike PACs, parties, and individual contributors, soft money groups exist outside of the federal campaign finance regime because they do not directly advocate the election or defeat of federal candidates.

13. Quoted in "Excerpts from Remarks on First Day of Campaign Finance Hearings," *New York Times,* July 9, 1997.

14. Wright, "PACs, Contributions, and Roll Calls"; and "Contributions, Lobbying, and Committee Voting"; Grenzke, "PACs and the Congressional Supermarket." For an alternative viewpoint see John Frendreis and Richard Waterman, "PAC Contributions and Legislative Behavior: Senate Voting and Trucking Deregulation," *Social Science Quarterly* 66 (1985): 401–412.

15. John W. Kingdon, *Congressmen's Voting Decisions* (New York: Harper and Row, 1981).

16. Aage R. Clausen, *How Congressmen Decide* (New York: St. Martin's Press, 1973).

17. Wright, "Contributions, Lobbying, and Committee Voting" and "PACs, Contributions, and Roll Calls."

18. The parties of the golden age, especially the political machines, had shortcomings as well as strong points. Their shortcomings included undemocraticness, corruption, secrecy, and formal and informal barriers to the participation of women and various racial, ethnic, and religious groups. For some lively accounts of these parties see William Riordan, *Plunkitt*

of Tammany Hall (New York: E. P. Dutton, 1905) and Mike Royko, *Boss: Richard J. Daley* (New York: E. P. Dutton, 1971).

19. See Hibbing and Theiss-Morse, *Congress as Public Enemy,* esp. chap. 5.

20. Conference on Campaign Reform, Committee for the Study of the American Electorate, "Poll Finds Public Sour on Congress, Seeking More Bi-Partisanship on Issues and Reform, Uncertain and Divided on Details of Reform," press release, July 29, 1994.

21. On the roles of minor parties see Steven J. Rosenstone, Roy L. Behr, and Edward H. Lazarus, *Third Parties in America: Citizen Response to Major Party Failure* (Princeton, N.J.: Princeton University Press, 1984); David Gillespie, *Politics at the Periphery: Third Parties in Two-Party America* (Columbia: University of South Carolina Press, 1993); and the essays in *Multiparty Politics in America,* ed. Paul S. Herrnson and John C. Green (Lanham, Md.: Rowman and Littlefield, 1997).

22. L. Sandy Maisel, "Competition in Congressional Elections: Why More Qualified Candidates Do Not Seek Office," in *Rethinking Political Reform,* ed. Ruy A. Teixeira, L. Sandy Maisel, and John J. Pitney Jr. (Washington, D.C.: Progressive Foundation, 1994), 29.

23. Gary W. Cox and Michael C. Munger, "Closeness, Expenditures, and Turnout in the 1982 U.S. House Elections," *American Political Science Review* 83 (1989): 217–231.

24. The idea of giving candidates free television and radio broadcast time has been around for many years. See, for example, Twentieth Century Fund Commission on Campaign Costs, *Voters' Time* (New York: Twentieth Century Fund, 1969); and Campaign Study Group, "Increasing Access to Television for Political Candidates" (Cambridge: Institute of Politics, Harvard University, 1978).

25. Herrnson, *Party Campaigning,* 127.

26. Graber, *Mass Media and American Politics,* 53–55.

27. Larry J. Sabato, *Paying for Elections: The Campaign Finance Thicket* (New York: Twentieth Century Fund, 1989), 31.

28. The law currently requires broadcasters to make preemptive time available at the lowest unit rate; most candidates choose the more expensive nonpreemptible time slots.

29. Subsidized or free communications can also be used to induce certain desirable behaviors in candidates. They could be offered communications subsidies in exchange for participating in campaign debates or abiding by spending limits, for example.

30. See Ruth S. Jones and Warren E. Miller, "Financing Campaigns: Macro Level Innovation and Micro Level Response," *Western Political Quarterly* 38 (1985): 190, 192.

31. For countries and American states that offer citizens the opportunity to obtain tax credits for political contributions, see the case studies in *Campaign and Party Finance in North America and Western Europe.*

32. Marshall Ganz, "Voters in the Cross-Hairs: Elections and Voter Turnout," *The American Prospect,* winter 1994, 4–10.

33. Raymond E. Wolfinger and Stephen J. Rosenstone, *Who Votes?* (New Haven, Conn.: Yale University Press, 1980), 61–88.

34. J. Eric Oliver, "The Effects of Eligibility Restrictions and Party Activity on Absentee Voting and Voter Turnout," *American Journal of Political Science* 40 (1996): 498–513.

35. Candidates would also have to abide by spending limits in a runoff election, in the event that one were held.

36. In the event that the PAC ban was declared unconstitutional, a $1,000 contribution limit would be imposed as previously.

Index

Index